Music: A Social Experience

By taking a thematic approach to the study of music appreciation, *Music: A Social Experience*, Second Edition demonstrates how music reflects and deepens both individual and cultural understandings. Musical examples are presented within universally experienced social frameworks (ethnicity, gender, spirituality, love, and more) to help students understand how music reflects and advances human experience. Students engage with multiple genres (Western art music, popular music, and world music) through lively narratives and innovative activities. A companion website features streaming audio and instructors' resources.

New to this edition:

- Two additional chapters: "Music and the Life Cycle" and "Music and Technology"
- Essay questions and "key terms" lists at the ends of chapters
- Additional repertoire and listening guides covering all historical periods of Western art music
- Expanded instructors' resources
- Many additional images
- Updated student web materials

Steven Cornelius is Lecturer in Music at University of Massachusetts Boston.

Mary Natvig is Professor of Music History at Bowling Green State University.

MUSIC
A Social Experience

Second Edition

Steven Cornelius
University of Massachusetts Boston

with

Mary Natvig
Bowling Green State University

Routledge
Taylor & Francis Group

NEW YORK AND LONDON

Second edition published 2019
by Routledge
711 Third Avenue, New York, NY 10017

and by Routledge
2 Park Square, Milton Park, Abingdon, Oxon, OX14 4RN

Routledge is an imprint of the Taylor & Francis Group, an informa business

© 2019 Taylor & Francis

The right of Steven Cornelius and Mary Natvig to be identified as authors of
this work has been asserted by them in accordance with sections 77 and 78
of the Copyright, Designs and Patents Act 1988.

All rights reserved. No part of this book may be reprinted or reproduced
or utilised in any form or by any electronic, mechanical, or other means,
now known or hereafter invented, including photocopying and recording,
or in any information storage or retrieval system, without permission in
writing from the publishers. Printed in Canada.

Trademark notice: Product or corporate names may be trademarks or
registered trademarks, and are used only for identification and explanation
without intent to infringe.

First edition published by Pearson Education, Inc. 2012

Library of Congress Cataloging-in-Publication Data
Names: Cornelius, Steven, 1952– author. | Natvig, Mary, 1957–
Title: Music : a social experience / Steven Cornelius ; with Mary Natvig.
Description: Second edition. | New York ; London : Routledge, 2018. |
Includes index.
Identifiers: LCCN 2017061308 (print) | LCCN 2018000648 (ebook) |
ISBN 9781315222868 (ebook) | ISBN 9780415789325 (hardback) |
ISBN 9780415789332 (pbk.)
Subjects: LCSH: Music appreciation. | Music—Social aspects.
Classification: LCC MT90 (ebook) | LCC MT90 .C69 2018 (print) |
DDC 781.1/7—dc23
LC record available at https://lccn.loc.gov/2017061308

ISBN: 978-0-415-78932-5 (hbk)
ISBN: 978-0-415-78933-2 (pbk)
ISBN: 978-1-315-22286-8 (ebk)

Typeset in Sabon and Stone Sans
by Florence Production Ltd, Stoodleigh, Devon, UK

Visit the companion website: www.routledge.com/cw/cornelius

To our teachers and our students,
with great appreciation for all you
have taught us.

BRIEF CONTENTS

DETAILED CONTENTS

LISTENING GUIDES

Welcome to *Music: A Social Experience*, an innovative approach to exploring music in all of its aspects. Our approach encourages engaged listening and learning. This text is based on two simple observations:

- Musical experience unfolds in a web of social experience.
- We learn best by building on what we already know.

Music: A Social Experience takes advantage of these truths by beginning with familiar pieces or concepts, then expanding outwards to more distant musical sounds and contexts. By focusing on the social aspects common to all music, we engage with a wide range of musical styles, cultures, and historical periods. Rather than valuing one type of music over another, *Music: A Social Experience* demonstrates the role that all music plays in teaching us about ourselves and the world in which we live.

A social approach makes for intriguing juxtapositions. In our chapter on music and nation, for example, Jimi Hendrix's Woodstock performance of "The Star-Spangled Banner" opens a pathway to understanding the reception history of Ludwig van Beethoven's Symphony No. 9. The chapter on music and gender connects and juxtaposes 1960s "girl groups" with Wolfgang Amadeus Mozart's 1786 opera *The Marriage of Figaro* and with proscriptions against women performing gamelan music in Indonesia.

In this book we:

- Present music from a variety of time periods and cultures.
- Use cultural knowledge to promote musical understanding.
- Use musical knowledge to promote cultural understanding.
- Reveal music's deep relationship with individual and social conditions.
- Encourage self-reflection and independent thinking.

Why Should We Study Western Art Music?

Art music represents Western philosophical ideals and social values. By studying art music we gain insights into Western civilization as a whole. Our repertoire is carefully chosen to demonstrate ways in which music and society interact. Alexander Borodin's orchestral tone poem *In the Steppes of Central Asia* informs us about 19th-century European concepts of nation and otherness. Studying Bizet's sultry operatic character Carmen tells us about 19th-century gender expectations. Furthermore, by engaging with Western art music on both sonic and social levels we see how music of the past influences who we are today.

Why Study the Music of Other Cultures?

We study music of the non-Western world because it helps us to understand and empathize with alternative points of view. Ours is a world in which diverse cultures share geographic territories, though often not political, philosophical, or spiritual values. Because musical practices reflect and sustain those values, they offer us important insights into how people understand the world. We can investigate the bards of West Africa and hear their influence on American music. We can learn to hear the ways in which Tibetan Buddhist chant embodies spiritual beliefs. We can understand how and why 1960s Chinese opera was refashioned to serve Communist ideology.

Why Popular Music?

Because this is music of the moment, has wide appeal across cultures, and is based on vernacular sounds. It is also the music that most immediately reflects and gives form to young adults' hopes, needs, and desires. We hear Aretha Franklin demanding "R-E-S-P-E-C-T" and Roy Orbison and k.d. lang "Crying" for lost love. We wonder at vocaloid Hatsune Miku's rising popularity and the future of computer-mediated, even computer-generated, pop stars. We follow the glitzy politics that guide the annual Eurovision Song Contest. We learn that our musical choices do more than entertain; they tell us about who we are and who we strive to become.

These experiences are mutually reinforcing. At course's end, students will be:

- Prepared to think independently and critically about a variety of musical styles.
- Equipped with skills for listening to classical, popular, and world music.
- Able to make connections between musical experience and life experience.
- Empowered with the intellectual and creative skills necessary for lifelong musical learning.

Organization

Part 1, Music Fundamentals, includes Chapters 1–3. Chapter 1 introduces the power of music, how we perceive music in its cultural and historical context, and ways of categorizing musical styles. Chapter 2 introduces the basic vocabulary and meanings of the elements of music. Chapter 3 demonstrates how to apply the concepts learned in Chapter 2 by analyzing three short works.

Part 2, Musical Identities, includes Chapters 4–6. These chapters focus on how music *expresses* individual and group identities and, in turn, how music *shapes* social expectations of identity. Chapter 4 considers the human life cycle through musical experience. Chapter 5 investigates how musical ethnicities cross cultural, social, and geographical boundaries. Chapter 6 shows how gender is mirrored in music, in both performance roles and soundscapes. Chapter 7 explores music's connections to the sacred traditions of Buddhism, Christianity, Islam, Judaism, and the Yoruba.

Part 3, Musical Intersections, includes Chapters 8–10. Here we explore how music crosses into the social realms of politics, conflict, and love. Chapter 8 discusses how music reflects political ideologies and national identity. Chapter 9 examines music's use in, and response to, war. Chapter 10 shows how music can express various aspects of love: young love, unattainable love, obsessive love, betrayal, and fidelity.

Part 4, Musical Narratives, includes Chapters 11–15. These chapters focus on musical genres (theater, film, and dance), the concert experience, as well as the impact of technology on musical possibility. We investigate the social stories these narratives tell, as well as the histories of the genres themselves. Chapter 11 focuses on three significant works of American musical theater: *Show Boat*, *West Side Story*, and *Into the Woods*. Chapter 12 explores music's role in film, past and present, and Chapter 13 examines music's inextricable connection to dance. Chapter 14 focuses on the concert experience, with an emphasis on Western art music, but with excursions in jazz and North Indian classical music. Chapter 15 considers the impact of music technologies past and present, and wonders about our technological future.

Features

- *Music: A Social Experience* encourages engaged learning by including "Questions for Thought" and "Activities and Assignments" at regular intervals throughout the text. These features are meant to encourage you to reflect on and connect the knowledge of your own life experiences with the information presented in the text. They may also be used for class or small group discussions or activities.
- Boxes present concise summaries of people, places, things, or ideas that supplement the text's narrative. They may also serve as ideas for further research.
- Listening Guides provide structural road maps of featured works.
- Bolded terms are defined in the glossary.
- Web references refer to supplementary examples and materials on the companion website.
- Listening Guide examples are labeled as per the example shown here.

  Sound links are indicated by Listening Guide numbers on the companion website.

- Music elements discussed in Chapter 2 are enhanced on the companion website with links to sound examples and additional resources.
- The book is available in print and e-book formats.

New to this Edition

- Two additional chapters: "Music and the Life Cycle" and "Music and Technology."
- First edition chapters are updated and expanded.
- Essay questions and "key terms" lists at end of chapters.
- Additional repertoire and listening guides covering all historical periods of Western art music.
- Expanded instructors' resources.
- Many additional visual images.
- New boxes on a wide variety of topics.
- Updated student web materials.

Website Content: www.routledge.com/cw/Cornelius

- Listening Guide repertoire is posted by chapter under the STUDENT tab, and also under the INSTRUCTOR tab as a complete unit
  - Supplementary materials are linked to each chapter with items such as:
  - audio examples of musical elements (Chapter 2)
  - links to composers' biographies
  - bibliographies
  - links to outside readings, videos, blogs, related musical works
  - expanded discussions of chapter topics
  - chapter learning objectives

- Interactive, self-correcting quizzes for students
- Tips on writing about music
- Tips on how to study
- Instructors' resources
  - test bank
  - powerpoint slide shows
  - instructors' manual

To the Instructor

Students soar when listening to the music they know and like, but unfamiliar sounds and contexts often leave them flat. So how can we get our students to engage with musical styles that for them are aurally new and socially distant? This textbook, the result of two decades experimenting with teaching classes in music appreciation, is an attempt to solve that conundrum. Rather than making students come to us, we engage them on their own terms. First, we tap into their enthusiasm for music by starting with sounds and contexts they already experience, or can easily understand. Then, we redirect and widen the focus by exploring the sonic and cultural roots from which today's musical worlds grow.

Chapters focus on ideas, contexts, and cultural understandings. Each begins with music close to students' experience, and presents broadly applicable ideas about culture and identity. Thus fortified, students find that distant times and places no longer seem so shadowy, or representative composers and their music so inert. To put this into practice, chapters are based on social understandings (ethnicity, gender, nation, love, etc.) through which music may be engaged and assimilated.

This is a compelling strategy. First, it fits experience. We listen to music because we identify with it. Our choices confirm, confront, and energize social and emotional experience. Second, social understandings represent distinct, yet interconnected, ways of being within the world. For example, our chapter organized around the experience of love neatly places music from Disney's 1991 children's film *Beauty and the Beast* alongside works by Antoine Busnoys, Giacomo Puccini, Hank Williams, and others.

Like ace pilots in a time-traveling helicopter, instructors can plunk down students for pinpoint stopovers in musical landscapes conceptually related but culturally and stylistically removed, one from another. Stays are quick, but cogently organized—two to three pinpoint landings in a single class period. The frequent use of boxes allows peripheral topics to be quickly introduced and briefly developed. Lengthier repositories of historical and background information are housed on the internet. Listening guides map out musical examples.

Over the course of the semester, students will have experienced and come to appreciate a wealth of musical styles from times and places around the globe. Most importantly, they will have learned to make connections between disparate times and places. (Instructors can easily plug their favorite works and/or the latest popular tunes into such a scheme.)

The musical choices available for such a text are endless, but we strive to offer examples that fit together like a jigsaw puzzle, making a final cohesive picture that encourages a range of listening skills and prepares students for the ever-widening variety of music they will encounter in their future lives.

Finally, while the focus of this text is weighted toward the music of the Western traditions, the mix of examples reflects the ever-increasing integration and juxtaposition of global musics that comprise the American cultural experience. This broad focus is acutely practical for college students, most of whom will take only a single music course during their undergraduate career. No longer is jazz or pop music an afterthought at the end of the text. No longer is music of the Indonesian gamelan stuffed in as a sidebar to Debussy's Impressionist palette. Instead, all music is given equal treatment, not as "masterpieces" from particular times and places, but as examples that contribute to our understanding of the human experience of self and culture as embodied through art.

How to Use This Text

Instructors may use this book in a number of ways. In order to cover all of the text's material in class, the instructor would likely need three to four class periods per chapter. Many course schedules do not allow for such a pace. Therefore, the text can easily be used as follows:

- Instructors may select chapters of interest.
- Instructors may select only certain sections within the chapters.
- Instructors might discuss only certain sections of each chapter in class and have students be responsible for the remainder on their own.
- Instructors can easily incorporate alternate repertoire.
- The *Teacher's Guide* offers supplementary materials for every chapter.

Repertory List

Western Art Music

Medieval

Kyrie eleison (Chapters 2 and 7)

Perotin, *Sederunt principes* (Chapter 7)

Renaissance

Giovanni Pierluigi da Palestrina, Kyrie from *Pope Marcellus Mass* (Chapters 2 and 7)

Clement Janequin, "La guerre" (Chapter 9)

Antoine Busnoys, "Je ne puis vivre ainsy toujours" (Chapter 10)

Anonymous, "Branle des lavandieres" (Chapter 13)

Baroque

J.S. Bach, Bourrée from Suite in E minor, BWV 996 (Chapter 3)

J.S. Bach, excerpts from *St. Matthew Passion* (Chapter 7)

Salamone Rossi, "Elohim Hashivenu" from *Hashirim asher lish'lomo* ("The Songs of Solomon") (Chapter 7)

G.F. Handel, "La Réjouissance" from *The Music for the Royal Fireworks* (Chapter 8)

Giovanni Pergolesi, "Lo conosco" ("I can see it") (Chapter 10)

Antonio Vivaldi, "La Primavera" ("Spring") from Concerto in E major, op. 8 (Chapter 14)

Classical

W.A. Mozart, "Non so piu cosa son" from *The Marriage of Figaro* (Chapter 6)

W.A. Mozart, fourth movement from Symphony No. 40 in G minor (Chapter 14)

Franz Joseph Haydn, fourth movement from String Quartet in E flat major, op. 33, no. 2, "The Joke" (Chapter 14)

Romantic

Maurice Ravel, "Habanera" from *Rapsodie espagnol* (Chapter 5)

Georges Bizet, "L'amour est un oiseau rebelle" (Habanera) from *Carmen* (Chapter 6)

Richard Wagner, Act II, scene 2, from *Siegfried* (Chapter 6)

"All Quiet Along the Potomac Tonight," by John Hewett (Chapter 9)

"Ballad of the Green Berets," by Robin Moore and Staff Sgt. Barry Sadler (Chapter 9)

"La Vie en Rose," by Louis Guglielmi (music) and Édith Piaf (lyrics) (Chapter 10)

"Something There," from *Beauty and the Beast*, by Alan Menken and Howard Ashman (Chapter 10)

"Your Cheatin' Heart," by Hank Williams (Chapter 10)

World

"Alap and Gat-Tora," in Chatuttal Manj-Khamaj raga, performed by Ravi Shankar, Ali Akbar Khan, and Chaturial (North India) (Chapters 2 and 14)

"Tarawangsa" (Java) (Chapter 2)

"Tuvan Folk Melody" (Chapter 2)

"Nesaza Shirabe," performed by Tadashi Tajima (Japan) (Chapter 3)

"Ceurik Rahwana" (Indonesia) (Chapter 4)

"Kimísou yié" (Greece) (Chapter 4)

"Mă Guariţă" (Romania) (Chapter 4)

"Seeta Kalyana Vaibhogame" ("Sita's Wedding"), by Tyagaraja (South India) (Chapter 4)

"Kelefaba" and "Kuruntu Kelafa" (West Africa) (Chapter 5)

"Perets-Tants" (Klezmer) (Chapter 5)

Mekar Sari (Bali) (Chapter 6)

"Kol Nidre" (excerpt) (Chapter 7)

Eleggua (Cuba) (Chapter 7)

Naat-i-Sherif (excerpt): Taksim and Peşrev (Sufi) (Chapter 7)

"Song Boo Cherpa" (Tibet) (Chapter 7)

"Dilmano, Dilbero," by Philip Koutev (Bulgeria) (Chapter 8)

"My Heart is Bursting with Anger," scene 9, from *Hong deng ji* (China) (Chapter 8)

"Es iz geven a zumer-tog" ("It was a Summer's Day"), Rikle Glezer (text) (Chapter 9)

"Father Have Pity on Me" and "Light from Sun is Flowing" (Arapaho and Comanche) (Chapter 9)

Baamaaya (Ghana) (Chapter 13)

Steven Cornelius currently teaches at the University of Massachusetts Boston. Previous teaching positions include Phillips Academy (2013–2014), Boston University (2008–2012), Bowling Green State University (1991–2008), Bruckner-Konservatorium Linz (adjunct faculty, 1992–1997), and University of Wisconsin-Madison (1984–1986). Books include *Music of the Civil War Era* (2004) and *The Music of Santería: Traditional Rhythms of the Batá Drums* (with John Amira, 1991). From 1996 to 2006 he authored more than 1200 articles as music and dance critic for *The Blade*, Toledo, Ohio's daily newspaper. Performances as a percussionist include Metropolitan Opera, New York City Opera National Company, Radio City Music Hall, Oklahoma Symphony, and others. He holds a Ph.D. from the University of California Los Angeles.

Mary Natvig is Professor of Music History at Bowling Green State University where she has taught since 1990. Previous to that she was Visiting Assistant Professor of Violin at Hope College (1982–1984). Publications include an edited collection titled *Teaching Music History* (Ashgate, 2001/paperback, Routledge, 2017), as well as chapters, essays, and articles in various publications on diverse topics. Her Ph.D. is from the Eastman School of Music of the University of Rochester.

ACKNOWLEDGMENTS

We are grateful to the staff at Routledge (a member of the Taylor & Francis Group), especially to our editor, Constance Ditzel, and her senior editorial assistant, Peter Sheehy, for guiding us through this second edition. As is evident from the list below, we are indebted to numerous colleagues for their help and encouragement in preparing this text.

Vasile Beluska, Bowling Green State University (retired)

Jonathan Britt, Bowling Green State University

Susannah Cleveland, Bowling Green State University

Vincent Corrigan, Bowling Green State University (retired)

Allison Eckardt, Arizona State University

Robert Fallon, Philadelphia, PA

Heather Fischer, Saginaw Valley State University

David Harnish, University of San Diego

Clare Hu, Winter Park Florida

Peter Janson, University of Massachusetts Boston

Ellen Koskoff, The Eastman School of Music (retired)

Panayotis League, Harvard University

Sharan Leventhal, Boston Conservatory at Berklee

David R. Lewis, Bowling Green State University

Solungga Fang-Tzu Liu, Bowling Green State University

Katherine Meizel, Bowling Green State University

Adam O'Dell, Bowling Green State University

Elinor Olin, Northern Illinois University

Jamie K. Oxendine, Lumbee/Creek

Michael Pisani, Vassar College

Ulrike Präger, University of Konstanz

Mehmet Sanlikol, Brown University

Marilyn Shrude, Bowling Green State University

Andrew Martin Smith, Fredonia: State University of New York

Timothy Stulman, Full Sail University

Garret Tanner, Bowling Green State University

Sean Williams, The Evergreen State College

MUSIC
FUNDAMENTALS

CHAPTER GOALS

- To introduce music as a social and scientific object of study.
- To introduce various ways of understanding music.

CHAPTER ONE

Experiencing Music

QUESTIONS FOR THOUGHT

- What is music?
- What types of music do you enjoy? Why?
- How many genres of music can you name?
- How do you generally listen to music?
- What do you think about while listening?
- How does music function in your life?

Introduction

Ninety-three-year-old Veva Campbell slumps wordlessly in her wheelchair. Suffering from Alzheimer's disease, she has not spoken, walked, fed herself, or recognized friends and family for over two years. This afternoon, her granddaughter, an out-of-town musician, comes to visit. There is nothing to say or do, so she pulls out her violin and begins to play. Miraculously, Mrs. Campbell sits up and begins singing along to the traditional hymns and old-time songs she recognizes from her youth. When the music stops, Mrs. Campbell retreats back into a world of silence.

The story is not apocryphal. Mrs. Campbell was the co-author's grandmother. This demonstration of music's power, remarkable as it may be, is not an isolated example. All over the world music unites and heals, transforms and inspires. This appears to have been the case since the beginning of civilization.

"Music produces a kind of pleasure which human nature cannot do without."
—Confucius (ca. 551 BCE to 479 BCE)

Music and the Brain

The foundation of musical experience resides deep within the mind. Medical science is just beginning to document these complexities. Severe stutterers and those afflicted by aphasia, even those unable to get out single spoken words, can sometimes sing entire sentences. Therapists successfully used "melodic intonation therapy" to facilitate speech recovery for former Congresswoman Gabrielle Giffords, who was injured in a 2011 shooting in Tucson, Arizona. We also know that music can lower blood pressure and decrease stress. And we know that those with the neuropsychiatric disorder Tourette syndrome can sometimes calm their tics by participating in drum circles. @ 1.1

Evidently, music has the potential to help anyone. Research has shown that music may improve memory and cognition, strengthen the immune system, ease depression, and increase motivation. Music played before, during, and after surgery can reduce pain significantly. Music played during surgery appears to help the physicians as well.

There is much to learn. Scientists cannot explain the case of Tony Cicoria, a middle-aged physician who, after being struck by lightning, suddenly developed a passion and gift for playing the piano and composing. Nor can they explain the case of Clive Wearing, a British amnesia victim who, despite being able to remember just a few seconds into the past, can still play the piano, read music, and even direct choral rehearsals.

MUSIC HOTSPOTS IN THE BRAIN

- **Auditory cortex**: Perceives and analyzes sounds. Some neurons specifically respond to music.
- **Visual cortex**: Used when reading music or watching dance.
- **Somatosensory cortex**: Processes tactile feedback while playing or dancing.
- **Motor cortex**: Controls movement.
- **Prefrontal cortex**: Processes expression, behavior, and decision making.
- **Amygdala**: Processes emotions.
- **Cerebellum**: Active during movement.
- **Hippocampus**: Active during musical memories.
- **Corpus callosum**: A bridge allowing fluid communication between left and right brain. Music listening and training enhances these connections.

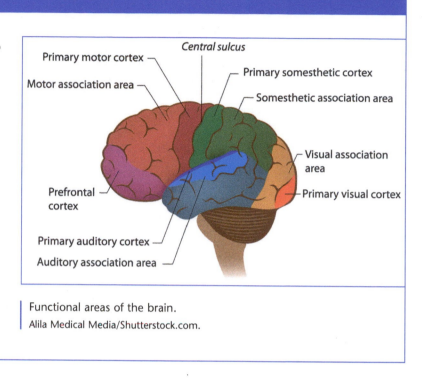

Functional areas of the brain.
Alila Medical Media/Shutterstock.com.

The human brain seems to be programmed for song. So fundamental is the human capacity for music that it may have evolved even before speech. Physiologists have shown that a mother's lullaby does double duty by lowering a child's arousal levels while simultaneously increasing the child's ability to focus attention. Music therapists have found that listening to music induces the release of pleasure-producing endorphins that ease the sensation of physical pain. Social scientists believe that music, by bringing people together to perform and listen, may have provided an early model for social cooperation, cohesion, and even reproductive success. If this is correct, then music would seem to be a fundamental building block in the development of culture.

Attentive listening is good for the brain. It helps us organize our thinking, give shape to consciousness, and focus ideas. These phenomena seem to happen for a variety of reasons and in a number of ways. Our involuntary nervous system—including heart rate, brain waves, and other basic bodily functions—automatically entrains to the sounds we hear. We also respond to music's emotional qualities. Lovely melodies softly played relax us; beating drums and searing trumpets excite us. A favorite song recalls times gone by; the sounds of a national anthem invite us to reflect upon identity.

In addition, musical training helps structure the analytical mind. Psychological studies suggest that studying music improves one's organizational skills and might even have a positive effect on IQ. Indeed, scientists hypothesize that while performing, musicians are actually engaged in high-powered brain calisthenics. These skills transfer to other areas of life.

EARS, BRAIN, AND FINGERS

The auditory cortex, which grows with musical training, can be up to 130 percent larger in musicians than in non-musicians. Brains grow when challenged with physical tasks as well. The part of the brain that governs a violinist's left-hand fingers will be larger than the part that governs the right-hand fingers. Presumably, Kurt Cobain and Jimi Hendrix, who both played the guitar "backwards," would have shown more brain growth for the right-hand fingers.

MUSIC'S NEGATIVE EFFECTS: TURN DOWN THE VOLUME!

Repeated exposure to loud sounds can affect your health and psychological wellness. Loud sounds cause hearing loss, but they also raise blood pressure, cause heart disease, increase the breathing rate, disturb digestion, and even contribute to low birth weight, birth defects, and premature birth.

Volume levels are measured in decibels (dB). Sounds louder than 80 dB are considered dangerous; those louder than 120 will cause pain. Extended exposure will cause permanent hearing loss. Fan noise from a number of football stadiums has reached volume levels exceeding 120 dB. Arrowhead Stadium in Kansas City has exceeded 140 dB, loud enough to cause immediate hearing damage.

Take care when listening. In the fall of 2007, students at Johns Hopkins University were given an assignment to calibrate noise levels in their environment. Surprisingly, they found that the highest noise levels were neither on a busy highway during rush hour nor at a symphony orchestra concert. The highest dB levels came from listening to music with earbuds. Levels often far exceeded the danger point.

MUSIC AND THE MIND

Some cultures fear music's power; others see it as a doorway to mystical experiences. For good reason. Music activates similar reactions in the brain as do food, romance, and addictive drugs. Listeners really do "get high" from music. Thousands of scientific studies have been undertaken in an attempt to understand music's remarkable impact on human consciousness.

Clearly, engaged musical experience affects consciousness in profound ways. But what does this mean for you? What if you do not play music, sing, or dance? The answer is clear. One need not perform to reap music's benefits. Simply engaging in listening (or dancing!) is enough to set the brain in high gear. And the best part of all this is that the effects of listening skills are cumulative. The better you learn to listen today, the more listening techniques you will have available tomorrow.

Music and Culture

Societies ancient and modern have recognized music's transformative agency. Indeed, Greek mythology tells us that music had power over death itself. When Orpheus's beloved wife Eurydice died and passed into the underworld, he followed. Empowered by the irresistible strains of his music, Orpheus swayed the will of the gods. Eurydice was allowed to return to the land of the living.

The idea of music's regenerative power remains relevant today. As was witnessed worldwide in the remarkable concerts following the tragedy of 9/11, music making often signifies a return to life, or the promise of life after death.

Cultures around the world have stories about the power of music. In the American Southwest, Hopi mythology tells of the primordial beings Tawa and Spider Woman, who sat together and sang humanity into existence. In India, the rhythmic dance of the Hindu deity Shiva is said to animate the universe. Music is also believed to have regenerative powers. Shamans of the Temiar ethnic group of Malaysia in Southeast Asia heal with songs received from spirit guides. To ensure a person's good fortune, Navaho ritual specialists perform the Blessingway Ceremony (*Hózhooji*), a cycle of hundreds of songs said to date back to the Creation itself. @ 1.2

Let's step back a minute. The preceding paragraph opened with the word "cultures," as if its meaning were obvious. In fact, culture is a difficult concept to digest. Anthropologists and sociologists have developed many definitions. We will start with that of British anthropologist Edward Tylor, who in 1874 defined culture as a "complex whole" that includes a people's acquired knowledge and beliefs, arts and morals, laws and customs. All groups of people everywhere have culture, said Tylor, but cultures differ significantly one from another.

Tylor saw culture as relatively static. Today, however, we understand that culture is fluid and adaptable. Culture involves material, social, and intellectual aspects of life. It is a people's way of living in the world.

Orpheus and Eurydice, August Rodin, 1893.
Courtesy of The Metropolitan Museum of Art, New York, gift of Thomas F. Ryan.

- Material aspects include the things we use and how we use them.
- Social aspects include the ways in which people interact with one another and go about organizing their communities.
- Intellectual aspects include the self-generated webs of meaning within which individuals and groups of people live their lives.

Some scholars contend that culture is deterministic, that culture is the matrix within which an individual is conditioned, and that one's fundamental nature is primarily formed by our social environment; other scholars believe that while we all live within a cultural matrix, we as individuals are free to (and are responsible for) what we become. Today, many scholars believe that fundamental notions of truth and justice, right and wrong, are relative, and that judging a cultural outsider's actions from one's own cultural perspective may lead to serious misunderstandings.

What constitutes a culture? Drawing cultural boundaries is often a matter of perspective. It is easy to think of the above-mentioned Malaysian Temiar as culturally separate from the North American Hopi or as separate from a child growing up in Paris. But what about the differences in worldview between a child raised in New York City and another raised on a Montana cattle ranch? Or what about differences in worldview between American Catholics and American Protestant evangelicals? Might these last examples constitute different cultures? Perhaps yes, if their religious ideologies sufficiently impact fundamental understandings of the world.

There are micro cultures as well. Consider, for example, a large corporation such as Sony Music Entertainment. Top executives live in a very different world from the company's generally desk-bound workforce and from the company's free-wheeling contracted musicians, such as Beyoncé or Bruce Springsteen.

What might constitute a musical culture? Perhaps it is a group of people who share particular values that are reflected in the way they make, hear, and use music. In North America, for example, the music industry divides itself for marketing purposes into specific **genres**—top 40, bluegrass, jazz, world music, classical, blues, zydeco, country and western, hip-hop, and many more. These designations offer commercial boundaries. Do they also represent distinct musical cultures?

Cultural identities are flexible and constantly negotiated, especially in today's globalized and media-linked world. Individuals move from one cultural sphere to another as they pass through adolescence, go to college, learn new languages, enter the workforce, travel, or get married. Some people will use music to reinforce their identities or to form stronger links to their cultural heritage. Teenagers, however, often use music to break free of cultural expectations. For teens, listening habits often represent an expression of individuality and independence.

GLOBALIZATION AND CULTURAL APPROPRIATION

Globalization refers to the increasingly integrated worldwide flow of material goods and ideas. Music, both because of its universal appeal and accessibility through mass media and the internet, is one of culture's most penetrating, wide-ranging, and free-flowing artifacts. Many music traditions spread through commerce and reciprocal exchange. When members of a dominant culture take or adopt elements of a minority culture, these actions are sometimes seen as cultural appropriation: trivializing, exploiting, "exoticizing," and even stealing cultural identity. In response to these critiques, adopters might claim they are promoting diversity or showing admiration for another culture. These issues remind us of the complexities of social context, privilege, and power.

As you progress through this text, think about the ideas presented here. Which musical compositions are designed to wield power? To persuade? To soothe? Do they succeed? How do these works fit into the artists' cultural milieu? And finally, how might considering music from the composers' or performers' social perspectives enhance your understanding of the world and influence your own listening choices?

Classifying Music

There are any number of ways to classify music, from very broad categories to very specific ones. For example, you and a friend might have many of the same tunes on your electronic devices, but organize them into very different playlists. We present below one common and very broad tripartite categorization system. Look carefully at the three sections. Do they make sense to you? Can you see any problem areas?

World Music or Global Music

In the early 20th century, Hungarian composer Béla Bartók (1881–1945) and other music researchers developed a new field of science called comparative musicology, which sought to study and quantitatively compare musical traditions from different parts of the world, particularly those traditions that were considered to be ethnically pure and unadulterated by outside influences. Soon, however, scholars were developing theories about change, about how musical traditions spread and develop, or sometimes entrench and stagnate. In the 1950s, the field's name was changed from comparative musicology to ethnomusicology, reflecting the emerging focus on music in its social context.

In the 1960s, the term "world music" emerged. Today, the best-known definition of world music is the one used by the commercial music industry. The term refers to local or regional music traditions outside the spheres of Western popular and art music genres. World music 1) is transmitted orally/aurally, 2) may be commercial or non-commercial in its local/everyday usage, 3) is generally categorized by geographic region (such as Africa, Asia, India, Eastern Europe), and/or 4) is generally categorized by ethnic origin (Tejano, Celtic, Afro-Cuban).

Obviously, the term world music is highly problematic. A European rock band falls under the category of popular music, not world music. But West African pop stars like Salif Keita and Youssou N'Dour, both of whom have a large European following, are considered world music artists. The problems do not end there. American "folk" music from the 1960s, for example, might be classified as world music or pop music depending on who was doing the singing, Pete Seeger or Bob Dylan.

Some scholars advocate discarding the "world music" label in favor of "global music," a term that shakes off a half century of artificially static classification problems (nation, region, ethnicity, commerce) by replacing them with fluid concepts of process and globalization, concepts that fit much better with the way we now transmit, explore, share, and collect sounds from around the planet.

Popular Music

Popular music is distinguished by these facts: 1) it is closely associated with the music industry; 2) it is distributed through the mass media; and 3) it is generally designed to appeal to a wide audience (though its commercial attraction may be short lived). Although today's top-40 music marketed to teens and young adults most closely fits the above definition, genres that may comprise popular music range from folk to film, country and western to jazz, and blues to Broadway.

Eighth-century Mayan ceramic crocodile rattle.
Courtesy of The Metropolitan Museum of Art, New York, Museum Accession.

Western Art Music

Western art music (often called "classical music") refers to a specific body of works composed mostly by Europeans and peoples of the European diaspora from the 9th century to the present. Because of its long history, the music is stylistically diverse, but in general we can say the distinguishing feature of this music is that it is composed by individuals and notated. Scholars divide Western art music into six historical periods.

The Medieval Period (ca. 400–ca. 1430)

Late 13th-century Italian manuscript page (Nativity).
Courtesy of the J. Paul Getty Museum.

The Medieval Period (or Middle Ages) refers to European history from the 5th-century collapse of the Roman Empire to the beginning of the Renaissance (ca. 1430). This period saw the development of Western musical notation, which was used in music composed for the Church and the nobility. Commoners also made music, of course, but because it was not written down, it was lost.

Early church music, sung in Latin and composed by anonymous **clerics**, had a twofold purpose: to enhance the texts of the liturgy and to inspire a connection with the divine. The music, which was called **plainchant** and consisted of a single free-flowing vocal line, also had its roots in oral tradition. Around 850, however, with the development of music notation, scribes began to write down the texts and melodies in manuscripts, as a way to preserve the repertory. It was also around that time that musicians began to decorate the original tunes by adding newly composed melody lines above and below the original plainchant. The practice of writing several independent melodies that sound at the same time is known as **polyphony**. Polyphonic music would reach extraordinary complexity during the Renaissance.

Music of the nobility consisted of secular songs in local dialects, such as the amorous **chansons** (songs) of the French **troubadours** and **trouvères**. Like plainchant, the early love songs consisted of a single melodic line, but with metric poetry and melodic and textual repetitions not found in chant. It is possible that these works may have been accompanied by instruments.

In the 13th and 14th centuries, the sacred and secular merged in a genre called the **motet** (from the French word, *mot*, meaning "word"). These polyphonic motets were in two, three, and four voices and could have a mixture of Latin (sacred) and French (secular) texts sung simultaneously. According to the medieval music theorist Johannes de Grocheo (ca. 1255–ca. 1320), motets were meant for "learned persons" who could understand their subtlety and take pleasure in their sound.

The Renaissance Period (ca. 1430–1600)

The term "Renaissance" means re-birth. It refers to a time of renewed interest in the writings, philosophies and art of ancient Greece and Rome. The era's humanist movement valued empirical evidence and reasoning, and its music was characterized by textures of complex intertwining melodies. Both Church and nobility were important patrons of music.

Because instrumental music was often improvised, much of the music that survives, both secular and sacred, is for voices. Although chant remained the most common music of the church, composers were often called upon to write lavish polyphonic settings of the **Mass Ordinary**, the parts of the Mass that use the same texts every day: the Kyrie, Gloria, Credo, Sanctus, and Agnus Dei. Polyphonic Mass settings were written for special sacred or courtly occasions.

The early polyphonic Mass was usually written for four voice parts and sung by a small group of clerics. Boys or men (singing in the **falsetto** voice) would perform the top line. (Nuns in convents also took part in singing, but generally did not perform in public settings.) Fifteenth-century composers, such as Guillaume Dufay (ca. 1397–1474), began to unify the Ordinary by placing a borrowed melody (either a sacred chant or secular tune) in the **tenor** line of each section. This melody was called a **cantus firmus** (or firm song) around which composers would then write new melodies for the cantus (or **soprano**), **alto**, and **bass** lines. In reaction to the Protestant Reformation at the end of the 16th century, Catholic Church officials banned the use of secular cantus firmi. They also called for clear text settings so the devotional texts could be understood.

German music thrived during the **Protestant Reformation**, in part because Martin Luther (1483–1546) believed that music sung in the vernacular was essential to worship. Luther developed a new genre, the **chorale**, which was a tune with sacred German text sung by the congregation. Many arrangements of chorales written during the Reformation form the basis for modern-day hymns.

Another important sacred genre was the Renaissance motet. These polyphonic works were often for four voices (five or six voices in the 16th century). In contrast to the Medieval motet, which could have had French and/or Latin texts, Renaissance motets were in Latin. Many were used for sacred ceremonies.

During the 15th century, the dominant secular genre was the French chanson, usually for three voices. In the 16th century more voices were added to the chanson and a variety of other national genres developed, including the **madrigal** in Italy and England. Solo songs accompanied by the lute were also popular in England as was **consort music**, works written specifically for instrumental ensembles.

The Baroque Period (1600–ca. 1750)

At the end of the 16th century, Italian humanists sought to revive the emotive power of ancient Greek drama. Their writings led to the invention, around 1600, of a new genre called **opera**. With plots taken from Greek mythology (in particular the love story of Orpheus and Eurydice), the earliest operas consisted of simple songs that were sparingly accompanied by a continuous bass line (**basso continuo**). To create variety, composers soon began to alternate speech-like sections of opera (**recitative**) with melodious songs (**arias**). Dancers, small choruses, and an increasingly involved instrumental accompaniment aided the genre's development. Baroque opera finales often featured a *deus ex machina*, a plot device in which any remaining (and seemingly insurmountable) problems were miraculously resolved, often by divine intervention.

Though opera was incredibly popular, it was banned in Catholic countries during the devotional season of Lent. Entertainment-hungry Baroque audiences found solace in **oratorio**, a sacred dramatic genre similar to opera, but not staged. Today, the most well-known Baroque oratorio is George Frideric Handel's *Messiah* (1741).

Many new instrumental genres arose in the Baroque period, including the **suite** (a collection of pieces based on courtly dances), the **sonata** (a work for either an unaccompanied soloist or for a solo instrument with basso continuo), and the **concerto** (a composition for soloist(s) and orchestra).

A feature that unifies the many genres and styles composed during the Baroque period is the above-mentioned basso continuo. Almost every genre, from large choral/orchestral works to accompanied song, is built on this foundational accompaniment played by a keyboard instrument (usually **harpsichord** or **organ**), and bass instrument (such as a **cello**). Another common practice in the Baroque era was the addition of decorative notes, called **ornaments**, to melodic lines, both vocal and instrumental. **Ornamentation** could either be written out by the composer or improvised by performers.

The Classical Period (ca. 1730–ca. 1820)

This period of history is more generally called the Enlightenment. The guiding principles were reason, individual rights and empowerment, and the guiding light of natural law. Along with widespread advancements in the sciences came the Industrial Revolution, which led in part to the rise of the middle class and to great changes in socio-political structures (including the American and French revolutions).

Classical period music was an "international" style that drew primary from Germanic and Italian tastes. It emphasized thematic development, clarity of line, structural symmetry, and formal balance—features reminiscent of the architectural ideals of Classical Greece from which the era gets its name. Composers relied on contrasting melodies and tonal areas to delineate formal sections. Common forms included **ternary** (ABA), **rondo** (ABACADA) and **sonata form** (exposition, development, recapitulation).

Although opera remained the most important vocal genre, new instrumental types—the **symphony** and **string quartet**—became concert staples. Performance gradually moved from private to public spheres as a growing middle class made its expanding aesthetic interests and economic power felt.

There were many gifted composers in the Classical Period, but history has canonized three in particular: Franz Joseph Haydn (1732–1809), Wolfgang Amadeus Mozart (1756–1791), and Ludwig van Beethoven (1770–1827), whose later work is generally considered to belong to the Romantic period. At various times in their lives, all three were closely associated with the city of Vienna, Austria. In part because these composers have enjoyed continuous popularity, all of Western art music is commonly referred to as "classical," though in strictest usage the term applies only to a relatively short period of music history.

The Romantic Period (ca. 1820–1900)

The Romantic Period coincided with the 19th-century rise of industrialization and nationalism, as well as the European drive for world colonization. In all the fine arts there was a focus on direct individual experience. Writers such as E.T.A. Hoffmann (1776–1822), the Brothers Grimm, Mary Shelley (1797–1851), and Edgar Allan Poe (1809–1849) explored the dark worlds of the supernatural. Visual artists like Francisco Goya (1746–1828), Caspar David Friedrich (1774–1840), J.M.W. Turner (1775–1851), and Eugene Delacroix (1798–1863) portrayed images of individuals immersed in a world pulsing with mystery and/or hyper-vitality.

Music, which was considered to be the highest of the arts (in part because it was the most ephemeral), became infused with emotional intensity. Extremes were embraced. Some performances featured soloists in private salons; others massed hundreds of musicians in outdoor venues for audiences of tens of thousands. Everywhere, virtuoso performers dazzled audiences with seemingly superhuman technique and bravura. The "universality" of classical balance gave way to the precarious uniqueness of the particular.

To meet these expressive demands, instruments were modified (even invented) as composers explored new sounds, textures, and harmonies. Orchestras doubled in size. The symphony remained a concert staple, but new genres also developed, including the **symphonic poem**, a type of **program music** that characterized themes from visual art and literature. Folk melodies and rhythms were often incorporated as composers colored their music with national or ethnic identities.

The concerto continued to be a popular concert work. Violinist Niccolò Paganini (1782–1840) played with such uncanny skill he was rumored to have sold his soul to the devil. Pianist Franz Liszt (1811–1886) moved his audiences to near hysteria.

Intimacy was also valued. The *Lied* (art song), for vocal soloist and piano, became a favorite of composers Franz Schubert, Robert and Clara Schumann, and Johannes Brahms. On the instrumental side, "Character pieces" for solo piano evoked specific moods or ideas, such as Robert Schumann's *Carnival* or Chopin's **mazurkas** (Polish folk dances).

The Twentieth-Century Period (ca. 1900–)

The Twentieth-Century Period saw remarkable changes in technology, medicine, and lifestyle. Most people born in the 1910s would not have had electricity, plumbing, or telephones in their homes. As children, they likely traveled by horse and buggy. Over the course of their lives they would see commercial air travel, the first man to land on the moon, personal computers, and the World Wide Web. They would also have lived through two world wars, nuclear proliferation, and the rise and fall of the Soviet Union.

Approaching the cusp of 1900, French painters and musicians developed an artistic style called **Impressionism**, which focused on atmosphere and mood. Shimmering colors characterized the style's

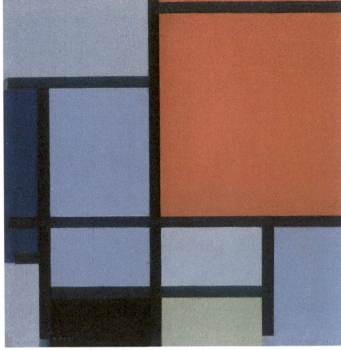

Oil on canvas, Piet Mondrian, 1921.
Courtesy of The Metropolitan Museum of Art, New York, Jacques and Natasha Gelman Collection.

The Abduction of Rebecca, Eugene Delacroix, 1846.
Courtesy of The Metropolitan Museum of Art, New York, Catharine Lorillard Wolfe Collection, Wolfe Fund, 1903.

painting; composers achieved similar effects with innovative tonalities and instrumental textures, setting the stage for a century or more of stylistic exploration.

In the century's first decades, Austrian composer Arnold Schoenberg and his students developed a new style of composition that reflected the aesthetics of **Expressionism,** a movement that sought to explore the dark reaches of the unconscious mind. Musical expressionism led to the abandonment of the major–minor scale system as composers explored **atonality,** music without a tonal center.

Alongside atonality, the 1950s and 1960s brought experimentation with electronic instruments such as the **theremin** and **synthesizer.** Tape recorders were also used to manipulate electronic, industrial, and natural sounds. The very definition of "music" was challenged. American composer John Cage was the art form's greatest iconoclast. In perhaps his most radical composition, *4'33''* (1948), the performer does nothing at all. Ambient noise in the concert hall—breathing (and perhaps someone's coughing), buzzing lights, and ventilation systems—provide the "music."

Perhaps the most notable style of late 20th-century art music was **minimalism,** a reaction against the intellectual complexities of the atonal **avant-garde,** which had come to the fore following World War II. Minimalism is characterized by harmonic consonance, steady pulse, and the slow, hypnotic transformation of musical phrases.

Perhaps it is too soon to characterize Western art music written in the early years of the 21st century. At present, it seems to embody a stylistic eclecticism that commingles disparate genres and geographic regions. Perhaps this reflects a world made small by the internet and social media. It is not extraordinary to hear references to hard core punk, bagpipe music, or Chinese *pipa* on the concert stage. Computers "performing" with live musicians is increasingly common.

QUESTIONS FOR THOUGHT

- Why do you enjoy some musical genres more than others? Have your favorites changed over time? If so, why?
- How do you think your cultural background influences or reflects the music you prefer?
- A national anthem is one obvious way in which people use music to express identity. Can you think of additional examples?
- The media often talks about different American cultures. Can you name some?
- Is all music associated with culture?

Conclusion

In this first chapter we have discussed ways in which music has a fundamental role in physiology, consciousness, and social identity. We have also presented an overview of major genres and historical periods. In the following two chapters, we complete the music fundamentals section by presenting basic theoretical concepts and terminology. After that, we shift focus to the role music plays in social experience.

By organizing our study according to universally experienced social categories—ethnicity, gender, the life cycle, politics, spirituality, love, and war—we are able to juxtapose music from the distant past and/or distant lands alongside music of the here and now. These pairings demonstrate connections between time and place that are not always apparent using chronological and mono-cultural approaches to understanding musical experience. As you read about the social contexts of the examples in the book, be sure to think about how the music you listen to communicates various social meanings.

Although we bring together a collection of wonderful music, this text is not primarily concerned with identifying and teaching an era's greatest "masterpieces" or even favorite works. Instead, we strive to give you tools for listening and for understanding music's place within the human experience. With these skills, the world will become your playlist.

Composers

The Medieval Period (ca. 400–ca. 1430)
Hildegard of Bingen (1098–1179)
Bernart de Ventadorn (ca. 1130–ca. 1200)
Leonin (fl. ca. 1150s–ca. 1201)
Beatritz de Dia (fl. late 1100s–early 1200s)
Perotin (fl. ca. 1200)
Adam de la Halle (ca. 1240–?1288)
Petrus de Cruce (fl. mid 1200s–early 1300s)
Philippe de Vitry (1291–1361)
Guillaume de Machaut (ca. 1300–1377)
Francesco Landini (ca. 1325–1397)

The Renaissance Period (ca. 1430–1600)
Guillaume Dufay (ca. 1397–1474)
Antoine Busnoys (ca. 1430–1492)
Josquin des Prez (ca. 1450–1521)
Giovanni Pierluigi da Palestrina (1525/6–1594)

Orlande de Lassus (1532–1594)
William Byrd (ca. 1540–1623)
Thomas Morley (1557/8–1602)
Carlo Gesualdo (ca. 1561–1613)
John Dowland (1563–1626)

The Baroque Period (1600–ca. 1750)
Claudio Monteverdi (1567–1643)
Jean-Baptiste Lully (1632–1687)
Johann Pachelbel (1653–1706)
Arcangelo Corelli (1653–1713)
Henry Purcell (1659?–1695)
Elisabeth Jacquet de La Guerre (1665–1729)
Antonio Vivaldi (1678–1741)
Georg Philipp Telemann (1681–1787)
Johann Sebastian Bach (1685–1750)
George Frideric Handel (1685–1759)

The Classical Period (ca. 1730–ca. 1820)
Wilhelm Friedemann Bach (1710–1784)
Carl Philipp Emanuel Bach (1714–1788)
Franz Joseph Haydn (1732–1809)
Johann Christian Bach (1735–1782)
Antonio Salieri (1750–1825)
Muzio Clementi (1752–1832)
Wolfgang Amadeus Mozart (1756–1791)
Ludwig van Beethoven (1770–1827)
   (early works)

The Romantic Period (ca. 1820–1900)
Ludwig van Beethoven (1770–1827)
   (mid and late period works)
Franz Schubert (1797–1828)
Hector Berlioz (1803–1869)
Felix Mendelssohn (1809–1847)
Frédéric Chopin (1810–1849)
Robert Schumann (1810–1856)
Franz Liszt (1811–1886)
Richard Wagner (1813–1883)
Giuseppi Verdi (1813–1901)
Clara Wieck Schumann (1819–1896)
Alexander Borodin (1833–1887)
Johannes Brahms (1833–1897)
Georges Bizet (1838–1875)
Pyotr Ilyich Tchaikovsky (1840–1893)
Giacomo Puccini (1858–1924)
Amy Beach (1867–1944)

The Twentieth-Century Period (ca. 1900–)
Claude Debussy (1862–1918)

Arnold Schoenberg (1874–1951)
Charles Ives (1874–1954)
Maurice Ravel (1875–1937)
Béla Bartók (1881–1945)
Igor Stravinsky (1882–1971)
Anton Webern (1883–1945)
Edgar Varèse (1883–1965)
Alban Berg (1885–1935)
Jerome Kern (1885–1945)
William Grant Still (1895–1978)
George Gershwin (1898–1937)
Duke Ellington (1899–1974)
Aaron Copland (1900–1990)
Ruth Crawford Seeger (1901–1953)
Dmitri Shostakovich (1906–1975)
Olivier Messiaen (1908–1992)
John Cage (1912–1992)
Benjamin Britten (1913–1976)
Leonard Bernstein (1918–1990)
Miles Davis (1926–1991)
Karlheinz Stockhausen (1928–2007)
Stephen Sondheim (b. 1930)
John Williams (b. 1932)
Krzysztof Penderecki (b. 1933)
Arvo Pärt (b. 1935)
Steve Reich (b. 1936)
Philip Glass (b. 1937)
John Corigliano (b. 1938)
Joan Tower (b. 1938)
Libby Larson (b. 1950)
Tan Dun (b. 1957)
Jennifer Higdon (b. 1962)

Key Terms

- alto
- appropriation
- aria
- atonality
- auditory cortex
- avant-garde
- bass
- basso continuo
- cantus firmus
- cello
- chorale
- classical music
- Classical Period
- clerics
- chanson
- concerto
- consort music
- culture
- deus ex machina
- Expressionism
- falsetto
- genre
- harpsichord
- Impressionism
- Lied
- madrigal
- Mass Ordinary
- mazurka
- Medieval Period
- minimalism
- motet
- opera
- oratorio
- organ
- ornaments/ornamentation
- plainchant
- polyphony
- popular music
- program music
- Protestant Reformation
- recitative
- Renaissance Period

- Romantic Period
- rondo
- sonata
- sonata form
- soprano
- string quartet
- suite
- symphonic poem
- symphony
- synthesizer
- tenor
- theremin
- ternary
- troubadour
- trouvère
- Twentieth-Century Period
- Western art music
- world/global music

Essay Questions

- How does music become meaningful to a listener?
- Is musical meaning inherent within the music or is it imposed from the outside?

CHAPTER GOALS

- To develop tools for listening.
- To understand the basic elements of music.
- To develop a vocabulary of musical understanding.
- To explore the relationships between musical sound and musical meaning.

CHAPTER TWO

Listening to Music

QUESTIONS FOR THOUGHT

- How does music communicate meaning?
- How might a composer portray heartbreak? Joy? Fear? Surprise?
- How might a composer maintain coherence in a long piece?

Engaged Listening

Music is culture-specific. It is found in every human society. Like language, each music culture has its own particularized grammar and syntax. Sounds that are important in one context may not be meaningful in another. Or, they may signify something quite different.

As children, we learned to make sense of the music around us, just as we did with our first spoken language. But to understand music's subtleties we have to actively train, or "tune," our minds to respond to the proper stimuli. This process is complex, but relatively easy to understand.

The ear itself takes in the enormous range of information from the soundscapes in which we live. But as the mind becomes engaged, we discover that not all sounds are equally important. As infants, *we learn to listen*: to identify (and make use of) relevant sounds and disregard others. This is how we learn to speak. It is also how we come to understand music.

Everyday experience offers us important listening opportunities. Consider all the elements involved when following a single conversation in a crowded and noisy room. You will:

- pinpoint the speaker's location and focus your attention in that specific direction
- single out the unique quality of the speaker's voice and tune out the others
- use context to fill in words you may have missed
- follow the speaker's lips, facial expression, or gestures for additional information.

Hearing happens automatically. Engaged listening, however, requires mental focus. It is also hugely rewarding. Let's reconsider the basic details of following a conversation, but this time in a quiet environment. Think back to a recent talk you had with a friend. You listened to words for their meanings, of course. But you also listened to much more. You took notice of your friend's tone of voice, tempo of speech, choice of words, grammatical syntax, and physical affects. From this, you deduced meanings hidden behind the words—for example, if your friend was confident or nervous, open or conspiratorial. All of this helped you to develop not only a rich interpretation of the conversation's true meaning and the speaker's true intent, but also how those meanings and intents affected you.

Compared with speech, music listening is more abstract, but the general process is the same. In music, besides the lyrics, we pay attention to the instruments used and their sound qualities, as well as to the melodies, harmonies, and rhythmic inflections. We listen for repeated patterns. Perhaps we tap a foot or sway to the rhythmic groove. If we are at a live concert, we notice the musicians' dress and stage demeanor, as well as the audience's reaction (i.e. the *audience's* performance). Moment by moment, we process this information in an attempt to figure out what the musicians are up to (what

> "Music is the art of thinking with sounds."
> —Jules Combarieu (1859–1916)

they are trying to express, and what they want us to think and feel) and what *we* are up to (how we respond and what we hope to gain from the experience).

The key to gaining a rich musical experience is to immerse oneself (mind and body) through *engaged listening*, an acquired four-part process that involves:

- attentiveness
- analysis
- interpretation
- inner awareness.

With a few moments of thought, you will notice that the four processes inform each other and occur virtually simultaneously.

Alas, practice will not make perfect. We will never become aware of everything. But engaged listening will guarantee an increasingly rich musical experience as we learn to notice ever-greater detail. As we train ourselves to follow multiple musical ideas simultaneously, we can even learn to distinguish a single player's melody amidst the sonic commotion of a full orchestra. And, of course, by directing attention inwardly we come to understand ourselves more deeply.

The Elements of Music

Performers rely on sonic road maps to navigate their way through a composition. This is true for every musical genre or style. Listeners use road maps too. The biggest difference between a performer's road map and a casual listener's road map is the level of complexity. A performer's map is necessarily intricate and multifaceted. It consists of many interrelated layers that are accessed to different degrees according to the musical demands. These layers include such basic elements as melody and harmony, rhythm and texture, and others. By comparison, a listener's map might initially include only general outlines and expectations—perhaps just the lyrics of a song, or the overall emotional feeling it projects, or the beat. It takes engaged listening to fill in the details of a musical landscape.

So how to build a sound map? We need specific tools, which we will learn to use in the following pages. Musical structures can be extremely complex, of course. Do not worry about that. Like a house made of bricks, complexity is built by combining relatively simple ideas. These ideas, or building blocks, constitute the six major "elements" or "fundamentals" of music:

1. Melody *pitches — org in times*
2. Rhythm
3. Harmony

4. Timbre *— tone*
5. Texture
6. Form *— what is playing*

In this chapter we focus on each element individually. In the next chapter we look at three compositions to see how these elements work together to construct musical meaning. As you read about each element, be sure to use the Student Supplement (@) on the text's website in order to hear examples of the concepts discussed.

Melody

At the most basic level, **melody** can be understood as a unit of **pitches** (or **tones**) sounded in succession. Stated in a more natural fashion, one might say that melody is the tune; it is the part of a **song** or **composition** you go away singing. @ 2.1

Melodies portray emotions. For example, a melody that moves between adjacent tones (**conjunct motion**) from one pitch to the next and is narrow in **range** (the distance between highest and lowest pitches) might represent calmness. Contrarily, a melody that has leaps between consecutive pitches (**disjunct motion**) might represent vigor or anxiety. Melodies that progress slowly downward often suggest relaxation, melancholy, or sadness. Melodies that move upward often represent resolve or optimism. (Experiment with these ideas by humming a favorite song. Also pay attention to how the melody fits with the lyrics.)

A melody is a sentence in tones. As you know from studying English grammar, sentences are organized into phrases and held together by periods, commas, and other punctuation. Nouns are stable; verbs suggest action. Other words function as articles and prepositions, adjectives and adverbs. In a well-constructed sentence, every word has a function—a place in the grammatical whole. So too with the tones that comprise melodies.

The Western melodic system is built upon the principle of tension and release. Each of the seven tones of the **major scale**—do, re, mi, fa, sol, la, ti (do)—embodies a different emotional tendency. "Do" (the home tone or **tonic**) and "sol" (the **dominant**) represent stability and rootedness (like nouns). Other scale degrees, particularly "ti" and "re," are relatively unstable and have action tendencies (like verbs). They generally create tension, such as a longing to return to "do." Each scale tone has its own distinct personality, as with the different colors of a rainbow or the green/yellow/red of a traffic signal.

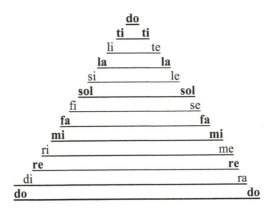

FIGURE 2.1 Chromatic scale: ascending and descending.

The term "scale" comes from the Latin *scala*, meaning ladder. Like a ladder, musical scales consist of ascending and descending steps; on each step resides a tone. The Western scale is divided into twelve equidistant steps called half-steps (or semitones). A scale that contains all twelve pitches is called a **chromatic scale** (Figure 2.1, major scale tones are in bold). The interval (or distance) from one tone to its upper or lower repetition (e.g. "do" to "do" or "sol" to "sol") is called an **octave**.

Most pieces of Western music use either major or minor scales, which consist of specific patterns of whole-steps (W) and half-steps (H). Both major and minor scales consist of seven individual tones (Figure 2.2).

Ascending
do—re—mi-fa—sol—la—ti-do
  W W H W W W H

Descending
do-ti—la—sol—fa-mi—re—do
 H W W W H W W

FIGURE 2.2 Major scale.

Minor Scales

In the Western melodic system there are three types of minor scales: natural, harmonic, and melodic. All three use a lowered third scale degree whereby "mi" becomes "me" (pronounced "may"). The differences among the three are in the raising and lowering of the sixth and seventh steps. In Figure 2.3, we present only the natural minor scale, which has lowered sixth and seventh degrees ("la" and "ti" become "le" and "te").

Ascending
do—re-me—fa—sol-le—te—do
 W H W W H W W

Descending
do—te—le-sol—fa—me-re—do
 W WH W W H W

FIGURE 2.3 Natural minor scale.

In Western art music, some hear the major scale as extroverted and joyful, the minor scale as introverted, even sorrowful. We shall see that this connotation is not always the case, but for now it might be helpful to think of major tonalities as bright in color and minor tonalities as relatively dark. Remember though, these descriptions are stereotypes that serve only as a starting point.

WESTERN MUSICAL NOTATION

Western musical notation was largely standardized during the 9th to 15th centuries. Pitch is indicated by placing symbols (called notes) on a five-line staff. Different clefs—treble and bass are most common—indicate the overall range of the staff. There are various ways to indicate the duration of notes. Notes of longer duration have empty note heads, shorter ones are black. Very short notes add "flags" on the stems. The more flags, the shorter the note. A **time signature** shows the meter (top number) and which type of note gets the beat (bottom number).

(A more detailed discussion of notation can be found on @ 2.2.)

FIGURE 2.4

"Summertime," from the opera Porgy and Bess *(1935)*

It is time for us to put some of this information to use. We begin by listening to and analyzing the song "Summertime," which has been performed by countless artists working in genres from opera to jazz to rock. We suggest you begin with a version in the style the composer intended. But as with this and every composition we study, you should explore the internet to compare and contrast different performances.

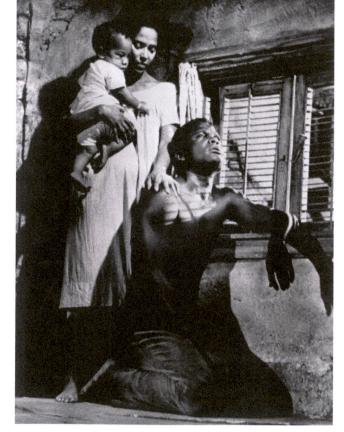

Sidney Poitier and Dorothy Jean Dandridge in *Porgy and Bess*, 1959.
Mondadori Portfolio/Getty Images.

"Summertime" from *Porgy and Bess*, by George Gershwin and DuBose Heyward

Texture: Homophonic
Meter: Quadruple
Form: Two verses, each with melodic phrases that follow ABAC pattern

The setting is a steamy evening along Catfish Row in Charleston, South Carolina. Listen to the first verse of lyricist DuBose Heyward's (1885–1940) "Summertime" from the opera *Porgy and Bess* (1935) written by composer George Gershwin (1897–1937), DuBose and Dorothy Heyward, and lyricist Ira Gershwin (1896–1983).

The verse consists of four complete sentences each of which divides neatly into two parts. Yet, none of the first three sentences seem capable of standing on their own. Each is strangely lethargic. Each requires more context. When we hear, for example, that "livin' is easy," we do not really know what to make of the news. Is easy livin' good? Bad? Indifferent? Why should we care?

We have similar emotional responses with sentences two and three. Fish seem to be plentiful, assuming one can catch them. High cotton suggests a healthy crop, but it also brings to mind the harvest's labor history and the oppressive heat of late summer in the Deep South.

We are receiving lots of information, but what to make of it? Finally, there is resolution in the fourth sentence ("Hush little baby . . ."). Now we have context. This is a lullaby. And with that knowledge perhaps we feel inner disquiet. Why tears from an innocent baby if life is so placid?

Maybe it is not.

Listen to Gershwin's melody. Mirroring the poetry, Gershwin divides the music into four melodic sections or **phrases** (Figure 2.5). After each, there is a short pause, allowing time for the singer to breathe and time for the listener to reflect.

Notice that the first and third phrases are virtually identical in terms of melodic contour. For purposes of analysis, we will label them as "A" phrases. Also notice that both A phrases meander downward in an easy manner.

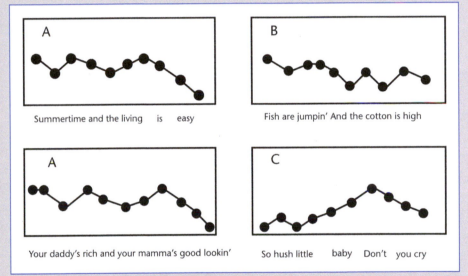

FIGURE 2.5 Melodic map of "Summertime."

Relaxed though they are (and like the lyrics they enhance), the phrases do not provide a sense of resolution. Why? Because the phrases end on the pitch "sol," the dominant, rather than "do," the tonic. The listener is left suspended in mid-air.

The second phrase (the "B" phrase) is similar in shape and general downward direction to the A phrases, but the range is narrower. As B begins, we wonder if it will provide the anticipated resolution to the initial A phrase, but by ending on "re," it does not.

Do you see how Gershwin (as did Heyward) is delaying satisfaction? He makes us continue to listen to the complete story.

The awaited resolution finally comes with the fourth phrase (the "C" phrase), which begins on the same low pitch that ended the A phrases. Notice that in contrast to the first three phrases, which all begin on the same pitch and move

continued

downward, the C phrase has a generally upward direction, though in the end it too relaxes downward, but now to "do," the tonic.

Notice the tidy balance of the ABAC format. Four distinct sections divide neatly into two main groupings: AB and AC.

Take a moment to consider what a strange, wonderful, and emotionally complex world the song has created. It is as if the plain meanings of everyday life have been suspended in a dream, the implications of which are just out of conscious reach. Such is the power of a well-constructed composition. (For more about Gershwin's *Porgy and Bess*, see @ 2.3.)

Melody in the Non-Western World: An Example from North India

We have seen that Western melodies are built on specific concepts and expectations. Composers engage those ideas when writing music. The Western system is not universally employed, however. In the classical music of India, for example, melodies are based on pitch collections called *ragas*. @ 2.4

- A raga is a collection of tones (*svaras* or *swaras*), each of which has a name: *sa–re–ga–ma–pa–dha–ni–sa*).

- Individual ragas are associated with specific emotions or spiritual states. Some are linked to particular times of the day or night.

- The distance between the tones, except for the foundational interval between sa and pa, may be slightly larger or smaller from one raga to the next. Thus, a raga's tones, which might fall between the measured half- and whole-steps of the Western scale, sometimes sound unusual to the Western ear.

Plaque with dancer and veena player, 1st century, BCE.
Courtesy of The Metropolitan Museum of Art, New York, Samuel Eilenberg Collection, Gift of Samuel Eilenberg, 1987.

- There are rules governing the way the pitches are used. For example:
  o Ragas may be characterized by the movement between pairs of tones.
  o Melodic sequences may require that tones be altered, skipped over, repeated, or left out.
  o The ascending form of a raga may be different from its descending form.
  o Even though two ragas may contain the same pitches, they can be distinguished by melodic emphasis or characteristic melodic combinations.

Generally speaking, classical Indian music begins with an improvised and rhythmically free section known as *alapana* (or simply, *alap*). It is here in the alap that the raga's various tonal, melodic, and emotional characteristics are introduced. We will listen to a brief alap excerpted from a longer performance by *sitar* player Ravi Shankar (1920–2012) and *sarod* player Ali Akbar Khan (1922–2009). The two musicians take turns interjecting brief musical ideas.

SITAR AND SAROD

Mid 19th-century sitar.
Courtesy of The Metropolitan Museum of Art, New York, The Crosby Brown Collection of Musical Instruments, 1889.

Sarod, ca. 1885.
Courtesy of The Metropolitan Museum of Art, New York, The Crosby Brown Collection of Musical Instruments, 1889.

Both of these plucked stringed instruments are members of the **lute** family and are associated with the North Indian (Hindustani) music tradition. The instruments share many commonalities, but also have significant differences in both sound and construction. The sitar's resonating body is made of gourd (on the back) and wood on the face (and sometimes has a second gourd attached to the neck); the sarod's resonating body has a teak back and a goatskin face. A sitar has moveable frets along the neck; a sarod has no frets at all (like a violin). Both use "melody" strings, drone strings, and numerous high-pitched sympathetic resonance strings, which add richness to the tonal spectrum. The sounds are easy to distinguish. The sitar—first made popular in the West by Shankar, and soon after by George Harrison of The Beatles (and other rock musicians)—has a shimmering tone quality; the sarod's tone is relatively dark and unadorned.

WHAT IS A LUTE?

German lute, 1596.
Courtesy of The Metropolitan Museum of Art, New York, Gift of Joseph W. Drexel, 1889.

Lutes are one of the world's most common instrument types. Guitars, banjos, mandolins, and violins are types of lutes. In all of these instruments, the strings are attached to and then run across and parallel to the resonating body. Strings are then stretched along a neck. There is also an instrument simply called "lute," which was fashionable in Europe in the Renaissance and Baroque periods. The lute intersected with popular culture when the English rock musician Sting (b. 1951) recorded 16th-century songs for voice and lute on his album *Songs from the Labyrinth* (2006).

LISTENING 2.2 GUIDE

Excerpt in Chatuttal Manj-Khamaj raga, performed by Ravi Shankar (sitar) and Ali Akbar Khan (sarod)

Texture: Biphonic and heterophonic
Meter: Unmetered
Form: Open

ALAPANA

0:00	The music begins with the soft sound of the *tambura*, a large resonant four-string lute that plays a **drone** on the pitches "sa" and "pa." The tambura continues throughout the composition and has the essential role of providing the never-changing tonal atmosphere into which all other pitches of the raga are projected and understood. The drone is omnipresent, like a garden's scent. Even so, once the other instruments enter, the tambura's tones are hardly noticed.
0:05	The sarod player strums his open strings. Moments later, the sitarist does the same. Notice the difference in the instruments' tone colors.
0:09	The sarod introduces the tones of the raga, which are similar to a Western major scale. There are small differences, however. Listen carefully and you will notice alterations of the 4th and 7th scale degrees (the 4th, or "ma," is sometimes raised; the 7th, or "ni," is sometimes lowered. These inflections might go unnoticed in casual listening, but not only do they help define the pillar tones (degrees 5 and 1) immediately above, they are also important contributors to the raga's mercurial quality.
0:18	The sitar follows with a similar melodic gesture. (Make sure you identify the tone color [timbre] difference between sarod and sitar.) Note that both sarod and sitar melodies begin and end on "ga," the 3rd scale degree. The instrumentalists play different melodies, but common beginnings and ends unite them. Notice how both musicians bend pitches higher and lower.
0:33	A melodic conversation begins between the two instrumentalists. Sometimes one will echo the other; other times, new ideas are introduced, always in the spirit of conversation. Notice the continued emphasis on the pitch "ga." Also notice the fluidity of the melodic gestures. There is no steady pulse.
1:02	The sarod embarks on an extended improvisation. Notice the temporal space between tones.
1:40	The sitar takes over. Do you feel the tension of the raised 4th scale degree briefly sounded at 1:48?
2:00	Sitar moves down the scale for a full octave.
2:17	Sarod enters. Sitar briefly answers at 2:24. Sarod continues. Higher tones are presented. Do not be impatient. Think of this as a gentle introduction to the raga's tones and emotional qualities. We are on an unfolding adventure of discovery.
3:33	The two instruments play together in melodic and rhythmic unison. This marks the introduction of the pre-composed melody that will be prominent in the composition's next section. We will return to this music in Chapter 14.

Rhythm

Rhythm refers to the ways in which music is organized into distinct time units. 🌀 2.5 To illustrate this, we will study the hymn tune "Amazing Grace," which is built on a general pattern of short and long tones (Figure 2.6).

A crucial element of rhythm is pulse, or **beat**. Understanding beat is simple; it is what you tap your foot to, what you step to when you dance, and what soldiers march to.

Beats are generally organized into repeated groups (**measures**, or "bars") of strong and weak pulses. In most Western music, the first beat of every measure (the **downbeat**) is strongest. The number and accentuation of beats in each measure determines a composition's **meter**. Meter is a fundamental

ACTIVITIES AND ASSIGNMENTS

- Use the internet to listen to many different versions of "Summertime." Besides different operatic versions, listen to versions by Billie Holiday (1915–1959), Nora Jones (b. 1979), Ella Fitzgerald (1917–1996) and Louis Armstrong (1901–1971), and Janis Joplin (1943–1970), and more. Which do you like best? Why? Finally, listen to the remarkable recording by Albert Ayler (1936–1970). What was Ayler up to? How does knowing these other versions help you understand his?

- Take a familiar song and map its melodic phrases. Which phrases sound final? Which sound incomplete? On what pitch does the melody want to end? Where in the phrases are the highest notes? The lowest? Is the melody conjunct or disjunct? Is the range narrow or wide? How do these characteristics affect your emotional response?

- Use the internet to find examples of traditional music from non-Western cultures. Does the melodic language sound different from what you are used to? Describe the differences using the concepts above.

organizing principal, a temporal yardstick that organizes rhythm's various elements into a cohesive whole, like organizing inches into feet, or feet into yards.

short	long	short	long	short	long	short	long
A-	**ma-**	zing	**grace;**	how	**sweet**	the	**sound.**

FIGURE 2.6
"Amazing Grace" rhythm pattern.

To find the beat and meter in "Amazing Grace," recite the lyrics above and tap out a steady pulse that gives one tap to the "short" tone and two taps to the "long" tone. When long and short patterns are thus combined we get a repeating pattern of three pulses, called triple meter. Music that groups into two beats per measure is called duple meter; four beats per measure is quadruple meter.

So far, the concept of rhythm seems pretty simple. But there is one more issue to tackle. Where does the meter begin? On which pulse? Meter is rooted by the downbeat, but many compositions begin elsewhere. For example, "Amazing Grace" begins on beat three. With a moment's thought, you will see why.

Say the word "amazing" and notice that the second syllable, not the first, is the strongest. So, if lyrics and meter are going to align (and they must), "ma" has to fall on the downbeat. This means that the first syllable ("A") must fall on a preparatory beat leading to one. Thus, the syllable "A" is on the **pickup** beat to the meter's beginning (Figure 2.7).

short	long	short	long	short	long	short	long
A-	**ma-**	zing	**grace;**	how	**sweet**	the	**sound.**
3	1	2	3	1	2	3	1	2	3	1	2

pickup note

FIGURE 2.7
"Amazing Grace" metric analysis.

Notice that lyricists almost always place the most important words or naturally accented syllables on strong beats. Thus in "Amazing Grace" the accented syllable "ma" is placed on the strong beat one, as are the colorful words "sweet" and "sound."

"Amazing Grace" is a beloved hymn, and because the rhythm is so clear it is an excellent tune by which to introduce the concept of meter. But the fact is, triple meter songs are relatively unusual today. Almost all popular music in the United States (even the world) is organized into two- or four-beat units, duple or quadruple meter.

The last aspect of rhythm we need to discuss here is **tempo**. @ 2.6 Simply put, tempo refers to the pace at which the beats go by. It is fine to refer to tempos as fast or slow, but classically trained musicians, who follow a European system developed over centuries, often use Italian terms, such as adagio (at ease), andante (walking tempo), and allegro (lively). These are the words you will generally see in the program book for a recital or symphony orchestra concert, even in English-speaking counties.

Tempo might stay steady throughout an entire work. Or it might vary. Tempo can change gradually or suddenly. Often tempo changes signify a shift in emotional focus, or a shift from one musical section to another.

Rhythm in the non-Western World: An Example from Southeast Asia

RAMAYANA

The *Ramayana* (*Rama's Journey*) is an epic Sanskrit poem of 24,000 verses, the authorship of which is attributed to the poet Valmiki, who lived during the 4th century BCE.

Valmiki tells the story of Rama (a worldly incarnation of the Hindu deity Vishnu) who lives on Earth unaware of his divine heritage and worldly mission. Through his life, Rama endures hardships and learns many difficult lessons.

Rama's greatest trial begins when his wife Sita is kidnapped by the many-headed demon Ravana, who desires Sita for himself. With the help of the monkey god Hanuman (according to some mythology, an avatar of the Hindu deity Shiva) and Hanuman's monkey army, Rama is able to defeat Ravana.

Just as concepts of melody vary from culture to culture, rhythmic organizations also differ. A contrasting approach to rhythmic organization can be found in Bali, Indonesia, an island famous for its physical beauty, bronze **gamelan** orchestras, and interlocking rhythms. @ 2.7 These interlocking patterns can be heard in *Kecak* (pronounced ké-chak), a composition for narrator and men's chorus.

Kecak, which is drawn from the Hindu epic the *Ramayana* (*Rama's Journey*), tells of Lord Rama's battle with the demon Ravana. The chorus takes on the role of a monkey army, which chatters away with great energy. To achieve this effect, the men divide into groups and shout "monkey sounds" ("cak") in interlocking rhythmic patterns. Each pattern includes short spaces for breathing, while an adjacent pattern fills in the empty space of the other. This interlocking technique is called *kotekan*, a foundation of Balinese music making. Kotekan may be performed vocally (as in *Kecak*) or between the instruments of the gamelan.

A standard kotekan pattern for three groups of *Kecak* performers is diagrammed in Figure 2.8. Give it a try by forming a trio (or a duet using patterns 1 and 2). Reading from left to right, sing the patterns while clapping the steady beat. For familiarity, first have everyone sing each of the lines together. Then, divide the parts so that each person (or group) sings a different line. You will notice

Kecak dance in Bali, March 28, 2016.

Cmichel67/Wikimedia Commons/CC-BY-SA-4.0.

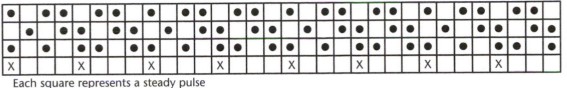

Each square represents a steady pulse
Clap the beat on X
● Represents "cak"
☐ Represents silence

FIGURE 2.8
Kotekan pattern.

that all the patterns have the same exact sequences of sounds and silences, but because each pattern fits differently against the underlying pulse, each *feels* different. When the patterns are performed together, every temporal subdivision is filled with a sound. (This is also the case when patterns one and two or patterns two and three are performed together.)

QUESTIONS FOR THOUGHT

- What would a composite diagram of all the kotekan parts look like?
- Notice in "Amazing Grace" that the full syllable is "maz," but that when sung the "z" is moved back and attached to the "ing." Experiment singing the phrase both ways. Why does the "z" get moved?
- How do you identify meter in music without words? What are the cues?
- Tap out the beats to a song you know. Is there a pickup beat? Do the beats group into twos/fours (duple/quadruple) or threes (triple)? Have one person clap the rhythm of the piece and one person tap the beat. What's the difference between the rhythm and the beat?

ACTIVITIES AND ASSIGNMENTS

- Compose an interlocking pattern for two people. Perform it for the class.
- Find a video of *Kecak* on the internet. Do you hear a pulse?

Harmony

Harmony occurs when at least two different pitches sound at the same time, such as when two people sing together with different material or when a musician strums the strings of a guitar. Harmonies that sound pleasing to our ears are said to be **consonant**. Those that sound harsh or clash are said to be **dissonant**. As a general rule, dissonant harmonies are used to produce feelings of anxiety or tension. @ 2.8

Different cultures and time periods have different standards of what is consonant and dissonant. A musician in the 12th century, for instance, would likely find the works of Wolfgang Amadeus Mozart (1756–1791) to be jarringly dissonant. Today, however, we consider Mozart's music to be quite soothing.

In Western art music, three or more pitches that sound at the same time create a **chord**. Chords are built according to specific rules. The most basic rule is that a simple three-tone chord, or **triad**, is built upward from the bottom (or "root") in alternating scale tones. Thus, a triad built on "do" will skip "re," include "mi," skip "fa," and end on "sol." The resulting triad will be do–mi–sol.

Chords function in a manner similar to melodic scale tones in that they too have varying degrees of stability. A chord built on the first scale degree (do–mi–sol) is the most stable. This is called the "tonic" or (Roman numeral) I chord. Most pieces in the Western tradition begin and end on the

I   IV   V   I

FIGURE 2.9
I–IV–V chord
progression.

tonic chord. The "dominant," or "V" chord, is second in foundational importance to the tonic chord. It is built on the fifth scale degree (sol–ti–re). The dominant chord has a tendency to return home to the tonic. Third in foundational importance is the "**subdominant**," or "IV" chord (fa–la–do). The subdominant tends to move either to the tonic or the dominant (Figure 2.9).

These three chords make up the harmonic backbone of Western music. If you string these together (subdominant [IV], dominant [V] and tonic [I]), you get a common ending formula known as a **cadence**. Slightly more complex (and more common) are cadential progressions based on the chord series I–vi–ii–V–I. George Gershwin's hugely popular song "I've Got Rhythm" (1930) followed this pattern almost throughout. Even today, musicians call the sequence "rhythm changes." It remains a standard progression in both jazz and pop music.

ACTIVITIES AND ASSIGNMENTS

- Keeping the alternating-scale-tones rule in mind, build a triad based on "re"; build a triad based on "la." Notice that chords often share tones with one another. Triads built on "do" (do–mi–sol) and "la" (la–do–mi) have two tones in common. Triads based on "fa" (fa–la–do) and "do" (do–mi–sol) have one tone in common.

Timbre

Every sound has a particular color or **timbre**. It is through timbre that you can tell the difference between your grandmother's voice and your girlfriend's, a flute and a violin, and (if you listen carefully) even distinguish one violin from another. During the course of the semester we will find that timbre can identify not only the individual or instrument producing the sound, but perhaps also the particular culture from which the music derives. In vocal music, for example, certain cultures value purity of tone while others value tones that are grainy or strongly nasal. So too, some instruments have a harsher quality than others. An instrument's timbre depends on a combination of three factors: 1) the size of the instrument, 2) what it is made of, and 3) how the sound is produced. Playing styles can also influence timbre.

DYNAMICS

Dynamics refer to the volume of a note or passage of music. In Western art music, Italian terms are used to indicate how loudly or softly to play.

forte (*f*) = loud

piano (*p*) = soft.

Other dynamic markings include:

fortissimo (*ff*), louder than *forte*

mezzo-forte (*mf*), moderately loud

mezzo-piano (*mp*), moderately soft

pianissimo (*pp*), softer than *piano*.

The term *crescendo* means to get louder; *decrescendo* means to get softer.

MUSICAL INSTRUMENT CLASSIFICATION SYSTEMS

Musical instruments are categorized in many ways, though the most common in the Western system is that used in the modern orchestra: **strings, woodwinds, brass,** and **percussion**. The early 20th-century German scholars Kurt Sachs and Erich von Hornbostel created a more formal classification system based on five large categories: **chordophones** (stringed instruments: guitar, violin, etc.), **aerophones** (wind instruments: flute, trumpet, etc.), **membranophones** (drums), **idiophones** (shaken or struck instruments: maracas, xylophones, gongs, etc.), and **electrophones** (synthesizers, radios, theremins, etc.). @ 2.9

QUESTIONS FOR THOUGHT

- Do you see potential weaknesses in the above musical instrument classification systems?
- The first classification system presented above is based on the instruments' role in the orchestra. The second is based on how the sound is produced. What others systems might work?
- Where does an acoustic instrument leave off and its electric counterpart begin? Rock guitarists, for example, create many new sounds through electronic effects.
- Theater companies, TV and movie producers try to save money by reproducing the sounds of instruments electronically rather than paying musicians. What effect does this have on the music? On the musicians? On the economy?
- In the 17th and 18th centuries, the trombone was associated with the underworld and death. Are certain instruments associated with particular ideas today?
- Notice how people change the timbre and pitch of their voices when talking to babies, yelling at a sports referee, or talking in front of a crowd. How and why do you change the timbre of your voice?

ACTIVITIES AND ASSIGNMENTS

- Bring an instrument into class and perform. Have your classmates describe the sound.
- Make an idiophone with things in your backpack or on your desk. Can you make a chordophone? An aerophone?
- As you listen to the pieces discussed in later chapters, describe the timbres you hear (nasal, clear, rough, etc.). Then consider how timbre affects meaning.

Texture

The ways in which different musical parts fit together is called **texture**. Music can have different textures. @ 2.10 A large orchestral texture might be described as thick, like velvet. A solo flute might be silky thin. Music theorists categorize texture according to five different characteristics:

1. Monophony
2. Polyphony
3. Homophony
4. Heterophony
5. Biphony.

Monophony consists of a single musical line without accompaniment. Even though many voices or instruments might be involved, as long as all are sounding the exact same line, the texture is monophonic.

Polyphony involves several independent lines sounding simultaneously. The simplest kind of polyphony is a round (also called a canon). A good example is the children's song "Row, Row, Row Your Boat" in which everyone sings the same melody at a different time.

In more complex examples of polyphony, the independent melodies are not necessarily the same tune. Instead, complementary lines are

Kyrie eleison

LISTENING 2.3 GUIDE

This setting of Kyrie eleison is an example of a monophonic, sacred chant from the Middle Ages (see Chapter 7: Music and Spirituality). Notice that all of the voices are singing the exact same melody.

LISTENING 2.4 GUIDE — Kyrie from the *Pope Marcellus Mass,* by Giovanni Pierluigi da Palestrina

Listen to the six-voice polyphonic setting of the Kyrie eleison text by the Renaissance composer Giovanni Pierluigi da Palestrina (ca. 1525–1594). Notice how each voice enters separately, one after the other.

soprano 1 _____

alto 2 _____

tenor 1 3 _____

tenor 2 4 _____

bass 1 5 _____

bass 2 6 _____

FIGURE 2.10
Diagram of vocal entrances in Palestrina's Kyrie eleison.

LISTENING 2.5 GUIDE — "Amazing Grace," performed by the Robert Shaw Festival Singers

Listen to the Robert Shaw Festival Singers singing "Amazing Grace." Concentrate on the texture, particularly the relationship between the melody and the accompanying chords.

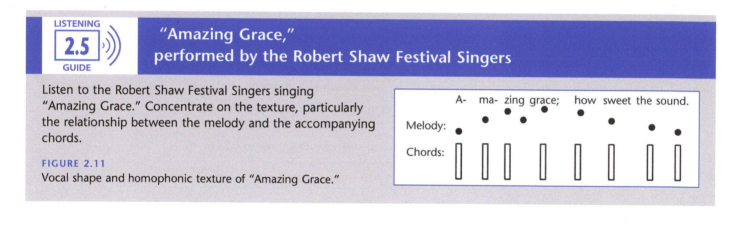

FIGURE 2.11
Vocal shape and homophonic texture of "Amazing Grace."

woven together like threads in a tapestry. Much of the music of the Renaissance and Baroque periods was written polyphonically. Composers relied on a strict set of compositional rules to combine the different lines. Later composers often used polyphony to indicate a "learned" or elevated style of music.

Homophonic texture consists of a melody plus chordal accompaniment, such as a guitar-strumming folksinger. The basic idea behind homophony is that the accompanimental tones sound together as a whole rather than as individual parts. For example, when a musician strums a six-string guitar, the listener hears a single event comprising six tones, rather than six individual tones each with its own particular identity. In the Western tradition, the vast majority of hymns, folk tunes, and popular songs are set in a homophonic texture. More complex homophonic textures may be found in symphonic works and other pieces from the Western art music tradition, but these, too, are considered to be homophonic since they are based on an underlying chordal foundation.

Heterophony is heard when a single basic melody is performed slightly differently by two or more performers. For instance, one singer/player might add embellishments to his version of the melody in order to differentiate it from that of another musician. Or, he might perform it with slightly different rhythms from the other performer. This texture is uncommon in Western music, but is often used in Middle Eastern, Asian, and Native American cultures.

Biphony refers to two separate lines consisting of a melody plus a drone. Biphonic music is often found in world music repertories. Bagpipes use drone pipes along with the melody pipe. A **harmonic singer** can produce both a drone and a melody. Most Indian music uses a drone instrument to establish the tone "sa."

"Tarawangsa," performed by S.B. Manchakai

LISTENING
2.6
GUIDE

In this excerpt, one musician plays the *tarawangsa*, a two-stringed fiddle, while the other plays a small zither called a *kapaci*. As the kapaci player plucks the main tones of the melody, the tarawangsa player uses a bow to perform an embellished version of the same tune.

"Tuvan Folk Melody"

LISTENING
2.7
GUIDE

In this Tuvan folk melody, a vocalist produces a melody above an unchanging drone. How does he do it? First, he produces the drone pitch with his vocal chords. Then, by moving his lips and tongue in various ways, he changes the shape and size of his oral cavity. As this resonating chamber is reshaped, different overtones are emphasized. These overtones make up the melody.

ACTIVITIES AND ASSIGNMENTS

- With a partner, read the following words aloud in exact unison: "Monophonic music requires perfect blend." If you succeeded in being in unison, you performed in a monophonic style. Now, choose a new sentence that your partner does not know. Say it aloud and have your partner repeat what you say as she hears it. Inevitably, she will speak her words slightly behind yours, maybe even leave out or change a word. This is heterophony.

MUSICAL GENRES

The word "genre" means "type" or "kind." Most cultural artifacts (art, literature, cinema, music, etc.) are labeled according to genre (novel vs. poem; watercolor vs. oil painting, for example). The following list includes the more common genres of Western art music; those you are likely to encounter in a concert setting.

Song: a work for a solo vocalist, usually with piano accompaniment (note that the term "song" is not a generic term for all pieces of music. Generally, if you do not hear singing, you are not hearing a song. Use the terms "piece" or "work" as a good substitute for "song.")

Symphony: a large-scale work written for a symphony orchestra, usually consisting of separate sections called movements.

Concerto: a work for a solo instrument accompanied by a symphony orchestra, usually in three movements.

Sonata: a multi-movement piece either for solo piano or for piano plus one other instrument. For instance, a violin sonata would be for violin and piano.

Opera: a staged drama told in music.

Chamber music: any number of instrumental combinations usually written for nine or fewer players. The most prevalent is the string quartet, written for two violins, viola, and cello.

Form

Form refers to the overall shape or structure of a piece of music. Composers generally have a basic form in mind before starting to write. Occasionally the form is the invention of the composer, but usually it conforms to a traditional structure. Examples of traditional Western art music forms include **binary** (two parts); **ternary** (three parts); and **rondo**, in which a familiar **refrain** alternates with new material. Forms common to Western popular music include **32-bar song form** and **12-bar blues**. Composers use their full arsenal of musical elements to distinguish different sections of a form, including: melody, rhythm, harmony, texture, and timbre. Through repetition, contrast, and development, composers can both set up and thwart expectations. They can create tension or relaxation, chaos or order. We will consider these forms in subsequent chapters. @ 2.11

QUESTIONS FOR THOUGHT

- Why might composers use forms for their music? Why not just write whatever comes into their heads?

ACTIVITIES AND ASSIGNMENTS

- Find artworks or poetry (or create your own) that illustrate the equivalent of binary, ternary, and rondo forms. How are the different sections delineated?
- Experiment with writing your own music. Try to incorporate aspects of each of the musical elements discussed in the text.

Conclusion

This chapter equipped us with a vocabulary comprising the basic tools used to describe, order, and analyze our listening experience. In subsequent chapters we put these tools to use in making sense of our musical world. The repertoire is wonderfully diverse, but general analytical techniques can be applied universally. With practice we will hear new complexities within single compositions, as well as connections between different musical genres, musical cultures, and historical eras.

Key Terms

- 12-bar blues
- 32-bar song form
- alapana
- beat
- binary
- biphony (biphonic)
- composition
- conjunct motion
- consonant
- dominant
- disjunct motion
- dissonant
- downbeat

- drone
- form
- gamelan
- genre
- harmony
- heterophony (heterophonic)
- homophony (homophonic)
- kotekan
- measure (or bar)
- melody
- meter
- monophony (monophonic)
- octave

- phrase
- pickup
- pitch (or tone)
- polyphony (polyphonic)
- raga
- range
- rondo
- rhythm
- sarod
- scale (major, minor, chromatic)
- sitar
- song

- subdominant
- tambura
- tempo
- ternary
- texture
- timbre
- tonic
- triad

Essay Questions

- How might an understanding of musical elements encourage engaged listening?
- How might a composer or lyricist create multiple layers of meaning?
- Physicality and space are essential elements in the formation and experience of visual art (painting, sculpture, architecture). What elements are essential in the formation and experience of sonic art?

CHAPTER GOALS

- To demonstrate how the ideas introduced in Chapter 2 apply to musical examples from three different musical traditions.

CHAPTER THREE

Three Listening Examples

In Chapter 2 we undertook a general overview of musical terminology. Now we apply these tools by studying three compositions. Each is from a different time and culture; each has a different social purpose. As you listen to the examples, keep in mind the various musical elements and how they express meaning.

"Bourrée" by J.S. Bach

If during a eulogy for German Baroque-era composer Johann Sebastian Bach (1685–1750) someone had stated that 250 years after his death the composer would be considered one of a handful of giants in Western art music, the Protestant mourners, though sure to remain respectful, would have found the idea incomprehensible. Bach was a skilled musician to be sure, but others, now mostly forgotten, were more highly regarded. Nevertheless, the eulogist's words would have been true. Few composers have cast a shadow as broad and enduring as J.S. Bach.

Bach lived his life within a limited geographical area. @ 3.1 He was born in the town of Eisenach, spent most of his life in small towns, and never left Germany. Large in creative spirit, but humble in ego, Bach was content to labor in the background. He considered himself a craftsman and a hard worker. Neither fame nor fortune interested him. In their own lives (and even that of their father's), four of his sons were far more prominent composers than he.

Bach was best known as a skilled improviser and keyboardist. As a Lutheran church organist, he was accustomed to extemporizing preludes and elaborating on hymn tunes for church services. These, however, were skills expected of any reasonably accomplished church musician.

How good an improviser was Bach? Indicative is a story from May 1747 when he visited the Potsdam court of Frederick II of Prussia (Frederick the Great, 1712–1786), who was himself an accomplished amateur musician. During an evening of chamber music, the king presented Bach with a melody that he had composed. Bach took the melody, sat down at the keyboard, and effortlessly improvised an intricate polyphonic composition called a **fugue**. The melody continued to hold Bach's attention. He went on to write thirteen pieces, each a complex elaboration of the original melody. Bach dedicated the collection, known as *The Musical Offering*, to Frederick II. @ 3.2

Bach's compositional output was extraordinary. His catalog of works (*Bach-Werke-Verzeichnis*, or BWV) lists over 1000 compositions; the complete recorded set fills 153 CDs. Bach wrote for nearly every imaginable combination of instruments and voices. From works for solo violin to pieces for chorus and orchestra, Bach's output was of universally high quality. Many of his compositions— such as his sonatas and partitas for violin solo, a collection of pieces for **harpsichord** called *The Well-Tempered Clavier*, and the *Brandenburg Concertos*, to name just a few—are considered among Western art music's greatest achievements.

Bach's first important job came in 1708 when the Duke of Weimar hired him as organist, chamber musician, and eventually as first violinist in the court orchestra. Six of his twenty children were born in Weimar. It was there that Bach wrote the first of his didactic works, the *Little Organ Book*, for his eldest son and future composer, Wilhelm Friedemann Bach (1710–1784).

Bach left Weimar in 1717 to accept a position in the court of Prince Leopold of Cöthen. The transition was not easy, however. At first the Duke of Weimar refused Bach's resignation and even

"When I don't like a piece of music, I make a point of listening to it more closely."
—Florent Schmitt (1879–1958)

Portrait of J.S. Bach seated at the organ, 1725.

imprisoned him for "too stubbornly forcing the issue of his dismissal." After nearly four weeks in detention, Bach was granted an "unfavorable discharge" and allowed to move his family to Cöthen.

Once there, work went well. The prince was an amateur musician who enjoyed having music at court, but he was also a Calvinist, with little use for music in worship. Therefore, Bach's Cöthen output was mainly secular. He wrote mostly instrumental works for members of the court orchestra, including his six Brandenburg concertos.

In 1723 Bach moved his family to Leipzig, a cosmopolitan city of 30,000. Bach spent the last twenty-seven years of his life there, serving as music director at the St. Thomas Church and as the city's director of music. Those duties included composing, rehearsing, and performing music for the city's four main churches; overseeing music for the town council and university; and providing musical training for the fifty to sixty boys at the boarding school attached to St. Thomas Church.

As much as we revere Bach's music today, it was rarely performed in the years immediately following his death. Bach lived at a time when audiences were more interested in what was new; the past was invariably out of fashion. That attitude took a seismic shift in 1829 when 20-year-old German composer and conductor Felix Mendelssohn (1809–1847) put together a performance of the *St. Matthew Passion*, one of Bach's most important works (see Chapter 7: Music and Spirituality). The audience was moved and intrigued by what it heard. Thus began not only the reintroduction of Bach's music to the public but also an interest in historical music in general.

LISTENING 3.1 GUIDE

"Bourrée" from Suite in E minor, by Johann Sebastian Bach

Texture: Polyphonic
Meter: Duple
Form: Binary

Though the bourrée originated as a 17th-century French folk dance, by the mid-18th century it was commonly danced by the nobility. Bourrées were cheerful and lively, used both as a social courtship dance and in theatrical entertainments. They were in duple meter and usually began with a pickup beat. The dance began with a plié (a slight bending of the knees), which provided the impetus to rise gracefully onto the balls of the feet and flow into a variety of gliding steps. Gentle leaps and hops often separated the steps. @ 3.3

Bach and other composers of the Baroque period wrote bourrées (as well as other popular dances) and included them in instrumental **suites**. Comprising four to six different dances, a suite was meant for listening only. Even so, each dance retained its representative meter and character, thus reminding listeners of the social dances they knew so well.

PART 1 (A)	0:00	Phrase one (a)
	0:06	Phrase two (b)
PART 1 (A) Repetition	0:12	Phrase one (a)
	0:17	Phrase two (b)

Part 1 (A) consists of two angular phrases. Both begin in the upper register on "do," ascend to "me" and then meander up and down, eventually heading toward the bottom of the melody's range. The first phrase ends on "do," an octave below the first note of the phrase. Notice the octave leap that results when moving to phrase two. The second phrase

begins like the first, but ends on "me," which briefly becomes the new home tone, or tonic of a parallel major scale. This momentary "home away from home" pivots the listener either back to the beginning (for the repeat) or on to the next section.

Try conducting the beat. Or better yet (since this is a stylized dance), walk to the beat so that you can feel the rhythm in your entire body. How quickly should you step? Let your body and intuition tell you which rate is most appropriate. Perhaps you have noticed that the rhythm is extremely repetitive—short–short–long, short–short–long, etc.—and also extremely propulsive. Notice how the two quick tones push the melody (and your stepping body) forward.

PART 2 (B)	0:23	Phrase one (c)
	0:29	Phrase two (d)
	0:35	Phrase three (e)
	0:41	Phrase four (f)

The B section is longer, with four separate phrases whose melodies differ from those in the A section. The short–short–long rhythmic motive carries over from the first section, but here the melodic contours are more jagged, or disjunct. The harmonies are also less stable than in the A section, creating a unified drive to the end of the last phrase. This section is then repeated.

PART 2 (B) Repetition	0:47	Phrase one repeated (c)
	0:53	Phrase two repeated (d)
	0:59	Phrase three repeated (e)
	1:04	Phrase four repeated (f)

The overall form of this piece is AABB, or more simply, AB, known as binary form. There are many ways form can be delineated, but usually it is based on the concept of "same" and "different." Our brief example above is organized according to same/different melodies. In the case of large-scale works, many more musical elements would work together to delineate the different sections.

So far we have concentrated on the music's melody, rhythm, and form. What else is happening? You may have noticed another line of music below the melody. It has less rhythmic interest than the top part, mostly moving along by keeping a steady beat. However, it has its own melodic character and could function independently as a separate tune, albeit a less interesting one. As we have learned, when two or more independent lines sound together, the resulting texture is polyphonic.

Finally let's return to the social context of Bach's "Bourrée." How might this piece remind listeners of the dance? Can you envision the steps and hops? Why did Bach choose to emphasize the short–short–long rhythmic pattern? And considering that the bourrée was a cheerful dance, why did Bach write this work in a minor key? Here is a case where the minor scale does not correspond to its oft-associated "sad" affect. Perhaps Bach was trying to portray a more serious bourrée, one befitting the dignified expressions expected of the nobility. Or perhaps Bach's bourrée is simply more reflective than cheerful—evoking the reminiscence of the dance, rather than the dance itself.

Our example features a guitar, but Bach actually wrote the piece for a keyboard instrument. Today, one can hear this piece on almost any instrument and in a variety of styles. It was a favorite of Led Zeppelin guitarist Jimmy Page (b. 1944), who often attached it to his improvised solo in the song "Heartbreaker." It was also a favorite of Ian Anderson (b. 1947), flutist in the 1960s rock group Jethro Tull. This bourrée remains one of Bach's most recognized pieces. @ 3.4

QUESTIONS FOR THOUGHT

- Why do you think the A section is shorter than the B section?
- Notice that each phrase becomes less active at its end, as if it ran out of energy. Why might this be?
- Where does the bottom line play faster notes than the top line? How would the piece feel different if the bottom line kept its regular pace?
- What do you imagine the dance to look like? Many performances can be found on the internet. Do they meet your expectations?
- Any thoughts as to why this music is still so well known?

ACTIVITIES AND ASSIGNMENTS

- Notice that some phrases of the "Bourrée" do not feel quite complete, as if they end with a comma or question mark. Others end more definitively, with the musical equivalent of a period, sometimes even an exclamation point. Make a diagram of where these different endings occur.
- Look up Bach's "Bourrée" on the internet. How many performances can you find? How do different performances affect the emotional quality of the piece? (A few of them may surprise you.)

Music from Japan

Our discussion of the "Bourrée" demonstrated some basic principles in the composition of Western art music. Many of those principles are employed in traditions around the world. But not all, of course.

Japanese musicians, attributed to Kusakabe Kimbei, 1870s–1890s.

Courtesy of the J. Paul Getty Museum

Our next example, a composition for the Japanese *shakuhachi*, a five-tone-hole bamboo flute, offers a different set of compositional principles and aesthetics.

First, however, some history. Though long associated with Japan, the shakuhachi may have been invented in China (where it was known as the *chiba*) or perhaps in the Middle East. What is certain is that the instrument was brought from China to the Japanese islands in the 8th century as part of a mixed instrumental ensemble used to accompany the courtly music and dance genre *gagaku*. @ 3.5

Though gagaku has continuously thrived in Japan, the shakuhachi apparently did not. The marriage of instrument to genre ended by the 10th century. At that point, the shakuhachi mostly disappeared from the historical record until the 14th century.

During the late 17th and 18th centuries, however, the shakuhachi again rose to prominence when it became associated with the Fuke sect of Zen Buddhism. Apparently, the instrument was used to facilitate *suizen*, or blowing meditation. It was also during this time that it attained its contemporary physical form. The modified instrument was thicker and heavier than earlier versions and had a slightly flared end.

"Nezasa Shirabe," performed by Tadashi Tajima

LISTENING 3.2 GUIDE))

Texture: Monophonic
Meter: Unmetered, breath governs phrase length
Form: No set form; this work relies on melodic expansion and contraction to give it shape.

"Nezasa Shirabe," like nearly all traditional shakuhachi music, is built on a **pentatonic** (five-tone) scale: do–re–me–sol–ley, which, to the Western ear, gives the impression of a minor tonality.

As you listen to the piece, try to breathe in sync with the musician. Notice how long your breaths become, perhaps how time itself seems to expand. The music has no rhythmic pulse, no meter. Instead time seems to float alongside the slow rhythm of the breath.

Nezasa is a branch of northern Japan's Kinpū sect; a shirabe is a short introductory piece, generally of a meditative character. Sometimes a shirabe stands alone; other times it may be attached to the beginnings of longer compositions. The music is designed to warm up both shakuhachi and performer. A particular trait of this piece is the *komibuki* (pulsating breath), a technique designed to focus the mind.

0:00	The opening gesture is a downward movement: a short upper **grace note** followed by a long held tone (sol–re). We cannot know it yet, but the gesture lands on the lowest pitch in the composition. It will also be the tone on which the music concludes. Notice how Tajima colors the tone by constantly changing its inflections through komibuki, vibrato, dynamics, and subtle pitch bending.
0:11	The second gesture is more or less opposite the first in that it leaps up to, and then sustains, the same tone that served as the grace note at the music's beginning (sol–re–sol).
0:20	A movement to "ley" (though only the third of five possible pitches) gives complete shape to the pentatonic scale, which an experienced listener will now hear in his inner musical road map. "Do," a new high point in the melody, is briefly sounded, then a return down to "sol."
0:37	As Tajima continues his slow upward exploration, it seems as if every movement upward is followed by another small one in the opposite direction. He reaches a new high pitch, "re," then settles back down to "do" before continuing to move upward to "me" at 0:54, "sol" at 1:12, and "ley" at 1:20.
1:25	The composition, just short of halfway complete, reaches its upper limit sitting on the tones "do" and then "re" at 1:35. This is the music's climax, which is followed by a meandering descent to the original pitch area.
2:33–2:42	Finally, repeating the gestures with which the composition began, the melody returns to its opening tones. The return signals the music's end.

Perhaps these were aesthetic choices. Equally possible was that the changes accommodated the instrument's secondary use as a defensive weapon. Wearing basket-like hats (*tengai*) over their heads to hide their identities, Komoso (Fuke) monks (many had once been samurai warriors) walked the dangerous countryside playing their shakuhachis and begging for alms. Also, or so it is speculated, some worked as spies on behalf of the government.

Whatever the monks' political motives, they apparently became formidable instrumentalists. It was also during this time that a standard repertoire developed. Many of these compositions were written down and preserved. They are still taught today.

Following the end of feudalism with the Meiji Restoration of 1868, a wave of modernization spread across Japan. One consequence was the banishment of the Fuke sect and a proscription against using the shakuhachi for religious purposes. Once again, the instrument was adapted to fit new interests. The repertoire was secularized and music notation improved. New theoretical ideas were developed. Compositions began to be written for ensembles of different-sized instruments.

This last development might seem strange, since the word shakuhachi (taken from *i shaku ha sun*) specifically refers to the instrument's size. A *shaku* is a little less than one foot in length; *hachi* stands for 8/10 of a shaku. Thus, a shakuhachi equals a length of just under 1.8 feet. Today, while this size remains common, a shakuhahi may come in a variety of lengths, ranging from just over one foot to more than three feet.

The shakuhachi proves that simplicity of design is no guarantee of ease of performance. It is notoriously difficult to play. Breath control can take years to master. Pitch inflection, which is achieved by changing the angle of the breath or by partially uncovering any of the five finger holes, is a subtle and essential aspect of performance.

Japan today has a number of shakuhachi playing schools. Each is associated with a characteristic style and a particular lineage of teachers. Although the instrument has lost many of its sacred connotations, links to Zen Buddhism remain. This can be heard in the slow unfolding tempo of performance and the common practice of focusing on just a single extended tone, despite the instrument's range of about three octaves.

We have heard that the piece unfolds along an undulating arc moving generally from low to high and back down again. We have also noticed that the same melodic and rhythmic gestures open and close the composition. How else might you describe the music? Meditative? Austere?

Finally, notice that many of the skills used to understand Bach's "Bourrée" are useful in understanding "Nezasa Shirabe." In both we hear the outlines of organized form, the use of repeated melodic gestures, and applications of rhythmic gestures. Despite the many obvious differences in mechanical application, social use, and emotional focus, the pieces also have much in common.

QUESTIONS FOR THOUGHT

- "Nezasa Shirabe" ends where it began. What might be the symbolism behind this choice?
- Why might monks choose a wind instrument to play rather than a stringed instrument?
- What is the emotional effect of the music's lack of metric pulse?

ACTIVITIES AND ASSIGNMENTS

- There are many recordings of "Nezasa Shirabe" (though the spelling varies slightly). Find another recording to compare and contrast.
- Construct a shakuhachi from PVC pipe.

Understanding American Popular Song: "Over the Rainbow"

In 1938, at the age of 16, child filmstar Judy Garland (1922–1969) was cast as Dorothy Gale in the Metro–Goldwyn–Mayer film *The Wizard of Oz* (1939). It was the role of a lifetime for a young woman with a once-in-a-generation voice. The movie's signature song, "Over the Rainbow," by composer Harold Arlen (1905–1986) and lyricist E.Y. Harburg (1896–1981) became an American standard and one of the most recorded songs ever.

We close this chapter by analyzing two different "Rainbow" recordings. The first is Garland's original from the motion picture soundtrack. The second was recorded by jazz pianist Art Tatum (1909–1956). The performances, which could hardly be more different, give an idea of the interpretive range that skilled musicians bring to their work.

Judy Garland and Terry (Toto), 1939.

"Over the Rainbow," by Harold Arlen and E.Y. Harburg, performed by Judy Garland

LISTENING
3.3
GUIDE

Texture: Homophonic
Meter: Quadruple
Form: Strophic, 32-bar song form—AABA

We begin with the Garland version, not just because it came earlier, but also because it is by far the easier performance to understand. (We offer an audio version of the song on our website, but for context we suggest you find a film clip on the internet.) Listen to the first stanza (or verse) and its graceful melody, which begins with the inspirational upward leap of a full octave from "do" to "do" on the word "Somewhere." The leap echoes this Kansas farm-girl's dreams of the world she hopes someday to see. From there, the melody loops downward slightly, but finishes the line ("rainbow") back at the upper tonic. The second phrase ("Way up high") also begins on "do" but lacks the energy of the full octave leap. Instead it jumps to "la" before settling on "sol" (the scale's fifth degree) with the word "high." It seems that "high" is not so high after all, at least not as high as Dorothy's dreamy "Somewhere."

The pause on "sol" is structurally important. It sets up a downward near-octave fall from one phrase to the next—that is, from the word "high" to "There's" on the pitch "la" below the opening "do." With that tone Arlen has given the limits of the song's melodic frame, nearly an octave and one-half. Also notice the symmetry—the leap upward to the song's highest note has been balanced by a fall downward to its lowest note. With the final syllable of "lullaby" the melody ends back home, on the same pitch that it began.

What about the accompaniment? Soft tones from orchestral strings and winds contribute to the dreamy atmosphere. There are no stark lines; there is little sense of meter. Counter melodies enhance Garland's singing.

"Somewhere . . ."	Stanza 1 (A)
"Somewhere . . ."	Stanza 2 (A)
"Someday I'll wish . . . "	Stanza 3 (B)
"Somewhere . . . "	Stanza 4 (A)
Coda	

Find the complete lyrics on the internet and take notice of Harburg's equally well-crafted words. Stanzas one, two, and four begin the same, with the line "Somewhere over the Rainbow." All three stanzas also rhyme lines two and four (high/lullaby, blue/true, fly/I) creating a rhyme scheme of ABCB. Notice also that stanza four returns to the long "i" vowel rhymes of stanza one, yet another one of the song's many symbols of returning home.

continued

Contrast stanzas one, two, and four with stanza three, which is the odd one out. Here the words come faster and the rhymes are more complex. The opening line's closing word "star" is rhymed with an interior word "far" in the following line. This allows Harburg to complete the rhyme scheme with "me," "drops"/"tops," and finally returning to "me," thus creating a stanza rhyme scheme of A(A)BCCB.

You have probably noticed that stanzas one, two, and four all have the same melody and that stanza three is different. Building from this we can analyze the large-scale melodic material of the four stanzas as fitting a model of AABA.

Now, listen to the song again and conduct time (four beats to each measure) along with the melody. If you follow through the entire song, you will notice that all four stanzas are exactly the same length—eight complete measures. Your beats should fall in the following places:

Some . . .	(beats 1 and 2), *where* . . .	(beats 3 and 4)	measure 1
Over . . .	(beats 1 and 2), *rain* . . .	(beats 3 and 4)	measure 2
Way . . .	(beats 1 and 2), *up* . . .	(beats 3 and 4)	measure 3
High . . .	(beats 1 through 4)		measure 4

Finally, we are in a position to give the song's structure a name. It is 32-bar song form, consisting of four equal-sized sections of eight measures in the melodic framework of AABA. Many thousands of songs have been written in this form, from 19th-century art songs to rhythm and blues.

Perhaps you noticed that the song's final two lines break the 32-bar pattern. These closing lines are an optional addition to the form, called a **coda** ("tail"). If a performer were to expand on the general 32-bar form, perhaps with improvisation or by adding additional stanzas, the coda would not be played until song's end.

What other things might you choose to listen for? We suggest you listen to Garland's voice, to the way she inflects the melody, to her use of vibrato, and to the general character of her voice. Is she convincing in her delivery? Does she sound like a young girl?

Art Tatum, Rochester, NY, May 19, 1946.
Photo by William P. Gottlieb/Library of Congress Prints and Photographs Division [LC-GLB13- 0831]

Art Tatum

Burdened with near blindness from early childhood but blessed with perfect pitch, pianist Art Tatum was an iconic and controversial figure in the world of jazz. Fans and fellow musicians found his vivid and eclectic musical imagination unsurpassed. So too were his technical skills. No jazz pianist, before or since, has gotten around the piano keyboard with a more formidable combination of spontaneity, power and lightness, speed and groove. Curiously, Tatum's critics found fault with the same qualities his supporters admired. They found his imagination rich, but undisciplined, and his technical facility so highlighted as to overwhelm the music itself. Although these controversies continue, today Tatum's large catalog of recordings, the vast majority done on a single take, serves as a sonic textbook for both aspiring and well-established musicians.

A child prodigy, Tatum was born and raised in Toledo, Ohio. And like so many successful black American musicians, he grew up in the shadow of the church. Both parents were musically involved at Toledo's Grace Presbyterian Church, where his mother was the pianist. Tatum learned to improvise on church hymns while still a small boy. Elsewhere, he received formal instruction in classical music, the results of which can be heard in his penchant for lightning-fast melodic runs, tempo shifts, and complex harmonies—

qualities also central to the music of Europe's 19th-century virtuoso pianist/composers, such as Frédéric Chopin (1810–1848) and Franz Liszt (1811–1886).

However strong Tatum's early attraction to classic music may have been (he often improvised on classical melodies), those sounds could not offer a career path for an African American in the 1920s. Jazz did. While still in his teens, Tatum got his own radio show. He was also a regular performer, often with Jon Hendricks, at the Waiters and Bellman's Club, a "black and tan" (i.e. racially integrated) nightclub that formed the heart of Toledo's then vital jazz scene. Tatum moved to New York City in the early 1930s where he spent much of the rest of his brief life.

Stylistically, Tatum's music is hard to categorize. He performed mostly as a soloist. (Perhaps describing him as a one-man band is most accurate.) Playing alone allowed Tatum the freedom to give his musical eccentricities full range. Though he began his career as a **"stride"** pianist (a style in which the left hand moves between bass line and chords) and he could "swing" as well as anyone, Tatum often abandoned stride's muscularity to insert lush chords and idiosyncratic runs. While he occasionally played the blues (Chapter 5: Music and Ethnicity), the pianist seemed most at home with the more intricate harmonies characteristic of the **American Songbook**, music drawn from musical theater and film and **Tin Pan Alley,** the one-time center of the New York City songwriting industry.

> "I used to close my eyes when we worked together, thinking that maybe if I couldn't see, I might learn to hear like Art."
> —jazz vocalist Jon Hendricks (b.1921–2017)

"Over the Rainbow," performed by Art Tatum (1939)

LISTENING 3.4 GUIDE

"Over the Rainbow" is an American Songbook classic, of course. It was also a staple in Tatum's repertoire. He recorded the song on multiple occasions, each time differently. The first surviving recording comes from a live radio broadcast made just six weeks after the movie was released. This is the least complex of the various available recordings, and the one we will examine.

First, listen to the recording all the way through. So thick are the textures and so extravagant the melodic additions and harmonic alterations that the first time through you may feel rather overwhelmed, if not altogether lost. Keep the original melody in mind and try to follow the AABA form.

| 0:00 | Introduction |
| 0:07 | First stanza (A) |

The performance begins with introductory sounds (perhaps raindrops?). Tatum then plays the song's melody ("Somewhere, over the rainbow . . . "). The song's original harmonies are embellished and the rhythmic movement is jagged—pushing forward, then falling back. (Tatum's melodic imagination disguises this, but the rhythmic instability will become apparent if you attempt to conduct time.) For Tatum, however, the line "Way up high" seems to have demanded a melodic response in the downward run, which is greatly embellished. The original melody is obscured under Tatum's improvisatory filigree. Notice how Tatum rushes through the final words of the stanza ("Once in a lullaby").

0:23	Second stanza (A)
	The same basic strategy is followed for stanza two (A).
0:36	Third stanza (B)
	In the B stanza ("Someday I'll wish..."), Tatum's improvisatory abstractions virtually subsume the original melody. Exotic harmonies are introduced; the tempo rushes forward only to pull back a moment later. Try to find the melody tones. Most of them are there, but they are hidden inside thick chords and sometimes displaced across octaves.
0:57	Fourth stanza (A)
	Stanza four (A) begins with the same stop and start rhythmic feel, but halfway through (at 1:10), he switches to a rhythmically stable stride style with the left hand keeping strict time and the right hand embellishing the melody.
1:18	First stanza (A)
1:37	Second stanza (A)

continued

	Tatum briefly fragments the melody with isolated tones, like points in space. The sounds are abstract, almost mathematical.
1:57	Third stanza (B)
	Tatum drops the stride for the first half of the section, then returns to stride style.
2:17	Fourth stanza (A)
	Notice how the music becomes a bit more abstract with each stanza.
2:36	First stanza (A)
2:58	Second stanza (A)
3:16	Third stanza (B)
	Pulsing chords
3:34	Fourth stanza (A)
	Tatum interrupts the B section with a wild drive to song's end.

Tatum's performance is fresh and nonchalant, almost conversational. He is as comfortable improvising music as we are talking with a best friend. Almost all of Tatum's recordings were made on a single take. He sometimes recorded dozens of tracks in a single day.

QUESTIONS FOR THOUGHT

- Which performance, Garland's or Tatum's, do you prefer? Why?
- What does your choice suggest about your musical tastes?
- Might your choice reflect your cultural background?
- How does social context affect a performance? Give examples.
- What constitutes creativity in musical performance? Does a performer need to improvise to be creative?
- Can musical elements (melody, harmony, rhythm, etc.) be compared to other fundamental building blocks in the visual arts or literature?
- Bach and Tatum were both virtuoso improvisers. Imagine a musical meeting between the two. What would it be like?

ACTIVITIES AND ASSIGNMENTS

- Pick a piece of music you know well. Map the form and label the musical elements that distinguish each part.
- Find two pieces of music that express opposing emotions. Identify how the musical elements are used to create the mood.
- Listen on the internet to all four Tatum recordings (1929, 1948, 1953, 1956) of "Over the Rainbow." How are they similar? Different? Do you have a favorite? If so, why?
- Find still more recordings of "Over the Rainbow." What values does each reflect? Which do you enjoy the most? Why?

Conclusion

We have seen that while musical compositions may be extremely complex in the aggregate, they are built from many separate, and relatively simple, elements. By investigating these elements individually through careful listening and thoughtful analysis, even highly intricate music becomes understandable.

In the following chapters we will look at many different kinds of music. We will explore the technical make-up of representative works in order to understand how they were conceived and composed. We will also study how music reflects and influences the social world in which it is created and performed. We will learn that musical sounds and functions vary considerably according to time and place, social identity, and aesthetics. Finally, we will come to understand how exploring our musical world offers rich insights into the human condition.

Key Terms

- 32-bar song form
- American Songbook
- bourrée
- coda
- fugue
- gagaku
- grace note
- harpsichord
- komibuki
- pentatonic scale
- shakuhachi
- stride piano
- suite
- suizen
- Tin Pan Alley

Essay Questions

- The musical examples in this chapter are very different, one from the other. What traits do they have in common?
- How does musical form help contribute to musical understanding?
- How might understanding one style of music help you to understand a different style? Might familiarity with one musical style impede the understanding of another?

MUSICAL
IDENTITIES

CHAPTER GOALS

- To highlight our important and ever-changing relationship to music as we move through life's stages.

CHAPTER FOUR

Music and the Life Cycle

QUESTIONS FOR THOUGHT

- What is your earliest musical memory? Why did this event stay in your mind?
- How have your musical tastes changed over time? Why did they change?
- How many different social contexts can you name in which music is important?

After a rousing opening with drums beating and cymbals crashing, Sir Edward Elgar's (1857–1934) *Pomp and Circumstance March No. 1* (1901) settles into an austere long-melodied processional march. Almost certainly you recognize this music. Odds are you walked to it at your high school graduation; there is a good chance you will do so again at college commencement. In the United States, graduates have processed to this music since 1905, when it was first performed at the Yale University commencement in which Elgar was given an honorary doctorate. In England, Elgar's home, the melody is perhaps best known as the song "Land of Hope and Glory," which has been arranged for both government and popular occasions.

What would grand public affairs be without music? Less grand for sure. More importantly, they would be emotionally diminished. So would most aspects of life. Music accompanies us through the dependency of infancy and the possibilities of early childhood. It supports us through the trials of teenage angst and romance, the reversals of adulthood, then on to old age and death. Music is essential in life's major transitional rituals: initiations, graduations, weddings, and funerals.

"When children listen to music, they don't just listen. They melt into the melody and flow with the rhythm."
—Michael Jackson (1958–2009)

Our Earliest Music

Because music is known to reduce labor pain, some babies come into the world with music playing. But in fact, sound experience begins well before birth. The organs for hearing are fully formed around twenty-five weeks after conception. Because amniotic fluid is a good sound conductor, a fetus is exposed to the same sounds (though distorted, as if hearing under water) as is the mother. What is more, a fetus is constantly immersed in the rhythms of life—the beating of its mother's heart and the whooshing sounds of blood in the arteries. It will also be calmed by its mother's voice.

No research clearly shows positive effects of fetal music exposure, but since musical experience can lower stress levels during pregnancy, one might assume what is good for the mother is good for the fetus. Music delivered in too heavy doses can be a bad thing, however. Fetal exposure to loud sounds over extended periods may result in premature births, lower birth weight, and even high-frequency hearing loss. Moms should not put earphones over their bellies; it may be best to avoid loud concerts during pregnancy. @ 4.1

Union City, New Jersey's class of 2010.

Photo by Luigi Novi/Nightscream/ Wikimedia Commons/ CC-BY-SA-3.0.

NAMING CEREMONIES

Some ethnic groups celebrate the naming of a child with a musical ceremony. The Wolof people of Senegal, West Africa, for example, hold a ceremony called *ngente*, a day-long event of drumming and dancing. Some Senegalese groups hold a more elaborate ngente, called a *bekete*, which is also designed to protect the infant from evil influences.

Baby's Lullaby, Mary Cassatt, ca. 1887.

Courtesy of The Metropolitan Museum of Art, New York, H.O. Havemeyer Collection, Bequest of Mrs. H.O. Havemeyer, 1929.

Infancy

Even minutes after birth, a newborn responds to its mother's voice. Newborns also respond to music. Amazingly, research suggests they seem to know the difference between singing specifically directed at them and an indiscriminately sounded song. That makes sense. The most successful music making unfolds as an interactive experience. In the nursery, when a sensitive singer correctly responds to an infant's reaction, a flexible bond of give and take is initiated. @ 4.2

There is more to this story than feel-good bonding. Infant exposure to lullabies has been connected with mitigating infant stress, reducing pain, and stimulating early language development. Can't carry a tune? Don't let it stop you from singing. Infants do not seem to care if the singer is out of tune or even tone deaf; to baby it is the singer's commitment that counts. Babies thrive on musical simplicity, familiarity, and repetition, not golden voices.

Lullabies

Every culture has lullabies. They all share certain traits. Most melodies are narrow in range and consonant. Phrases fit to natural breath lengths. Rhythms are soothing. As for topics, lullabies can be about anything. Whether the song is about sugar canes or hungry crocodiles, baby does not care.

We will explore just one lullaby example, a lovely Greek song titled "Kimísou yié." As is common in lullabies from Asia Minor, the melody is built on the *Hijaz* (do, ra, mi, fa, sol, la, te, do) melodic mode, which is part of the *maqam* tonal system of the Middle East (for more detail on maqam, see Chapter 7: Music and Spirituality). In this song we hear only the four lowest tones of Hijaz (the lower tetrachord, C–D-flat–E–F). Notice the emotional relaxation felt as the singer ends each phrase. (If you hum the lowest tone while listening to the lullaby, you will get a good sense of the tetrachord's emotional feel.)

As you listen, first notice that the melody is repeated six times, once for each line of verse. Each iteration begins and ends on the lowest tone of the tetrachord. Many words are sung using **melismas** (with many tones to a single syllable). Finally, consider the song's rhythmic framework, which though presented in unmeasured beats, follows the singer's relaxed breathing, one breath to each phrase.

"Kimísou yié"

LISTENING
4.1))
GUIDE

Texture: Monophonic
Meter: Unmetered
Form: AAAAAA coda

Kimísou yié mou, kala yié,	Sleep well my son, my son,
ómorfe diamantári.	My beautiful diamond.
kimísou pou na se charí	Sleep, so that the young woman who you'll marry
i niá pou tha se pári.	can rejoice in you.
náni mesa stin kouniá sou	Sleep in your cradle,
kai sta paliá ta paniá sou.	and in your old sheets.
ee-ee-ee	ee-ee-ee

QUESTIONS FOR THOUGHT

- Can you think of an event in your life that would have been greatly diminished without music?
- Does listening to *Pomp and Circumstance* call up memories? If so, what kind?
- Do you remember any lullabies sung to you or your siblings?
- Would you rather sing for someone else or be sung to? Why?

Childhood

As children grow up, their lives are filled with music, through the internet and media, in stores, at school, and in the home. Much of the music they hear is directed at the adults around them, but some is directed expressly at children. In North America, entertainers such as Pete Seeger (1914–2014), Ella Jenkins (b. 1924), Raffi Cavoukian (b. 1948), Tom Chapin (b. 1945), Elizabeth Mitchell (b. 1968), and many others have composed and performed for generations of children.

There are classic children's songs far too many to mention, like "Wheels on the Bus," "La Cucaracha," "Old McDonald," and so many more. Some of them come from folk culture, such as "She'll Be Coming 'Round the Mountain." Some share melodies. "Twinkle, Twinkle, Little Star," "Baa Baa Black Sheep," and "The Alphabet Song" are all set to the melody of the 18th-century French folksong "Ah! vous dirai-je, maman." @ 4.3

Young violinists.
Photo by Mary
Natvig.

Some songs are obviously didactic, like "The Alphabet Song" and "Fifty Nifty United States." But for children, every musical experience is educational, especially if it is participatory. After all, any musical participation requires cooperation, which builds social and emotional intelligence. Also, because playing a musical instrument is difficult, the process of learning enhances problem-solving skills, develops fine motor skills, and builds discipline, patience, and tenacity.

A number of "classical" composers have written works designed to introduce children to the orchestra and its instruments, including: *Carnival of the Animals* (1886, by Camille Saint-Saëns), *Tubby the Tuba* (1945, by Paul Tripp and George Klinsinger), and *Young Person's Guide to the Orchestra* (1946, by Benjamin Britten). Perhaps most beloved of all is the story of *Peter and Wolf* (1936) by Russian composer Sergei Prokofiev (1891–1953), who wrote both the story and music for a Moscow-based children's theater.

In this work, a narrator tells Peter's story, which includes a cast of eight: four humans and four animals. Each character is associated with a particular instrument(s) and melody (see leitmotifs in Chapter 6: Music and Gender). As for the humans, we have the adventurous Peter (portrayed by joyful strings), his slow-moving grandfather (a stiff-sounding bassoon), and a pair of trigger-happy hunters (booming kettle drums). The animals include a flighty bird (flute), a careless duck (oboe), a goofy cat (clarinet), and a ravenous wolf (horns).

Here is a brief synopsis of the story. One morning, Peter opens the gate of his family compound and goes into the meadow. Behind him waddles the family duck, who wants to go for a swim.

LISTENING 4.2 GUIDE

Peter and the Wolf, by Sergei Prokofiev, narrated by David Bowie

Texture: Complex homophony
Meter: Varies
Form: Follows the narrative

We do not really need a listening guide to this composition. After all, the musical form and themes are intimately tied to the story. What is particularly interesting, however, is that for Prokofiev (as he recorded in his diary), "the story was important only as a means of inducing the children to listen to the music." So let's discuss just enough of the piece to get our bearings and understand how Prokofiev invites us to listen:

- Introduced one by one are the characters, and instruments that represent them. Notice the particular timbre and personality of each instrument.

- The story begins with Peter and his musical theme played by the string section. Notice how the music portrays Peter's gentle and optimistic character. (Quadruple meter)

- Next we meet the bird (flute solo). (Duple meter)

- The narration continues as the orchestra intersperses bird tweets with Peter's music. (Quadruple meter)

- We meet the duck (oboe). Listen to him waddle as he heads toward the pond. Be sure to listen for the occasional bird tweet. (Triple meter)

- The story continues.

The range of narrators who have recorded *Peter* attests to the music's wide and lasting appeal: from former First Lady and human rights activist Eleanor Roosevelt (1884–1962) to former president Bill Clinton (b. 1946), and from goth rock-star Alice Cooper (b. 1948) to Shakespearian actor Patrick Stewart (b. 1940), and from English new-wave rocker Sting (b. 1951) to American actress Sharon Stone (b. 1958). Our example is narrated by David Bowie (1947–2016).

On his way to the pond, the duck argues with the bird about the nature of "birdness" (one swims; one flies). Immersed in the argument, the careless bird is almost caught by the cat. Peter's grandfather sees the boy outside alone, makes him come home, and then locks the gate. Meanwhile, the wolf shows up, eats the duck, and makes plans to eat the cat as well. Peter, looking on from the courtyard, decides to help. He grabs a rope, climbs a tree, and catches the wolf by the tail. Just then, the hunters arrive, with guns blazing. Peter intervenes. Rather than shooting the wolf, the hunters and Peter take the animal to the zoo. The story's lessons are clear. Protect the innocent; do not fight; kindness overcomes cruelty; and most important of all, be true to yourself.

Coming of Age

For many, musical experience is most powerful during the emotions-driven teen years and early twenties. Especially then, music lights us up. Literally. As we listen, neurons in the brain's auditory cortex begin to fire. If we sing along and focus on lyrics, neurons in the premotor and parietal cortexes are set off. If a song is connected to memories, the prefrontal cortex swings into action. Dance along, and music becomes a full brain/body experience.

As we discovered in the first paragraphs of Chapter 1, music is an open door to the past. That is why oldies radio is so popular. For adults living through their thirties, forties, and fifties, the music they grew up with remains deeply imprinted in their consciousness. Even for a 93-year-old (remember Mrs. Campbell from Chapter 1), listening to sounds from her youth may bring memories pouring in as if the events happened just yesterday.

For teens, music provides a private space in which identities may be tried on, love imagined, and real-life rejection assuaged. The Beach Boys, a California-based garage band that made it to superstardom, understood this when they recorded "In My Room" (1963), a plaintive dirge of teenage angst. For the singer, his bedroom is "a world" in which he can go and "tell my secrets to." For thoughtful listeners, the song itself becomes that place. Though perhaps saccharine by today's standards, "In My Room" resonated with untold numbers of lonely teens.

The teen years are a time of awakening and struggle. Home life, which once nurtured, now constrains. As teens strive for independence and struggle to break from their parents' control, music plays a role in that rebellion. For more than sixty years, commercial music about the desire/need for freedom has given voice to that emotion. Unconstrained movement, even if embodied only in a song, came to symbolize the power to do as one wants.

In some cultures, ceremonies or rituals mark a teenager's passage to adulthood. Such rituals are relatively rare in the United States, where neither turning 16 nor the responsibility of legal adulthood at age 18 is accompanied by a specific ceremony. We do find them in religious and ethnic communities, however. Some Christian denominations mark full membership into the church through the rite of confirmation. Jewish girls and boys may mark their transition into adulthood with their bat/bar mitzvahs. For some Hispanic girls, *quinceañera* parties (fifteenth birthday celebrations) mark their entrance into adulthood. Debutante balls continue to usher "young ladies" into the opportunities and responsibilities of high-society life.

MUSIC AND THE AGING BRAIN

"If you want to firm up your body, head to the gym. If you want to exercise your brain, listen to music." So say researchers at Johns Hopkins University. They suggest three strategies.

1. Listen to music that is new to you. Doing so will push your mind to make sense of new sound combinations.
2. Pay attention to how your body reacts to the music. Not only will you become more self-aware, but you will also be more likely to find a good emotional fit.
3. Listen to music that is familiar and remember back to the time when you first heard it.

Strategy three has proven to be particularly effective for Alzheimer patients, even those with severe disability. For many patients, though not all, hearing music that was important in the distant past can unlock long-term memories. In some cases, positive effects will last for hours. @ 4.4

Although in many areas around the world, coming of age traditions are weakening in the wake of urbanization and modernization, ceremonies marking the entrance into adulthood continue to take place. Some ceremonies are being rekindled, and others are adapting to fit changing times. Consider the Yankton Sioux *Isnati Awica Dowanpi* coming-of-age ceremony for girls, which was recently revived after many years of dormancy. An example of adaptation is the Inuit coming-of-age ceremony on North Baffin Island, which was once open only to boys but now includes girls.

QUESTIONS FOR THOUGHT

- Did you have a particularly important song during your early teens? If so, listen to it and pay attention to the memories that come flooding in. You may even experience smells and tastes. Why is the song important to you?

- Did you pass through a coming of age ceremony, religious or otherwise? If so, are you glad you did? If not, do you wish you had? Why? Do you remember the music?

ROLLING TOWARD FREEDOM

Photo collage by Mary Natvig.

In 1950s rhythm and blues and 1960s rock 'n' roll, car songs like Jackie Brenston's "Rocket 88" (1951) and Steppenwolf's "Born to be Wild" (1968) represented the raw vitality of unbridled freedom. Each generation has its classic car songs, including: War's "Lowrider" (1975), Bruce Springsteen's "Racing in the Street" (1978), Rush's "Red Barchetta" (1981), LL Cool J's "The Boomin' System" (1990), and the Grammy Award-winning songs "Life Is a Highway" (1991) and "Fuel" (1997), by Tom Cochrane and Metallica respectively. Many rap videos empower the protagonist by putting him behind the wheel.

Marriage

In the traditional American wedding of yore, emotions ran high as the groom stood at the altar awaiting his future wife. Ceremonies often began with a music cue: the "Bridal Chorus" ("Here Comes the Bride") from German composer Richard Wagner's (1813–1883) opera *Lohengrin* (1848). Stepping with the music, the bride entered the ritual space on the arm of her father. At ceremony's end (promenading once again to music), she would leave as wife, arm in arm with her husband.

Compared with other parts of the world, American weddings are rather simple affairs. Consider the rituals that, until 1970, surrounded traditional Chinese weddings. The "Six Rites and Three Covenants" took days to perform. A wedding match could be confirmed only after extensive interfamily negotiations and astrological probing. The wedding ritual itself began with the bride's three-day seclusion in her family home, during which time she sang songs lamenting her fate. On her wedding day, the bride was carried in a sedan chair to her future husband's home. Halfway there, submission complete, she threw out a white handkerchief. A threshold crossed, her songs of sorrow were done. A new life was beginning.

Why sing laments at a wedding? Life transitions can be frightening, especially for a woman living in a traditional culture where weddings mark stepping into new worlds, forming new allegiances, and leaving the past behind. With social loss defined and the future uncertain, wedding laments were once common throughout the world, especially where arranged marriages were customary. They are still sung today.

> ## *ASHRAMA* AND THE HINDU STAGES OF LIFE
>
> Hinduism divides the life cycle into four distinct stages, or ashramas. The first two ashramas signify deepening engagement with the material world; the second two signify withdrawal from it. The first stage, *Brahmacharya*, is the student phase, a time of gaining worldly knowledge and building moral character. The second stage, *Grihastha*, begins with marriage and the duties of adulthood that accompany it. Stage three, *Vanaprastha*, begins when one's children have themselves attained adulthood and external responsibilities begin to lessen. At this point, one's inner life is vitalized by a focus on meditation and sacred literature. The final stage, *Sannyasa*, is the period in which one renounces the material world.

Rama's Wedding

Of course, weddings also transform love's longing into love's consummation. Perhaps no wedding, mythological or otherwise, has been more recounted and celebrated than the story of Sita and Lord Rama. In the Hindu epic poem, *The Ramayana* (*Rama's Journey*) (Chapter 2, Box: *The Ramayana*), the wedding represents a turning point for the protagonist—from adolescence to manhood. Here we enter the story during Rama's final adolescent days, when he receives mantras and learns the lessons of courage and forbearance that prepare him for adult life and its responsibilities.

The Lead-up to Rama's Wedding

When the sage Vishvamitra travels to the court of Rama's father, King Dasarath, Vishvamitra asks the king to allow Rama to travel with him so the youth might learn important lessons that will prepare him for the duties of adulthood. Vishvamitra says Rama must battle, and defeat, a powerful

King Dasaratha and his retinue proceed to Rama's wedding: folio from the Shangri II Ramayana Series, ca. 1620–1710.

Courtesy of The Metropolitan Museum of Art, New York, Purchase, The Dillon Fund, Evelyn Kranes Kossak, and Anonymous Gifts, 1994.

demon. Though fearing for his son's life, Dasarath reluctantly accedes to the sage's wishes. Rama is joined by his brother, Lakshamana, and the three men depart.

Along the way, Vishvamitra teaches the brothers hymns that assure protection, endurance, and wisdom. Then he sends them into their first battle. Once victorious, Vishvamitra initiates the brothers into the mysteries of the sacred weapons wielded by the gods and teaches the spells that empower them. After another battle of (literally) cosmic proportions, their training is complete. Rama and Lakshamana have arrived at the cusp of manhood. Accordingly, Vishvamitra takes the men to Mithila, a city (in present-day Nepal) ruled by King Janaka, Sita's father. Housed in Mithila is a bow that once belonged to the Hindu deity **Shiva**. It is a weapon so heavy that 500 men are required just to move the chest in which it is stored. Such is the bow's potency that those of impure heart find themselves incapable of even approaching it.

Knowing that a mere mortal will never complete the task, Sita's father has made it known that he will give his daughter in marriage to whomever can lift and string the weapon. Although Rama himself does not yet know it, he is no mere mortal. He is an avatar of the Hindu deity **Vishnu**, one of the deities that make up Hinduism's *Trimurti*, or holy trinity (Brahma, Vishnu, and Shiva).

After appraising the bow's beauty, Rama effortlessly picks up the weapon and flexes it to attach the string. But when he draws the bow to test its power, it breaks in half. Witnessing this, Sita modestly puts a garland around Rama's neck, a signal that she accepts his proposal. They will marry. And so begins Rama's transition from *Brahmacharya* to *Grihastha* (adolescence to manhood).

There is much to do to arrange the wedding. First, King Janaka must send an envoy to King Dansarath, Rama's father, to tell him the news. Dansarath is relieved that Rama is safe and delighted to hear about the proposed marriage. He sets out with an entourage to Mithila, where the kings will council.

One of the necessary wedding rituals is the recitation of the groom and bride's lineage. Vishvamitra does this for Rama; Janaka does this for Sita. Lineages shared and found satisfactory, Vishvamitra

THE "TRINITY" OF KARNATIC COMPOSERS

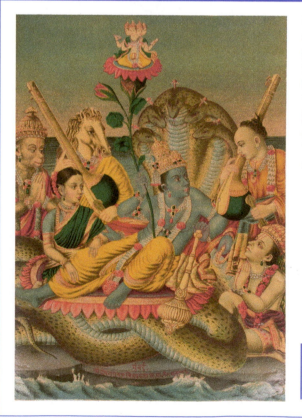

Muthwswami Dikshitar (1776–1835), Syama Sastri (1762–1827), and Tyagaraja (1767?–1847) are venerated as Karnatic music's greatest composers. Tyagaraja is perhaps the most beloved of the three. A devotee of Rama, he was a humble and devout man who believed that music was an ideal way to experience god. Tyagaraja wrote over 600 songs (*kriti*) devoted to Rama. Every January in Thiruvarur, Tyagaraja's birthplace, thousands gather to commemorate the composer in a music festival called the Tyagaraja Aaradhana. Tyagaraja festivals are also held annually in Cleveland (Ohio), Salt Lake City (Utah), and Chicago (Illinois).

Vishnu on the divine serpent Shesha, with Laksmi and the sage Narada (probably modeled on Tyagaraja), by Shri Sheshanaraya, 1886.
Courtesy of The Metropolitan Museum of Art, New York, Gift of Mark Baron and Elise Boisanté, 2012.

suggests a quadruple wedding. Rama and Lakshamana will marry Janaka's daughters; Rama's half-brothers will marry the daughters of Janaka's brother.

After the exchange of priceless gifts and the singing of hymns, the four grooms, their heads shaved, sit and await the arrival of their brides.

South Indian Karnatic Music

Like many aspects of Indian culture, musical traditions are split between north and south. Northern musicians perform in the Hindustani tradition; southern musicians perform in the Karnatic (or Carnatic) tradition. The roots of both traditions reach back to the *Natya Shastra*, a 2000-year-old treatise that still serves as the principle authority in the production of Indian traditional music, dance, and theater.

While Hindustani music focuses on instrumental performance, Karnatic music is vocally based. The driving force behind Karnatic song is the expression of *bhakti*, or religious devotion. Almost synonymous with bhakti is the composer–saint Tyāgarāja, who dedicated his life and nearly all of his music in supplication to Lord Rama.

Like music in the Hindustani north, Karnatic music divides into three parts: drone, melody (raga), and rhythm (*tala*). Acting like gravity, the drone sounds the tonic pitch, thereby providing a stable foundation upon which the raga can unfold. Traditionally, the four-stringed, long-necked chordophone called the tambura (or tampura) sounds the drone. Today, however, a *śruti box* (miniature organ) often replaces the tambura.

A Karnatic vocalist will usually be shadowed by an instrumentalist who loosely follows the singer's melody, thereby creating a heterophonic texture. Often, the instrumentalist will also provide improvisatory interludes. Karnatic melody instruments include the *venu* (a transverse bamboo flute), violin, and *veena*, a lute-family instrument with four melodic strings and three drone strings. The veena is darker in tone color than the Hindustani sitar and sarod, instruments to which we were introduced in Chapter 2. Like the sitar, the veena has moveable frets on its neck. Unlike sitar players, however, veena players often sing while accompanying themselves on the instrument.

As for the other Karnatic melody instruments mentioned above, the south Indian violin is the same instrument as the Western violin, though it is tuned differently. The venu flute has eight finger holes. By regulating the breath and adjusting the embouchure positions, a performer can achieve the pitch subtleties required to perform different ragas.

The *mridangam* is a double-headed drum, and Karnatic music's main percussion instrument. The drum's heads are of different sizes and pitches. To each is attached a paste that changes the way the drum head vibrates, which allows the drummer to create a variety of tones and timbres.

Although they apply the ideas differently, both Hindustani and Karnatic rhythmic structure is governed by the tala system. Here we focus on Karnatic rhythmic structures.

Because of their length and complexity, tala cycles are broken up into smaller units of one, two, or more pulses. Listeners keep their place within the units by following along with specific hand motions as indicated below:

- *Anudhrutam*: one pulse, notated by "U." Right hand, palm down, taps the thigh (or taps the other hand as in a gentle clap).

Vina (Veena), late 18th century.

Courtesy of The Metropolitan Museum of Art, New York, Gift of Michael Pellettieri, in memory of Y.G. Srimati, musician and artist, 2009.

- *Dhrutam*: two pulses, notated by "O." Right hand, palm down, taps the thigh (or taps the other hand), then tap again with palm up.
- *Laghu*: variable number of pulses, notated by "I" followed by a number that indicates the total number of pulses. Beat one is palm down, followed by counting beats with the fingers, starting with the little finger.

The most common Karnatic cycle is *Adi* tala, which consists of eight pulses organized as laghu/dhrutam/dhrutam (notated I_4 O O). Figure 4.1 shows how it is performed.

FIGURE 4.1
One Adi tala cycle.

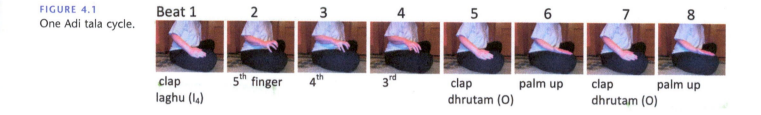

clap   5th finger   4th   3rd   clap   palm up   clap   palm up
laghu (I₄)   dhrutam (O)   dhrutam (O)

"CHUNKING" RHYTHM

Psychologists have found that short-term memory begins to falter when a subject is asked to remember more than seven distinct objects. Memory can be greatly extended by a process called "chunking," in which items are combined into groups. For example, three groups of four (twelve) unrelated objects are easier to remember than one group of eight unrelated objects. Karnatic musicians also "chunk" groups of pulses (*aksharas*), a trick that allows them to handle large akshara groupings easily. For example, *jhampa* tala has ten aksharas, too many to keep track of if not chunked, but the tala becomes manageable when the aksharas are grouped into three sets: one set of seven, one set of one, and one set of two (7 + 1 + 2 = 10).

LISTENING
4.3)))
GUIDE

"Seeta Kalyana Vaibhogame" ("Sita's Wedding"), by Tyagaraja

Texture: Heterophonic
Meter (tala): *Khanda chapu*—five aksharas (pulses) per *aavartanam* (cycle).
Rhythmic grouping: *dhrutam anudhrutam dhrutam* O U O (clap – clap clap –)
Raga: *Sankarabharanam* (sa-re-ga-ma-pa-dha-ni-sa, the same pitches as a major scale)
Form: Kriti

The *kriti* (sacred song) "Sita Kalyana Vaibhogame" is a beloved composition in India. This song can be heard on traditional Karnatic concert programs, a wide range of recordings (stylistically from classical to pop), and in numerous **Bollywood** films.

A kriti generally consists of three sections:

- *Pallavi* is the first verse, which can reappear throughout the performance.
- *Anupallavi* is an optional "small pallavi."
- *Charanam* is the last and longest verse(s), which can be repeated several times.

Even when a singer is not present, instrumentalists may perform a kriti without its words. They will maintain the kriti's text-based form and its associated melodies.

| 0:00 | Our performance begins with the raga's pillar tones "sa" and "pa" sounded by a tambura. The mridangam, tuned to "pa," strikes a few tones. Notice the music's austere tone and firm processional quality. |

0:10 PALLAVI

Sita Kalyana Vaibhogame.
Sita Kalyana Vaibhogame.
Rama Kalyana Vaibhogame.

The grand celebration of the marriage of Sita.
The grand celebration of the marriage of Sita.
The grand celebration of the marriage of Rama.

A finger cymbal sounds on the syllable "yan" (0:11), thereby marking beat one of the five-beat cycle. Though not played consistently, a small tambourine (*kanjira*) generally marks the rhythmic groupings: O U O.

Notice the melody's narrow range: sa sa . . . sa re . . . sa (actually a quick alteration between ni–sa–ni–sa–ni–sa). Because the singers sing with a wide vibrato in a heterophonic style, the melody feels extremely active. Adding to the texture is a harmonium, which also embellishes the song's melody and increases the heterophonic density.

0:53 CHARANAM

This section introduces a new, more expansive, upward-reaching melody.

Pavanaja Stuti Patra Pavana Charitra.
Pavanaja Stuti Patra Pavana Charitra.
Ravi Soma Vara Netra Ramaniya Gatra.

He who is praised by Hanuman, the son of wind,
He who has a very holy story.
Whose sacred eyes are the Sun and the Moon.
He whose bearing is grace.

1:22 CHARANAM

Pavanaja Stuti Patra Pavana Charitra.
Ravi Soma Vara Netra Ramaniya Gatra.

1:38 PALLAVI

Sita Kalyana Vaibhogame.

Mridangam emphasizes beat one with a low tone (1:39).

1:55 CHARANAM

Nigamagama Vihara Nir-Upama Zarira.
Nigamagama Vihara Nir-Upama Zarira.
Naga Dharagha Vidara Nata Lokadhara.

He who lives in sacred books and Vedas.
He who has an incomparable body.
He who is the soul of great Ragas.
He who takes care of devotees.

2:20 PALLAVI

Sita Kalyana Vaibhogame.

| 2:29 | Mridangam plays a *mohra*, a thrice-repeated rhythm that marks the end of a section. (The same technique is called a *tihai* in Hindustani music) |

2:34 CHARANAM

Paramesa Nuta Gita, Bhava Jaladhi Pota.
Tarani Kula Sajjata Tyagaraja Nuta.
Tarani Kula Sajjata Tyagaraja Nuta.

continued

He who is sung in prayers by Lord Shiva himself.
He who removes the problems of domestic life.
He who understands the human beings.
And is sung by sage Tyagaraja.

3:07 **PALLAVI**

Sita Kalyana Vaibhogame.
Rama Kalyana Vaibhogame.
Vaibhogame.
Vaibhogame.

3:37 Mridangam signals the performance's end by playing a second mohra.

QUESTIONS FOR THOUGHT

- What does Jhampa (7+1+2) tala look like using the symbols for Anudhrutam (U), Dhrutam (O), and Laghu (I_x)?
- Imagine if the tambura player did not sound raga's tonic. How might the listener's perception of the raga change?

SUNDA

Centered on the island of Java, the Sundanese ethnic group consists of some 35 million people. Most Sundanese practice Islam, though remnants of earlier religious beliefs are still found. Hinduism, which arrived from India centuries before Islam, constitutes one such layer. While Hindu religious practice has mostly been displaced, the Hindu epics retain an important place within the culture.

End of Life: Making Amends and Assuaging Grief

Almost all of us will exit the world to the strains of music. A funeral service without music is almost inconceivable, even if the tones are as austere as a military bugler playing "Taps." We explore two musical scenarios: first, a song depicting the last moments of life; second, an actual burial.

Contrition

We return to Indonesia with the song "Ceurik Rahwana" ("The Tears of Ravana," pronounced "**Cheu**-rik Ra-**wa**-na"). We met Ravana, Sita's abductor in Chapter 2. Now the story has advanced. A battle

The Combat of Rama and Ravana, late 18th century.

Courtesy of The Metropolitan Museum of Art, New York Purchase, Friends of Asian Art Gifts, 2008.

has been fought and Rama has rescued Sita. Ravana is dying and seeks forgiveness from Banondari, the still-beloved wife whom he has betrayed.

"Ceurik Rahwana" is drawn from the vocal music genre *tembang Sunda,* which developed in the 19th-century Sundanese court of Cianjur (Chi-**an**-jur) on the island of Java, Indonesia. Though little known, even in greater Indonesia, this music genre remains prized among urban Sundanese who value the way the music subtly mines the emotions of melancholy and loneliness. When performed in traditional fashion, songs feature a vocal soloist accompanied by two or three instruments: the *kacapi indung* (a large plucked zither), the *suling* (a bamboo flute), and possibly a *kacapi rincik* (a small plucked zither).

"Ceurik Rahwana" ("The Tears of Ravana")

LISTENING
4.4
GUIDE

Texture: Heterophonic and homophonic
Meter: Duple
Form: Strophic

"Ceurik Rahwana" is in the *rarancagan* style, with its emotional texts and impassioned delivery characterized by *cacagan* (a pulsing and jagged vocal vibrato). "Ceurik Rahwana" consists of a five-verse dialog between Ravana and Banondari. The lyrics are supported by a motoric ostinato produced by the kacapi indung. The singers deliver the lyrics within a narrow melodic range in syllabic chant-like phrases. Vocal lines are accompanied heterophonically by the suling. Singers use subtle pitch inflections to enhance the sense of extreme emotion.

0:00	Running scalar patterns in the kacapi indung introduce the tones that identify *sorog* as the song's pentatonic tuning system. The Sundanese conceive of their musical scale as building downward from high to low. So, we too will organize the tones in that fashion. Rather than using the Sundanese tone syllables da-mi-na-ti-la (high to low) we use the Western syllables fa-mi-re-te-la.
0:11	Kacapi indung sounds a central motive (mi . . re mi . . . . . . <u>la</u> . . te . . re . . fa mi . . . la . . fa la fa mi).
0:12	Suling enters.
0:16	**Verse 1** *Banondari anu lucu, boho kakang anu geulis. (geunig, duh anu geulis.)* Banondari who is beautiful. My lovely wife. (Oh, who is lovely.) *Kadieu sakeudeung geuwat, akang rek mere pepeling. (aduh geulis, mere pepeling.)* Here, just a second. I wish to give a message. (Oh lovely one, I give a message.) *Geura sambat indung bapa, samemeh akang pinasti.* Go summon mother and father before I perish.
	As the verse begins, the vocalist focuses the phrase on "mi," which forms the melodic center for the entire first line. With the second line, the vocalist begins higher, but gradually drifts back down to "mi." The third line relaxes down toward resolution on "la." Each succeeding verse follows the same melodic framework.

1:04	**Verse 2**
	
	Aduh engkang buah kalabu sembaheun lahir jeung batin.
	    (geuning, lahir jeung batin.)
	Oh beloved fruit of my heart, dedicated body and soul.
	    (Oh, body and soul.)
	
	Aya naon pengeresa tara-tara ti sasari. (aduh geuning, ti sasari.)
	How should one feel from now on? (Oh, from now on.)
	
	Nyauran ragrag cisoca, abdi mah saredih teuing.
	Calling, streaming down tears, I am devastated.

continued

1:54	**Verse 3**

Aduh Enung anu ayu nu geulis pupujan ati. (guelis, puypuhan ati.)
Oh Darling who is so delicate, who is so lovely, praiseworthy heart.

Akang tangtu ngababatang, samemeh akang pinasti. (aduh geulis, akang pinasti.)
I am fated to die. But before I perish. (Oh my lovely, I perish.)

Arek menta dihampura, lahir tumeka ing batin.
Let it be that I ask to be forgiven, body as well as soul.

2:42	**Verse 4**

Duh engkang panutan kalbu, teu kiat abdi wawarti. (geunign, abdi wawarti.)
Oh object of my heart. I am not strong, I warn you. (I warn you.)

Ulah sok ngumbar amarah antukna kaluli-luli. (aduh, geuning, kaluli-luli.)
One must not follow anger, [instead] one must forget/forgive.
    (Oh, forgetting all.)

Nu matak mawa cilaka, kaduhung ngajadi bukti.
[Anger] leads to catastrophe. Regret becomes proof.
[Not forgiving leads to sorrow.]

3:31	**Verse 5**

Kaduhung kakang kaduhung, kataji nu lain-lain. (geulis, nu lain-lain.)
Regret, I regret, I was drawn by an extraordinary other.
    (Yes, Lovely, by an extraordinary other.)

Kaiwat goda rancana, kagembang ku Sintawati. (aduh geulis, ku Sintawati.)
Ensnared and seduced by tempation, enchanted by Sita. (Oh Lovely, by Sita.)

Geuning kieu karasan, malindes malik ka diri.
This is how it feels when the suffering (that one inflicts on others) returns
    to oneself.

Mourning the dead in Bulgaria.
KUCO/Shutterstock.com.

A Funeral Lament

Singing funeral laments is usually the prerogative of women. Typically, laments are passed on by **oral tradition** and performed by female relatives of the deceased. In some traditions, a professional lamenter may be hired. In the Middle East, for example, hired lamenters are the norm since it is generally believed that for a relative to lament a death would question God's perfect will.

Lamenting practices vary throughout the world. Stylistic characteristics are closely tied to geographic region. Some trace roots back to ancient classical Greece and Egypt. Others, like the Finnish-Karelian laments from northern Europe and Russia, exhibit vestiges of ancient female-centered folk religions.

The laments of eastern Europe are sung for practical reasons. For the living, they facilitate mourning and celebrate lives well lived. For the

FUNERAL MUSIC

Classic funeral songs performed in the United States include: "Amazing Grace" (Chapter 2), and "Precious Lord" (Chapter 5), and "Nearer My God to Thee" (Chapter 9). Since its appearance in the soundtrack of the Vietnam War film *Platoon* (1986), many associate Samuel Barber's (1910–81) *Adagio for Strings* with death.

Popular music songs often performed at funerals include: "Yesterday" (Lennon and McCartney), "Imagine" (Lennon), "What a Wonderful World" (Thiel and Weiss), "Simply the Best" (Turner), "My Heart Will Go On" (Horner and Jennings), the Christian hymns "For All the Saints" (Vaughn Williams), "On Eagles Wings" (Joncas), "Will the Circle be Unbroken" (Gabriel and Habershon), and countless others.

"Mă Guariţă"

LISTENING 4.5 GUIDE

Texture: Monophonic
Meter: Non-metric
Form: Strophic

In Transylvania (a region of Romania), laments are called *bocete* (singular, **bocet**, pronounced "**bo**-chet"), which literally means "to cry with tears." Bocete are performed by close female friends or relatives of the deceased during the first three days following a death. They may be sung in the home, during the funeral procession, or at the burial. They are also performed on subsequent visits to the cemetery and on special days designated to remember the dead. Bocete are fully or partially improvised, but follow a recognizable formula. Sometimes, as in our listening example, mourners will mumble or elide words and mix crying with singing.

The lament below consists of fifteen short melodic phrases separated by pauses. All of the phrases end on the same pitch, with a vocal "ah" sound at the end, sounding much like a sigh. The melody is simple and uses just four pitches. Phrases follow a general pattern of falling from the fourth scale degree stepwise to the tonic. The text setting is **syllabic**, as if the lamenter is half speaking, half intoning her thoughts. Some of the phrases are ornamented with oscillating pitches, especially those that call out the name of the lamenter's brother, "Guariţă" (Georgie). Not all the words, or their meanings, are clear.

0:00	*Mă Guariţă Guariţă draga*	You Guarita, dear
0:05	*Guariţă, Guariţă fratele meu drag*	Guarita, my dear brother
0:13	*Spune-mi dragă spune-mi cum ai mai facut*	Tell me dear how were you?
0:21	*Mă Guariţă mă . . .*	You Guarita, you . . .
0:27	*Pînă la Brasov mă Guariţă mă*	All the way to Brasov [a town in Transylvania], you Guarita
0:34	*Că . . . te-ai mai dus pe . . .*	You indeed took me on . . .
0:41	*Pînă la coadra, Guariţă, Guariţă*	All the way to [the forest?] Guarita, Guarita
0:48	*Cine . . . apa*	Who . . . water
0:54	*La ceasul mortii mă Guariţă mă*	The hour of death. You, Guarita, you
1:01	*Gata lumea dragă toată la . . .*	[You] are finished with the whole World . . .
1:08	*De pe lumea . . . Guariţă dragă*	From this world . . . Guarita, dear
1:15	*Vino dragă vino vino noaptea in vis*	Come dear, come at night in dream
1:23	*Sa te . . . sa mă racoresc*	To . . . cool me off [soothe me]
1:29	*Mă Guariţă Mă ia . . .*	You Guarita, you, take . . .
1:36	*Pînă la coadra sa-mi vin si ea dragă.*	All the way to [the forest?] for me to come as well, dear.

dead, they are believed to assist the soul's transition from life to the afterlife. Singers are often said to possess magical or shaman-like powers.

Performers often utilize wailing, sobbing, speech-like song, and non-tonal pitch inflections to invite emotional catharsis. In the Finnish-Karelian tradition, lamenting is called "crying with words." Romanian lament singers are expected to perform with tears in their eyes.

QUESTIONS FOR THOUGHT

- Can you think of other songs in which reconciliation is sought before death?
- Should Banondari forgive Ravana? Why or why not?
- What emotions did you experience while listening to "Mă Guariţă"? Why?
- Why do you think lament singing might be more socially acceptable for women than men?
- What ethical issues might arise when recording a lament singer?

ACTIVITIES AND ASSIGNMENTS

- Ask a grandparent to describe his/her early childhood musical memories. What music was popular during adolescence? Did your grandparents have a favorite song? Did they like to dance?

Conclusion

As we moved through this chapter you may have noticed that as music accompanies us through life, the same music can function in multiple contexts. John Lennon and Yoko Ono's song "Imagine" fits as well in the context of a funeral or political rally as it does for a first kiss.

Meanings change even if the context remains the same. Years ago your parents may have processed to *Pomp and Circumstance*, but the piece will invoke very different emotions if they hear it again at your own college graduation.

The music that comforted you as a child will stay with you through adulthood. Someday, you may pass it on to your grandchildren. We age, but music is a gift that stays new, always fresh, and ready to come to our aid in celebration and sorrow. Whether we are young or old, music lights up our lives.

Key Terms

- Ashrama
- bar/bat mitzvah
- bhakti
- bocet (pl. bocete)
- Bollywood
- Brahmacharya
- cacagan
- Grihastha
- Hindustani music
- Isnati Awica Dowanpi
- Karnatic (Carnatic) music
- kriti
- lament
- maqam
- mohra
- mridangam
- *Natya Shastra*
- oral tradition
- quinceañera
- raga
- *Ramayana*
- sorog
- śruti box
- syllabic
- tala
- tambura
- tembang Sunda
- tihai
- Trimurti
- veena
- venu
- Vishnu

Essay Questions

- Suppose you are planning the music for a wedding or funeral. What considerations would impact your choices?
- Create a musical playlist that represents your entire life. What music would that include? Why?

CHAPTER GOALS

- To investigate the way in which music supports and reflects ethnic identity and values.
- To explore the ways in which musical ethnicity crosses and bridges both cultural and social boundaries.
- To become familiar with musical expressions of ethnicity in selected times and places.

CHAPTER FIVE

Music and Ethnicity

QUESTIONS FOR THOUGHT

1. **What is your ethnic background or heritage? Does your family express this background in particular ways? In music or dance, cooking styles or fashion? If so, when and how?**
2. **Have you ever spent a holiday or special occasion with a family whose ethnicity is different from your own? How did this experience compare with the way things are done within your own home?**
3. **Look up definitions of ethnicity and race. What are the differences?**

Lima, Ohio

Buffalo steaks sizzle on grills as crowds stroll toward the sounds of Great Plains-style singing and drumming emanating from the nearby performance ring. The dancers, who have come to the powwow from cities and towns across North America, wear the traditional clothing of their various Native American ethnic groups, including Lumbee, Cherokee, Lakota, Navaho, and many more. A blond-haired, blue-eyed dancer borrows the emcee's microphone and tells the audience that she is proud to be Native American. Not genes, but life experience and worldview make us who we are, she says.

"[I]f I interfere in the profession of griots, this is to ask them to pardon me, and let me play a little music so I can eat."
—Salif Keita (b.1949)

Fourteenth Woodland Indian Celebration 2016, Perrysberg, Ohio.
Courtesy of Black Swamp InterTribal Foundation, Jamie Oxendine.

Sociologists tell us that ethnic groups are bound by shared culture, including social customs, values, and beliefs, and perhaps common language, religion, and ancestry. As our blond-haired dancer contends, looks can be deceiving. Today's social realities are not easily encapsulated. Ethnic borders are often porous and can be difficult to delineate.

This is the second of four chapters that explore the ways in which music reflects and gives shape to social identity. Here we focus on the concept of ethnicity, a central building block in the establishment of one's sense of self, home, and community.

In order to develop a better understanding of ethnicity in general and of "ethnic music" in particular, we draw examples from a tiny sampling of the world's many ethnic groups. As we do so, you might sense that the distinctions between ethnicity and race are blurry. Perhaps you will even begin to wonder if you might best identify yourself as belonging to more than one ethnic group.

ACTIVITIES AND ASSIGNMENTS

- **Search the internet for videos of powwows. You will discover a wide range of dances and musical styles.**
- **Attend a powwow.**

Africa and the Diaspora

The movie *8 Mile* (2002) tells the story of Jimmy "B-Rabbit" Smith Jr. (played by Eminem), a struggling white wanna-be rapper living in a predominantly black Detroit neighborhood. The film's final scene, set in a nightclub, features a rap competition. It is on stage that B-Rabbit finally finds himself, not by rapping tough-guy verse, but by highlighting his outsider status (he's "white trash," lives in a trailer with his mother, recently got beat up, and has friends who act like fools). Unfettered by acknowledging the truths of his troubled life, he not only wins the contest, but also takes a step toward becoming his own man.

Writers generally place rap's beginnings in New York City's 1970s South Bronx, but seeds can be found in many places, ranging from the civil-rights era recordings of The Last Poets to African-American storytelling to insult competitions ("The Dozens"). African-American musical and verbal traditions draw heavily from West Africa, where we now go.

The *Jalolu*: Musician/Historians of West Africa

Seated inside a family compound in the Gambia, West Africa, a *jali* (pl.: *jalolu*, Fr.: *griot*), remembers the life of an elderly Mandinka chief recently deceased. There is much to say. One by one, the chief's many accomplishments are recounted. The jali's tale gradually expands outward to include the man's family and friends. Genealogies are traced, life histories expounded. Sometimes the praise singer's meaning is clear. Other times, words are cloaked in symbolism that only the elders understand. The performance continues long into the night.

Perhaps the jali tells the history of the Mandinka ethnic group itself, a tale that crosses centuries and details the rise and fall of civilizations. The jali might reach all the way back to the warrior/king Sundiata Keita (ca.1217–ca. 1255), founder of West Africa's vast Mali Empire (1234–1600) and spiritual father of the Mandinka people. As the story unfolds, the jali links past to present, thus offering insights on how best to prepare for the future.

The jali accompanies himself with the *kora*, a plucked 21-stringed chordophone. With a range of three octaves, the kora's soft interlocking melodies provide a kaleidoscopic tonal foundation for song. Between vocal lines, the kora comes to the musical foreground, perhaps echoing a melody just sung, perhaps improvising sounds altogether new. Together, voice and kora form a balanced pair, each supporting the other.

For at least 800 years, the jalolu have sung the history of the Mandinka. Born into their profession, training begins for these "casted bards" in early childhood. Learning is a lifelong enterprise that involves memorization of social history, skill in rhetoric, and training as a singer and/or instrumentalist. A jali's most important characteristic, however, is courage. No matter what, a jali must not be afraid to tell the truth.

In the past, the jalolu were attached to chiefs. But with the political decline of chieftaincies, along with the rise of the nation-state and market-based social systems, the jalolu's clientele has broadened. Today's jalolu sing for politicians, businessmen, religious leaders, and community members. They perform at naming ceremonies, weddings, funerals, and all other socially important events. A number have developed successful careers in the world-music industry.

Although the kora is the instrument that has most captured the imagination of Western listeners, it is only one of a number of melodic instruments a jali might play. Others include the *balafon* (xylophone), the five-stringed *ngoni* lute, and the *bolon*, an arched harp. Traditional gender roles dictate that female jalolu generally do not play instruments, but they are considered to be excellent singers. Men provide instrumental accompaniment for women, other male vocalists, and themselves. Generally, a solo singer takes a leading role in presenting the historical narrative. Other jalolu may support the soloist by singing a repetitive refrain. Music scholars call this solo/chorus song style "**call and response.**"

Kora.
Photo by Kevin Walsh/Flickr/ CC-BY-SA-2.0.

Jalolu music making consists of sets of balanced oppositions: verse/refrain, song/narrative, male/female roles, instrumental/vocal combinations, and more. Kora playing itself divides into two categories: accompanimental (*kumbengo*) and soloistic (*birimintingo*). Kumbengo melodies support song by providing an unobtrusive tonal backdrop. Because there is no singing during birimintingo improvisations, these virtuosic sections provide opportunities for listeners to reflect on details of the jali's story.

Jalolu also divide vocal styles into two categories: *donkilo* and *sataro*. Donkilo is the composition's basic tune, often consisting of a short phrase that is repeated time and again throughout the performance. If, for example, a jali were telling the story of Sundiata Keita, he might set to the donkilo melody the words, "the lion of Mali." With each donkilo repetition, the idea of Sundiata's power is reaffirmed. Over time that concept of power is woven inseparably into the story and into the listeners' minds. With words so closely associated to a particular melody, the phrase's meaning will be heard in the kora's melody alone.

Sataro is speech-like verse that includes proverbs, praise, and other commentary. It flows free of the kora's established melody and rhythmic meter. In sataro, information can be quickly distributed. Therefore, a jali will move to sataro when s/he has much to say, wants to move the story forward, or simply wants to increase the dramatic pace.

"Kelefaba" and "Kuruntu Kelafa" (medley), performed by Foday Musa Suso

LISTENING
5.1
GUIDE

Texture: Homophonic
Meter: Duple
Form: Strophic

0:00   (The recording begins in the midst of a performance.) Kora fades in with a series of kumbengo-style accompaniment figures. Listen to the repeating bass line that provides foundation for the tones above.

continued

0:24	Improvisation in the birimintingo style.
0:34	Kora begins a simple kumbengo-style accompaniment figure, a signal that singing will soon commence.
0:40	Foday Musa Suso sings "Kelefaba" in donkilo style

| Mindolo banta, Malama la mindolo banta. | The millet beer is finished,
The millet beer is finished. |
| Kelefaba la mindolo banta. | The great Kelefa's millet beer is gone. |

The song tells about the exploits of the 19th-century Mandinka mercenary Kelefa Sanneh, who fought along the Gambia River for the kingdom of Nyomi against neighboring kingdom of Jokadu. Notice the general downward trend of the melody (do–ti–la–sol . . . sol–la–sol–fa–mi . . . and all the way down to "do").

1:16	Extended birimintingo solo.
1:50	Short kumbengo section.
2:00	Birimintingo.
2:30	Kumbengo.
2:36	Closing section of "Kelefaba." (Notice the same melody as at 0:40).
2:52	New song: "Kuruntu Kelefa" ("Trailing Kelefa").

Kora plays in the kumbengo style as the singer **riffs** in donkilo style on the phrase:

| Mansa jalo kuma fo baga le,
"Kari siya jama, a kela man siya." | The king's jali says,
"Those who talk are many, but those who act are few." |

Legend says that this song was played by Kelefa's personal jali as he followed his master in various exploits.

| 3:02 | Kora in birimintingo style. |

QUESTIONS FOR THOUGHT

- The sound of the kora is very beautiful in its own right. Imagine a kora performance without song. Would this be complete? Why or why not?
- Imagine that you are a jali. What would you sing about? How much of your own family's history could you tell? What about the history of your home town?
- Think about the music you know well. Can you identify any instrumental melodies to which you automatically hear the implicit words?

ACTIVITIES AND ASSIGNMENTS

- Find jalolu performances on the internet. Compare and contrast them.
- View Malian kora virtuoso Toumani Diabaté's *The Mande Variations*, a short film usually available on the internet. Although Diabaté does not name them as such, he demonstrates kumbengo and birimintingo. The film also includes a section on kora construction.

Ethnicity in a Changing World

We introduced the jalolu as representatives of the Mandinka, an ethnic group of some eleven million people found across West Africa in coastal countries stretching from Senegal to Côte d'Ivoire and inland to landlocked Mali. The Mandinka are bound together by common ancestry, language, and tradition. Farming forms the basis of their economy. Islam is nearly universally practiced, though it is generally infused with older beliefs and rituals. The Mandinka have their own language, but no written script. Their oral histories, as sung by the jalolu, are some of the world's richest. The Mandinka are an ethnic subgroup of a still larger group of West African people known as the Mande, which includes the Bafour, Malinke, Kpelle, Dyula, and other subgroups. Anthropologists generally speak of Mande as a cultural group made up of a variety of ethnicities.

In the section that follows we trace aspects of West African ethnic heritage across the Atlantic Ocean to the United States, where it was transformed to fit new surroundings, social needs, and personal interests. Next, we present case studies of musical ethnicity in Europe. In each example we will see how music is adopted and adapted according to specific needs of time and place, values and identity. At chapter's end, we return to Africa.

QUESTIONS FOR THOUGHT

- **Ethnicity is often seen through the political lens of nation. In the United States, for example, we speak of African Americans, Asian Americans, etc. What sorts of differences do these terms imply? Are those implications accurate?**
- **Can one identify musical differences among American ethnic groups?**

The Blues

Four and one-half centuries of trans-Atlantic slavery resulted in as many as twelve million Africans captured, chained, and transported to the Americas where they were sold as chattel. African slaves brought almost no material culture with them to the New World. What they did bring, however, was something that could not be taken away from them: a rich and vital social culture. African ways of thinking and acting, of cooking and farming, and of making music and dance all took root across the Americas. In this chapter section we focus on the **blues**, a form that grew out of the African-American experience in the Mississippi Delta. In later chapters we will investigate African-derived New World religious and dance traditions.

The blues genre began in the late 19th century as a rural tradition with roots in African-American work songs, field hollers, and spirituals. African aspects of these sources are apparent in social values (storytelling, group participation, and improvisation) and musical style (call and response, rhythmic groove, and sliding pitches). The blues echoes the jalolu/kora tradition in the importance of storytelling and the close relationship between singer and instrument.

In the 1920s and 1930s, blues singer/guitarists such as Lead Belly (1888–1949), Charlie Patton (1891–1934), Robert Johnson

Portrait of Bunk Johnson, Lead Belly, George Lewis, and Alcide Pavageau, Stuyvesant Casino, New York, ca. June 1946.

Photo by William P. Gottlieb/Library of Congress Prints and Photographs Division.

(1911–1938), and others codified the blues into the form we know today. They honed their repertory in traveling shows and town squares, **juke joints** and nightclubs. The emerging blues style was rough, but distinctive. It was simple in form, but capable of endless nuance. Like the jalolu an ocean away, blues artists focused on human experience. Songs spoke of everyday life, often of broken love and troubled times.

The blues changed as its popularity grew and as it moved from the rural South to northern cities, like Chicago and New York. The instrumental and vocal sounds remained muscular, but the packaging became sleeker. Performance formats grew from solos and duos to small ensembles. Arrangements became tighter, improvisation more formalized.

There are a number of standard blues forms. The most common is the **12-bar blues,** which divides neatly into three sections of four measures (bars) each. Over the course of twelve measures, the song's lyrics go through a single cycle, as does the harmonic progression.

Generally, the lyrics of a 12-bar blues song contain two different lines of text. The first line is sung across the first four measures, then more or less repeated over the next four. The second line is sung in the final four measures. Thus, the lyric form of 12-bar blues is AAB.

Consider the lyrics from "Cross Road Blues," by Robert Johnson. @ 5.1 The first line sets the scene and serves to attract the listener's interest:

(A) *Was standin' at the crossroad, tried to flag a ride.*

Think about the lyrics' implications and imagine the scene. Why a crossroad? Why is he hitchhiking? Where is he going? What does a Mississippi Delta crossroad look like?

"CROSS ROAD BLUES"

Robert Johnson's "Cross Road Blues" is a classic early blues song, covered countless times over the past seventy years. Listen to Johnson's recordings and you will notice that he does not follow the 12-bar form exactly. Some phrases are longer than expected; others are shorter.

What is the song about? Ask five people and you may get five different answers. Folk legend says that Johnson went to the crossroads to make a bargain with the devil—his soul in exchange for guitar virtuosity. Others say the crossroads is a religious symbol associated with Legba, a West African trickster spirit. Still others reject the African connections, but accept the idea that danger lurks at crossroads—places were ideas and people intersect, and where decisions (right or wrong) are made. Another theory argues that the song is about the danger that African Americans felt when traveling in the white South. Still others will say the song is simply about hard times, about trying to hitchhike when nobody stops.

Perhaps there is truth in all of these interpretations. Blues lyrics are often ambiguous, open to a variety of readings. A good blues song invites you to reflect upon your own experiences, or perhaps to compare and contrast your experiences with those of the singer.

For a very different interpretation of "Cross Road Blues" listen to "Crossroads" as recorded in 1968 by the British rock band Cream, which featured guitarist Eric Clapton (b. 1945). Footage of Cream performing "Crossroads" can be found on various internet sites.

BLUES AND THE RECORDING INDUSTRY

In August 1920, Mamie Smith (1883–1946), primarily a **vaudeville** singer, was hired by Okeh Records in New York City to record a song titled, "Crazy Blues." In doing so, she not only became the first African American woman to record "the blues," but she also helped jumpstart the "**race record**" industry, music recorded for African-American consumption. In fact, "Crazy Blues" is far closer to vaudeville and Dixieland jazz than Delta blues. Nevertheless, there is bluesy social dystopia and ultimately racial militancy in the song's lyrics, which range from "the man I love/He don't treat me right" to "Gonna get myself a gun/And shoot myself a cop." This was powerful stuff just a year removed from the 1919 "Red Summer" race riots.

Rather than provide answers, Johnson repeats the line. As is common in the blues, he alters the words slightly:

(A) *Ooo eeee, I tried to flag a ride.*

Okay, but there must be more to the story. We want to know what happened. What was he doing there? Did he get where he was going? With the B line, the singer partially satisfies our desire for more information:

(B) *Didn't nobody seem to know me. Everybody pass me by.*

Certain themes pop up repeatedly in the blues. Songs are about hard times, social isolation, sex (mostly good), love (often gone bad), money (mostly needing it), and patient endurance in the face of hardship. Early blues musicians seem to have lived by their own rules, beyond the constraining effects of social norms. They also had a powerful effect on the American imagination. Robert Johnson and other early blues singers would supply the prototype for images developed by rebellious rockers from Elvis Presley (1935–1977) to Steven Tyler (b.1948) to Kurt Cobain (1967–1994).

Fifteen-times Grammy Award-winner guitarist B.B. King (1925–2015) was born into poverty in the Mississippi Delta; his parents were share croppers and King picked cotton as a boy. A 10th-grade

---

"Sweet Little Angel," performed by B.B. King

LISTENING 5.2 GUIDE

Texture: Homophonic
Meter: Quadruple
Form: 12-bar blues

The song "Sweet Little Angel" is a 12-bar blues classic. It has been recorded under various titles, the first being in 1930 as "Black Angel Blues" by Lucille Bogan. Our recording by King begins with a 12-bar introduction, followed by twenty-four bars of vocals (two cycles), followed by twelve bars of the band playing riffs, then twelve bars of King soloing on guitar. Follow the chordal harmony (I–IV–I–I, IV–IV–I–I, V–IV–I–V), which fits one chord to each bar. To hold your place within the form, conduct along or use the snare drum back-beat, which plays on beats two and four of each bar.

0:00	Instrumental introduction twelve bars

0:48   A (bars 1–4)
    (1) I've got a sweet little angel,   (2)
    I   IV

 . . . . . .
    (3) I love the way she spread her   (4) wings
    I   I

1:03   A (bars 5–8)
    (5) I've got a sweet little angel,   (6) . . . . . . I love the
    IV   IV
    (7) way she spread her wings.   (8) . . . . . .
    I   I

1:17   B (bars 9–12)
    (9) When she spreads her wings around me, (10) . . . . I get joy
    V   IV
    (11) in everything.   (12) . . . . .
    I   V

King exploits a variety of vocal timbres as he bends pitches and jumps back and forth between **chest voice** and **falsetto**.

B.B. King live at the Audimax at the University of Hamburg, Germany, November 1971.

Heinrich Klaffs/Wikimedia Commons/CC-BY-SA-2.0.

dropout and married at age 17, he had to grow up fast. The next year, King had put the fields behind him and was performing six nights a week in a West Memphis juke joint. There he heard, and backed up, many of the early great blues guitarists, including electric guitar innovator T-Bone Walker, whose sound the up-and-coming King sought to assimilate. King did, and more. He went on to create a guitar timbre and style—simultaneously conversational and wailing—that was immediately recognizable and deeply influential.

ACTIVITIES AND ASSIGNMENTS

- Sing the root (bottom) tones of the chord changes along with the recording.

I	IV	I	I	//	IV	IV	I	I	//	V	IV	I	V
do	fa	do	do	//	fa	fa	do	do	//	sol	fa	do	sol

- Sing the words along with King. Then, sing the words during the solos. See if you can hold your place inside the form.
- Improvise your own melody. You might start small by singing little interjections against the words or the guitar.
- Consider the meaning of the words. What sort of "angel" is this woman?
- Write a verse about your own "angel," big or little.

QUESTIONS FOR THOUGHT

- Is social experience an important aspect of the blues? If a Japanese garage band covers "Crossroad Blues," is that still the blues?
- Robert Johnson used just his guitar to play the blues. B.B. King uses a band comprising highly skilled sidemen. What effect might solo versus ensemble performance have on blues form?
- Are words an essential part of the blues?
- Lucille Bogan's "Black Angel Blues" can be found on the internet. How does her recording compare with King's?
- Does the choice of musical instruments matter? Is the blues still "the blues" if performed by a symphony orchestra? "Composed" by a computer program?

Jazz

American music need not be in the blues format to reference African heritage. Consider the classic 1937 composition "Caravan," by Juan Tizol (1900–1984) and Edward Kennedy "Duke" Ellington (1899–1974). Still today, this piece invokes a mysterious atmosphere laced with feral possibility.

The Ellington Band with Ray Nance, Tricky Sam Nanton(?), Johnny Hodges(?), Ben Webster(?), Otto Toby Hardwick(e), Harry Carney, Rex William Stewart, Juan Tizol, Lawrence Brown, Fred Guy(?).
Photo by William P. Gottlieb/Library of Congress Prints and Photographs Division.

How are these effects achieved? First, there is Tizol's restlessly chromatic and undulating melody. Behind this, Ellington adds harmonies that are simultaneously lush and dissonant. Finally, there is Ellington's **orchestration**. Gongs shiver and "African" tom-toms beat; a trumpet growls. Taken as a whole, "Caravan" presents a shimmering soundscape of unprecedented exoticism, one that seems to invoke America's deepest imaginings about the place once called the Dark Continent.

Using music to create powerful imagery was standard procedure for Ellington, who wanted his music to have what he called "representative character." Nearly everything he wrote—whether the subject matter was love, city life, dance, or spirituality—was meant to inspire a vivid sense of place and attitude. Invariably, Ellington's music reflected the life he lived and the world his audiences imagined.

Part of Ellington's genius was that his music made use of the unique backgrounds, talents, and personal styles of his bandsmen. Each musician was encouraged to contribute his own individual personality. Some band members, such as drummer Sonny Greer (1895–1982) and trumpeter Arthur Whetsol (1905–1940), had been Ellington's childhood friends. Others brought to the group a wealth of regional styles. The earthy sounds of New Orleans can be heard in the playing of trumpeter Bubber Miley (1903–1932) and clarinetist Barney Bigard (1906–1980). Trombonist Joe "Tricky" Sam Nanton (1904–1946), along with trumpeters Miley and Charles "Cootie" Williams (1911–1985), specialized in "jungle" growls. Puerto Rico-native Juan Tizol added Caribbean colors and grooves.

"Caravan," by Juan Tizol and Duke Ellington, performed by the Duke Ellington Orchestra (recorded in 1937)

LISTENING **5.3** GUIDE

Texture: Homophonic
Meter: Quadruple
Form: 32-bar song form (AABA)

0:00	The recording begins with drummer Sonny Greer beating out "jungle" rhythms on the tom-toms. Cymbals and gongs (a reference to the Silk Road?) punctuate each new two-measure cycle. At the end of the cycle, Ellington's piano chords replace the gongs.
0:13	**A Section** Trombonist Juan Tizol enters with the song's chromatic main melody, a long undulating tune that seems to drift across the pulse-like shifting desert sands. Tizol's vibrato is fast and wide, filled with emotion. The melodic phrase itself is oddly unbalanced, consisting of seven alternating sections of held tones and movement—stasis, action, stasis, action, stasis, action, stasis. During the stasis sections, baritone saxophonist Harry Carney (1910–1974) interjects a counter melody. A trumpet growls as the section comes to an end.

continued

0:31	**A Section**
	Tizol repeats the melody.
0:50	**B Section**
	Woodwinds sound held chords over which Tizol's solo continues.
1:06	**A Section**
	Clarinetist "Barney" Bigard takes over the A section melody. The feel is lighter and jazzier than in Tizol's version. The accompaniment—now woodblocks and muted brass instruments—has changed as well. Bigard's improvised flourish at the end seems to abandon the melody altogether.
1:24	**A Section**
	Trumpeter Cootie Williams (1911–1985) has been growling in the background all along. Now he takes the lead with a jazzy solo both brisk and sharply punctuated.
1:42	**A Section**
	Williams's solo continues, but now he exploits his plunger mute. The tones are longer, more flowing. It sounds as if he is telling a story with his trumpet.
1:59	**B Section**
	The sequence of featured soloists is broken as the spotlight is given to the saxophone section as a whole. Musical individuality has been replaced by the voice of community.
2:16	**A Section**
	Carney takes over the melody. The ensemble growls its approval. Greer moves back from woodblocks to tom-toms.
2:27	**A Section: Conclusion**
	Tizol interrupts Carney. The band drops out. Rhythmic time stops while Tizol plays a short operatic-like cadenza. Notice the lack of tonal resolution in both melody and harmony. A gong strike closes the song, but one might feel that the stop is temporary, a moment of stasis between action.

Ellington's songs often referenced African-American heritage and culture. Early compositions include "Black and Tan Fantasy" and "Creole Love Call," both from 1927. Middle-era works included "Reminiscing in Tempo," (a 1935 ode to his recently deceased mother) and "Harlem Airshaft" (1940). In his later music, Ellington often took European themes and reshaped them to fit his own social world. Among these works is *Harlem Nutcracker*, a thoroughly adult dance suite drawn from Russian composer Pyotr Ilyich Tchaikovsky's (1840–1893) ballet, *The Nutcracker* (1892). Ellington became increasingly religious in his later years, a period in which he wrote and performed a series of sacred concerts.

QUESTIONS FOR THOUGHT

- "Caravan" is considered a highpoint of Ellington's "jungle" sound, yet the song seems to be referencing the nomadic life of the North African desert, or further east still. What location does the sound texture suggest to you?
- Consider the song's trajectory from an exotic "other" to jazz to closing cadenza. What might the range suggest?
- Regional music styles are far less distinctive today than they were in the 1930s. Why might this be?

ACTIVITIES AND ASSIGNMENTS

- "Caravan" has been recorded over 1000 times by artists ranging from pop crooner Bobby Darin (1936–1973) to Phish to The Skatalites, a Jamaican ska band. The rapper Afrika Bamaataa (b. 1957) sampled "Caravan" in "Jazzy Sensation (The Jazz Mix)." Search out these or other recordings and compare and contrast them to the original.

Western Art Music: William Grant Still (1895–1978)

Known as the "Dean" of African-American composers, William Grant Still successfully navigated his way through the socially conservative (and, at the time, almost exclusively white) realm of classical music. @ 5.2 He was the first African American to conduct a white American orchestra; he was also the first African-American composer to have a symphony performed by one. Early in his career, Still worked as an arranger for jazz orchestras and Broadway shows. He went on to compose eight operas, along with other classical works.

Still's best-known composition is the "Afro-American" Symphony (1930). Although written for a symphony orchestra—a medium of European heritage—the composition presented a distinctly African-American voice. His goal was to compose music for orchestra that did not show Caucasian influence. In particular, Still said he wanted to demonstrate that the blues, "often considered a lowly expression, could be elevated to the highest musical level." Accordingly, he opened the symphony with a 12-bar-blues theme. The second theme is in the style of an African-American spiritual, a genre that Still considered more Caucasian, less African, than the blues. Both themes are original.

William Grant Still.
Photo by Maud Cuney-Hare, 1936.

SYMPHONY ORCHESTRA

A symphony orchestra (or sometimes just called "symphony," "orchestra," or "philharmonic") is a Western art music ensemble consisting of string, woodwind, brass, and percussion instruments. In the 18th century, when these ensembles were first established, the typical orchestra rarely had more than thirty players. Over the years, as concert halls became larger and as composers imagined new textures and timbres, the orchestra grew. Today's ensembles may include 100 or more instrumentalists.

In the United States alone there are nearly 2000 such ensembles, ranging from unpaid community groups to prestigious full-time ensembles employing some of the finest musicians in the world. In the 2014/15 season, attendance at New York Philharmonic concerts alone topped 500,000. Many orchestras also perform in the "background" of course, providing music for ballet, theater, and film scores.

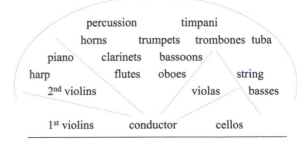

Orchestral seating layout.

SONATA FORM

Sonata form, an instrumental form that developed in Europe in the 18th century, provided a flexible grid upon which composers could lay out their musical ideas for easy understanding. It consists of three main sections:

- Exposition—where the composer introduces contrasting musical themes or tonal areas.
- Development—where these themes are developed and expanded.
- Recapitulation—where the original ideas return.

To get a sense of the structure's logic, it may help you to compare sonata form with the format of a research paper: introduction, body, and conclusion.

Exposition		Development	Recapitulation	
Key area 1 (transition)	Key area 2 (closing)	Composer plays with materials from the exposition	Key area 1 (transition) Key area 2 (closing)	
Tonic key	Related key		Both areas now in tonic (home) key	
Harmonically stable	Harmonic shift	Harmonically unstable	Harmonically stable - - - - - - - - - - - - -	
(section repeated)- - - - - - - - - - - - - - - - - -				

FIGURE 5.1
Sonata form.

QUESTIONS FOR THOUGHT

- Still wanted to compose an orchestral score free of Caucasian influence. Is this possible?
- Why do you think Still wanted to elevate the blues "to the highest musical level?" What do you think he meant by that idea? Do you think he succeeded?
- Who was Still's audience? What was he trying to say to them?
- In what ways might the blues be more African than a spiritual? (Consider both musical and social possibilities.)

LISTENING 5.4 GUIDE

First movement (Moderato assai) of "Afro-American" Symphony, by William Grant Still

Texture: Homophonic
Meter: Quadruple
Form: Sonata (loosely followed)

0:00	Introduction Melody played by English horn
0:22	Exposition Theme 1 (blues) begins and is played by a sultry muted trumpet.
0:54	Theme 1 repeats twelve bars later, this time with a clarinet taking the lead. Notice how the other instruments in the orchestra seem to answer.
1:25	The blues form evaporates. Still chops up and embellishes his thematic material. At 1:33 the full orchestra has one last go at thematic material before easing into theme 2.

2:05	Theme 2. For this inward-looking theme (an emotional quality typical of second themes) he borrows from the style of the spiritual. The music then proceeds through a series of transformations in style and attitude. Some are inward looking, some extremely jazzy and extroverted.
3:23	Development Recasting of ideas from theme 2.
4:28	Recapitulation (notice that the thematic order is reversed) Theme 2.
5:05	A jazzy version of theme 1. Listen to the conversation between the muted trumpets and the riffing woodwinds. This lasts for 12 bars.
5:36	Coda Expansion of theme 1 ideas.

HARLEM RENAISSANCE

The Harlem Renaissance sought to celebrate Afro-American experience and heritage. Important figures in the movement included philosopher Alain Leroy Locke (1885–1954), writer Langston Hughes (1902–1967), folklorist Zora Neale Hurston (1891–1960), composers Duke Ellington and William Grant Still, and many others. The movement, which coincided with the Great Migration of African-American families from the rural South in search of work in the urban North, is generally dated from 1919 until the mid-1930s.

Identity and Ethnicity in 20th-Century Europe

The affirmation of one's roots can be an empowering experience. But what about the weakening of one's roots? For some, this might offer a sense of independence and freedom; for others, however, it might create a sense of unease, even inspire a search for identity. Drawing from the European experience, we now look at three examples of 20th-century music making. Each can be understood as a different response to the complexities of ethnic identity. Each is represented by a distinctive flowering of musical ideas.

Maurice Ravel (1875–1937)

Composer Maurice Ravel's ethnic and cultural heritages drew from a variety of sources. Although his mother was Basque (an ethnic group residing in the Pyrenees Mountains along the border of Spain and France), she was raised in Madrid. His father was Swiss. Ravel was born in the Basque village of Ciboure, but raised in Paris, at the time the world's most cosmopolitan city.

While still in his early teens, Ravel attended the Paris-based 1889 Exposition Universelle, a summer-long world's fair attended by over thirty million people. @ 5.3 The event featured exhibits from cultures around the world, including: a Cairo bazaar, a 400-person *village nègre* (Negro village), a Javanese gamelan orchestra, and American sharpshooter Annie Oakley performing in Buffalo Bill's Wild West Show. The Eiffel Tower was one of many structures built for the exhibition.

As the success of the Exposition suggests, *fin de siècle* Europe was fascinated with the "exotic" ways of distant ethnicities and cultures. Composers were quick to incorporate newly discovered cultures and soundscapes into their own work. For Ravel, that interest would resurface throughout his creative life. He invoked ancient Arabia in his orchestral song cycle *Shéhérazade* (1903) and ancient Greece in his ballet *Daphnis et Chloé* (1909–1912). He drew ideas from Roma (Gypsy) musical culture in *Tzigane* (1924, for violin and orchestra), and African-American blues in his Sonata for Violin and Piano in G major (1923–1927). Other compositions were influenced by sounds of Spain, Asia, and Africa.

Eiffel Tower, 1890s.
Courtesy of The Metropolitan Museum of Art, New York, Museum Accession.

HUMAN ZOOS

Ethnic imaginings sometimes took shocking turns. The 400-person village nègre of the 1889 Exposition Universelle was just one of hundreds of similar exhibits presented between the 1830s and the early 1900s. A 1906 exhibit at New York City's Bronx Zoo presented the caged central African Mbuti pygmy Ota Benga (1883–1916) as the "missing link" in the evolution between ape and man. Other exhibits in other times and places have displayed Inuits and Apaches, Filipinos and Samoans. For a more recent "human zoo" exhibit, see the film documentary *Couple in a Cage* (1997).

Ota Benga, a pygmy from the Congo brought to the United States for the 1904 World's Fair.
Library of Congress Prints and Photographs Division.

The sciences were also on the move. The dawning century heralded a time of new explorations, both outward and inward. Some journeys involved traversing wide geographies; others unfolded on a psychologist's couch. Scholars in the newly created field of anthropology searched the globe for "primitive" cultures where they hoped to discover the secrets of pre-rational existence. Psychologists stayed in their laboratories where, following Sigmund Freud (1856–1939), they traveled inward in hopes of mapping the unconscious. Meanwhile, physicist Albert Einstein's (1879–1955) theory of relativity revolutionized the most fundamental ideas of space and time. The firm ground of 18th-century **Enlightenment**-era rationalism, which held that truth was immutable and accessible by reason alone, was crumbling.

Visual artists of the time were also intrigued by the idea of capturing events beyond everyday experience. Painters explored a style known as **Primitivism**. Their canvases were vivid, with thick textures. Subjects were often taken from unsullied nature. Paul Gauguin (1848–1903), for example, traveled to Tahiti and other "exotic" lands to escape the "artifice" of European culture.

Other artists, who remained closer to home, developed an inward-looking painting style called **Impressionism**. @ 5.4 Shimmering light, glistening pastels, and blurred edges characterized the style. From a distance, the pixel-like brush-stroke techniques appear relatively conventional. But get closer and the viewer detects blotches of paint, bold individual brush strokes, and striking juxtapositions of color. Artists such as Edouard Manet (1832–1883), Claude Monet (1840–1926), and Pierre-August Renoir (1841–1919) were considered radical for breaking with conventional painting methods.

Ia Orana Maria, Paul Gauguin, 1891.
Courtesy of The Metropolitan Museum of Art, New York, Bequest of Sam A. Lewisohn, 1951.

Just as the visual artists experimented with color, Ravel and fellow French composer Claude Debussy (1862–1918) experimented with tone. Both were deeply affected by the shimmering Javanese gamelan music they had heard at the Exposition Universelle. @ 5.5 Both attempted to recreate the aesthetic with Western instruments, thus developing what some have labeled Impressionist music. To achieve the desired sonic effects, Ravel and Debussy experimented with unconventional scales, rich chordal combinations, and striking instrumental groupings that mirrored the iridescent colors of the gamelan (Chapter 6: Music and Gender).

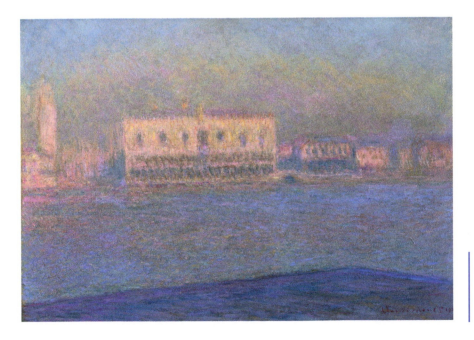

The Doge's Palace Seen from San Giorgio Maggiore, Claude Monet, 1908.
Courtesy of The Metropolitan Museum of Art, New York, Gift of Mr. and Mrs. Charles S. McVeigh, 1959.

Rapsodie espagnol: "Habanera"

Ravel's orchestral composition *Rapsodie espagnole* is a masterpiece of Impressionist imagery. It consists of four **movements**: "Prélude à la nuit," "Malagueña," "Habanera," and "Feria." Each movement (a prelude and three dances) is a study in tone color. Here we examine "Habanera," which is modeled on a dance genre of the same name. (We return to the habanera when we take up the story of the operatic protagonist Carmen in Chapter 6: Music and Gender.)

The roots of the habanera are diverse. It is known as a Cuban dance, though it came to the island by way of French refugees escaping the early 19th-century Haitian wars of independence. Once in Cuba, the habanera was adopted by Afro-Cuban slaves who infused it with African rhythmic nuances. The dance soon became popular across Cuba with peoples of all ethnicities and social classes. From Cuba, it spread to South America and back across the Atlantic Ocean to Spain.

Ravel reframes the dance as if filtered through a tinted soft-focus sonic lens. Like Bach did with his "Bourrée" and Still would soon do with the blues, Ravel removes the music from its original setting and places it in the concert hall. Ravel's dance takes place in the imagination alone.

LISTENING 5.5 GUIDE

"Habanera" from *Rapsodie espagnol*, by Maurice Ravel

Texture: Polyphonic
Meter: Duple
Form: ABA

0:00	Notice the texture's soft-edged and non-rhythmic ethereal quality. The tones of the muted strings evoke dreamy distance suggestive of the Impressionist aesthetic. Perhaps we also hear Ravel referencing the shimmering textures of a Javanese gamelan.
0:22	A gentle pulsing melody begins in the oboes, English horn, and clarinets. Hear how the melody seems first to rush upward and then fall back (but always falling less than it rises). It feels as if the music is trying to get something started, but cannot quite muster the energy.
0:43	The melody becomes more energized. Listen to the typical habanera rhythm (long/short/short/long). The energy quickly dissipates until . . .
1:10	The horns play a long drawn-out chord.
1:24	Solo clarinet and violins play the rising/falling melody heard earlier in oboes, English horn, and clarinets. Melody and rhythms echo throughout the orchestra.
1:54	The habanera rhythm is expanded and developed with accents from a tambourine and snare drum. The woodwinds have the melody for two cycles.
2:14	Then the strings enter.
2:26	And finally the horns.
2:38	The opening texture returns. The music evaporates, like a vague scent gently dispersed.

Béla Bartók (1881–1945)

A similar fascination with ethnicity pervaded the thinking of Ravel's near contemporary, the Hungarian composer and pianist Béla Bartók. @ 5.6 Yet Bartók's response could hardly have been more different from Ravel's. As we have seen, Ravel was working in Paris at the powerful and outward-looking center of the European world. From that socially confident perch he tried on a variety of musical ethnicities with the ease of one being fitted for a new wardrobe.

Bartók, working at Europe's eastern periphery, did not share Ravel's confidence in world-ranging eclecticism. Instead, he, like his Hungarian contemporary Zoltan Kodaly (1882–1967), decided it

Bartók recording in Transylvania.
DEA/A. DAGLI ORTI/De Agostini/Getty images.

was important to champion his own ethnic background within the international style of Western European art music. The aim is simple enough, but there was a problem. "Real" Hungarian music—that is, the pure ethnic music of the Hungarian "folk"—was no longer heard in urban Hungary, where Romani (Gypsy) musicians dominated "traditional" performance styles. Although Bartók was attracted by the idea of ethnic music's social purity and potency, it was not clear what an "authentic" Hungarian tune actually sounded like.

"Allegro Barbaro," by Béla Bartók

LISTENING
5.6
GUIDE

Texture: Homophonic and polyphonic
Meter: Duple
Form: ABAB

0:00	Hammering alternating chords create a relentless rhythmic **ostinato** (repeated phrase).
0:03	Theme 1 sounds over the ostinato.
0:11	Theme 1 again, this time at a higher pitch level and in a more expansive form.
0:29	Ostinato alone, as in the beginning only on a lower pitch.
0:33	Theme Group 2, four ideas derived from theme 1's extension material. Each idea is separated by the ostinato figure growling away in the low register. The ostinato gradually disintegrates.
0:59	Theme 1 returns, now with a thinner texture.
1:19	Theme 2 ideas intermingle with the ostinato but finally come to a halt around 1:35.
1:35	Theme 2 material in the lower register joins with the ostinato and theme 1 extension material.
1:48	Right-hand flourishes momentarily disrupt the obsessive pounding of the ostinato.
1:57	Theme 2 material restarts the rhythmic engine.
2:12	Ascending scalar passage. A final statement of the ostinato pattern.

THE SOLO PIANO

The piano was invented in the early 18th century and offered an alternative to the harpsichord, the main keyboard instrument of the day. Nineteenth-century composers in particular were enamored with the instrument. Hungarian Franz Liszt (1811–1886) and Polish-born Frédéric Chopin (1810–1849) wrote virtuosic music that greatly expanded the instrument's expressive range. Both incorporated elements of their respective ethnic homelands into their music.

In 1904, at age 23, he decided to find out. The plan, he wrote to his sister, was "to collect the finest Hungarian folksongs and raise them . . . to the level of art-song." In the process, he hoped to find his own musical voice, one grounded in the songs of the common people.

Thus began for Bartók a decades-long process of song collection, analysis, and musical transformation. Equipped with pencil and paper, sometimes also with hundreds of pounds of primitive recording equipment, he documented peasant musical life, collecting thousands of songs and dances. Some of them he arranged for the concert hall.

Virtually all of Bartók's composition was influenced by the folk music he collected. His work is filled with locally derived scales, brash dissonances, and regional dance rhythms. The harmonic style was spare and dissonant. Rhythms reflected the **agogic** (durational) accents of the Hungarian language. Sometimes unbalanced rhythms pounded violently, as if animated by the vigorous cadences of life lived close to the earth. All of this is heard in Bartók's "Allegro Barbaro" (1911) for solo piano.

QUESTIONS FOR THOUGHT

- How do Ravel's and Bartók's musical languages differ from one another? Might this be a reflection of ethnicity?
- Bartók and Still both sought to infuse art music with their ethnic heritage. How else might they be seen as similar? How might they contrast with Ravel?
- What might make a musical style authentic? What might make it inauthentic?

ACTIVITIES AND ASSIGNMENTS

- Investigate the sounds of Hungarian folksongs. What characteristics of this music do you hear in Bartók?

Klezmer

The setting is Anatevka, a *shtetl* (village) in Czarist Russia. Life is hard for the Jews who live there. Tevye the milkman struggles to support his wife and five daughters. His horse is lame; money is short. Keeping one's footing is precarious in such a world—like a fiddler on the roof, he says.

All this we learn in the first minutes of composer Jerry Bock (1928–2010), lyricist Sheldon Harnick (b. 1924), and author Joseph Stein's (1912–2010) 1964 Broadway musical *Fiddler on the Roof*. By show's end, Tevye's three eldest daughters have married, mostly against their father's wishes, and the Jewish populace has been forced to leave Anatevka. Yet even amidst the setbacks and failed hopes, life goes on. Tevye and his wife will start again, in America, a land of immigrants in which everyone, or so Tevye hopes, is given a fair chance, whatever his ethnicity.

Tevye and Anatevka were fictitious, of course. But the Jewish experience that the show describes was not. Nor were the distinctive sounds that made this Broadway show so memorable. Bock drew his materials from the traditions of the Ashkenazic **klezmer** musicians of Eastern Europe. The style's raucousness was softened for Broadway, but the plaintive appeal of its harmonic and melodic language remained.

Klezmer is a Yiddish term. It refers to both Jewish professional musicians and the music they play. The word derives from two Hebrew words, *kley* (instrument) and *zemer* (song). Klezmer came to the United States with waves of Eastern European Jewish immigrants in the early decades of the 20th century. The music was essential at Jewish weddings and other celebratory events.

Klezmer music virtually disappeared in Europe during the years of the Nazi-driven Holocaust. In the United States during the same period, klezmer faded as immigrants and their descendants assimilated into American culture. Even so, the Jewish sound prevailed in other ways. Echoes of klezmer's exuberance and tonal personality can be heard in the improvisations of jazz clarinetist Benny Goodman (1909–1986), the melodies of George Gershwin and Irving Berlin (b. Israel Baline, 1888–1989), and countless other Jewish American performers and composers.

Today, klezmer music is undergoing a resurgence across both Europe and North America. But while the musical sound remains closely connected to Jewish culture, contemporary performers come from a variety of ethnic backgrounds. Klezmer is also an important category in the "world music" commercial genre.

In the past, the violin formed the heart of a klezmer ensemble. Today that role is often taken by the clarinet. Other popular instruments include **cimbalom** (hammered dulcimer), bass or cello, flute, accordion, trumpet, trombone, drums, and most any other instruments that might be available.

Today's klezmer ensembles tend to be highly eclectic in both membership and musical approach. Consider, for example, the New York City-based group The Klezmatics. Formed in 1986, the ensemble forged its sound by emulating klezmer recordings from the 1930s and 1940s. To this they added a dash of social activism, a pinch of Jewish mysticism, and sounds (from jazz to punk) of the city in which they live and perform. The ensemble has collaborated with artists ranging from folksinger Arlo Guthrie (b. 1947) to classical violinist Itzhak Perlman (b. 1945) to "Beat" poet Allen Ginsberg (1926–1997). When not playing klezmer music, band members are busy following other endeavors. Some compose for theater, film, and television. Others perform in a variety of ethnic music styles from North America, the British Isles, and Eastern Europe.

Klezmer musicians at a wedding, playing an accompaniment to the arrival of the groom, Ukraine, ca. 1925.

Photo by Menakhem Kipnis.

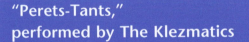

"Perets-Tants,"
performed by The Klezmatics

LISTENING
5.7
GUIDE

Texture: Polyphonic/Homophonic
Meter: Duple
Form: Intro / AA / BB / CC / DD / CC / DD / E / AA / BB / CC / DD / CC / DD

0:00	Introduction. The music opens with a vamp-style dialog between trumpet and violin over an animated rhythmic groove and static harmony from the accordion and clarinet. Listen to how the two solo instruments trade ideas back and forth, sometimes even overlapping.
0:25	A new section begins with the entrance of drums. This is a four-measure phrase that repeats. Since it is the first material of the main body of the piece, let's call it A. Since it repeats (at 0:32), the entire section is AA.
0:39	Section B. Notice that the complete phrase of four measures is actually two contrasting sections of two measures. It might seem like nitpicking to be so exacting, but it is not; there is a reason for the distinction. The musicians shortened the phrase length to speed up the sequence of events. Increased pacing translates into increased excitement. The B phrase repeats at 0:45.

continued

0:51	Sections CC. Call this the **"stop-time"** section; the rhythm instruments play accents. Notice the countermelody embellishment the second time through (repeat begins at 0:58).
1:04	Sections DD. Violin and trumpet exchange four-measure solos.
1:17	Sections CC. Similar to original CC, drummer plays on woodblock.
1:30	Sections DD. Violin and trumpet play together.
1:43	Section E. This section is sixteen bars. So now the pace of musical change has been slowed down. Saxophone solo. The section serves as a bridge back to the beginning of the form.
2:09	Return of AA, slightly embellished.
2:22	Return of BB, slightly embellished.
2:35	Return of CC, slightly embellished.
2:48	Return of DD. Violin and trumpet exchange four measure solos.
3:01	Return of CC, slightly embellished.
3:14	Return of DD. Violin and trumpet play together.

ACTIVITIES AND ASSIGNMENTS

- Interview an elderly family member and ask about ethnic heritage. Do any pre-American cultural traditions survive today? Recipes? Holiday songs? Were any practiced when your interviewee was a child?
- Interview students from another country. Ask about the kinds of music they listen to. Ask about the music their parents and grandparents listen to. Ask if their musical tastes have changed since coming abroad.

Return to West Africa

We have seen how music on three continents is used to strengthen ethnic roots and imagine new ones. The simple reality is that cultural interaction invariably influences those on both sides of the equation, even if one group might dominate another. The thirty million people who attended Paris's 1889 Exposition Universelle were changed by their exposure to non-Western cultures. So were the actors, musicians, and dancers who came from around the world to share their traditions.

Such is the case today. The roots of African-American blues and jazz are clearly found in the ancient musical and social cultures of West Africa, but influences flow both ways. In the 1960s, for example, soul singer James Brown (1933–2006) achieved superstar status in West Africa. Brown's music served as a model for Nigerian musician/political activist and Afro-beat creator Fela Anikulapo Kuti (1938–1997) (Chapter 11: American Musical Theater). In the 1970s and 1980s, the revolutionary politics of Jamaican reggae were heard

Salif Keita.
SIMON MAINA/AFP/Getty Images.

across the African continent. In today's Africa, values traditional and modern intersect and merge in ways both vital and unpredictable.

Journey today through the dusty neighborhoods of Bamako, Mali in West Africa and one is sure to come upon musicians. Some have traded traditional instruments for guitars and amplifiers. But their craft remains the same. Songs of the past offer gateways to the future. Bamako is a center for West African popular music. The city has served as a base for singer/guitarists Ali Farka Touré (1939–2006) and Baubacar Traoré (b. 1942), kora player Toumani Diabaté (b. 1965), and many others.

It is also the home of Salif Keita (b. 1949), whose Mandinka family claims royal descent dating back to the 13th-century reign of Sundiata Keita. Normally, such a powerful lineage would prevent one from working in the relatively low-status profession of musician. After all, a jali's traditional role is to *serve* royalty.

Life dealt Keita a different set of rules, however. He is albino, a sign of bad luck among the Mandinka. An outcast in his home town of Djoliba and rejected in his own family, as a teenager Keita made his way to Bamako where he joined the Rail Band, one of the city's most popular groups. In 1972, Keita became a member of Les Ambassadeurs, which had a high profile all across West Africa. Keita moved to Paris in 1984. Today he divides his time between Bamako and Europe.

Keita considers himself a pop musician, not a jali. His inspiration comes from traditional African styles, but also African-American musicians such as Chuck Berry (1926–2017), Little Richard (b. 1932), and James Brown (1933–2006). Keita generally delivers a more socially conscious message than his American models, however. Like the jalolu, he is committed to singing about social needs and truths. His songs tell of the importance of love, justice, and community. He talks about the difficulties of making a living as an artist, about the importance of values, and standing up for justice.

Keita's song "Baba" is typical of both his general musical style and his socially complex approach to music making. The song tells of Malian millionaire Babani Sissoko, who is admired for giving money to impoverished musicians. Keita acknowledges that Sissoko has also been accused of being a swindler. Maybe he is; maybe he is not, says Keita. But whatever he may be, he shares with those less fortunate.

ACTIVITIES AND ASSIGNMENTS

- Numerous music videos of Salif Keita can be found on the internet. Search them out and try to understand his approach to music making.
- Search the internet for video clips of other Bamako pop stars. What do the videos share in common? How do they compare with American music videos?

Conclusion

When considering ethnic music in the United States, we tend to think of sounds produced by people outside the Western European core upon which the early nation developed. But what about a movie soundtrack by John Williams or a song performed by Taylor Swift? Might that also be ethnic music? Your answer depends at least in part on the lens you use for analysis.

Ethnicity has always played a role in American social consciousness. Communities often formed along ethnic divisions. Majorities oppressed minorities along lines of skin color, language, cultural heritage, and religion. For many, the easiest way to avoid discrimination was to assimilate. Children learned English—the language of public school education—and wore the local fashions. Old World traditions were replaced. Achieving a certain level of conformity may have been an essential ingredient for building national identity, but much was lost.

Today, many Americans are searching for ethnic roots nearly forgotten. Family trees are constructed, old recipes tried, and songs rediscovered. In some cases, second-, third-, and even fourth-generation Americans hold to Old World traditions, even as those still living in the original "homeland" have moved on. A Polish visitor to the United States, for example, might not recognize the carefully preserved dances and songs performed at a Midwestern Polish American heritage festival.

We have seen that music is one way in which people express ethnic identity. Sometimes that expression is conscious; often it is not. In the following chapters we explore other ways in which music shapes and is shaped by other sorts of cultural and personal perceptions of identity.

Key Terms

- 12-bar blues
- agogic
- balafon
- birimintingo
- blues
- bolon
- call and response
- cimbalom
- Delta blues
- donkilo
- Enlightenment era
- *fin de siècle*
- Impressionism
- jali (pl.)
- jazz
- juke joint
- klezmer
- kora
- kumbengo style
- movement
- ngoni
- orchestration
- ostinato
- powwow
- Primitivism
- riff
- sataro
- sonata form
- stop-time

Essay Questions

- **How might one compose music that has no ethnic connections or connotations? Would listeners hear it as such?**
- **How might the reception of a piece of music be affected by its perceived closeness to a particular ethnic group?**

CHAPTER GOALS

- To understand relationships between gender, music, and culture.
- To learn how music reflects and shapes cultural understandings about gender.
- To become familiar with important trends, composers, and compositions that exemplify gender issues in music.

CHAPTER SIX

Music and Gender

QUESTIONS FOR THOUGHT

- What does it mean to be "feminine"? To be "masculine"? Is music gendered?
- Can objects or actions be seen as feminine or masculine? Musical instruments (flute vs. tuba)? Art (sculpture vs. watercolor?), Professions (nursing vs. construction)?
- How do you portray your masculine side? Your feminine side?

Introduction: Understanding Gender

Author J.M. Barrie (1860–1937) conceived Neverland as a boy's playground, an island populated with pirate hoards and mermaids, fairies and Indian bands. Neverland is home to Peter Pan, for whom life is little more than an endless series of adventures. Sometimes, when Peter is lonely, he visits our world. Should Peter arrive at your window some night, let him in. If he likes you, he might even take you to Neverland. If he does, and you are a boy, all of his adventures will be yours. But if you are a girl, he will expect you to play the mom.

> "I won't forget when Peter Pan came to my house, took my hand. I said I was a boy; I'm glad he didn't check."
> —folksinger Dar Williams (b. 1967)

Peter Pan lives in a gendered world, like the ones inhabited by all our fairytale heroes and heroines. As a child you might have learned the story of Little Red Riding Hood, and how she needed a beefy woodsman to save her from the wolf. You might have read about Sleeping Beauty, who remained dead to the world until kissed by a charming prince. Perhaps as a child you experimented with gender roles by playing with Barbie dolls or G.I. Joes.

Gender roles are learned. They differ from one culture to the next, sometimes even from one generation to the next. In a future telling, maybe it will be the charming prince who helplessly awaits a woman's animating touch. Maybe a woodsman will need Red to come to his rescue. G.I. Jane now fights alongside G.I Joe.

Gender is performed. We place gender on display when we put on dresses or pants, shirts or blouses, perfume or aftershave. We perform our gender through the way we carry our body when we walk or sit, through the ways we use our hands, and through the ways we speak and interact.

Gender is stamped into our earliest experiences. Baby girls are often dressed in pink, boys in blue. Breaking gender conventions comes with a price. As country and western singer/songwriter Johnny Cash (1932–2003) observed, life is going to be tough for "A Boy Named Sue" (1969).

We opened the chapter with a quote from folksinger Dar Williams's song "When I Was a Boy" (1993). Williams sings of the increasingly stringent gender restrictions that confine us as we grow from childhood toward adolescence and on into adulthood. She sings of a childhood relatively unconstrained by gender, of a time when she could be herself, even if hers was "boy" behavior. She played pirate games, climbed trees, and even rode her bike shirtless.

Listening in, we feel for Williams. Perhaps we remember the freedoms of our own lost childhoods. The song's kicker comes at the end, when she includes the perspective of her male friend. He too, it turns out, once enjoyed a time unconstrained by gender restrictions.

Gender norms are constantly evolving, but unevenly fluid. Working women are highly respected. Dads who quit their jobs to raise children are fodder for television comedies. From college class-

Story of Golden Locks, Seymour Joseph Guy, ca. 1870. Courtesy of The Metropolitan Museum of Art, Gift of Daniel Wolf and Mathew Wolf, in memory of their sister, the Honorable Diane R. Wolf, 2013.

rooms to the pages of *Vogue*, women's fashion continues to explore domains once reserved for men. In Japan, make-up-wearing "genderless *danshi*" (young men) are prominent in the entertainment industry. Most of their fans are teenage girls.

Not surprisingly, gender pervades musical sounds and music-related activities. Composers use strings and woodwinds to express the "gentle" feminine. Brass and percussion instruments often represent the "brawny" masculine. In many places, we also encounter gender-restricted music making. It was not until 1997 that the Vienna Philharmonic orchestra allowed women into its membership. Women have been barred from playing ritual drums in some Sub-Saharan African cultures, playing in the Balinese **gamelan** ensemble, and playing the **didgeridoo** in Australian Aboriginal ceremonies. Men face proscriptions as well. Musical activities controlled exclusively by women include singing laments in Eastern and Northern Europe, and the *Muheme* drumming tradition in Tanzania.

In the following pages we look at the ways in which music gives voice to gender. @ 6.1 We listen to "masculine" and "feminine" music and study how each reflects and shapes cultural ideals. We learn about individuals who embodied gender expectations and others whose expressive lives were stunted by gender restrictions. We encounter still others who confronted these restrictions head on and forced society at large to reevaluate fundamental notions of identity.

QUESTIONS FOR THOUGHT

- **Many songs take a position on gender. Examples might include Bo Diddley's (1928–2008) "I'm a Man" (1955), Helen Reddy's (b. 1941) "I Am Woman" (1972), and Ciara's (b. 1985) "Like a Boy" (2006). Can you think of others? Can you think of gender-fluid songs?**
- **What music-related gender expectations have you experienced in your own life?**

Female Composers and Western Art Music

"Perhaps for Felix music will become a profession, while for you it will always remain but an ornament; never can nor should it become the foundation of your existence."
—Abraham Mendelssohn in a letter to his daughter Fanny

Until the last half of the 20th century, women composers of Western art music were few. Musical training for "ladies" was usually limited to the home or convent. Playing wind and percussion instruments was considered unfeminine. Some men thought too much creative work might affect a woman's sanity. In spite of this, women made significant contributions to art music's development. But they were largely ignored by historians.

Today, restoring these women to the historical narrative (**reclamation history**) is an important scholarly focus. @ 6.2 Early important women composers include Hildegard of Bingen (1098–1179), Comtessa de Dià (late 12th–early 13th century), Isabella Leonarda (1620–1704), and Elizabeth Claude Jacquet de la Guerre (ca. 1666–1729).

German abbess Hildegard of Bingen wrote sacred works exclusively for the women in her convent. She also composed the first musical drama, *Ordo Virtutum*, a play about a young soul who wrestles with good vs. evil. Isabella Leonarda, also a nun, was the first woman to publish a collection of instrumental sonatas. Jacquet de la Guerre came from a family of prominent musicians. She was both a composer and a **virtuoso** harpsichordist at the court of Louis XIV.

In the 19th century, artistic skill was expected for young women of the upper middle-class. But their performances and compositions were generally confined to the home's parlor. This was the case

The Music Room, Mihály Munkácsy, 1878.

Courtesy of The Metropolitan Museum of Art, Bequest of Martha T. Fiske Collord, in memory of her first husband, Josiah M. Fiske, 1908.

for Fanny Mendelssohn Hensel (1805–1847), sister of composer Felix Mendelssohn. Few of Hensel's compositions were published during her lifetime but many were performed in the family's salon, where intellectuals and artists often gathered, and where talented women could respectably display their talents.

One 19th-century woman who ventured into professional music making was German composer and pianist Clara Wieck Schumann (1819–1896). Schumann came from a middle-class family, which allowed her more professional leeway than her female upper-class contemporaries. Indeed, her domineering father was determined to exploit the fact that professional female musicians were such a rarity. Schumann made her professional debut in Leipzig at age 9 with a program of virtuoso pieces and two of her own compositions. By 1830, she was famous across Europe. After a long courtship, one vehemently opposed by her father, Clara married composer Robert Schumann (1810–1856). Despite bearing eight children and supporting her husband's career, she continued to perform and compose, including the beautiful 1841 song, "Liebst du um Schönheit" (we will explore this in Chapter 10: Music and Love).

Clara Schumann not only contributed to the day's concert life, but also helped change social perceptions about women. By the late 19th century, music conservatories were matriculating women. Though still a minority, many of today's prominent composers are women, including: the Russian Sophia Gubaidulina (b. 1931), as well as the Americans Joan Tower (b. 1938), Ellen Taafe Zwilich (b. 1939), and Julia Wolfe (b. 1958) to name just a few. In some of today's professional orchestras, women outnumber men, up from 5 percent in 1970.

Gender in Popular Music

With the rise of television in the years immediately following World War II, the look and behaviors of American popular musicians became nearly as important as the music they performed. Along with this came controversy. Elvis Presley (1935–1977) was the catalyst. In mid-1950s television appearances, the singer's gyrating hips and spaghetti legs dazzled teens and shocked parents. His 1956 performance on the *Milton Berle Show* was "tinged with a kind of animalism," said New York's *Daily News*.

CAROLE KING (b. 1942)

When NYC disc jockey Alan Freed told teenaged songwriter-hopeful Carole King to start calling record companies if she wanted get her music played, that is exactly what the gutsy Brooklyn-born daughter of a NYC firefighter did.

"I had no fear. I don't know why. I was never brought up to be fearful or to think I couldn't do anything, for any reason. But certainly not because I was a girl," she remembers. King was only seventeen (and pregnant) when she and her lyricist husband Gerry Goffin wrote their first No. 1 Billboard hit, "Will You Love Me Tomorrow." What followed was a torrent of 118 charting songs, including (with Goffin or by herself): "Take Good Care of My Baby," "Run to Him," "Crying in the Rain," "The Loco-Motion," "Up on the Roof," "You've Got a Friend," "It's too Late," and many others. In 1968, Aretha Franklin recorded King's "(You Make Me Feel Like) A Natural Woman," a song Franklin performed for King when the latter was honored in 2015 at the John F. Kennedy Center for the Performing Arts in Washington, D.C. *Beautiful: The Carole King Musical* opened on Broadway in 2014. The show earned two Tony Awards and a Grammy Award.

Carole King sings "Locomotion" to the crew of the USS *Enterprise*, December 23, 1998.

Some thought Presley was hyper-masculine; others found him effeminate. For many, the combination was intoxicating. Life at gendered extremes was central to Presley's success. Fellow performers took notice. Ever since, the popular music industry has made the performance of gender a central aspect of an artist's public persona.

Early rock 'n' roll was dominated by white male performers, writers, producers, and audiences. A milestone in the early 1960s was the introduction of "girl groups." Typical ensembles consisted of three to six vocalists, sometimes teenagers and often black. The girl group run was short but significant, in particular because the women appealed to both black and white audiences at levels that only a handful of black men—such as Chuck Berry (1926-2017), Little Richard (b. 1932), and Chubby Checker (b. 1941)—had previously achieved.

Most girl groups were careful to conform to the period's gender expectations. Marketed as "girls" rather than "women," even their names were diminutives. There were, for example, The Bobbettes, The Ronettes, The Marvelettes, and The Primettes (the original name of The Supremes). These "girls" also knew their place. Song lyrics portrayed a restrictive social world of carefully constructed gender roles. The focus was often on a teenaged girl's romantic fantasies. Self-worth was often measured by whether or not she had a boyfriend. Girls were depicted as dependent on, even reverential toward, their boys. Boys also met a wall of expectations. The girls wanted them strong, brave, and faithful. Often they were not.

Consider the lyrics to the first No. 1 Billboard hit by an all-female group, The Shirelles' "Will You Still Love Me Tomorrow?" (1961), written by Carole King (b. 1942). On the one hand, the piece is an admission of a teenage girl's sexual desires—a groundbreaking topic for teen music in the early 1960s. At the same time, however, pre-marital sex is coupled with the fear of abandonment. As portrayed by The Shirelles, the young woman, who has far more to risk from a sexual encounter than her fancy-free boyfriend, is anxious and apprehensive.

Similar anxieties are heard in the record debut of 16-year-old Lesley Gore (1946–2015), whose single "It's My Party" (1963) reached No. 1 on the Billboard pop music chart. Told is the story of a girl who watches her boyfriend leave her birthday party with a rival girl.

In the early 1960s, less than a quarter of the No. 1 hit songs were sung by women, and many of them expressed reliance on men, even men who hurt, abandoned, or ignored them. But gender roles were changing. Teenage girls would soon have a wider range of role models than did their 1950s and early 1960s counterparts.

The same year that "It's My Party" was released, social activist Betty Friedan (1921–2006) published *The Feminine Mystique*, a book that helped spark second-wave feminism of the 1960s and 1970s. It was during this period that women made important and lasting inroads into male-dominated professions and institutions. Harvard, Yale, and Princeton became co-educational; women began to insist on economic equality and reproductive freedom.

Over the next decade, the women's movement would gain momentum with the 1966 formation of the National Organization for Women (NOW), protests at the 1968 Miss America Pageant, a 1970 sit-in at the headquarters of the *Ladies Home Journal*, and the establishment of *Ms. Magazine* (1971). Women's Lib, as it was called then, did not meet with unanimous popularity. Some saw it as a threat to traditional values, and even the American way of life.

In spite of the social advancements made by second-wave feminists, the movement is often criticized for ignoring the experiences of African-American women. African-American women also had their spokespersons, however, including the hugely influential Aretha Franklin (b. 1942), who grew up singing in Detroit's New Bethel Baptist Church, where her father was pastor.

In the mid-1960s, Franklin signed with the R&B-oriented Atlantic Records and shifted her attention from gospel to soul. Working with producer Jerry Wexler, Franklin recorded a string of hits that blended gospel with pop music's increasingly open expression of sexuality. These included "I Never Loved a Man (The Way That I Love You)," "Respect" (which won two Grammy Awards), "Chain of Fools," "Think," and many others. Franklin never totally left singing for the church. Her LP *Amazing Grace* (1972) became the biggest-selling gospel record ever.

In 1967, Franklin recorded "Respect," one of her greatest commercial hits. The song was written by rhythm and blues singer/songwriter Otis Redding (1941–1967), who recorded it in 1965 to moderate commercial success. Redding's recording portrays a man on the defensive. He cannot control his free-wheeling woman; nor can he find the strength to leave her. Franklin's recording, however, turned the predictably gendered world of the 1960s upside down. She and her backup singers ooze authority. In Franklin's rendition, she is the one who controls the money. She is also in charge of domestic life. Her man may have been messing around in the past, but that was going to stop. Now.

Aretha Franklin, ca. 1967.
GAB Archive/Redferns/Getty Images.

BEYONCÉ (b. 1981)

Beyoncé Knowles's album *Lemonade* (2016) focused on failed love and its attendant responses—hurt, anger, and the desire for vengeance. Therein, she unveiled in her work a newly broadened persona that combined vulnerability with moxie. The album followed up the singer's 2016 Super Bowl performance of "Formation," a militant demonstration of black pride and female empowerment, one clearly related to the Black Lives Matter movement and made more compelling by the fact that it was a woman (with a phalanx of female dancers) who delivered the message. "No matter your race, gender, or sexual orientation. This is a fight for anyone who feels marginalized," she wrote on her website (July 7, 2016).

Beyoncé at Superbowl XLVII.
Arnie Papp/Wikimedia Commons/CC-BY-SA-2.0.

Franklin was not alone in challenging quickly evolving sexual mores and gender roles. In 1968, the San Francisco rock band Jefferson Airplane recorded David Crosby's (b. 1941) "Triad," in which lead singer Grace Slick (b. 1939) suggested to her men, with their "long hair flowing," that they "try something new," living and loving as a threesome.

LISTENING 6.1 GUIDE

"Respect," by Otis Redding, performed by Aretha Franklin

Texture: Homophonic
Meter: Quadruple
Form: Strophic

0:00 **Introduction**
Four-measure instrumental introduction. The wind instruments trade riffs with the electric guitar across a two-measure cycle. The drummer plays a strong 2 and 4 back-beat on the snare drum. As the second two-measure cycle concludes, the drummer's fill signals the vocal entry.

0:09 **Verse 1**
Franklin's trio of backup singers lead off with the vocable "oo." The sound is placed hard on the downbeat, taut yet sweetly aggressive. Franklin enters and the backup singers continue their pressure. "Listen up," they seem to be saying. (Could "oo" stand in for "you"?) When Franklin demands respect, the trio echoes the demand. They scold with, "Just a little bit . . . Just a little bit."

Listen carefully to Franklin's authoritative and expressive voice. On occasion she breaks into a kind of sung shout, as with the word "need" in the second line. Franklin is audacious. She takes risks and holds nothing back.

Pop music tends to unfold in eight-measure phrases. "Respect" could easily fit that mold, but each sung verse tacks on an additional two measures. The change allows the backup singers time to fully reinforce Franklin's demands. Count through all ten measures so you internalize the form.

0:29 **Verse 2**
Same format, though the backup singers do not enter at the verse's beginning.

0:52 **Verse 3**
Notice how the trio's words ("just a, just a . . . ") are being used for their color and rhythmic energy.

1:13 **Interlude**
Saxophone solo. The saxophone, though easily conceived as a powerful "male" instrument, sounds thin when juxtaposed against Franklin's commanding vocal presence. Thus, even the saxophone's timbre reinforces the song's message of female strength. Without the backup chorus's scolding, there is no need to extend the section to ten measures. It is eight measures long.

1:29 **Verse 4**
Franklin opens with a long "oo." The vocable works in two ways. First, it echoes the language of the backup singers. (These women are united.) Second, it slows the dramatic pace of the lyrics, as if Franklin too had time to reflect during the saxophone solo.

1:50 **Break**
In case her back-sliding man still does not get it, Aretha literally spells out the word for him.

R–E–S–P–E–C–T. This section is a Franklin addition that does not appear in the Redding original. Backup singers intone: "Sock it to me . . . Sock it to me . . . " and as the song fades out, they chant: "Re—re—re—re—." Like the "oo" at song's beginning, the "Re" probably has a double meaning. The chorus is clearly chanting the opening syllable of "respect." But they also seem to be chanting (A)*re*(-tha). And why not? No other pop song came close to portraying women in so powerful a light.

Musicians continued to play with sexuality and gender, but it was becoming harder and harder to shock. Just four years after "Triad," New York City-based singer/songwriter Lou Reed (1942–2013) released "Take a Walk on the Wild Side." Reed devoted each verse to a different real-life person associated with The Factory, pop artist Andy Warhol's (1928–1987) infamous New York production studio. Despite unmistakable references to transsexuality, drugs, and prostitution, the song garnered considerable radio airplay, even became a top 40 hit.

Reed's song coincided with the early 1970s emergence of glam rock, a movement that continued the journey toward androgyny begun by Elvis Presley and his contemporaries. Performers like David Bowie (1947–2016) wore make-up and jewelry, sported long carefully coiffed hairdos, and sometimes strutted about the stage in platform shoes. @ 6.3

Cultural theorists have offered various explanations for the look, including shock value, an attempt to portray an "alien" and exotic persona, and a symbolic rejection of capitalist society (even as the musicians raked in millions of dollars). Perhaps all of these factors contribute to the answer, but there has to be more to it. Maybe these guys were popular because they were just plain sexy, a status they achieved in part by daring to live outside social norms and within the ever-perilous world of gender ambiguity.

David Bowie, 1980.

Jack Kay/Hulton Archive/Getty Images.

QUESTIONS FOR THOUGHT

- Choose a favorite song. Can you identify masculine and/or feminine elements in the sound of the music? Do these sounds reinforce the lyrics?

- Get on the Internet and view some of Elvis Presley's early performances. Do you find them gendered? Why or why not? Some critics found Presley effeminate. How do you see him?

- Have your own evolving musical tastes reflected changing ideas about gender?

- Make up some diminutive names for 1960s "guy" groups. How do the name changes affect our perception of their masculinity? "The Four [Small] Tops"? "The [Minor] Temptations"? "Temptation[ette]s"? "The Rolling Pebbles"? What about "Little Stevie Wonder"?

- How are gender issues expressed in popular music today? Do certain styles of music reflect general worldviews?

ACTIVITIES AND ASSIGNMENTS

- A fascinating song from the 1960s is Nancy Sinatra's "These Boots are Made for Walking." Search the internet for a video of a performance. Compare it with Jessica Simpson's video of the same song.

- Survey your class members to see what types of music they like. Are there gender-delineated trends?

- Watch *Dreamworlds 3: Desire, Sex and Power in Music Video* (2007 by Sut Jhally). Does Jhally's premise hold true today?

- Compare and contrast The Shirelles's version of "Will You Still Love Me Tomorrow?" with King's own as it appears on the album *Tapestry* (1971).

- Compare and contrast Mötley Crüe's "Girls, Girls, Girls" with Shakira's "Hips Don't Lie."

Gender in the World

Balinese Gamelan

Balinese Gamelan, 1910–1931.
Tropenmuseum, part of the National Museum of World Cultures/Wikimedia Commons/CC-BA-SA-3.0.

Girls dancing *Tari Kelinci* (rabbit dance) during a women's gamelan performance.
Photo by Mary Natvig.

Earlier in the chapter we noted that a person's sex can limit musical activities. Such is the case on the Indonesian island of Bali. There, playing in a gamelan orchestra has been traditionally considered men's work.

Although Indonesia as a whole has the largest Muslim population in the world, nearly all Balinese practice Hinduism, a religious philosophy that requires a delicate balance of male and female energies. Many aspects of Balinese culture reflect that belief. For example, men care for certain animals; women care for others. For meals, men cook the meat; women cook the rice and vegetables. Trades and crafts are generally the province of men, but making certain kinds of religious offerings is a task exclusively for women.

Gamelan instruments are arranged in complementary pairs of male and female. Female instruments are tuned slightly lower, male instruments higher. Some say this arrangement reflects women's closeness to the earth. Whatever the reason, both male and female instruments must sound together in order to attain the desired shimmering effect that is essential to the gamelan's sound.

Until the late 20th century, women were prohibited from playing the gamelan. One of the reasons for this was the Balinese essence known as *gaya* (style). Gaya is a projection of energy, showmanship, and vigor, which the Balinese consider to be masculine qualities. Furthermore, gamelan playing is essential in Hindu temple festivals. Because of their menses, women were often expected to remain outside.

Beginning in the early 1980s, women began forming their own gamelan orchestras. @ 6.4 Several factors contributed to this, most notably, a government-sponsored mandate for co-education. Suddenly, music students at both high school and university levels found themselves playing in mixed ensembles. Greater exposure to Western ideas of sexual equality probably also helped open doors. At first, women played for personal enjoyment or for tourists. Slowly emboldened, they began to set up gamelans around temple perimeters in order to participate in religious festivals. Yet even today, women's gamelans remain outside the temple.

An astute observer will find differences between women's and men's gamelan performances. Women generally play more slowly and their performances are less polished. There are reasons for this. First, boys are initiated into playing gamelan at a very young age, often while sitting on their father's laps. Girls start much later. In addition, gender norms dictate that women conduct themselves demurely and modestly. Flashy expressions of gaya are socially inappropriate for women. Faced with this dilemma, women may prefer to sacrifice flair for propriety.

Where female performance aesthetics do dominate, is in dance. Many dances are meant specifically for women, whose controlled and elegant motions are highly valued.

Mekar Sari, Women's gamelan

LISTENING
6.2
GUIDE

Texture: Polyphonic

This video was taken in the summer of 1997 on a research trip to the town of Peliatan, Bali. Featured is *Mekar Sari* (Essence of Flower), a women's gamelan that performs weekly for tourists in an outdoor pavilion. Notice that while there is a protective roof, there are no walls. Performances are informal by Western standards. The audience is free to come and go, wander around, and even talk. Sounds of traffic and gamelan intermingle.

Scene 1	Pre-concert preparations. Performers ready the stage by distributing offerings to the Hindu gods; water is sprinkled in order to purify the performing area. A boy (one of the performer's sons) sneaks on stage and plays the reyong. (*fade out*)
Scene 2	The warrior dance *Baris*. Usually the warrior is danced by a grown man. But since the women usually perform with children, a boy takes the role. His gestures and poses are typically male. The dancer's movements also control the orchestra, which follows danced cues. (*fade out*)
Scene 3	*Tari Kelinci* (rabbit dance). This is one of several dances that became popular in the 1990s. Movements portray a variety of animals, including: deer, birds, and in this case, rabbits. *Tari Kelinci* is danced by pre-pubescent girls, usually ages 6 to 9. Girls have always been essential to the dance tradition. (*fade out*)

ETHNOMUSICOLOGY AND FIELDWORK

Ethnomusicology, a scholarly discipline closely related to anthropology, seeks to understand music from a cultural perspective. Usually, but not always, the object of study is a living tradition outside of Western art music. In the early years, the focus was on collection. Ethnomusicologists—loaded down with bulky recording devices, pencils, and staff paper—journeyed to far-away places where they sought to document and catalog the world's music.

Our Bali video is a field recording. Although not exactly technologically "primitive," like the early wax cylinder audio recordings, picture quality is low in comparison to today's high-definition digital recordings. Fieldwork documentations also often suffer from bumps from bystanders, ambient noises, visual impediments, and the level of experience of the cinematographer, who is usually a scholar rather than a trained videographer.

QUESTIONS FOR THOUGHT

- In your culture are some types of music considered to be more "feminine" or more appropriate for women to perform/compose? Are any styles off limits for one sex or the other?
- Listen to a piece of music by a woman composer. Would you be able to tell the sex of the composer if you did not know?
- "History is written by the winners," wrote author Alex Haley (1921–1992). How might that idea be reflected in the historical discourse on women in music in both the 19th century and today?

ACTIVITIES AND ASSIGNMENTS

- Watch the film *Songcatcher* (2001), a fictional portrayal of a woman ethnomusicologist from the early 20th century who documents English ballads in Appalachia. Note the style of singing, the use of wax cylinders, and the moral conflict inherent in "taking" other people's traditions for one's own gain.
- Find a video of a men's Balinese gamelan on the internet. Compare the concept of gaya in the male ensemble to the women's group in Listening Guide 6.2.

Gender on Stage

In **opera**, gender issues are worked out on stage. Non-conformity often leads to mayhem, even death. Witness the case of poor Lucia Ashton from Italian composer Gaetano Donizetti's (1797–1848) opera *Lucia di Lammermoor* (1835). Lucia has secretly sworn herself to another, but is forced to marry her family's political ally. Shamed and overwhelmed by the guilt of her infidelity, in her bridal chamber she plunges a knife into her hapless husband. Moments later, crazed and bloodied, she appears center stage, sings a virtuosic **aria** (this is opera, after all), then drops dead, presumably another victim of vapors, hysteria, and other overwrought emotions supposedly common to 19th-century women. Lucia's demise is not an isolated case. She is just one of many female characters who attempt to stand against social imperatives but pay for it with their lives. @ 6.5

A Leading Lady: Carmen

Let's consider the case of the sultry gypsy Carmen, perhaps opera's most sensuous leading lady and the protagonist in the opera *Carmen* (1875), composed by Frenchman Georges Bizet (1838–1875). Viewed from one perspective, Carmen is the ultimate *femme fatale*, a seductress and a criminal. From another perspective, she is a free spirit unwilling to be bound by social convention.

These associations provide for colorful crowd scenes and lively choruses, but the real drama has to do with Carmen's tempestuous relationships with two lovers—the sturdy (though thick-skulled) soldier Don José and the passionate matador Escamillo. As one might expect, things go poorly for Don José after he falls for Carmen. He lands in jail, deserts his regiment, rejects the entreaties of his mother regarding his faithful girlfriend Micaela, and is finally humiliated and scorned by Carmen and her gypsy clan. In the opera's final scene, Don José takes revenge on the object of his desire, fatally stabbing Carmen as she attempts to enter the bullring where Escamillo is performing.

Listen to this **chromatically** inflected and rhythmically seductive habanera ("L'amour est un oiseau rebelle"), the music that first introduces us to Carmen and her cigarette girls.

Carmen's death, rehearsal at Chorégies d'Orange opera festival in southern France, 2015.
BORIS HORVAT/AFP/Getty Images.

"L'amour est un oiseau rebelle"
from the opera *Carmen*, by Georges Bizet

LISTENING
6.3
GUIDE

Texture: Homophonic
Meter: Duple
Form: Strophic

Carmen's aria begins with a brief introduction featuring the hypnotic rhythm of the Cuban habanera (Chapter 5: Music and Ethnicity). For French audiences of 1875, the opera's Seville setting was sure to convey a sense of mystery, perhaps social danger. More provocative still would have been the habanera, with its boundary-crossing Afro-Cuban genesis. Bizet's habanera is laden with sensuality.

As the scene unfolds, Carmen is flirting with the young men gathered in the town square. Soon, however, her attention focuses on Don José, who, once locked into Carmen's Siren-like sights, is destined to fall. Note the interjections of the cigarette girls. In warning bystanders to beware of Carmen's love, they function much like the all-knowing choruses of ancient Greek tragedy.

Carmen's character is mirrored in the music through a combination of elements rhythmic, melodic, and textual. Just as the habanera's sensual lilt invites physicality, the falling chromatic melody suggests seduction. Then there are the lyrics. Love, says Carmen, is untamable, flighty like a bird, and not subject to any law. Just like her.

0:00	*Carmen*	
	L'amour est un oiseau rebelle	Love is a rebellious bird
	Que nul ne peut apprivoiser,	That nobody can tame,
	Et c'est bien en vain qu'on l'appelle	And it's simply no good calling it
	S'il lui convient de refuser.	If it suits it to refuse;
	Rien n'y fait, menace ou prière,	Neither threat nor prayer will prevail.
	L'un parle bien, l'autre se tait;	One of them talks, the other holds his peace,
	Et c'est l'autre que je préfère;	And I prefer the other one!
	Il n'a rien dit, mais il me plaît.	He hasn't said a word, but I like him!
0:40	*Chorus*	
	L'amour est un oiseau . . .	Love is a rebellious bird . . .
0:43	*The chorus continues in the background with Carmen's melody while Carmen sings:*	
	L'amour! L'amour! L'amour!	Love! Love! Love!
0:56	*A reduced orchestra, with pizzicato strings centers the focus on Carmen:*	
	L'amour est enfant de Bohème,	Love is a Gypsy,
	Il n'a jamais connu de loi.	It has never been subject to any law.
	Si tu ne m'aimes pas, je t'aime;	If you do not love me, I love you
	Si je t'aime, prends garde à toi!	If I love you, take care!
1:13	*Chorus—a bold and cautionary interjection, with full orchestra!*	
	Prends garde à toi! . . .	Take care! . . .
1:16	*Listen to Carmen dwell on "pas"—"if you do NOT love me . . ."*	
	Si tu ne m'aimes pas, je t'aime;	If you do not love me, I love you
1:22	*Chorus*	
	Prends garde à toi! . . .	Take care! . . .
1:24	*Carmen*	
	Si je t'aime, prends garde à toi!	If I love you, take care!
1:37	*Chorus*	
	L'amour est enfant de Bohème . . .	Love is a Gypsy . . .

continued

1:52	Prends garde à toi! . . .	Take care! . . .
1:54	*Carmen*	
	Si tu ne m'aimes pas, je t'aime;	If you do not love me, I love you;
	Si je t'aime, prends garde à toi!	If I love you, take care!
2:00	*Chorus*	
	Prends garde à toi! . . .	Take care! . . .
2:01	*Carmen and chorus*	
	Si tu ne m'aimes pas, je t'aime;	If you do not love me, I love you;
	Si je t'aime, prends garde à toi!	If I love you, take care!
2:21	*Here the music from the beginning repeats.*	
	Carmen	
	L'oiseau que tu croyais surprendre	The bird you thought to surprise
	Battit de l'aile et s'envola;	has spread its wings and flown;
	L'amour est loin, tu peux l'attendre;	Love is far away, you may wait for it;
	Tu ne l'attends plus, il est là!	When you've given up waiting, it is there!
	Tout autour de toi vite, vite,	All around you, quickly, quickly,
	Il vient, s'en va, puis il revient;	It comes, goes, and comes again.
	Tu crois le tenir, il t'évite;	You think you've caught it, it escapes you;
	Tu crois l'éviter, il te tient!	You think to escape it, you are caught!
2:54	*Chorus*	
	Tout autour de toi . . .	All around you . . .
2:56	*Carmen*	
	L'amour! L'amour! . . .	Love! Love! . . .
3:14	L'amour est enfant de Bohème . . .	Love is a Gypsy . . .
3:28	*Chorus*	
	Prends garde à toi! . . .	Take care! . . .
3:30	*Carmen*	
	Si tu ne m'aimes pas, je t'aime;	If you do not love me, I love you;
3:36	*Chorus*	
	Prends garde à toi! . . .	Take care! . . .
3:38	*Carmen*	
	Si je t'aime, prends garde à toi!	If I love you, take care!
3:52	*Chorus of girls*	
	L'amour est enfant de Bohème . . .	Love is a Gypsy . . .
4:06	Prends garde à toi!	If I love you, take care!
4:08	*Carmen*	
	Si tu ne m'aimes pas, je t'aime;	If you do not love me, I love you;
4:16	Prends garde à toi!	If I love you, take care!
4:18	*Carmen and chorus*	
	Si je t'aime, prends garde à toi!	If I love you, take care!

A Leading Man: Siegfried

How might opera portray a heroic young man as he comes of age? For this, we look to German composer Richard Wagner's (1813–1883) epic four-opera cycle, *Der Ring des Nibelungen* (*The Ring of the Nibelungen*), first performed in its entirety in 1876, one year after *Carmen*'s premier. Thirty years in the making, the cycle represents the culmination of the composer's philosophy concerning drama. Wagner believed that opera was the greatest of the art forms and that it should strive not only to unify all of the arts (music, visual art, drama, and poetry), but also to portray the inner psychological workings of humankind. *The Ring Cycle* (as it is called, or sometimes just *The Ring*) is the realization of that ideal.

The cycle's complex story was drawn from Northern European epic poetry and mythology. Characters include gods and humans, and giants and dwarves, and even a dragon. The plot centers on the theft, and ultimate return, of a cache of magic gold that is taken from the depths of the Rhine River. Whoever controls the gold has power over the entire world. But there is a catch. One can only obtain the gold by renouncing love. This is the metal's corrupting curse.

The gold is stolen, then forged into a ring of power. Thereafter—and amidst murder and mayhem—the ring is vied for by every class of character. In the end, Brünnhilde (the famous opera character often depicted wearing a winged helmet) sacrifices her life in order to return the ring to the Rhine River. With that, the reign of the gods is ended and the era of man begins.

The Young Siegfried, Julius Hübner, 1839.
Courtesy of The Metropolitan Museum of Art, Purchase, Guy Wildenstein Gift, 2010.

In accordance with his desire to unify all of the arts, Wagner expanded the expressive range of the orchestra. He increased and diversified the instrumentation, and employed a bold, even revolutionary, musical language. Thus fortified, the orchestra gained a status almost equal to that of the voice. The orchestra itself became a storyteller, capable of foreshadowing and revealing ideas and happenings of which even the characters on stage were not always aware.

Wagner accomplished this in part through the use of **leitmotifs** (leading motives), short musical figures representing people and places, things and ideas. Because of their extreme brevity, leitmotifs are easily folded into the orchestral texture where they enhance the story being acted out on stage. Wagner manipulates and juxtaposes the motives so that they take on considerable dramatic significance.

The third of the four *Ring* operas is titled *Siegfried* (1871), after the protagonist, the half-human grandson of the god Wotan. Siegfried is naïve in the ways of mankind, but he is honest and fearless. As the opera opens, Mime (*Mee-muh*), Siegfried's surrogate father, is attempting to forge a sword powerful enough to slay Fafner the dragon, who currently possesses the ring. Mime hopes to coax Siegfried into killing the dragon, after which he plans to murder the lad. Mime will half succeed. Sword in hand, Siegfried heads off toward the dragon's lair. He blows his horn to awaken the beast and the battle begins.

Act II, Scene 2 from the opera *Siegfried*, by Richard Wagner

LISTENING
6.4))
GUIDE

Texture: Homophonic
Meter: Quadruple
Form: Open

Siegfried plays his famous horn tune. It is a call to battle, a leitmotif representing Siegfried's heroic nature and boundless energy. We hear the motive three times. Then Siegfried switches to a more personal tune, one that was first heard at the beginning of the opera. The melody differs from the initial horn call in that it is contemplative, dark, and less youthful. Perhaps this represents the tragic Siegfried who, despite all of his bravery and good intentions, is destined to succumb to deception and a murderous end.

0:00	We hear a series of horn calls meant to awaken the dragon.
1:37	Fafner awakens. The orchestra enters with Fafner's awakening. The music is thick, ominous, and tonally unstable. A chromatic melody creeps upward as Fafner drags himself out from the bowels of the earth. The music tells us that the creature is feral and brutal.

Contrast these sounds to the tonal clarity of Siegfried's horn call. The horn, an instrument of the hunt and the military, represents a socially acceptable show of masculine power. It soars above Fafner's mucky sludge.

1:52 *Siegfried*

Haha! Da hätte mein Lied	Just look, my tune has
Mir was Liebes erblasen!	Brought me something lovely.
Du wärst mir ein saubrer Gesell!	You would be a pleasant friend for me.

Tremolo in the strings and timpani alert the audience to trouble, though Siegfried is fearless.

2:04 *Fafner*

Was ist da?	What is that?

2:09 *Siegfried*

Bist du ein Tier,	Well, now, if you're an animal
Das zum Sprechen taugt,	That's learned talking,
Wohl ließ sich von dir was lernen?	Perhaps I can find out something from you.
Hier kennt einer	Someone here knows
Das Fürchten nicht:	Nothing about fear:
Kann er's von dir erfahren?	Can he learn it from you?

2:20 *Fafner*

Hast du Übermut?	Are you being arrogant?

2:29 *Siegfried*

Mut oder Übermut,	Brave or arrogant—
Was weiß ich!	How do I know?
Doch dir fahr' ich zu Liebe,	But I'll cut you to shreds,
Ehrst du das Fürchten mich nicht!	If you don't teach me fear.

2:40 *Fafner*

Trinken wol7lt' ich:	I wanted a drink:
Nun treff' ich auch Fraß!	Now I've found food, too.

2:59 *Seigfried*

Eine zierliche Fresse	That's a pretty maw
Zeigst du mir da,	You're showing off;
Lachende Zähne	Teeth laughing

Im Leckermaul!	In a dainty mouth!
Gut wär' es, den Schlund	It would be a good thing
Dir zu schliessßen,	To stop the gap for you.
Dein Rachen reckt sich zu weit!	Your jaws are gaping too wide.

3:14 *Fafner*

Zu tauben Reden	At empty chatter
Taugt er schlecht:	They're no good.
Dich zu vershlingen,	But for gobbling you up
frommt der Schlund.	My throat is just right.

3:34 *Siegfried*

Hoho! Du grausam	Ho ho! You gruesome
grimmiger Kerl!	Angry fellow!
Von dir verdaut sein,	Being digested by you
Dünkt mich übel:	Seems to me a bad idea.
Decisive, quick string chromatic scales.	
Rätlich und fromm doch scheint's	But it seems sensible and decent
Du verrecktest hier ohne Frist.	For you to drop dead without delay.

3:48 *Fafner*

Pruh! Komm,	Bah! Come on,
Prahlendes Kind!	Bragging child.

3:54 *Siegfried*

Hab acht, Brüller!	Watch out growler.
Der Prahler naht!	The braggart is coming.

Siegfried wields his sword and, with crash of cymbal, plunges it into Fafner's heart.

Da lieg, neidischer Kerl:	Lie there hateful fellow!
Notung trägst du im Herzen!	You've got Notung [the sword] in your heart.

QUESTIONS FOR THOUGHT

- Some opera scholars see Carmen's fate as a reflection of 19th-century European social mores. Women were to be submissive. If they were not, they were doomed. How do you see Carmen's life and death? Might Don José also be a victim of gendered stereotypes?

- How is Carmen's sexuality portrayed in the opera? How is sexuality portrayed in music today?

- Siegfried challenges a dragon to test himself. What are today's "dragons"? Is challenging them how we judge masculinity today? How does the composer's music suggest that, at least in this case, Siegfried's behavior was appropriate?

- *The Ring Cycle* continues to cast its powerful spell on Western culture. See how many references to Wagner's operas you can find in popular media (film, cartoons, computer games, comic books, etc.).

- How is masculinity portrayed in movie soundtracks? How do you know when a male character is strong and heroic as opposed to weak and timid?

Gender Confusion: Castrati and Pants Roles

What is the ideal masculine voice? A stentorian bass? A soaring tenor? How about a luminous soprano? Three hundred years ago, the male soprano was Europe's operatic hero of choice. But how does a man sing soprano? One way to preserve a boy's soprano voice is to deny puberty, which was once accomplished through castration. Such was the fate of more than a few 17th- and 18th-century boys who showed exceptional vocal promise. With their supposedly "unearthly" voices, the greatest castrati achieved fame and fortune singing both male and female operatic roles.

Although the practice of castration had generally ended by the early 19th century, there were a few castrati singing in the Catholic Church up into the early 20th century. Today, castrati roles are sung either by women or **countertenors** and **sopranists** (men who have developed their falsetto voice and can sing in the alto and soprano ranges).

Another common operatic practice was composing male roles designed to be sung by women. The classic "pants," or "breeches role" character is a handsome boy at the cusp of manhood, with hormones raging. Often he is a character of relatively low status, perhaps a servant or court page, and is hopelessly in love with a leading lady who treats him as the mere boy he is. Female characters adore him for his gentle beauty and naïve charm; adult male characters are less enthralled.

For the story's action, of course, the character's gender is not in question. Things are not so clear in the audience, however. Theater, after all, is artifice. While we may enter fully into the characters we watch, sophisticated viewers are simultaneously engaged with the actor/actress playing the role. This being the case, what to make of the allure of a lovely boy/man who is actually a woman? All of this provides tantalizing gender-bending ground for composers and audiences alike.

FARINELLI (1705–1782)

The castrato Carlo Broschi (Farinelli) attained superstar status singing on operatic stages in Italy, France, and England. In 1737, he gave up the stage to work for Philip V of Spain. The king, who was plagued by depression, required Farinelli to sing to him every evening. In addition, Farinelli directed the king's chapel music and staged Italian operas. Farinelli remained in Spain for over twenty years, then retired to a villa in Bologna, Italy.

A fictional account of Farinelli's life was presented in the French film *Farinelli* (1994) directed by Gérard Corbiau. The task of recreating the castrato sound was given to the Institute de Recherche et Coordination Acoustique/Musique (IRCAM), an organization otherwise known for its pioneering efforts in electronic music. After much experimentation, IRCAM digitally blended the voice of a male countertenor with a female **coloratura** soprano to replicate the now only-imagined castrato sound.

The Marriage of Figaro: Cerubino

One of the greatest pants role characters is Cherubino ("the little cherub") from Wolfgang Amadeus Mozart's (1756–1791) opera *Le Nozze di Figaro* (*The Marriage of Figaro*, 1786), libretto by Lorenzo da Ponte (1749–1838). Cherubino is a stock character: the hormonally driven adolescent. Time and again, the poor fellow, a page in Count Almaviva's court, is overwhelmed by his sexual desires and fantasies.

The Countessa, Cherubino, and Susanna, Salzburg Festival dress rehearsal, 2007.
STRINGER/AFP/Getty Images.

"Any woman makes me change color; any woman makes me quiver," he confesses in the aria "Non so piu cosa son." From the get-go, Cherubino's antics offer plenty of mayhem to all the characters on stage. The Countess and Susanna (Figaro's bride to be) treat him as little more than a doll, even dressing him up as a young lady.

WOLFGANG AMADEUS MOZART (1756–1791) AND *THE MARRIAGE OF FIGARO*

The Salzburg, Austria-born Mozart was a child prodigy—an accomplished harpsichordist and violinist at age 4, a composer at age 5, and a guest of both France's Louis XV and England's George III by age 8. As an adult, however, Mozart struggled. He pasted together a successful career by working as performer, teacher, and composer, but was often in debt. He wrote over 600 compositions, including symphonies, concertos, sacred works, string quartets, and other chamber pieces.

His twenty-some operas reveal a musical and dramatic imagination that is unsurpassed. *The Marriage of Figaro*—based on a 1784 play by Pierre Beaumarchais (1732–1799)—is the first of three operas on which Mozart collaborated with librettist Lorenzo da Ponte (1749–1838). Beaumarchais's play, which satirized the aristocracy during a time of political instability (the French Revolution was just a few years away), was initially banned in Vienna. Nearly 200 years later, the overture was used in another comedic satire about social class, the film *Trading Places* (1983), which starred Eddie Murphy and Dan Aykroyd.

Leopold Mozart and his children, Wolfgang and Maria Anna (1763–1764).

MEN WITH HIGH VOICES

The era of castrati is long over, but we still enjoy listening to men sing in falsetto. Some of these artists are simply goofy, such as scraggly haired, ukulele-strumming Tiny Tim (born Herbert Khaury, 1932–1996). Others mix falsetto with chest voice. Included in this list are Justin Bieber, Prince, Justin Timberlake, Frankie Valli, Brian Wilson of the Beach Boys, Curtis Mayfield, David Ruffin of The Temptations, and Bobby McFerrin.

"Non so piu cosa son" from Act I from the opera *The Marriage of Figaro*, by Wolfgang Amadeus Mozart

LISTENING
6.5
GUIDE

Texture: Homophonic
Meter: Duple
Form: ABAC

Listen to the orchestra's accompaniment and the syncopated rhythms of the violins, perhaps a mirror of Cherubino's racing heartbeat. His vocal line is quick with excitement, almost breathless, and in an upper range. It rises even higher with the line "any woman makes me quiver."

0:00	*Cherubino*	
	Non so piu cosa son, cosa faccio,	I don't know any more what I am, what I'm doing,
	Or di foco, ora sono di ghiaccio,	Now I'm fire, now I'm ice,
	Ogni donna cangiar di colore,	Any woman makes me change color,
	Ogni donna mi fa palpitar.	Any woman makes me quiver.
0:18	Solo ai nomi d'amor, di diletto,	At just the names of love, of pleasure,
	Mi si turba, mi s'altera il petto,	My breast is stirred up and changed,
	E a parlare mi sforza d'amore	And a desire I can't explain
	Un desio ch'io non posso spiegar.	Forces me to speak of love.
0:48	Non so piu . . .	

Here Cherubino pours out his heart. Notice the dramatic pauses, the melodic peaks, and the repeated phrases, all of which suggest adolescent exuberance and yearnings. In the last two lines, Cherubino echoes the near universal fate of love-struck adolescents, "And if there's nobody to hear me . . . I speak of love to myself."

1:08	Parlo d'amore vegliando,	I speak of love while awake,
	Parlo d'amor sognando,	I speak of love while dreaming,
	All'acqua, all'ombra, ai monti,	To the water, the shade, the hills,
	Ai fiori, all'erbe, ai fonti,	The flowers, the grass, the fountains,
	All'eco, all'aria, ai venti,	The echo, the air, and the winds
	Che il suon de'vani accenti	That carry away with them
	Portano via con se.	The vain words.
	Parlo d'amore vegliando . . .	I speak of love while awake . . .
	E se non ho chi m'oda,	And if there's nobody to hear me,
	Parlo d'amor con me!	I speak of love to myself!

ACTIVITIES AND ASSIGNMENTS

- Is there such a thing as non-gendered music? Find a piece or song that you consider to be non-gendered. Be sure to take its historical context into account.

- Are the gender concepts discussed in the operatic examples above found in contemporary music videos?

- Gender confusion reigns in the romantic comedy *Tootsie* (1982), which starred Dustin Hoffman as an actor pretending to be a woman in order to land a television role. Watch the movie and pay particular attention to the song "It Might Be You." Part of the song's considerable charm stems from the fact that the lyrics give no clue to the many romantic possibilities the movie presents.

LGBTQ Issues

In many parts of the world, gays and lesbians continue to endure cultural oppression that ranges from exclusion to outright violence. How does this affect their artistic voice? Are the pressures of Pyotr Ilyich Tchaikovsky's closeted sexual life audible in his music? Do we witness Elton John's (b. 1947) sexuality in his songs? American anti-homosexual sentiments in the 1950s and 1960s kept many gay composers close to the closet. Aaron Copland's (1900–1990) homosexuality was not widely

THE AIDS SYMPHONY

Inspired by seeing the AIDS Memorial Quilt, Pulitzer Prize-winning composer, John Corigliano (b. 1938) composed his Symphony No. 1 (The AIDS Symphony) as an elegy to friends who had died of the disease. The piece was commissioned by the Chicago Symphony Orchestra and received its first performance in 1990. Since then it has received nearly 1000 performances by orchestras around the world.

BILLY TIPTON (1914–1989): PERFORMING GENDER

Jazz pianist and saxophonist Billy (*nee* Dorothy) Tipton performed at a time when finding employment as a female jazz instrumentalist was extremely difficult. In order to live her dream, she decided to cross the line. At age 19, Dorothy became Billy.

At first, Tipton's male identity was more of a disguise than a lifestyle; her friends knew "he" was a she. But as Tipton moved from job to job and city to city, she gradually assumed a full-time male identity. She bound her breasts and claimed that a car accident had resulted in both sterility and permanently unhealed ribs. Throughout the 1930s and 1940s Tipton played with various West Coast dance bands. In 1954, he formed the Billy Tipton Trio and led the group for more than ten years. Eventually, Tipton moved to Spokane and worked as an entertainment agent. He and his fifth wife adopted three sons. The couple led a typical family life. Tipton even served as a scoutmaster.

In the end, however, Tipton's life was marked by poverty and isolation. The marriage broke up and Tipton's health declined. Having avoided any kind of paperwork that would reveal his sex, Tipton was unable to collect Social Security or Medicare benefits. He avoided physicians. At age 74, Tipton collapsed in his trailer. As his son looked on, paramedics undressed the musician to administer CPR. Tipton's longest and most remarkable performance was finally over.

1000 Panels of the AIDS Memorial Quilt on the Ellipse.
Photo by David/Flickr/CC-BY-SA-2.0.

known until after his death. Important gay or bisexual American composers of the succeeding generation included John Cage (1912–1992), Samuel Barber (1910–1981), and Leonard Bernstein (1918–1990).

In the pop music world, there are many more "out" lesbian and female bisexuals than openly gay males. Melissa Etheridge (b. 1961), k.d. lang (b. 1961), Indigo Girls, and Ani DiFranco (b. 1970) have provided lesbians and bisexuals with a level of visibility unknown in previous generations. (Leslie Gore came out in 2005. "You Don't Own Me" is a favorite at gay-pride celebrations.)

One of the ways that gay musicians, especially those in the popular realm, have expressed their sexual orientation is through a specific kind of humor known as "camp." Camp can be difficult to define, though it may include elements such as self-mockery, theatricality, exaggerated gendered mannerisms, absurdity, vulgarity, silliness, and banality. Camp has often served as a code, safely signaling homosexual themes for those in the know while leaving others oblivious to the subtext. Musical examples include female impersonator Jean Malin's (1908–1933) Columbia recording "I'd Rather

Be Spanish (Than Mannish)" (1933), Cole Porter's (1891–1964) "Anything Goes" (1934), and Little Richard's "Tutti Frutti" (1955, though Richard's lyrics were changed for the recording).

One of the most openly gay musical activities is the gay and lesbian chorus movement, which began during a vigil following the murder of San Francisco councilman Harvey Milk (1930–1978). Today there are over 200 gay and lesbian choruses, with over 10,000 singers involved internationally. The choruses are civic as well as musical organizations. Members work to promote tolerance and generate social awareness.

Preceding the gay choral movement by two years was the Michigan Womyn's Music Festival (MWMF). (Womyn, with a "y," implies there are no "men" in womyn.). For one week every August (1976–2015) the MWMF was home to over 4000 women who collectively organized and maintained the campgrounds, support systems, and entertainment. The festival had a controversial women-born-women policy, which ultimately contributed to its demise. Neither men, nor transgendered nor transsexual women were allowed on the grounds. The contention was that being born in a female body was essential to understanding patriarchal oppression.

Social norms regarding gender are rapidly changing. Dustin Hoffman's much-loved cross-dressing character in the 1983 film *Tootsie* earned him an Academy Award nomination, but the mainstream early 1980s American audience remained secure in knowing his character was a sham. In 2014, after an earlier two-year run off-Broadway, the once controversial rock musical *Hedwig and the Angry Inch*, the musical story of an East German transsexual who marries (and divorces) an American serviceman, opened on Broadway.

ACTIVITIES AND ASSIGNMENTS

- In the film *Arizona to Broadway* (1933), Jean Malin played the character of actor Ray Best, whose stage show was an obvious send-up of sexpot comedienne Mae West (1893–1980). Popular in 1960s was actor Flip Wilson's character Geraldine in the comedy television show *Laugh-In*. Search out other cross-gender impersonators.

- Compare the women-only ideology of the MWMF with Dar Williams's point of view in "When I Was a Boy." Williams opened the festival in 2007.

Conclusion

We opened the "Gender in Popular Music" section of this chapter with a discussion of Elvis Presley, "girl groups," and changing social norms from the 1950s into the 1970s. Perhaps as you read that section you were thinking of songs or musicians that broke with the general trends we outlined. Perhaps you thought of Roy Orbison's (1936–1988) plaintive ballad "Crying" (1961), which tells the story of a man who cannot stop loving the woman he has lost. The song broke with the time's mainstream attitudes. Girls cry, not men.

Audiences did not seem to mind. Orbison was an enigmatic figure. His voice ranged from deep baritone to falsetto, and was warmed with a rich vibrato. On stage, he presented the quiet, yet stalwart, and even tragic persona of someone who could cry without endangering his manhood.

There is not much of a story to glean from the lyrics to "Crying." Orbison has lost his lover, but we do not know why. He sings a soliloquy in which he describes a world imploding.

In 1987, Orbison re-recorded the song with feminist, activist, and out-lesbian k.d. lang. Watch a video of the collaboration between Orbison, the feminized male, and lang, the masculinized female. Are they simply two lonely voices in the night, bound by hurt but nothing else? Or might they be singing about the same woman? Or perhaps, could Orbison and lang themselves be the unhappy couple? The social ambiguities add to the performance's restless despair.

Throughout this chapter we have seen that music is rarely, if ever, gender neutral. Indeed, it is through subtle (and sometimes not so subtle) projections of gender that much of music's emotional power is cultivated. This should not be surprising. After all, gender is a cornerstone of personal and social identity. Composers and performers inevitably (though not always consciously) reflect that identity in their music. Sometimes they do so by reinforcing accepted social constructions. Often, however, their music challenges social norms. As sensitive listeners, conceptualizing these various representations gives us a wealth of opportunity through which to re-imagine the gendering of our own inner and social lives.

Key Terms

- aria
- chromatic
- countertenor
- didgeridoo
- gamelan
- gaya

- gender
- girl groups
- leitmotif
- librettist
- opera
- pants role

- reclamation history
- sopranist
- strophic song
- virtuoso
- vocable

Essay Questions

- How might one attach the concept of gender to the following music-related experiences? Composing. Performing. Listening. Researching. Dancing. Explain the criteria you used to form your answers.
- Do you have a preference for female or male musicians? Why or why not?

- To understand how humankind uses music to express spirituality.
- To investigate musical relationships between the sacred and the secular.
- To become familiar with select works that exemplify spiritual traditions in music.

CHAPTER SEVEN

Music and Spirituality

QUESTIONS FOR THOUGHT

- **What makes music sacred? Does music need to have religious text in order to be sacred?**
- **Are there particular types of music that you consider to be spiritual?**
- **Are there any styles of music you believe to be inappropriate for religious services?**
- **Is there a difference between spiritual music and religious music? How so?**

Kathmandu, Nepal

Buddhist monks chant ancient texts. The sound is strange to the Western ear—pulsing speech-like vowel tones over which swirling high-pitched harmonics can often be heard. The monks' goal is not to make music as such. Instead, they chant verses to memorize and meditate upon the Buddha's teachings, to center their minds, and to sublimate improper desire. The monks seek enlightenment, the awareness of the divinity of all things.

> "Music is the harmonious voice of creation; an echo of the invisible."
> —Giuseppe Mazzini (1805–1872)

The Buddhist religion reaches back to Siddhartha Gautama (ca. 563 to 483 BCE), who, after years of meditation and moderate living, attained spiritual enlightenment and became the Buddha. He spent the rest of his life teaching, particularly the Four Truths:

1. *Dukkha*: Material life is suffering.
2. *Samudaya*: Improper desire is the cause of suffering.
3. *Nirhodha*: Ending improper desire will bring an end to suffering.
4. *Magga*: Suffering's end can be achieved by following the Noble Eightfold Path, along which one works to develop correct: 1) understanding, 2) thought, 3) speech, 4) action, 5) livelihood, 6) effort, 7) mindfulness, and 8) concentration.

Buddhist musical practice has generally remained simple. The focus is on scriptural meaning rather than sonic beauty.

Various sects of Buddhism employ a type of **harmonic singing** in which a singer produces two tones simultaneously. The technique is not complicated, but is physically subtle. Success requires precise (and relaxed) positioning of jaw, tongue, and lips. @ 7.1 When the proper shape and resonance is achieved, some vocalists can even produce overtone melodies (Chapter 15, Music and Technology).

In our listening example, pay attention to the shifting overtones and how they are affected by changing vowels and consonants. This will require careful listening. To most Westerners, overtone effects are not immediately obvious.

The monks' vocal technique can be described in mechanical terms. But how might chanting be a gateway to spiritual experience? Here are some ideas to consider:

- Texts deal with sacred topics. Chanting, which brings the sacred to mind, is a type of meditation.

Temple altar in Kathmandu.
Photo by Howard Leventhal.

- Chanting requires focus, which disciplines the mind and removes it from the doings of everyday life.
- Chanting regulates breathing, which may have an ordering effect.

Can you think of additional ways in which chanting might enhance consciousness?

The monks' texts are subtle and capable of multiple interpretations. Consider the phrase "*Om mani padme hum.*" This text, universally known throughout the Buddhist world, is closely associated with Avalokitesvara, the much loved **bodhisattva** (one who dedicates one's life in service to others) of compassion and mercy. The text is both enigmatic and recursive. According to Tenzin Gyatso (the 14th Dalai Lama and current leader of the Gelug Buddhist order), the syllable "om" represents the body, speech, and mind of both the devotee and the enlightened Buddha. "Mani" embodies the "jewel" of altruism; "padme" embodies the "lotus-flower" perfection of wisdom. "Hum" represents the idea of unity or indivisibility. Taken as a whole, the phrase presents the idea that impurities of existence can be overcome through the unifying power of compassion and wisdom.

In the remaining sections of this chapter we investigate the many ways in which music is used to enhance spiritual experience. Some spiritual practices use music to quiet mind and body; others use it to excite. Some focus on words, others on melody, and still others on rhythm and dance. In each case, music is used as a lens to focus experience.

BOUDHANATH STUPA

Bhudda's eyes oversee a pilgrim circumambulate the stupa and spin its prayer wheels—Boudhanath.
Photo by Jorge Láscar/Flickr/CC-BY-SA-2.0.

Rebuilt in the 14th century after its destruction by Mughal invaders, Boudhanath is Nepal's largest and most important Tibetan stupa (a site containing holy relics). Many Tibetan refugees have settled in the immediate area.

The stupa's construction is highly symbolic. Different aspects of the building (ascending from bottom to top) represent the elements: earth (base), water (dome), fire (pyramid), air (parasol), and ether (upper-most spire). Between the dome and the pyramid one sees Buddha's all-seeing eyes gazing in each direction.

When looking down on the stupa from above, one sees a **mandala**, a geometrically shaped image representing the cosmos. After Boudhanath was severely damaged in Nepal's 2015 earthquake, repairs began almost immediately.

"Song Boo Cherpa," recorded at the Boudhanath Temple in Kathmandu, Nepal

LISTENING
7.1
GUIDE

Texture: Heterophonic
Meter: Unmetered
Form: Open

0:00	Sounds of the *Rgya gling* (Tibetan oboe), *dung-dkar* (a conch shell), and a drum precede the chanting. This fanfare serves as announcement to the gods that the chanting is about to begin. It is hoped that the gods, now aware of the ensuing event, will grace the ceremony with their presence.
0:23	The chant asks God for blessings. Notice (by Western standards) the initially disorganized character of the chanting. Throats are cleared; individuals occasionally speak in the background. At first, voices overlap with little sense of order. The pace of the chant is generally steady. Listen for the overtones the monks produce with just their voices.
1:05	A bell sounds. Its resonant tone warns evil spirits to stay clear of the sacred space. (Bells are also said to represent *Dharma*—the Buddha's teachings, a blueprint for cosmic law and truth.) The chant continues.

Temple bells outside Boudhanath.
Photo by Howard Leventhal.

SAND PAINTING

Chanting is just one of numerous meditative endeavors undertaken by Buddhist monks. Another is the construction of mandalas made of colored sand. Although a sand mandala can take many days to create, it is destroyed shortly after completion. For the monks, the process of creation and destruction is a meditation in itself, a days-long rumination on life's complexity and impermanence.

Masters of ceremony assist His Holiness Dagchen Rinpoche holding a vajra and bell while praying, closing the colorful Hevajra sand mandala, after the empowerment, Tharlam Monastery of Tibetan Buddhism, Boudha, Kathmandu, Nepal.
Photo by Wonderlane/Flickr/CC-BY-SA-2.0.

QUESTIONS FOR THOUGHT

- Do you think Buddhist chant is sacred when performed as part of a ritual ceremony? What if the same chant were performed in New York City's Carnegie Hall as part of a fund-raising concert?
- There are dozens of versions of "Om mani padme hum" available on the internet. Compare and contrast some of them. How are they the same? Different?
- Adam Yauch of the Beastie Boys practices Buddhism. In 1995, the group released "Bodhisattva Vow." Might this be characterized as spiritual music?

ACTIVITIES AND ASSIGNMENTS

- Investigate overtone singing (often referred to as "harmonic" or "throat" singing) on the internet. You will find numerous sites offering instruction on how to learn the technique as well as examples from cultures around the world.
- David Hykes helped popularize overtone singing in the West. Visit his website or search for recordings.
- Many overtone singing styles are heard in Tuva, a Russian republic along the border with Mongolia. Many video clips are available online. Also of interest is the documentary film *Genghis Blues*, the story of American bluesman Paul Pena's 1995 trip to Tuva where he participated in a singing competition.

Music and Spirituality in Christian Traditions

In the remaining sections of this chapter we investigate the ways in which music is used to enhance spiritual experience in a variety of traditions. We will encounter a number of different strategies. Some religions use music to quiet mind and body; others use it to excite. Some traditions focus on words, others on melody, and still others on rhythm and dance. In each case, music is used as a lens to focus experience.

First we study the Christian **hymn** (song of praise) "Amazing Grace." We examine three different musical performances, each of which reflects distinct social values. From "Amazing Grace" we travel back in time to Europe's Middle Ages where we begin our study of the development of Christian church music and, by extension, the roots of Western art music. Then we explore selections from Yoruba, Sufi, and Jewish religious traditions.

"Amazing Grace"

Many consider "Amazing Grace," with its sturdy **diatonic** melody and message of personal transformation, to be the ultimate musical testament to the Christian doctrine of salvation.

Though commonly sung in church services, the hymn is also performed at commemoratory events, particularly funerals. In 1838, for example, it was sung on a near daily basis during the notorious "Trail of Tears" march, when thousands of Cherokee Indians died during forced relocation from the Carolinas and Georgia to Indian Territory west of the Mississippi River. Today in San Francisco's Chinatown, traditional funeral processions open with the hymn performed by the Green Street Mortuary Band. Following the deadly New York City terrorist attacks of September 11, 2001, the city's police and fire department bagpipe ensembles repeatedly played the hymn during ceremonies honoring their fallen comrades.

Amazing grace, how sweet the sound
That sav'd a wretch like me!
I once was lost, but now am found,
Was blind, but now I see.

The hymn's text was written by Englishman John Newton (1725–1807), a slave trader who at age 23, and after surviving a violent storm at sea, converted to evangelical Christianity. It is often told that Newton's near-death experience immediately convinced him of the sins of slavery and he wrote "Amazing Grace" in response to that conversion. The story is not accurate. In fact, Newton continued in the slave trade for some years and only became an abolitionist late in life. "Amazing Grace" was written in 1772 for his own use in a sermon, and possibly also for a hymn-text writing competition. Newton did not compose the melody. He would have expected a congregation either to speak the words or to sing them to any commonly known melody that might have fit his text. It was not until around 1835 that text and melody, a tune then known as "New Britain," became inextricably bound.

The Freedom Singers, 1963, Bernice Reagon, second from the left. The Estate of David Gahr/Premium Archive/Getty Images.

We examine three very different recordings of the hymn. The first is led by Bernice Johnson Reagon (b. 1942). The second is a concert arrangement performed by the Robert Shaw Festival Singers. The third is by a group of Tennessee **shape-note** singers. Each performance promotes the same message of redemption, but the styles are vastly different.

"Amazing Grace," performed by Bernice Johnson Reagon

LISTENING **7.2** GUIDE

Texture: Heterophonic/polyphonic/homophonic. The performance is a cappella (voices only).
Meter: Undefined
Form: Strophic

The daughter of a Baptist minister, Bernice Reagon was born and raised just outside of Albany, Georgia. Through her involvement in the Civil Rights Movement, she became at age 20 a founding member of the SNCC (Student Non-violent Coordinating Committee) Freedom Singers. In 1973 she founded the singing group Sweet Honey in the Rock. @ 7.2

For Reagon, music is a link to heritage. In this recording she demonstrates a technique called **lining out** in which the song leader introduces the words the choir will then sing. Lining out was once an essential choral technique in non-literate America. It is used in many churches today.

Reagon performs the song's first verse only, which she divides into parts. She sings the first two lines of the stanza which are repeated by the choir. Notice that when lining out, Reagon offers only hints of the song's melody; the words are presented in a simple syllabic style with a narrow melodic range. The choral repetitions are elaborately melismatic. Reagon follows the same process with the next two lines. Notice that the text is slightly changed; "sound" has become "Son."

0:00	Reagon lines out the lyrics:
	Amazin' grace, how sweet the Son
	That save[d] a wretch like me.
0:09	Lines repeated chorally in expanded form.
0:59	Reagon lines out the next lines:
	I once was lost, but now I'm found.
	Blind, but now I see.

continued

1:07	Lines repeated chorally.
1:56	Reagon continues: *'Twas grace that taught my heart to feel.* *And grace my relief.*
2:08	Lines repeated chorally.

Now we compare Reagon's performance with a choral performance led by conductor Robert Shaw (1916–1999). Under Shaw's direction, improvisation is replaced by order, individuality by unified forces. Shaw served as music director of the Atlanta Symphony from 1967 to 1988, but his greatest impact was as a choral music conductor, for which he earned fourteen Grammys and the National Medal of Arts (1992).

Vocalists on this recording are music professionals who were in residence at the Robert Shaw Institute. Though in session for only a few weeks in the summer, the Institute drew from across the nation choral music conductors seeking advanced training under Shaw's guidance. Each residency culminated in the recording and release of an album under the name of the Robert Shaw Festival Singers.

THOMAS DORSEY (1899–1993)

Paving the way for the gospel sound was Thomas Dorsey, considered by many to be the "father" of gospel music. Dorsey grew up in his father's Baptist ministry before going on to a successful career in jazz. When a nervous disorder interrupted his career, however, Dorsey returned to sacred music. In 1931 he founded the Thomas A. Dorsey Gospel Songs Music Publishing Company, the first African-American gospel music publishing house. At the time, African-American church music was marked by an increasingly restrained vocal style. Dorsey interrupted that trend by infusing his music with a rhythmic aesthetic built on improvisation, spontaneity, and heartfelt emotion.

Dorsey's gospel masterpiece is "Take My Hand, Precious Lord," which he wrote in a hotel room in 1932 after receiving a telegram stating that his wife had died during childbirth. The song's words came "like drops of water from a crevice of a rock above," said Dorsey. Over time,

Dorsey (third from left) with Ma Rainey, Chicago 1923.
Michael Ochs Archives/Getty Images.

"Precious Lord" not only attained a central place in the African-American church, but became an anthem for the 1960s Civil Rights movement. Mahalia Jackson (1911–1972) sang the song at the funeral of her friend Dr. Martin Luther King Jr. (1929–1968). Aretha Franklin sang it at Jackson's funeral.

"Amazing Grace," performed by the Robert Shaw Festival Singers

LISTENING 7.3 GUIDE

Texture: Homophonic
Meter: Triple
Form: Strophic

Notice the characteristics of the professionally trained voices: vibrato and careful text articulation.

0:00	Verse 1	A tenor soloist sings the melody with chordal accompaniment provided by the chorus's tenors and basses.
0:43	Verse 2	The full chorus enters.
1:25	Verse 3	The tenor soloist returns.
2:07	Verse 4	The full chorus sings again.
2:48	Verse 1	The tenor soloist sings the words to verse 1 again, slightly embellishing the melodic line.
3:36	Coda	The chorus's male voices conclude the hymn by repeating the last two lines of the verse.

Sacred Harp

Finally, we listen to an arrangement of "Amazing Grace" as performed by sacred harp singers. @ 7.3 Sacred harp, also called "shape-note," singing is an American folk tradition dating back to the late 18th century, when friends would gather at the local church or meeting hall to socialize and sing hymns. They used song books that facilitated music reading by having different-shaped notes represent different pitches (e.g. mi = ◆, fa = ◢, sol = ●, la = ■), hence the term "shape-note" singing. The earliest of these books were used as teaching tools in New England singing schools, America's first musical training institutions.

New Britain: shape notes. Photo by Mary Natvig.

Sacred harp singing emphasizes the natural voice (the "sacred harp"). The vocal timbre is untutored, often strident. No instruments are used and the melody line is often sung by tenors, or sopranos and tenors an octave apart. Singing focuses on face-to-face interaction with vocalists sitting along the perimeter of an open square and facing the middle. Participants take turns leading from the center. Community spirit and honest expression are valued above individual vocal skill.

Historically, sacred harp flourished primarily in the South, where in rural areas the tradition survives relatively unchanged. It is currently enjoying a revival in urban centers across the country, however. Those who participate do so for the love of singing. They remark upon the physicality of facing one another, singing in a full voice, and feeling the great waves of sound reverberate throughout the room. With most of today's shape-note singing there is no denominational association. Even so, participants often remark on the deeply spiritual emotions engendered by the experience.

Take some time to compare and contrast our three performances. Some listeners will find that Reagon's improvisatory style speaks directly to the heart, to the needs of the individual in the here and now. Others, however, will find the Festival Singers' controlled aesthetic to be quintessentially worshipful. Still others might label the sound too polished, and prefer the shape-note singers. Can any of them be considered "better" or "more sacred" than the other?

It is remarkable that all three of these examples, different as they are, come from contemporary American traditions. Imagine how differences will magnify as we travel back in time or to different cultures and religious practices. This is the journey we now undertake.

LISTENING 7.4 GUIDE — "Amazing Grace," performed by the Old Harp Singers of Eastern Tennessee

Texture: Homophonic
Meter: Triple
Form: Strophic

In a fashion reminiscent of Reagon's lining out, the leader begins each verse slightly before the rest of the singers. The choir quickly joins in and all sing together. Voices are untrained and uninhibited; some stand out as shrill and nasal. Enthusiasm is valued over blend. Singers tend to slide from one note to the next.

The hymn is sung in four-part harmony, but the texture sounds even thicker. This is because the various lines are being sung by men and women alike. Thus, the bass part is doubled up an octave by the women and the soprano is doubled down an octave by the men. The triple meter pushes forward with soldier-like regularity (ONE two *three*; ONE two *three*, etc.).

0:00	Verse 1.
0:38	Verse 2.
1:15	Verse 3.
1:53	Added verse

(Not original to John Newton. These words were first connected to "Amazing Grace" by Harriet Beecher Stowe in her 1852 anti-slavery novel *Uncle Tom's Cabin*.)

When we've been there ten thousand years,
Bright shining like the sun,
We've no less days to sing God's praise
Than when we first begun.

QUESTIONS FOR THOUGHT

- Is there such a thing as a "definitive" recording of "Amazing Grace"? Can one performance be more "correct" than another? If so, what might be the criteria?

- How many different performances (recordings, movies, TV shows, internet videos) can you find of "Amazing Grace"? How do these different performances reflect the values of their audiences?

- Think to a time in a religious service (or perhaps during the singing of "The Star-Spangled Banner" at a sporting event) when the person next to you sang horribly out of tune. (Perhaps you were that person.) What did you think of the performance? Would you have rather s/he did not sing at all? Should "bad" singers be barred from participation? What is most important, sound or intention?

As we move through the rest of this chapter, keep in mind the people for whom the musical examples are meant. What is their worldview? What is their spiritual view? What are their particular needs and desires? And especially, how does music represent and fortify their spiritual understandings?

Music in the Early Christian Church

From the early Middle Ages, up until the early 1960s, most of the individual elements (collectively called the **liturgy**) in the Catholic **Mass** were chanted. Chant (or plainchant) ranged in style from simple text recitation on just one or two notes to long, soaring, and undulating melodies. Most chant was sung by clerics: monks and nuns in churches, monasteries, and convents. As with the chanting of the Gyuto monks, plainchant was a tool for connecting with the sacred.

Chant was originally performed for voice alone, which was thought to be God's "perfect instrument." The language was Latin, the melodies were monophonic and rhythmically free. Chants usually had smooth melodic contours and sounded in one of the eight church melodic **modes** (rather than in the major and minor scales we use today). 🌀 7.4 Plainchants were composed anonymously and passed on by oral tradition. This started to change in the 9th century when Western musical notation began to develop in European monasteries. From then on, the music would be written down.

Listen to a plainchant of Kyrie eleison. The text is Greek, a vestige from the early Byzantine church, and the only part of the Mass that was not in Latin.

Kyrie eleison

LISTENING 7.5 GUIDE

Texture: Monophonic
Meter: Unmetered
Form: ABA CDC EDE[1] (E is extended)

0:00	*Kyrie eleison* (3 times)	Lord have mercy
0:36	*Christe eleison* (3 times)	Christ have mercy
1:03	*Kyrie eleison* (3 times)	Lord have mercy.

Notice that the words are set melismatically. The "e" of the final "eleison" spans nearly forty pitches. This technique of stretching the words allows the listener time to assimilate the spiritual message. The rhythm is without meter, free and flowing. The melodic contour is conjunct and forms gentle arches. Each line of text is repeated three times, a symbolic representation of the Trinity.

GREGORIAN CHANT

There are many plainchant traditions. Gregorian Chant, the most recognized type today, developed in Western Europe in the 8th century. It is likely that the repertory developed because Charlemagne (747–814), the first Holy Roman Emperor, wanted to unify his territory and strengthen ties with Rome. The chant is named for Pope Gregory I (ca. 540–604), who supposedly received the chants from the Holy Spirit (symbolized in literature and painting with a dove). Thus, one of Catholicism's most sacred musical genres likely developed from political aspirations rather than purely religious intentions.

Gregorian Chant was used in the Catholic Church until the Second Ecumenical Council of the Vatican (known as Vatican II), held from 1962 to 1965. In many Catholic churches, especially in North America, folk-style music replaced the Latin chants. In 2007, however, Pope Benedict XVI suggested reviving the pre-Vatican II plainchant Mass.

The Birth of Polyphony

The idea of adding new vocal lines above or below a chant was likely a technique first improvised by creative Medieval clerics to enhance the liturgy of important religious ceremonies. The first written evidence is from a 9th-century treatise in which the new genre was called **organum (pl. organa)**. Eventually, the genre developed into two basic varieties: **discant organum**—where the added voice(s) moves at the same pace as the original chant; and **florid organum**—when each chant tone is drawn out (i.e. held for a long time) while the other voice(s) sings many tones against it. By the mid-12th century, organum was a highly cultivated art form, particularly in and around Paris's Notre Dame Cathedral. Here they also developed the first rhythmic notation since the Ancient Greeks. The writing of an anonymous student cleric (known as Anon. IV) tells of a great book (the **Magnus Liber**) in which organa and other new polyphonic genres of Parisian composer-clerics were first written down. He names only two composers: Leonin (1150s–ca. 1201) and Perotin (fl. 1200), whom he considered the genre's greatest masters, but other clerics were surely involved.

Listen to the opening section of *Sederunt principes* an **organum quadruplum** (four-part organum) probably composed by Perotin. The voice on the bottom staff sings a fragment of the original chant with the text: "Se . . . de . . . runt," though each tone is held so long that the word and original melody are virtually unrecognizable. In an actual church service, the rest of the chant would have been sung monophonically, with the inserted organum section functioning as a sonic embellishment to the liturgy.

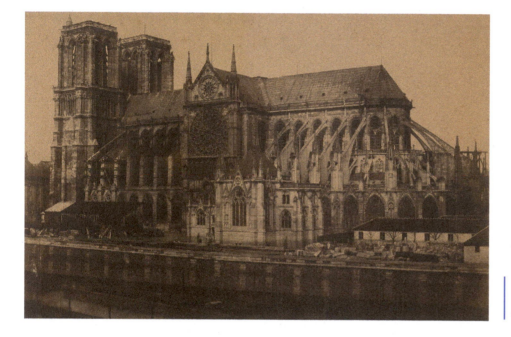

Notre Dame Cathedral, Paris; photo by Edouard Baldus, 1850–1960.
Courtesy of the J. Paul Getty Museum.

LISTENING 7.6 GUIDE

Sederunt principes (excerpt), by Perotin

Genre: Organum quadruplum
Texture: Polyphonic
Meter: Quadruple (with triple subdivisions)
Form: Alternating sections of organum and chant

0:00	All four voice parts begin on an open sounding consonance (do and sol), almost as if they are "tuning up" or organizing themselves for the work ahead.
0:06	The upper three voices begin a rhythmic pattern of "long–short–long; long–short–long" with rests in between each phrase. The bottom voice, on the syllable "Se-" sings the original chant on a long tone. The upper voices sing a neutral "eh" sound.
0:20	The upper voices change the rhythmic patterns with each voice taking a unique rhythm. At each subsequent phrase, the voices switch patterns with each other—a compositional technique called "voice exchange."
1:11	The bottom voice moves to the second note of the original chant, on the syllable "de-." Listen for the last syllable of "Sederunt."
2:50	The organum section ends and the voices continue to sing the plainchant monophonically.

The excerpt ends here, but the piece continues with alternating sections of organum and monophonic plainchant.

The Renaissance Mass

By the **Renaissance**, composers were writing elaborate polyphonic settings for the **Ordinary** of the Mass—the parts of the liturgy in which the texts never changed: Kyrie, Gloria, Credo, Sanctus, and Agnus Dei. The rest of the Mass, the **Proper** (with texts that changed from day to day), continued to be chanted. Polyphonic Mass settings peaked during the Renaissance, but even today some composers set these traditional texts. @ 7.5

Kyrie from the *Pope Marcellus Mass*, by Giovanni Pierluigi da Palestrina

LISTENING
7.7
GUIDE

Texture: Polyphonic
Meter: Quadruple
Form: text: ABA; music: through-composed

Palestrina (1525/26–1594) lived during the Counter Reformation, a time of renewal in the Catholic Church which was in response to the Protestant Reformation. Leaders of the Counter Reformation sought a return to religious basics. For music, that meant purging the Mass from secular tunes that had infiltrated polyphonic settings and making sure the sacred text could be understood. Palestrina's music was held up as a good example of reform aesthetics.

This excerpt is the first part of Palestrina's *Missa Papae Marcelli* (Mass of Pope Marcellus), named for the Pope who died in 1555, after just three weeks in office. The Mass is written for six independent voice parts and is performed a cappella. The six voice lines include soprano, alto, two tenors, and two basses; the upper lines would have been sung by boys or male sopranos since women, generally, did not sing publicly in churches at this time. Palestrina's Kyrie divides into three sections dictated by the text. Each section begins with a thin contrapuntal texture that thickens as new voices enter. The text is repeated as melodic lines are echoed and reshaped throughout the music. The feeling is calm but metered, and forward in its rhythmic direction.

0:00	*Kyrie eleison* Lord, have mercy upon us
	The voices enter in the following order: tenor 1, soprano, bass 1, alto, tenor 2, and bass 2. Listen for the distinctive upward leap in each voice. It is easiest to hear in the soprano, but all of the voices are singing it.
1:10	All of the voices gradually converge on a sustained chord that signals the end of the section.
1:18	*Christe eleison* Christ, have mercy upon us
	This section begins with three of the voices singing homophonically (all together, not imitatively).

First page of Palestrina's *Pope Marcellus Mass*, Kyrie, from Missarum, Liber 2, 1567 Roman print.

continued

	Soon, however, more voices enter and the texture once again becomes polyphonic with independently moving lines intertwining one with another.	
2:37	Once again, the voices converge on a long note to signal the end of the section. This chord does not sound resolved, however, so we know the piece is not over.	
2:44	*Kyrie eleison*	Lord, have mercy upon us
	As with the opening Kyrie, all of the voices enter by imitating one another.	

Music of the Protestant Reformation: From Luther to Bach

In 1517, the Catholic monk Martin Luther (1483–1546) nailed his "Ninety-Five Theses" to the door of the Wittenberg Castle Church in Saxony (now Germany). The document, which began the Protestant Reformation, emphasized (among other things) salvation by faith and criticized the Catholic policy of selling indulgences (monetary payments to the church so sins might be forgiven).

Some reformers thought that music represented luxurious excess and limited its use. Not Luther, who used music to instruct and to worship, and who wrote that "next to the Word of God, the noble art of music is the greatest treasure in the world." The Lutheran Church introduced a new genre, the German chorale, which was a strophic congregational song with a singable melody. Luther himself wrote many chorale texts and a few melodies. Some chorales had their roots in the Catholic Church and even in secular works. Both were the case with the chorale "O Sacred Head, Now Wounded," which we now study.

This chorale's text dates back to the 12th century. Originally in Latin, the text is attributed to Bernard of Clairvaux (1091–1153), an influential monk remembered for his elegant sermons, theological treatises, and hymn texts. The music, if there was any, no longer exists.

The Latin text was translated into German (*O Haupt voll Blut und Wunden*) for use in the early Lutheran Church. Words were then paired with the melody of a secular love song. "O Sacred Head, Now Wounded" is now a standard hymn in many Christian denominations.

St. Matthew Passion (1739)

Two hundred years after Martin Luther, Johann Sebastian Bach would spend most of his career working within the Lutheran Church. Many of his works make use of traditional chorale tunes. The melody of "O Sacred Head, Now Wounded," for example, appears in at least seven of his works, most notably in the *St. Matthew Passion* (1739).

The *St. Matthew Passion* is an **oratorio**, an unstaged and uncostumed musical play. Specifically, it is a passion oratorio, which tells the biblical account of Jesus' last days. The narrative is told through the evangelist—additional soloists sing the parts of Jesus, Pilate, Judas, and other characters; two choruses take the parts of the soldiers, the disciples, and the crowd. The composition takes almost three hours to perform.

For Bach, the *St. Matthew Passion* functioned both as a way to tell the historical narrative of Jesus' suffering and as a vehicle for spiritual reflection. The insertion of chorale tunes signified the music's specifically Lutheran origins.

Today, this work is performed in the concert hall, though in keeping with its original purpose, it is often programmed just before Easter. Thus, the *St. Matthew Passion* now functions on even more levels than it did in Bach's time. One may simultaneously see the work as:

- Bach's individual testament of religious faith
- an example of 18th-century Lutheran spirituality
- a vehicle for personal religious reflection
- one of the greatest examples of late-Baroque artistic achievement.

St. Matthew Passion (excerpts), by J.S. Bach

LISTENING
7.8
GUIDE

Texture: Homophonic
Meter: Quadruple
Form: AABC

Listen first to the chorale "O Sacred Head, Now Wounded." The first two musical phrases are the same (AA), ending without resolution on non-tonic chords. The melodic leap at the beginning of each phrase (perhaps a metaphor for the desire for heavenly ascent) gives the melody a yearning quality, as does the even larger leap in the middle of the phrase. To add contrast, as well as increase dramatic motion, the last two phrases are different (BC). While both begin in a high melodic range and descend to the same ending pitch, their respective harmonizations present different emotional feelings. The B phrase sounds bright, but incomplete. The C phrase offers conclusion.

		(familiar English version)
	Phrase 1 (A)	
0:00	O Haupt voll Blut und Wunden,	O sacred Head, now wounded,
	Voll Schmerz und voller Hohn	With grief and shame weighed down,
	Phrase 2 (A)	
0:11	O Haupt, zum Spott gebunden	Now scornfully surrounded
	Mit einer Dornenkron',	With thorns, thine only crown:
	Phrase 3 (B)	
0:23	O Haupt, sonst schön gezieret	How pale thou art with anguish,
	Mit höchster Ehr' und Zier,	With sore abuse and scorn!
	Phrase 4 (C)	
0:36	Jetzt aber höchst schimpfieret;	How does that visage languish
	Gegrüßet sei'st du mir!	Which once was bright as morn!

The chorale melody appears five times in Bach's *Passion*, all in the second half, where the focus is on Christ's trial and crucifixion.

Texture: Homophonic
Meter: Free (follows the pace of the text)
Form: Free

The next excerpt begins with the Evangelist describing the last minutes of Christ's life. As darkness settles over the land, Jesus cries his famous words, "*Eli, Eli, lama sabachthani?*" ("My God, my God, why have you forsaken me?").

As the narrator, the Evangelist sings in **recitative** style. The organ accompanies him, beginning with a chord that gives the singer his first pitch. Then he sings alone in a speech-like manner, with organ interjections. The organist sounds a clear cadence at the end of the sentence.

0:00	*Evangelist*	
	Und von der sechsten Stunde an	Now from the sixth hour there was
	war eine Finsternis über das ganze Land,	darkness all over the land until the
	bis zu der neunten Stunde.	ninth hour.

Next the narrator becomes more animated, his voice gets higher and louder.

0:30	Und um die neunte Stunde schrie	And about the ninth hour,
	Jesus laut und sprach:	Jesus cried in a loud voice, saying:
	Eli, Eli, lama asabthani?	"My God, my God, why have
		you forsaken me?

This phrase ends on an unresolved chord and there is a pause, letting the question sink in. Notice how the narrator sings at a higher pitch the second time he says, "my God."

continued

0:55	*Evangelist* Das ist, "Mein Gott, mein Gott, warum hast du mich verlassen?"	That is to say, "My God, my God, why have you forsaken me?"

Now the narrator describes the crowd:

1:13	Etliche aber, die da stunden, da sie das höreten, sprachen sie:	Some of them that stood there, when they heard that, said:

The chorus, accompanied by orchestra, comments on the action. The fast tempo, melodic leaps, and short interjections reveal the crowd's agitation. See if you can determine the texture, meter, and form of the following section.

0:00	*Chorus* Der rufet dem Elias!	He calls for Elias!

Back to recitative while the narrator tells the story.

0:00	*Evangelist* Und bald lief einer unter ihnen nahm einen Schwamm und füllete ihn mit Essig und steckete ihn auf ein Rohr und tränkete ihn. Die andern aber sprachen:	And immediately one of them ran, and took a sponge, and filled it with vinegar, and put it on a reed, and gave it to him to drink. The rest said:
0:00	*Chorus* Halt! Laß sehen, ob Elias komme und ihm helfe?	Stop, let us see whether Elias will come to save him.
0:00	*Evangelist* Aber Jesus schriee abermal laut und verschied.	Jesus, when he had cried again with a loud voice, yielded up the ghost.

The singer ends this phrase inconclusively . . . in a ghostlike way. The organ provides the final resolution.

Finally, we hear the last appearance in the *Passion* of the famous chorale tune. The words have been changed to suit Jesus' thoughts in the last moments of his life. Notice how Bach changes his harmonization in the second verse to fit the sentiments of the text. This is especially noticeable on the words, *allerbangsten* (languish), *Angsten* (anguish) and *Pien* (woe).

0:00	*Chorus* Wenn ich einmal soll scheiden, So scheide nicht von mir Wenn ich den Tod soll leiden, So tritt du denn herfür!	Be near me, Lord when dying. O part not Thou from me! And to my succor flying, Come, Lord, and set me free!
0:26	Wenn mir am allerbängsten Wird um das Herze sein, So reiß mich aus den Angsten Kraft deiner Angst und Pein!	And when my heart must languish In death's last awful throe, Release me from mine anguish, By Thine own pain and woe.

QUESTIONS FOR THOUGHT

- What constitutes a "good" or "beautiful" voice? Are the criteria different in religious music than in commercial music? Why might this be so?
- Are there any similarities between Tibetan and Western chanting?
- How does the function of chant differ from that of a hymn such as "Amazing Grace" or the chorale "O Sacred Head, Now Wounded"?
- What were the advantages and disadvantages of using plainchant for so many years in the Catholic Church?
- Why do you think composers only set the Ordinary of the Mass polyphonically?
- Some traditions do not use music in their services. Why might this be?

Yoruba Religion throughout the African Diaspora

We journey now in both time and place to the modern-day **Yoruba,** a large and influential ethnic group that resides in the central and coastal areas of Nigeria. The Yoruba (and related ethnic groups) practice a complex religion that, because of dispersion through the slave trade, has had considerable impact not just in Nigeria, but also on religions in the Americas, including: Brazilian Candomblé, Trinidadian Shango, Cuban Santería, and Haitian Vodún.

The Yoruba have a complicated and mythologically rich belief system. At the top of the Yoruba cosmology is Olodumare (God Almighty), a being too great to be comprehended by the human mind. Stationed just below are the *òrìsà* (literally, "sacred heads"), powerful entities who embody specific aspects of Olodumare. It is the òrìsà, rather than Olodumare, whom the Yoruba worship (see Figure 7.1).

Like the gods of classical Greece and Rome, the òrìsà have distinct human-like personalities. They are generally associated with forces of nature. For example, there is the virile thunder god Şàngó (similar to Zeus/Jupiter), the sensual river goddess Ochún (similar to Aphrodite/Venus), Obalúaiyé (associated with disease and death), and literally hundreds more. Some, like those mentioned above, are acknowledged all across Yorubaland. Others are recognized and worshipped only in specific regions.

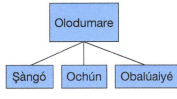

FIGURE 7.1

A small subset of the Yoruba religious hierarchy. Each of the hundreds of òrìsà embodies aspects of God Almighty. Each òrìsà is associated with specific praise poetry called oríkì.

The òrìsà like to involve themselves directly in the affairs of humans. Thus, a believer might pray or offer sacrifices to an òrìsà in exchange for assistance in life's daily events. The most dramatic contact is accomplished through possession trance, an event in which an òrìsà "mounts" and takes control of the mind and body of a human medium. While mounted on its human "horse," an òrìsà will generally give advice, both mundane and profound, to anyone who dares approach.

For a variety of reasons, music—especially drummed music—holds a central place in Yoruba worship. First, good music attracts the attention of the gods. Second, drum rhythms support worship through song and dance. Third, rhythms are believed to be a sonic representation, or manifestation, of a deity's character. Fourth, because Yoruba drums are capable of "speaking," musicians can praise an òrìsà through drummed words. Praise ensures the deity's beneficence.

The drums speak by imitating the inflections of the Yoruba language. Yoruba is tonal—the same vowel/

Bata drums (from left: Okónkolo, Iyá, Itótele).
Photo by Kenneth Ritchards.

DESI ARNAZ (1917–1986)

Cuban actor and musician Desi Arnaz was closely associated with the song "Babalú" (Obalúayé), composed by Margaria Lecuona. Arnaz occasionally sang the song as part of his nightclub act on the 1950s television show *I Love Lucy*, in which he played bandleader Ricky Riccardo.

Desi Arnaz with his conga (Congalese) drum.

consonant combination will take on different meanings according to its inflected pitch. Thus, in Yoruba the same syllabic combination might signify something completely different when spoken with a high tone versus a rising, low, or falling tone (e.g. *àlà* is a white cloth; *àlá* is a dream). By imitating the rhythmic and melodic patterns of speech, drums "talk."

The most important phrases that drums communicate are traditional *oríkì* (praise poems). An òrìṣà might be associated with hundreds of oríkì, each of which describes a particular aspect of the deity's personality. Drumming or singing an oríkì not only honors an òrìṣà, but is also believed to attract him or her to a ceremonial event. Once the òrìṣà is in the vicinity, possession trance can occur. The likelihood of trance is further enhanced through dance, an activity the òrìṣà enjoy.

The Yoruba use two types of drums to create speech melody. The most versatile talking drum is the two-headed hourglass-shaped *dùndún*. Leather strings run along the length of the drum from one head to the other. When the strings are squeezed, the drum's pitch rises.

Less adaptable to speech are *bàtá* drums. Although also double-headed, the drum's pitch cannot be changed while playing. So instead, drummers build high tone and low tone patterns by interlocking their rhythms, one drum with another, generally in sets of three or four. The drums are said to be owned by Ṣàngó. The instrument's shape resembles the head of Ṣàngó's thunder axe and the sound of a drum strike is said to represent a thunder clap.

Ritually blessed bàtá drums are rich in symbolism. @ 7.6 They are constructed with only organic materials (wood, rope, animal skin) and are treated as living objects. Drums are sometimes adorned with brass bells, which symbolize the goddess Ochún, Ṣàngó's most important lover. There is also a wealth of gendered symbolism. For example, the largest instrument is the *iyá ilú* (mother drum) and the instrument's interior is said to be a womb from which sonic/spiritual energy is born. Drummers are sometimes said to impregnate the drums with their hand strikes.

Yoruba religious beliefs traveled to the New World with the slave trade. In Cuba, the Yoruba belief system merged with other African systems as well as Catholicism. The latter mix eventually formed *Santería* (also known as *Regla de Ochá*), a syncretic religion combining

LISTENING 7.9 GUIDE))) *ELEGGUA*

Meter: Duple

Eleggua (or Èsù) is the first òrìṣà honored at any religious ceremony. He resides at the crossroads and is said to open or close all pathways. Because crossroads are places where new possibilities exist and where one must make decisions. All human decisions fall under Eleggua's purview.

The bàtá drums play the following brief oríkì: Èsù látopa, Èsù gongo.

0:00	The iyá ilú, the lowest-pitched drum, calls the rhythm.
0:03	The middle-pitched drum enters with the tones "gongo."
0:04	The drums combine to play the first line: Èsù látopa (Èsù waves a stick).
0:06	The drums combine to play the second line: Èsù gongo Èsù gongo (gongo refers to an elongated head shape).
0:08	The phrase repeats with minor variations.
0:34	Fade out.

TRANCE

What is possession trance like? Mediums—that is, those who actually become possessed—admit that even they do not know. This is because once the possession occurs, the individual's personality is displaced. Thus, the possessed person has no memory of the experience. People sometimes do remember the onset of possession, however. The following description comes from activist, writer, and filmmaker Maya Deren. The event happened in Haiti, where she was making *Divine Horsemen: The Living Gods of Haiti*, a documentary film about Vodún rituals. Deren was not a believer but attended ceremonies as her work required. She was not seeking to go into trance:

> The white darkness moves up the veins of my leg like a swift tide rising, rising; is a great force which I cannot sustain or contain, which, surely, will burst my skin. It is too much, too bright, too white for me; this is its darkness . . . The bright darkness floods up through my body, reaches my head, engulfs me. I am sucked down and exploded upward at once. That is all.

(*Divine Horsemen: The Living Gods of Haiti*.
McPherson & Company 1953. p. 260.)

Catholic and Yoruba beliefs. For a practitioner of Santería, a statue of Saint Barbara also represents Şàngó; a statue of Saint Lazarus also represents Obalúayé. Santería is increasingly practiced in the United States, particularly in Miami and New York City. Some North American practitioners are looking to "purify" the religion by extricating the Catholic influences and focusing on Yoruba principles.

QUESTIONS FOR THOUGHT

- Yoruba religious practice and thought thrives in many parts of the Americas. Yet, there is considerable variation from one location to another. What factors might account for these differences?

- Might one version of Yoruba religious practice be more authentic than another? Is religious practice in Nigeria more authentic than religious practice in Havana or Miami? Consider arguments on both sides.

- Yoruba drums speak by imitating speech inflection. Western music also creates a strong connection between pitch and words. Try the following experiment. Hum a well-known song to a friend. Then, ask her if she hears the song's words in her mind. The answer is almost certainly yes. How does this additive process contribute to understanding?

- Are there clear boundaries between sacred and secular music? If Bach's *St. Matthew Passion* is performed in a concert hall, does it remain sacred music by virtue of its subject matter? What about a bàtá rhythm? What if the performers themselves are agnostic?

The Whirling Dervishes of the Mevlevi Sufi Order

The art of music may never have had a more enthusiastic supporter than the Persian poet, philosopher, and mystic Mevlana Celeladdin Rumi (1207–1273). Rumi wrote that melody animates the soul, that rhythm once stirred the universe into existence. After his death in Konya, Turkey, followers honored him by founding the *Mevlevi* order, often known today in the West as the Whirling Dervishes.

The Mevlevi are a sub-order of *Sufism*, the mystical branch of Islam. There are numerous Sufi orders, each with its own particular rites. But all the orders share a belief in a universal God with whom it is possible to experience direct spiritual union. Sufi orders use a variety of techniques to achieve this, particularly meditation and contemplation. The Mevlevi place a strong emphasis on music, which sends the practitioner's physical body into a slow dance of graceful and ecstatic turning. @ 7.7

Mevlevi worship unfolds in a highly formalized and many-sectioned ceremony known as *Samā'* (or Sema, "listening" or "presence"). The ceremony, which is highly symbolic, enacts a soul's passage

"Hearken to the reed flute, how it complains, Lamenting banishment from its home."

—Prologue from Rumi's *Mathnavi*

MUSIC AND ORTHODOX ISLAM

Contrary to common belief in the West, the Qur'an (Koran) does not explicitly condemn music. In fact, evidence suggests that Muhammad himself enjoyed music. Even so, music's sensual power has long been a cause of concern for orthodox jurists. Beginning shortly after Muhammad's death, music was disallowed in certain religious contexts. Concerns were further heightened in the 9th century with the introduction of music and dance into the Sufi's ecstatic ceremonies. Today, music is not a part of orthodox Islam.

This proscription can be confusing to those outside the religion. After all, the chanting of both the Qur'an and the **ezan** (Turkish: call to prayer; **adhan** Arabic) sounds like music to a non-Muslim American listener. Both chant forms also follow strict melodic rules. Within Islam, however, neither chanting nor the ezan are considered to be music.

In Islam, the notion of what constitutes music is complex. The term **musiqa** refers to secular instrumental music, whereas the term **ghina'** refers to secular vocal music. **Samā'** suggests listening with moral presence. Koranic recitation, which is not music, is broadly known as **qira**. The term **tartil** refers to simple recitation, whereas the term **tajwid** refers to recitation that is highly ornamented.

Today, Qur'anic recitation is taught in formalized schools that are open to men and often women. Interestingly, many secular singers get their training by learning diction and melody in the religious schools. @ 7.8

to God. This metaphorical journey begins with the first flowering of the soul's awareness of divinity, which precipitates a gradual loss of self that ultimately leads to a mystical ascent to God's side.

Symbolism is pervasive in the Samā'. A *samazan*'s (Samā' practitioner) attire and actions reflect the ideal of surrendering one's individual identity to the all-encompassing universalism of God. For example, a samazan will wear tall headgear that represents a tombstone for the ego; his white skirt represents the ego's shroud. The samazan's body is treated symbolically as well. The samazan enters the performance space slowly, with arms crossed and hands on shoulders, a posture meant to represent the oneness of God. As the counter-clockwise *ayin-i şerif* or *mukabele* (spinning dance) begins, the samazan's arms are opened outward. The right palm is turned heavenward to receive God's blessings; the left palm is turned downward to transmit that power into the earth. Thus, the spinning dervish, like the reed flute in the Rumi verse above, becomes a conduit through which the divine is made manifest in the world.

The Inside of a Mosque, the Dervishes Dancing, William Hogarth, 1723–1724.

Courtesy of The Metropolitan Museum of Art, Harris Brisbane Dick Fund, 1932.

The Samā' ceremony unfolds through a series of distinct sections:

- *Naat-i-Sherif*: Praise given to the prophet Muhammad.
- *Kun*: Drum beats represent the sound of the creation.
- *Taksim*: An improvisation performed on the *ney*, an end-blown reed flute.
- *Devr-i Veled*: The samazen perform salutations. They are accompanied by a *peşrev* ("that which precedes"), an instrumental composition.
- The four-part *Ayin* section:
  - o   The birth of spiritual awareness.
  - o   Rapture.
  - o   Submission to God. (This is the section in which the samazen spin.)
  - o   The return to a life of service.
- A reading from the Qu'ran.
- After a prayer, the samazen return to their chambers for meditation.

Additional instruments that might be heard in a Samā' ceremony include the bowed **kemençe** (often replaced by the Western violin); various plucked lutes, including the **ud, saz,** and **tanbur;** the **kanun,** a plucked or hammered zither; and percussion instruments. Sung verses are drawn from religious poetry or from the Qu'ran.

Since the 16th century, almost all Mevlevi musical practice developed alongside Turkish secular art music. As with traditional music throughout the Middle East, the style is monophonic or heterophonic. Mevlevi melodies are lengthy and rhythmically complex.

Melody and rhythm are governed by intricate theoretical schemes called maqam and **usul** respectively. Maqam provides the blueprint for Turkish melody. In addition to designating a set of usable pitches (as does a Western scale), maqam employs rules governing how those pitches are to be combined in performance. Thus, a specific maqam (like an Indian raga [Chapter 2: Listening to Music]) might be identified not only by the pitches being used, but also by the characteristic ways in which a musician moves between them. Another difference between maqam and Western scale is found in the distance between pitches. Like raga, maqam uses intervals that are both smaller and larger than the half- and whole-steps of the Western system.

The usul system governs rhythm. Cyclical patterns from two to ten beats are common, though ones as long as twenty-eight beats are occasionally heard. In theory, usul patterns could be much longer still.

In order to aid memory and provide a sonic map of rhythmic progress through the cycle, usul patterns are subdivided into short groupings of two or three beats that are further distinguished by low (*dum*) and high (*tek & ka*) drum tones. Examples of two-beat patterns include:

1	2		1	2 +
Dum	tek	*and*	dum	tek-ka.

Examples of three-beat patterns include:

1	2	3		1	2	+	3	+
Dum	tek	tek	*and*	dum	tek	ka	tek	ka.

These basic patterns can be highly embellished and developed through improvisation. The following example consists of a simple development of the two-beat subdivision across an eight-beat cycle:

1	2	3	4	+	5	6	+	7	8	+
1	2	1	2	+	1	2	+	1	2	+
dum	tek	dum	tek	ka	dum	tek	ka	dum	tek	ka

LISTENING 7.10 GUIDE — *Naat-i-Sherif* (excerpt): Taksim and Peşrev

Instrumentation: ney, tanburs (bowed and plucked), kanun, kudüm, cymbals

TAKSIM in Maqam Bayati featuring the ney flute
Texture: Monophonic
Meter: Unmetered
Form: Open

The taksim allows the listener to become acquainted with the maqam's tonal structure. Our example is in the seven-toned maqam *bayati*. The bayati tetrachord (four related pitches) is characterized by a low second scale degree. Bayati is built on two tetrachords: bayati and *nahawand*. The tetrachords share pitch number 4, which is called *güçlü*.

do	ra	me	fa	sol	le	te	do
1	2	3	4				(1)
			4	5	6	7	

Bayati tetrachord **nahawand tetrachord**

0:00	Phrase one begins with an upward step to the *karar* (home pitch or "do"). From here the melody jumps up to the güçlü (fa), then drifts back down to the karar. Feel the downward pull of the lowered second scale degree. Also notice the strong presence of the musician's breath.
0:17	Phrase two leaps upward, then again drifts downward to karar (do).
0:34	Karar (do) is the starting point, then the melody moves up and down, eventually resting on the güçlü (fa) at 0:57.
1:00	The upper tetrachord is emphasized.
1:19	New pitches suggest that the performer has momentarily modulated to a different maqam, but he returns to bayati.
1:26	A gradually ascending stepwise pattern begins on karar (do). We will hear the same gesture in the ensemble section that follows.
1:38	A leap to the upper güçlü (fa). After a brief descent, the range expands upward.
1:56	Karar (do) is strongly stated. Then again the ascending pattern to the taksim's highest point at (2:15).
2:30	The phrase begins on güçlü (fa), which leads to final resolution on karar (do), where we began.

PEŞREV
Texture: Polyphonic
Meter: 28-beat usul
Form: A-B-C-B-D-B-E-B (Rondo)

A peşrev is an austere instrumental composition. This peşrev consists of four main sections (*hane* or houses: A, C, D, and E) with identical interludes (*teslim*: B) following. Each hane explores different aspects of the maqam, or temporarily modulates to another maqam. This peşrev was written by Neyaen Emin Dede (1883–1945). It is in *devr-i kebîr*, a 28-beat usul. If you count the beats, you will discover that each hane and the teslim lasts for exactly two 28-beat cycles. Be careful as you count. Phrase lengths and melodic turns may throw you off.

3:08	A	First hane. The hane is in two nearly identical halves. The second half, as well the second usul cycle, begins at 3:32.
3:55	B	Teslim. The second teslim usul cycle begins at 4:18.
4:40	C	The second hane covers two usul cycles but is not split into identical halves. The first half expands the upper melodic range and introduces new tones, perhaps suggesting a different maqam.
5:26	B	Teslim.
6:10	D	The third hane expands the melodic range and introduces new tone combinations.

6:54	B	Teslim.
7:35	E	The fourth hane stays in a lower melodic range and explores the melodic implications of a lowered güçlü.
8:18	B	Teslim.
9:00	A	Return to first hane (first half only).
9:23		Ney plays unmetered closing section.

QUESTIONS FOR THOUGHT

- Mevlevi ritual practice is rich with symbolism. This is true of religious music in general. What other religious symbolism have we encountered in this chapter? Are there commonalities? Important differences?

- As in the Yoruba religion, dance is a central ingredient of Mevlevi practice. How are these traditions similar? Different?

The Jewish Tradition

Every fall, on a date specified by the lunar calendar, Jews gather to commemorate the most sacred of High Holy Days: Yom Kippur, the Day of Atonement. During the holiday's 24-hour period, which spans sunset to sunset and focuses on repentance, there are several prayer services. The first takes place in the synagogue, just before sundown, as the holiday begins. Symbolism is pervasive. White is worn as a sign of purity. Men often wear *tallit* (prayer shawls), the fringe of which symbolizes the 613 *mitzvot* (commandments). Opening the service is a prayer called "**Kol Nidre**" ("All Vows"), which is sung three times by the *hazzan* (cantor)—first very softly, then louder with each repetition. The final Yom Kippur service ends with a single blast of the *shofar* (ram's horn) with the congregation exclaiming, "Next year in Jerusalem!" @ 7.9

Now we explore the music of Salamone Rossi (1570–1630), whose *Hashirim asher lish'lomo* ("The Songs of Solomon") is a collection of thirty-three polyphonic settings of psalms and synagogue songs. Although Rossi was a richly gifted composer residing in Mantua, then governed by one of Italy's most important arts patrons, Duke Vincenzo Gonzaga, anti-Semitism mostly kept Rossi an outsider to the court. Consequently, we know relatively little about his life. We do know that on Gonzaga's orders all Jews were required to live in a designated ghetto. Rossi may have died of the plague, which swept through Mantua in 1630.

Rossi's collection, perhaps a word-play on the composer's first name (none of the texts are actually from the "Song of Solomon"), are mostly drawn from the Old Testament. Written for three to eight voices, the music reflects the Italian polyphonic style of the day, although Rossi may also have borrowed melodic material from Jewish chants used in Italy. The text is sacred and is sung in Hebrew. The movement we study, "Elohim Hashivenu," is taken from Psalm 80: 4, 8, 20 and is organized into three distinct sections.

KOL NIDRE

The "Kol Nidre" has been used by composers as the basis for new compositions. The best known of these is German composer Max Bruch's (1838–1920) *Kol Nidrei (Adagio on Hebrew Melodies)*, op. 47 for cello and orchestra (1881). Though Bruch was a Protestant, his love for this beautiful music transcended religious divides.

LISTENING 7.11 GUIDE — "Kol Nidre" (excerpt)

Texture: Monophonic
Meter: Unmetered
Form: Through composed

The "Kol Nidre" asks that all individual vows made by petition to God or to the individual's own conscience be annulled. The recitation is a request for the forgiveness of sins and for renewal. The text is sung to an austere yet sorrowful melody that, though not notated until the 18th century, probably originated several hundred years earlier. There are many local variants to the tune, but the opening phrase of the melody is common to many traditions.

Hebrew:
Kol Nidre: Ve'esarei, Ush'vuei, Vacharamei, Vekonamei, Vekinusei, Vechinuyei.
D'indarna, Ud'ishtabana, Ud'acharimna, Ud'assarna Al nafshatana
Miyom Kippurim zeh, ad Yom Kippurim haba aleinu letovah
Bechulhon Icharatna vehon, Kulhon yehon sharan
Sh'vikin sh'vitin, betelin umevutalin, lo sheririn v'lo kayamin
Nidrana lo nidrei, V'essarana lo essarei
Ush'vuatana lo shevuot.

Translation:
All vows: prohibitions, obligations, oaths, and anathemas, whether called 'ḳonam,' 'ḳonas,' or by any other name, which we may vow, or swear, or pledge, or whereby we may be bound, from this Day of Atonement until the next (whose happy coming we await), we do repent. May they be deemed absolved, forgiven, annulled, and void, and made of no effect; they shall not bind us nor have power over us. The vows shall not be reckoned vows; the obligations shall not be obligatory; nor the oaths be oaths. (JewishEncyclopedia.com)

SHOFAR

Blowing the shofar on Rosh Hashanah.
slgckgc/Wikimedia Commons/CC-BY-SA-2.0.

The shofar is an ancient wind instrument made from a ram's horn. In biblical times, the shofar was also used as a signaling device. Today, the shofar is blown at various times of the religious year, including: the Hebrew month of Elul, Rosh Hashanah (the Jewish New Year), and Yom Kippur. There are four different sounds of the shofar: 1) *Tekiah*—one long, straight blast, 2) *Shevarim*—three medium notes rising in tone, 3) *Teruah*—nine quick staccato blasts in short succession, and 4) *Tekiah gedolah*—a single blast held as long as possible that sounds after a combination of Tekiah, Shevarim, and Teruah. The different sounds are meant to awaken the soul, inspire self-reflection, and spark a closer relationship with God.

"Elohim Hashivenu" from *Hashirim asher lish'lomo* ("The Songs of Solomon"), by Salamone Rossi

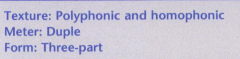

LISTENING
7.12
GUIDE

Texture: Polyphonic and homophonic
Meter: Duple
Form: Three-part

Although there is a clear rhythmic pulse, there is no sense of a steady meter. The music, which is highly melismatic, begins with the tenor voice followed imitatively by the bass, after which enter the remaining two voices.

0:00	Elohim hashivenu,	O God, restore us
	Y'haer panekha	And cause Your face to shine on us
	Y'nivvashe'a.	And we shall be saved.
0:56	Elohim tsevaot	O God of hosts,
	Hashivenu	Restore us
	Y'haer panekha	And cause Your face to shine on us
	Y'nivvashe'a.	And we shall be saved.
2:03	Adonai elohim tsevaot	O Lord God of hosts
	Hashivenu;	Restore us
	Y'haer panekha	And cause Your face to shine on us
	Y' nivvashe'a	And we shall be saved.

QUESTIONS FOR THOUGHT

• Rossi's "Elohim Hashivenu" is written in the style of 17th-century Italian polyphony, the same style used by Catholic composers of the time. What makes this music Jewish? Your answer may lead to a quite provocative question: is religious music ethnic music?

ACTIVITIES AND ASSIGNMENTS

• Search out additional recordings of "Kol Nidre." Here is some music that uses at least a portion of the famous melody:

  o David Axelrod's *Release of an Oath: Kol Nidre* (Electric Prunes, 1968).
  o Ludwig van Beethoven's *String Quartet in C sharp minor* op. 131 (opening bars of Adagio quasi un poco andante).
  o Nicolas Jolliet's *Kol Nidre Goes East* (2006).
  o Arnold Schoenberg's *Kol Nidre* (1938).
  o John Zorn's string quartet version of "Kol Nidre" (1999).
  o The film *The Jazz Singer* (1927) uses the "Kol Nidre" in its final scene (Chapter 12: Music and Film).

Conclusion

We have looked at a variety of ways in which religious cultures use music to enhance spiritual experience. The differences are vast. Some practitioners use music to focus the mind and body; others use it for its ability to attract benevolent spirits (or ward off evil ones). Some practitioners favor non-metric chant to quiet the body; others strive to excite the body with music that pulses with rhythm.

The boundaries between sacred and secular are permeable. Music originally conceived for performance in a temple, church, or synagogue often makes its way into concert settings. Individual belief or focus may or may not be relevant to our understanding of, and response to, spiritual music. Tibetan monks regard mental focus as an essential part of their chanting. But what about the experience of filmmaker Maya Deren? Though intrigued by Haitian Vodún, she was not a practitioner. She experienced possession trance nonetheless. Presumably, a Mevlevi dervish could perform *ayin-i şerif* or *mukabele* while thinking about the mundane matters of everyday life. How would we watching on ever know the difference?

Might certain sounds be inherently spiritual? One might be tempted to think so. Such a scenario would help explain Deren's trance experience, for example. But if so, how does one explain J.S. Bach's use of a secular love song in the *St. Matthew Passion*?

We began this chapter by asking what kind of music you consider to be spiritual. Perhaps working through this chapter has clarified your answer. Perhaps, however, it has only helped a tentative answer become more nuanced. The musical experience of spirituality is enormously complex. Every discovery seems to open new perspectives for understanding the human condition.

Key Terms

- a cappella
- bàtá drums
- bayati tetrachord
- bodhisattva
- Buddha
- dharma
- diaspora
- diatonic
- dùndún
- dung-dkar
- güçlü
- harmonic (overtone, or throat) singing
- hazzan
- hymn
- kanun

- karar
- kemençe
- lining out
- liturgy
- *Magnus Liber*
- mandala
- Mass (Proper and Ordinary)
- Mevlevi order
- modes
- nahawand tetrachord
- ney
- oratorio
- organum (discant and florid)
- organum quadruplum
- oríkì
- òrìşà

- plainchant
- recitative style
- Renaissance
- rgya gling
- sacred harp
- Samā'
- Santería
- saz
- shape-note
- shofar
- Sufism
- tanbur
- ud
- usul
- Yoruba

Essay Questions

- What is the difference between a piece of music that is "secular" and one that is "spiritual"? Is that difference apparent in the tones themselves?
- How does a piece of music become "spiritual"? How might a "spiritual" composition become "secular"?

MUSICAL INTERSECTIONS

- To explore overt and hidden political meanings in music.
- To see how music has been used for political aims.
- To examine how music helps to develop, form, reflect, and alter national identity.

CHAPTER EIGHT

Music and Nation

QUESTIONS FOR THOUGHT

- What kinds of music might be considered political?
- Does music need words to be political?
- How might music move us to embrace or reject political ideas?
- Music performance involves more than just sound. What other aspects of a performance might be used to invoke national ideologies?

As the wave of distortion faded away, a melody emerged with bell-tone clarity. It was a relaxed falling gesture followed by an upward sweep:

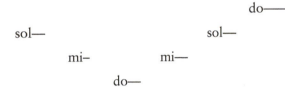

Every American recognizes the opening tones to "The Star-Spangled Banner." But who would have expected to hear it then and there—as the sun rose on Max Yasgur's New York farm on an overcast August morning in 1969? The Woodstock Music and Art Fair was officially over, but rain, mud, and the swell of 500,000 people had delayed the performances through the night. Jimi Hendrix, icon of 1960s psychedelia, was finally playing his set. Some in the audience probably sang along: "Oh, say can you see, by the dawn's early light . . . " @ 8.1

Hendrix took liberties with rhythm and pitch, but the tune was clear enough. Or at least it was initially. Soon, however, the song's melodic flow and formal structure disintegrated under a barrage of high-frequency and high-decibel distortion. Increasingly improvisatory, Hendrix's performance opened up the anthem to a series of audacious interpretations, ones that brought the anthem's most fundamental meanings and values into question. Following the line, "The rockets' red glare," Hendrix digressed into a 30-second improvisation of percussive disruptions and Banshee-like screams. The tone painting of the next line—"The bombs bursting in air"—was half again as long and twice as startling—replete with the sounds of incoming missiles, explosions, and screams. The postscript for the next line—"That our flag was still there"—was "Taps," the army bugle call to end the day and honor the dead. When "Banner" finally ended (after several more sonic excursions), Hendrix slipped into one of his signature hits, "Purple Haze."

What to make of such a performance in such an unlikely setting? Consider the time and place. Following the Tet Offensive of 1968, for the Americans the Vietnam War had spun out of control. The same year had also seen the assassinations of Dr. Martin Luther King Jr. and Senator Robert F. Kennedy. The streets rocked with anti-war and civil rights protests. The nation seemed at war both at home and abroad.

> "All I did was play it. I'm American, so I played it."
> —Jimi Hendrix (1942–1970)

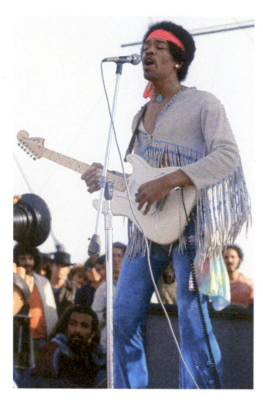

Jimi Hendrix at Woodstock Music and Arts Festival, 1969.

Barry Z Levine/ Premium Archive/ Getty Images.

Was Hendrix protesting as well? Not consciously, at least. "I thought it was beautiful," he later told late-night television talk-show host Dick Cavett, who asked about the performance. Many viewers saw it otherwise. They were deeply offended.

In this chapter we study the ways in which music is used as a vehicle for politics and a symbol for nation. We begin by comparing and contrasting anthems and other political music from various nation-states. Next, we study how "folk" music was used to promote national solidarity in 19th-century Russia, as well as 20th-century China and Bulgaria. From there we step further back in time and study how the German composer Ludwig van Beethoven (1770–1827) envisioned universal brotherhood in his Symphony No. 9 in D minor. We close the chapter with a look at the use of music in the still-simmering Zapatista revolutionary movement in Chiapas, Mexico.

THE MODERN NATION-STATE

Political scientists use the term "nation-state" to characterize sovereign entities that combine a high level of ethnic and cultural unity (nation) with a viable political system (state). In the history of human culture, however, the nation-state is a relatively new idea, arguably dating from the late 18th century.

National Identity

Like flags, songs of nation invoke powerful emotions. Director Michael Curtiz (1886–1962) understood this when he shot the remarkable "La Marseillaise" scene in the classic film *Casablanca* (1942), starring Humphrey Bogart (1899–1957) and Ingrid Bergman (1915–1982). @ 8.2 Set against the backdrop of World War II, the film mostly unfolds in the relative peace of Rick's Café, a bar frequented by German soldiers and French expatriates. Generally speaking, the French are cowed by the Germans. That changes, however, when a flurry of national pride and courage is unleashed in a battle of songs.

In one corner of the bar, German soldiers assemble around a piano. An officer pounds his fist on the instrument as the men sing in German "The Watch on the Rhine," a song dating from the 1870 Franco-Prussian War (and a war that Prussia won):

Es braust ein Ruf wie Donnerhall,	A voice resounds like thunder-peal,
wie Schwertgeklirr und Wogenprall:	Mid dashing waves and clang of steel:
Zum Rhein, zum Rhein, zum deutschen Rhein,	To the Rhine, the Rhine, the German Rhine!
wer will des Stromes Hüter sein?	Who guards today my stream divine?
Chorus	
Lieb Vaterland, magst ruhig sein,	Dear Fatherland, no danger thine;
Lieb Vaterland, magst ruhig sein,	Dear Fatherland, no danger thine;
Fest steht und treu die Wacht,	Firm and True stands the Watch,
die Wacht am Rhein!	the Watch at the Rhine!
Fest steht und treu die Wacht,	Firm and True stands the Watch,
die Wacht am Rhein!	the Watch at the Rhine!

On other nights, the French would have listened silently and miserably. Not this night, however. Encouraged by resistance leader Victor Laszlo (played by Paul Henreid, 1905–1992), they stand and sing as one while the nightclub's dance band plays "La Marseillaise," the French national anthem:

Allons enfants de la Patrie,	Arise children of the fatherland,
Le jour de gloire est arrivé.	The day of glory has arrived.
Contre nous de la tyrannie,	Against us tyranny's,
L'étendard sanglant est levé.	Bloody standard is raised.
Entendez-vous dans nos campagnes	Do you hear in the fields
Mugir ces féroces soldats?	The screams of the fierce soldiers?
Ils viennent jusques dans vos bras	They are coming into our midst
Égorger vos fils, vos compagnes.	To slaughter your sons, your countrymen

Chorus	
Aux armes citoyens!	To arms citizens!
Formez vos bataillons.	Form your battalions.
Marchons, marchons!	March, march!
Qu'un sang impur	Until the impure blood
Abreuve nos sillons.	Waters our fields.

The scene concludes in tears of joy and pride, and cries of "Vive la France!" Enraged, a German officer orders the café to close. It is an incredible scene, one that stirs the blood of moviegoers still today. Imagine its power in 1942 with the world at war and France on its knees.

Originally titled "War Song for the Army of the Rhine," "La Marseillaise" was written in 1792 by French army officer Claude Joseph Rouget de Lisle (1760–1836) as his country braced for a Prussian invasion. The song quickly became associated with the French Revolution. It was designated the national anthem in 1879.

Contrast the lyrics of "La Marseillaise" with Francis Scott Key's (1779–1843) text for "The Star-Spangled Banner" (1814), written after Key watched the American defense of Fort McHenry from Baltimore Harbor during the War of 1812:

Oh, say can you see, by the dawn's early light,
What so proudly we hailed at the twilight's last gleaming?
Whose broad stripes and bright stars, through the perilous fight,
O'er the ramparts we watched, were so gallantly streaming?
And the rockets' red glare, the bombs bursting in air,
Gave proof through the night that our flag was still there.
O say, does that star-spangled banner yet wave
O'er the land of the free and the home of the brave?

There are no notions of a fatherland, no impurities of blood, as in "La Marseillaise." Instead, the lyrics present a quieter notion of fortitude and hope throughout a long night of terror. Absent altogether is Hendrix's soundscape of terror, death, and suffering.

Francis Scott Key did not set out to write a national anthem, just a poem in response to his pride upon witnessing a night of stalwart bravery. In fact, "The Star-Spangled Banner" was not officially proclaimed the national anthem until 1931. As for the melody to which the words became linked, that was composed by Englishman John Stafford Smith (1750–1836) for a men's social club to which he belonged. Smith's song was titled, "To Anacreon in Heaven." @ 8.3

Disparate though their origins were, Key's words and Smith's melody were soon linked. Already by the American Civil War (1861–1865) the song had achieved a prominent place in the American consciousness. The song was so politically charged that in March 1861, just one month prior to the outbreak of fighting at Fort Sumter, George Tucker (1828–1863), a Secessionist Virginian, set the melody to pro-Confederacy words. He titled the song, "The Southern Cross." Would we all know this version today had the South been victorious?

Oh! Say can you see, through the gloom and the storm,
More bright for the darkness, that pure constellation!
Like the symbol of love and redemption its form,
As it points to the heaven of hope for the nation.

HYMN AND ANTHEM

Who could have imagined that a Christian hymn would become first a song of African resistance and later be incorporated into not one, but three African national anthems? That is what happened.

The song "Nkosi Sikelel' iAfrika" (Lord, Bless Africa) was written by 1897 by Johannesburg-based South African Methodist choirmaster Enoch Mankayi Sontonga (1873–1905). It is simultaneously a song of beseeching and pride:

Nkosi Sikelel' iAfrika	Lord Bless Africa
Maluphakanyisw' uphondo lwayo	May her glory be lifted high
Yiva imathandazo yethu	Hear our petitions
Nkosi Sikelela	Lord bless us
Thina lusapho lwayo	Us your children

In 1912, it was sung at the first meeting of the South African Native National Congress, the forerunner of the African National Congress (ANC), the political organization that struggled to gain civil rights for blacks in apartheid South Africa. The song soon became the anthem used to close ANC meetings. Today the melody is heard in the national anthems of Tanzania, Zambia, and South Africa. The current South African anthem, adopted in 1997, strives for ethnic inclusion. It is set in five different languages: Xhosa, Zulu, Sesotho, Afrikaans, and English. The anthem combines two melodies: "Nkosi Sikelel' iAfrika" and "Die Stem van Suid-Afrika," South Africa's anthem from the apartheid era.

Now radiant each star, as the beacon afar,
Giving promise of peace, or assurance in war,
'Tis the Cross of the South, which shall ever remain
To light us to freedom and glory again!

Sheet music, "Old Tippecanoe: A Patriotic Song," 1840.

Library of Congress, Music Division.

Tucker was not the only one to borrow this symbolism-laden melody. Italian composer Giacomo Puccini (1858–1924) used it to symbolize American hubris in his opera *Madama Butterfly* (1904) (Chapter 10: Music and Love). Other European composers who set the melody, though in decidedly more pro-American versions, were the Russians Serge Rachmaninoff (1873–1943) and Igor Stravinsky (1882–1971), and the German Kurt Weill (1900–1950).

Campaign Music and the American Presidency

Imagine yourself in Baltimore, Maryland on May 4, 1840. The Whigs (a once formidable American political party) are strutting into town to nominate William Henry Harrison (1773–1841) as their presidential candidate. Their parade, some 25,000 marchers strong, is led by a phalanx of vintage Revolutionary War-era artillery. Following behind are marching bands, a carriage housing wordsmith Daniel Webster (1782–1852), log-cabin floats, and hundreds of banners. To make sure the mood stays bright, the hard cider is free.

Emotions reach fever pitch when the parade passes Music Hall, where Democrats are joylessly confirming their own nominee, Martin Van Buren (1782–1862). The street rings with the ditty,

For Tippecanoe and Tyler too—Tippecanoe and Tyler too;
And with them we'll beat little Van, Van, Van;
Van is a used up man.
And with them we'll beat little Van.

In the end, William Henry Harrison was "sung into the Presidency," observed Whig politician Philip Hone (1870–1851).

Beginning with the Harrison campaign and lasting for more than a century, music was an essential ingredient in presidential campaigns. The songs were like today's media soundbites: utilitarian, simple in construction, easy to sing and remember, and (like "tweets") easily dispersed. Ideally, lyrics were clever. As often as not, however, they consisted of strings of banal, yet vivid clichés. Words were attached to well-known preexisting melodies, such as "Yankee Doodle," "Dixie," and any number of now mostly forgotten tunes. To make sure their message was disseminated, the Harrison campaign, like others to follow, distributed sheets or pamphlets of lyrics. Harrison's illustrated *Log Cabin Songbook* came with fifty-five sets of lyrics to well-known melodies.

Publishing campaign songs was a good business, albeit "seasonal." The crop had to be sown, harvested, and sold quickly. As the election grew near, the value would decrease, effectively reaching zero after the election.

With the emergence of television in the 1950s, campaign songs became less important, as did many of the material aspects of political culture. We still encounter political paraphernalia—elephants and donkeys, silly hats, posters, and buttons. But today's campaign rallies bring candidates on stage to the recorded sounds of songs by pop stars ranging from Dolly Parton to Van Halen. Almost nothing remains of the communal singing, banner waving, participatory atmosphere that typified campaign rallies of earlier generations.

QUESTIONS FOR THOUGHT

- Does "The Star-Spangled Banner" mean the same thing when performed by Jimi Hendrix at Woodstock as it does when played by the United States Marine Band? Or when sung by Fergie at the 2018 NBA All-Star Game?
- Do the anthems above reveal something about the national ideologies of Germans, French, South Africans, and Americans?
- Can you imagine the words to "La Marseillaise" being written today? Why or why not?
- Why might a nation decide to change its anthem?
- Sacha Baron Cohen reset the "Star-Spangled Banner" melody to new lyrics in his mockumentary *Borat* (2006). View the sequence. Do you find the scene offensive? Why or why not?
- Imagine that Congress decided to scrap "The Star-Spangled Banner" and designate a new national anthem. What elements would you like to see contained in the new anthem? Why?
- A national anthem is one musical device for promoting national identity and pride. What are some others?
- Presidential campaigns once relied on setting new words to melodies that would be universally recognized. Can you name five appropriate melodies that voting-age Americans of all backgrounds would recognize today?

ACTIVITIES AND ASSIGNMENTS

- There has been a push among some in the United States to change the national anthem. Investigate the reasons for the change and the musical alternatives that have been proposed.
- Listen to a selection of national anthems from other countries. What do they have in common? How do they differ?
- Visit *Trax on the Trail* (www.traxonthetrail.com), a website that examines presidential campaign music, past and present.

Of all the campaign songs of presidential races past, perhaps best remembered today is "Happy Days are Here Again" (1929), which was drawn from the 1930 movie *Chasing Rainbows*. Franklin Delano Roosevelt (1882–1945) used the song in his 1932 campaign. The song has been associated with the Democratic Party ever since.

Nineteenth-Century Nationalism

NINETEENTH-CENTURY NATIONALIST COMPOSERS

Central Europe
Bedrich Smetana (1824–1884)
Antonín Dvorák (1841–1904)
Leos Janácek (1854–1928)

Scandinavia
Edvard Grieg (1843–1907)
Carl Nielsen (1865–1931)
Jean Sibelius (1865–1957)

Russia
Mikhail Glinka (1804–1857)
"The Five" (or "Mighty Handful"):
   Alexander Borodin (1833–1887)
   Cesar Cui (1835–1918)
   Mily Balakirev (1837–1910)
   Modest Mussorgsky   (1839–1881)
   Nikolai Rimsky-Korsakov (1844–1908).

Spain
Isaac Albéniz (1860–1909)

The 19th century was a period of growing national identity and rivalry across Europe. Inspired in part by the era's overriding spirit of Romanticism, people sought to emphasize and develop their ethnic and social roots, even as those ties were being weakened by large-scale migration, industrialization, and urbanization. The political movement associated with these ideas became known as **nationalism.**

Across Europe, new political allegiances were formed; old ones were dropped or solidified. The Italian peninsula, which before 1870 was governed by a collection of city states, united to form a constitutional monarchy. Germany was united the following year. These large countries (as well as the long-united England and France) dominated the era's international politics and artistic movements. Increasingly, however, less powerful ethnic groups and/or nation-states—such as the Czechs and Bohemians, Norwegians and Danes, Poles, Hungarians, and Russians—sought to expand their influence.

All this made for complicated politics. After all, nationalism is a double-edged sword. On the one hand, it binds people together, celebrates common goals and heritage, and creates a sense of solidarity and social pride. On the other hand, nationalism is divisive. It reflects and fortifies an "us-against-them" mentality.

Nationalist composers strove to write music that highlighted and represented their heritage. To achieve their goals, composers often used folk melodies (or newly composed "folk-like" melodies) and folk-dance rhythms. Sometimes composers sought to tell a story with their music. In the orchestral repertoire, this led to the development of the **symphonic poem** (or tone poem). Such pieces had colorful names. The Bohemian composer Bedrich Smetana wrote *Ma Vlast* (*My Country*, 1874); Finnish composer Jean Sibelius wrote *The Swan of Tuonela* (1895, based on Finnish mythology); the Russian Alexander Borodin wrote *In the Steppes of Central Asia* (1880). These are just a few of many such compositions.

Borodin, a chemist by profession, was an important member of The Five (or Mighty Handful), a group of 19th-century Russian nationalist composers. Led by Mily Balakirev, The Five sought to create a repertory of art music with a sound that was characteristically Russian.

The question of course, was "What does 'authentic' Russian music sound like?" Balakirev contended that it had to be drawn from the "folk" and that it should sound unstudied so as to accurately reflect the native culture that it sought to promote.

In the Steppes of Central Asia (1880)

Russia at the end of the 19th century was the largest country in the world, in both land mass and population. It was also the most ethnically diverse. While size translated into potential economic and military power, it also worked against the creation of a central identity. Ethnic groups far from Moscow might easily feel stronger ties to their own local cultural heritage than to the more abstract concept of a Russian nation-state.

Perhaps we feel that tension in *Steppes*. Where exactly in the Central Asian steppes Borodin places us, we do not know. The area is vast; its peoples are many. Our immediate experience is clear, however. A caravan makes its way across the landscape. Soon, another caravan appears on the horizon. As the groups cross paths, they trade stories, maybe trade goods. Eventually, each continues on its journey. In the end, all that remains is the eternal landscape of Mother Russia.

The music is **programmatic,** that is, it tells a story. There are three main musical ideas: a "Russian" theme, an "Eastern" theme, and a "traveling" theme. The Russian theme has sweeping gestures; it is strong, but gentle. The Eastern theme, played on an "exotic"-sounding double-reed instrument, is relatively narrow in contour and rhythmically loose, as if it resists European conformity. Theme three, the traveling theme, is rhythmically steady and direct. Perhaps it represents the tread of powerful oxen teams moving across the seemingly endless landscape.

The Tibetan steppes, ca. 1911.

| *In the Steppes of Central Asia,* by Alexander Borodin | LISTENING 8.1 GUIDE |

In the Steppes of Central Asia, by Alexander Borodin

Texture: Complex homophony
Meter: Duple
Form: No standard form; unfolding themes

0:00	Strings sound a single pitch that provides a tonal reference point for the music to follow. Naturally, we assume that this single pitch, so prominent and pervasive, is "do," the tonic of the musical scale. Presumably, this texture represents the steppes, unchanging and eternal. Woodwinds—clarinet, then oboe—fade in and out on the same pitch. The interjections strengthen the idea of timelessness, like seasons that come and go.
0:08	A clarinet reenters and plays a two-part melody consisting of a downward falling phrase followed by a longer phrase at a higher pitch level. This is the "Russian" theme. Perhaps you are surprised by the melody's tonality, which tells us that our heretofore perceived tonic in the strings is actually "sol." Perhaps Borodin chose this deception to remind us that "home" is always relative, a matter of perception.
0:29	The horn enters with the same melody, but at yet another pitch level. Our imagined "do" turned "sol" in the strings now becomes "mi" when heard against the horn melody. It is as if our relationship to the unchanging landscape keeps shifting underfoot. It is hard to get a tonal footing.
0:47	Violas and cellos enter **pizzicato** (strings plucked, not bowed) with the "walking" theme. We move across the endless steppes, represented by sustained pitches in the woodwinds and brass. The music seems fragmented, without a clear personality. We seem to be suspended between worlds.

continued

1:11	Arrival. The English horn enters with the lilting "Eastern" theme (in ABA form). The range is narrow, the progression is slowly downward. This is the first half of the theme, the A section.
1:27	English horn continues with the B section of the melody.
1:40	English horn returns to a slightly shortened version of the "Eastern" theme's A section.
1:53	Sustained tones are echoed across the orchestra. We now know this sound. It is traveling music (both on the steppes and between musical themes). The pitch is raised, energy is briefly increased.
2:20	Clarinet returns with our familiar friend, the "Russian" melody. Notice the countermelodies.
2:41	Brass instruments take up the "Russian" melody; again, with countermelodies.
3:06	With an abrupt jump in dynamics, the full orchestra takes up the "Russian" melody. This is the loudest point in the piece.
3:30	More traveling music with instrumental punctuations. Transition.
3:53	Strings and English horn take up the "Eastern" theme. A section.
4:08	"Eastern" theme, B section.
4:21	"Eastern" theme, A section.
4:35	"Eastern" theme, A section. Sounds like a closing section (coda).
4:48	"Russian" and "Eastern" theme sound together. Oboe takes the "Russian" theme while first cellos then basses take the "Eastern" theme.
5:15	Reiteration of the dual themes. Violins take the "Russian" theme while horns take the "Eastern" theme.
5:29	Dual themes continue, but the instruments shift. Violins now have the "Eastern" theme.
5:43	The "Eastern" theme fades away. The "Russian" is fragmented and spread across different instruments in the orchestra. Cadence.
6:47	Strings return to opening texture representing the steppes.
6:50	Flute sounds the "Russian" theme one last time. Perhaps a memory left on the land? Sounds fade away.

Composing for the State

Kings and czars, dukes and duchesses have all employed musicians. During the Renaissance and Baroque periods in particular, European courts vied for the best artists, whose very presence was sufficient to increase a sovereign's political clout. Composers sought the best positions as well. To get them, they often curried favor with important rulers. Frenchman Jean-Baptiste Lully (1632–1687), for example, wrote operas that used allegory to glorify the deeds of his patron, King Louis XIV. In the 18th century, George Frideric Handel (1685–1759) wrote rousing choruses, which, though mostly based on biblical topics, in reality were thinly veiled tributes to the power of the British Empire. Handel's coronation anthem "Zadok the Priest" was one of four anthems written in 1727 for King George II. It has been sung at every British coronation service since. In the following sections we examine works that were either written for, or used as, agents of government policy.

Handel's *Music for the Royal Fireworks* (1749)

In Chapter 3 we introduced J.S. Bach; here we introduce his contemporary George Frideric Handel. The men had much in common. Both were German and born in 1685; both took music to new heights; and both were superb dramatists. But they were also very different.

Bach came from a musical family. He was deeply (and occasionally darkly) religious, conservative intellectually, and achieved a level of professional success far below his talent level. Bach's complex music could be remarkably dissonant, perhaps to the ears of his contemporaries even unpleasantly so.

Handel occupied a very different world. Handel's pragmatic father disapproved of his son's musical interests and wanted him to become a lawyer. Handel's temperament was also quite the opposite of Bach's. Handel was a gregarious, adventurous, well-traveled, and socially astute entrepreneur who often wrote music specifically designed to entertain. The two men never met.

Disobeying his father, as a child Handel practiced music in secret. In 1702, he set out to Hamburg, where he procured a position playing violin in the city's opera orchestra. Within a year he would compose a successful opera of his own. In 1706, determined to learn more about the Italian style, Handel traveled to Italy, opera's birthplace. He stayed until 1710, when he was offered a position as music director in the court of George Louis (then the Elector of Hanover), who was soon to become George I, King of England (1714).

His employer's ascendancy allowed Handel to move to London. The city would be Handel's home for the rest of his life. Composer, conductor, and savvy business man, Handel became rich. Today, Handel is best remembered for his 1741 oratorio *The Messiah*, a few of his operas, and the instrumental works *Water Music* (1717) and *The Music for the Royal Fireworks* (1749), written for George I and George II respectively.

Fireworks on the River Thames celebrating the peace of Aix-La-Chapelle. Handel composed his *Music for the Royal Fireworks* for this event, May 15, 1749.

Rischgitz/Hulton Archive/Getty Images.

Movement No. 4: "La Réjouissance" from *The Music for the Royal Fireworks*, by George Frideric Handel

LISTENING
8.2
GUIDE

Texture: Homophonic
Meter: Quadruple
Form: AABBAABB

To celebrate the 1748 Treaty of Aix-la-Chapelle, which ended the War of the Austrian Succession, England's King George II commissioned Handel to write music to accompany a fireworks show on the River Thames. The king, who did not enjoy string instruments, requested an ensemble of band instruments only, including oboes, bassoons, trumpets, horns, and percussion. (Handel added strings to later performances.) We listen to "La Réjouissance" ("The Rejoicing").

0:00	A Section A fanfare-like phrase of eight four-beat measures. Trumpets are featured.
0:18	A repeated Eight four-beat measures. Horns are featured. Notice the darker timbre
0:35	B Section Melodic ideas are more extended. Ten four-beat measures.
0:57	B repeats.
1:20	A Section with trumpets and horns.
1:37	A
1:54	B
2:17	B

Chinese Opera during the Cultural Revolution

Jiang Qing and Mao, 1930s.

BRIGHT SHENG
(b. 1955)

"There is something unique about my generation of Chinese artists," says composer and Shanghai-native Bright Sheng (b. 1955), who came of age during the Cultural Revolution. "They are tough and stubborn, with an unbreakable spirit of perseverance." Because of his musical gifts, at age 15 Sheng was sent to work with local musicians in Qinghai Province, bordering Tibet. There he discovered a love for folk music and composition. Sheng currently lives in Ann Arbor, where he teaches at the University of Michigan. He has written a number of operas, most recently *Dream of the Red Chamber* (2016), commissioned by San Francisco Opera.

A nation in crisis might be the best way to describe China from 1966 to 1976. The period, known as the Cultural Revolution, was a decade of terror. Loosely bound units of Red Guard youths roamed the streets seeking "closet capitalists," "bourgeois educators," and anyone else who dared think outside the Communist Party box. Millions died; and millions more were sent to labor camps to be "re-educated." Books were burned and artworks destroyed. Homes were ransacked and places of worship razed. Children identified their teachers, even their own parents, as traitors to the Party.

All this happened in the name of reform. Communist Party Chairman Mao Zedong (1893–1976) promised to rid China of what he called the "Four Olds"—old ideas, old culture, old customs, old habits. In their place he would create a new society purged of capitalist and imperialist influences.

The new Chinese society would need appropriate art. Accordingly, Mao's wife, the former actress Jiang Qing, embarked on an initiative using art to extol China's proletarian culture. The result was the **Yang Ban Xi** ("Model Plays")—originally eight works: five operas, two ballets, and one symphony. Plots centered on loyalists who worked selflessly for Communist Party ideals. The main characters were brave, wise, and kind. And, of course, they venerated Mao's vision for China. Follow-up compositions necessarily took these original eight works as their models. Performance of any work that did not conform was banned.

From 1967 to 1969, Jiang conducted a massive campaign to familiarize the population with the Yang Ban Xi. The works were performed frequently, played over the radio, turned into movies, and adapted to local dialects. Schoolchildren sang the tunes; all professional opera actors were required to learn the roles. Those who conformed exactly to Jiang's directions were paid handsomely and perhaps appointed to political committees. Those who did not were "re-educated," or eliminated. The most popular of the model works was the opera *Hong deng ji* (*The Red Lantern*). In 1967, shortly after the onset of the Cultural Revolution, *Hong deng ji* officially became one of the Eight Model Plays.

History: Jingju (Beijing Opera)

@ 8.4 Of the fifty or so long-established operatic traditions in China, Jingju emerged in the late 19th century as the dominant style. Its popularity was fueled by royal patronage and the 1909 declaration that Mandarin, Beijing's local dialect, would become the national language. Jingju includes singing, dialog, acrobatics, and martial arts. Costumes are brightly colored and elaborate. The sparse staging relies heavily on symbolism to indicate time and place.

There are four main character types in Jingju:

1. *Sheng* is the main male role. This character type is cultivated and refined. There are many subtypes depending on the character's age or social status. Sheng usually have a nasal quality to their voices.

2. *Dan* is the main female character type. Traditionally, only men played this role; make-up, costuming and gestures signaled their femininity. During the Cultural Revolution, women took on these characters. Today, both men and women sing Dan roles. Men sing in a stylized falsetto voice.

3. *Jing* is a powerful, courageous, and action-oriented male character. He wears a long beard. His face is painted according to personality traits: red for greatness, white for slyness, black for integrity and loyalty. Movements are exaggerated; the voice is powerful.

Sheng.
Courtesy of The Metropolitan Museum of Art, Rogers Fund, 1930.

Dan.
Courtesy of The Metropolitan Museum of Art, Rogers Fund, 1930.

Jing.
Courtesy of The Metropolitan Museum of Art, Rogers Fund, 1930.

Chou.
Courtesy of The Metropolitan Museum of Art, Rogers Fund, 1930.

4. *Chou* is an affable male clown whose ugliness and laughter wards off evil. White paint around the nose may symbolize either wit or slyness. The singing style is shrill, laced with colloquial speech. Chou roles are associated with percussion instruments.

Beginning in childhood, would-be performers undergo years of intense training in acting, singing, dance, martial arts, make-up, and gesture. A performer will specialize in one character type for an entire career. *Farewell My Concubine* (1993), a film by Chinese director Chen Kaige (b. 1952), chronicles the grueling preparation needed to become a Jingju artist. It also displays the genre's magnificent costumes, painted faces, and vocal styles.

Jingju utilizes two distinct aria types: *xipi* and *erhuang*. Each has specific meters and melodic characteristics. Xipi is lively and cheerful; erhuang is heroic. In both, percussion patterns punctuate speech and mark structural divisions. The **gu shi** (drum master) plays the **guban** (drum and clapper). He also serves as a conductor by signaling entrances and setting tempos. Other percussion instruments join in to accompany martial scenes. String instruments, especially the **jinghu** (bowed spike fiddle) accompany the melodies.

Reforms (Revolutionary Opera)

Jiang and Mao believed that Jingju should serve "the workers, peasants, and soldiers." Furthermore, it should be used as propaganda for the state, as a means to convert the masses to Communist ideas. These goals necessitated numerous changes to Beijing opera's traditional performance practice.

Accordingly, revolutionary opera was presented in vernacular Mandarin rather than the heretofore-used dialect of the upper class. Because Mandarin is a tonal language, this required changes in melody types. Xipi and erhuang aria styles were merged. Committees were put in charge of writing new arias and creating new aria types.

The four traditional character types were dissolved. New character types were divided into two categories: positive and negative. Elaborately painted faces that indicated personality and social class disappeared. Instead, positive characters were portrayed with warm, reddish make-up; negative characters wore colder, darker hues. Female characters were played by women. Costumes were simplified: peasants wore patched clothing; police and soldiers wore uniforms.

Staging became more elaborate with a focus on realism. Symbolic props and gestures mostly disappeared. Stylized dance movements were replaced by posed groups, which represented the struggles and rising power of the masses. As electrical grids became dependable, stage lighting became increasingly complex.

In addition to the traditional Chinese instruments used in Beijing opera, Jiang employed Western orchestral instruments. Why she did so is not clear. Some scholars contend that Jiang never liked traditional instruments; others suggest she was adhering to Mao's policy of "making foreign things serve China." In any case, Jiang clearly believed that the louder Western instruments sounded the revolutionary themes more forcefully. As in Western opera, a conductor now led the instrumentalists from an orchestra pit, thus diminishing the function of the gu shi.

Other Westernizations were the addition of an overture and the use of leitmotifs to unify the drama. Popular contemporary tunes, as well as "The Internationale" (an internationally recognized socialist anthem), were woven into several of the revamped operas. Performances were either free or available to the public at a low price.

Hong deng ji (The Red Lantern, 1964)

Hong deng ji performance, 1964.
Sovfoto/Universal Images Group/Getty Images.

Set during the Second Sino-Japanese War (1937–1945), *Hong deng ji* tells the stories of the railway worker Li Yu-he and his teenage daughter Tiemei. The two struggle on behalf of China against the Japanese invaders. As a Communist Party member, Li is assigned to transfer a secret code to guerrillas holding out in the mountains. Li is betrayed by spies, then captured and tortured by the Japanese. When he refuses to give up the code, he is killed. The task of delivering the code falls to Tiemei, who, against all odds, succeeds. In remembrance of her family's sacrifices, and with red flags flying, she joins the revolutionary army.

Tiemei's name, which means "iron-plum blossom," is symbolic. The hearty plum blossom blooms only in winter. Likewise, the iron-willed Tiemei matures to full beauty only under the bitter circumstances of loss and sacrifice. Tiemei served as a model of the youthful political devotion that Mao and Jiang cultivated during the Cultural Revolution.

LISTENING 8.3 GUIDE))) **"My Heart is Bursting with Anger," Scene 9, from *Hong deng ji***

Texture: Heterophonic and homophonic
Meter: Duple
(See @ 8.4 for a link to the full video)

Tiemei has seen her family members killed. She herself has barely escaped capture by Japanese spies. In the piercing voice characteristic of Jingju, she sings of her resolve to deliver the code to her comrades.

Tiemei reflects on what has happened. She unfolds each line separately and sings in taut nasal timbres. Orchestral interludes allow the audience time to digest the intensity of her passion. The melodic material is pentatonic. Rhythms are free.

0:05	Tíqǐ díkòu	When I think of my enemy . . .

Tiemei's fluttering hands reveal her nearly uncontrollable sadness. She quickly rallies, however, as percussion instruments—guban, gongs, and cymbals—sound her agitation.

0:15	Xīn fèi zhà	My heart and lungs are bursting . . .
0:44	Qiáng rěn chóuhén yǎosuí yá.	I keep the hatred inside me and in anger gnash my teeth.
1:08	Zéi Jiūshān qiānfāngbǎi jì bīqǔ mìdiànmǎ,	Jiushan [the Japanese chief of police] tried every possible way to get the code . . .
1:25	Jiāng wǒ nǎinai diēdiē lái qiāngshā.	My grandmother and father he has killed.

Each line begins slowly and freely. The last syllable of every phrase extends in a long melisma that emphasizes the word's power—"enemy," "bursting," "teeth," "code," and "killed." As Tiemei sings, the jinghu fiddles follow her lines heterophonically. Between the vocal lines, however, we hear a combination of Chinese and Western instruments—violins play in unison with jinghu; guban punctuates the drama.

In traditional Jingju, long pheasant feathers extended from the hats of female warrior characters. Gesturing with the feathers demonstrates anger or frustration. Tiemei gestures in a similar way, but with her long braid.

In the following section Tiemei's rage is portrayed by the extremely high vocal range. A steady rhythm begins and the pace quickens. The clapper articulates each word. Sentence after sentence, Tiemei's strength grows as she focuses her spirit. Only in the last lines does the extended melismatic characteristic of earlier lines return—now as she states her own name. Tiemei will defy her enemies.

1:45	Yǎozhù chóu, yǎozhù hèn,	Harbor the rage, harbor the hatred.
	jiáosuì chóuhèn qiáng yànxià,	These were forced down my throat.
	chóuhèn rù xīn yào fāyá,	Now they grow in my heart.
	bù kūqì, bù liúlèi,	No compromise! No hesitation!
	bùxǔ lèishuǐ sāibiān sǎ,	No tears on my cheeks.
	liúrù xīntián kāi huǒhuā	Instead, they flow inside and burst in my heart.
	Wànzhàng núhuǒ ránshāoqǐ,	The blaze of rage burns
	Yào bǎ hēidì hūntiān lái shāotā	So hard that sky and earth collapse.
	Tiě-méi wǒ, yǒu zhǔnbèi,	I, Tiemei, am prepared.
	bù pà zhuā, bù pà fang,	I don't fear capture! Don't fear exile!
	bù pà pí biān dǎ, bù pà jiānláo yā!	I don't fear lashing! Don't fear prison!
	Fěnshēnsuìgǔ bù jiāo mìdiànmǎ!	I won't turn in the code, even if my body is in pieces.
2:09	Zéi Jiūshān nǐ děngzhuó ba,	Jiushan, you wait,
	zhè jiùshì Tiě-méi gěi nǐ dì hǎo huídá!	this is the answer of Tiemei.

NIXON IN CHINA (1985–1988)

The opera *Nixon in China*, by American composer John Adams (b. 1947) and librettist Alice Goodman (b. 1958), tells the story of President Richard Nixon's 1972 visit to China where he met with Mao Zedong and other government officials. Act II includes a performance of one of the Yang Ban Xi. The opera's libretto is written in rhymed, metered couplets similar to Chinese theatrical styles; the music is **minimalist** in style.

QUESTIONS FOR THOUGHT

- With all of the changes made to Jingju during the Cultural Revolution, why do you think Jiang Qing still called the genre by its traditional name?

- Why would the new Revolutionary opera incorporate so many Western operatic conventions? Was there a symbolic message behind these appropriations?

ACTIVITIES AND ASSIGNMENTS

- **Watch *Farewell My Concubine*. Trace through the movie the political events that influenced the production of Beijing opera from 1924 to 1977.**

FOLK MUSIC

The term folksong (*Volkslied*) dates back to late 18th-century Germany. As originally coined, the term was said to represent music of the common people. Folk music was thought to have been communally composed, passed down orally from one generation to the next, and locally representative in its general aesthetic quality.

Notions of "folk" music evolved alongside growing sentiments of 19th-century nationalism. Collectors and composers saw this music as representing links to a rustic and idealized past. Thus, these varied styles, which tended to change considerably from one region to the next, were seen as vital source material for creating national music styles. Hungarian composer Béla Bartók collected music both to preserve it and to borrow ideas for his own compositions. British collector Cecil Sharp (1859–1924) scoured England and Appalachia in search of traditional melodies that might come to constitute a national style.

Bulgarian Concert Folk Music

A lad asks the pretty lass Dilmano to teach him how to plant his peppers. Push them deep into the soil and they will blossom, she answers. The dialog holds characteristics of **folksongs** found in many parts of the world—ordinary people striving to live in balance with both nature and their social world.

"Dilmono, Dilbero" is not a folksong in the traditional sense, however. Most folksongs are handed down orally over generations. This one was composed in the 1950s in "folk" style by Bulgarian musician Filip Koutev (1903–1982).

Bulgarian group performs at an international folk festival.

kpatyhka/
Shutterstock.com.

In times past, Bulgarian folk traditions often centered on love and courtship. Music and dance at traditional social events offered opportunities for introductions and close, but public, interaction. That was then. The 20th-century combination of technological innovation and modernization, of world wars and political totalitarianism, changed the social landscape. The village square no longer held the cultural currency it had in times past.

Folk music in this Southeast European republic was dying. Koutev sought to preserve the past by marrying it to the present. His idea was to rescue traditional music by bringing it into the concert hall. The new style would be called "Concert Folk Music," and he would write it.

But while Koutev drew from the folk imagination, his music was actually something altogether new. Regional differences of style were blurred; the harsh vocal timbres of earlier times were softened. Singers from villages across the country were trained together and formed into professional choirs. The goal was to create a unified "Bulgarian style." These so-called "authentic" folk ensembles would then sing their new songs in support of government policies.

In 1950–1951, Koutev established the National Folk Song and the Dance Ensemble Filip Koutev, an umbrella group that included a number of vocal and instrumental ensembles. In 1986, one of these groups, now working under a different director and known as Le Mystère des Voix Bulgares (The Mystery of the Bulgarian Voice), released to worldwide acclaim an album of the same name, *Le Mystère des Voix Bulgares*.

BULGARIAN FOLK MUSIC IN SPACE

In 1977, the Voyager I and II satellites were launched into space. They are now heading for two separate stars. Estimated time of arrival: 40,000 years. On board both crafts is the Voyager Golden Record, which includes messages in fifty-five languages, nature sounds, images, and music that portrays the diversity of life on Earth. On June 16, 1977, President Jimmy Carter said of the recording, "We cast this message into the cosmos . . . Of the 200 billion stars in the Milky Way galaxy, some—perhaps many—may have inhabited planets and space-faring civilizations. If one such civilization intercepts Voyager and can understand these recorded contents, here is our message: We are trying to survive our time so we may live into yours. We hope someday, having solved the problems we face, to join a community of Galactic Civilizations. This record represents our hope and our determination and our goodwill in a vast and awesome universe."

Among the ninety minutes of musical examples is a traditional Bulgarian folksong sung by Valya Balkanska from the Smolyan Province of Bulgaria.

"Dilmano, Dilbero" by Philip Koutev

LISTENING
8.4
GUIDE

Texture: Homophonic
Meter: Measures of eight and eleven beats
Form: Strophic

To the Western ear, perhaps the most striking aspect of this piece is its rhythm. Not only is the music fast, but also the accented pulse seems to constantly shift. Shift it certainly does, but in a highly ordered fashion consisting of two different patterns. The music opens with a rhythm consisting of eight quick pulses grouped in an accented pattern of 2–3–3 (heard twice). The second pattern, which begins with the line "Kazhi mi kak se sadi pipero," combines a group of eleven (combined into an accented pattern of 2–3–3–3) and the previous eight-pulses grouping (2–3–3).

We can hear both of these patterns articulated in the song's lyrics:

Dil	ma	no	Dil	be		ro

X x X x x X x x X x X x x X x x

| Ka | zhi | me | kak | se | sa | di | pi | pe | | ro |

X x X x x X x x X x x X x X x x x X x x

continued

Notice also the narrow vocal range and strident vocal style. The song's broad form is simple: Intro–A–A–B–Interlude–A–A–B. The A and B sections are further subdivided into individual phrases of aabb and ccdddd respectively. Perhaps all of these factors—dance rhythms, rough timbre, and simple form—contribute to the folksong-like quality that Koutev sought.

0:00	Instrumental introduction	
0:05	Dilmano dilbero, Dilmano, dilbero. Kazhi mi kak se sadi pipero. (2x)	Lovely Dilmano Teach me how to plant the peppers.
0:15	Dilmano dilbero, Dilmano, dilbero. Kazhi mi kak se sadi pipero. (2x)	Lovely Dilmano Teach me how to plant the peppers.
0:25	Da ts'fti da v'rzhe. Da ts'fti da v'rzhe, Da beresh beresh beresh kak sakash. (4x)	So they blossom and give fruit That one can have whenever one wants.
0:41	(Instrumental interlude)	
0:46	Pomuni go pobutsni go Eta kak se sadi sadi pipero (2x)	Put it in the soil and push. That's how you plant the pepper.
0:56	Pomuni go pobutsni go Eta kak se sadi sadi pipero (2x)	Put it in the soil and push. That's how you plant the pepper.
1:06	Da ts'fti da v'rzhe. Da ts'fti da v'rzhe Da beresh beresh beresh kak sakash	So they blossom and give fruit. (4x)

WOODY GUTHRIE (1912–1967) AND THE AMERICAN FOLK MUSIC REVIVAL

Rocked by the confluence of the Great Depression and the Great Dust Storm, 23-year-old Oklahoma native Woodrow Wilson (Woody) Guthrie left his wife and children and hopped a train for California. Like so many thousands of others, he went west seeking employment. What Guthrie found instead was music's power to affect social change. His songs championed the politically and economically disenfranchised, helped spur the labor movement, and served as a catalyst for the "American Folk Music Revival," which would include Pete Seeger (1919–2014), Odetta (1930–2008), Phil Ochs (1940–1976), Joan Baez (b. 1941), and Bob Dylan (b. 1941).

Guthrie's most famous song is "This Land is Your Land" (1940). Today we remember the song as an ode to the ideals of the American social contract. But the singer's tongue had a sharp edge when he sang about social injustice.

Woody Guthrie, March 8, 1943, New York World-Telegram and the Sun staff photographer.
Al Aumuller, Library of Congress Prints and Photographs Division.

Eurovision Song Contest

Over three evenings in May 2016, more than 200 million viewers tuned in to watch performers from twenty-six counties compete in the final rounds of the 61st annual Eurovision Song Contest, Europe's kitschy spectacle of pop music détente. Millions watched on television, but Eurovision's biggest devotees traveled to the contest site in Stockholm, Sweden. There they cheered on their favorites with a passion akin to English soccer fans. The winner was Ukraine representative Jamala, who performed (in English) the controversial song "1944," which appears to reference Soviet abuses against ethnic Tatars during World War II.

Started in 1956, the contest was conceived to help encourage national cooperation and offer a friendly musical competition between recent war-torn adversaries. The idea was to rise above politics, though that goal has often fallen short. Winners are decided by voting, but countries tend to vote for their allies. There have been accusations of international bribery as well.

As for the stage performances, sequins and light shows are requisite. Gay camp is certain to win fans but not necessarily votes (although the bearded Austrian drag queen Conchita Wurst won the 2014 contest). Eighteen-year-old Jaimie-Lee Kriewitz, Germany's popular 2016 entrant, sported an outfit inspired by Japanese comic book art.

Winning performers generally become stars across Europe, but few ever crack the American market. The exceptions include ABBA, which won for Sweden in 1974 with the song "Waterloo," and the French Canadian singer Celine Dion, who won for Switzerland in 1988 with the song, "Ne Partez Pas Sans Moi" ("Don't Leave Without Me").

Beethoven's Ninth Symphony (1824): Politics and Beyond

On Christmas day 1989, Germany was aglow in newfound hope. The hated Berlin Wall, which since 1961 had divided the city into East and West, had recently fallen. After nearly thirty years of forced separation, families were reunited. To celebrate this remarkable event, American conductor Leonard Bernstein led an international ensemble of musicians in a performance of Beethoven's Symphony No. 9 in D minor. @ 8.6

The symphony is a monumental composition, nothing less than a musical telling of the soul's journey from darkness to light. Perhaps the work's most extraordinary feature occurs in the final movement, where Beethoven introduces the human voice into the symphonic genre by setting Friedrich Schiller's poem "An die freude" ("Ode to Joy").

Think no more of sorrow, intones the baritone soloist as he introduces the poem:

> Freunde, nicht diese Töne!
> Sondern lasst uns angenehmere
> Anstimmen, und freudenvollere.
>   Freude!

> O friends, not these notes!
> Rather let us take up something more
> Pleasant, and more joyful.
>   Joy!

An exuberant chorus listens on, then almost shouts back:

> Freude!

> Joy!

For the Berlin celebration, Bernstein changed one word in Schiller's text—"Freude" became "Freiheit" (freedom). The concert was televised live in twenty countries to more than 100 million viewers. On that day, freedom sounded around the world.

Universal brotherhood is the central theme of the Ninth Symphony. Setting this lofty ideal to music proved no easy task. Beethoven made over 200 drafts of the "Ode to Joy" tune alone. The symphony took over eight years to complete.

Beethoven was German, of course, but no single nation or political movement can claim ownership of this great piece. Just months earlier, Chinese students had played the music during their fearless demonstrations in Beijing's Tiananmen Square. The symphony was performed repeatedly in memorials held in the aftermath of 9/11.

"Everything will pass, and the world will perish but the Ninth Symphony will remain."
—Michael Bakunin, 19th-century Russian revolutionary

LUDWIG VAN BEETHOVEN (1770–1827)

Ludwig van Beethoven.

German composer Ludwig van Beethoven lived by the principles of the Enlightenment, the late 18th-century intellectual movement that produced the ideals of rationality, political freedom, and personal liberty. His philosophy was directly reflected in his music, which was grander yet more introspective, more heroic yet more abstract, than anything written previously in the Western tradition. Such was the originality of his work that it took generations for composers and audiences alike to digest its implications.

Little came easily for Beethoven, who often struggled to compose. His sketchbooks reveal years of working out even a single theme. While still a young man, Beethoven began to lose his hearing. So devastating was the realization that he contemplated suicide. Happily for posterity, he carried on and gave musical voice to the struggle within. Many of his compositions were written after he was completely deaf.

Beethoven was a prolific composer. He wrote one opera, nine symphonies, five piano concertos, sixteen string quartets, thirty-two piano sonatas, ten violin sonatas, marches, songs, variations and many other works. His use of chromatic harmonies and expanded forms pushed the limits of the Classical style and ushered in the Romantic period. Upon his death, over 10,000 people lined the streets of Vienna to witness the funeral procession.

Repressionist regimes have also claimed Beethoven. Soviet leadership praised the composer for having given voice to the ideals and aspirations of the proletariat. A 1937 birthday party for Adolf Hitler included a Berlin Philharmonic performance of the Ninth Symphony. In 1974, the white minority rulers of Rhodesia (now Zimbabwe) set new words to the "Ode" melody for their new national anthem, "Rise O Voices of Rhodesia."

The idea of individual freedom dominated Beethoven's intellectual life. These interests came to the musical forefront in two other major compositions from the early 1800s: his Symphony No. 3 in E flat major (1804) and the opera *Fidelio* (1805). Both made political statements, though arguably both focused most strongly on inner psychological victories. As for Symphony No. 3, Beethoven originally subtitled it "Bonaparte," after Napoleon Bonaparte, the French general and people's champion. But when Napoleon proclaimed himself Emperor and invaded Austria, Beethoven was infuriated. He took a knife to the original inscription and renamed the work *Sinfonia eroica* (*Heroic Symphony*). Beethoven's opera *Fidelio* was no less idealistic. It tells the story of the political prisoner Florestan and his wife Leonore, who is willing to sacrifice her own life to save his.

LISTENING
8.5
GUIDE

Fourth movement (excerpt) from Symphony No. 9 in D minor, op. 125, by Ludwig van Beethoven

Texture: Complex homophony
Meter: Quadruple and Duple

0:00	Drum roll and agitated winds announce a short-lived "Fanfare of Terror."
0:08	As the sounds die away, the basses enter with a sturdy speech-like melody (0:11), as if they were "singing" an operatic **recitative**. This reference to a vocal genre in a symphony would have sounded odd to Beethoven's audience, but it also prepared them for the true vocal section to come.

0:21	"Fanfare of Terror" interrupts.
0:31	Once again, the basses enter. Changing instruments and timbres seem to flip the emotional mood back and forth between darkness and light.
0:40	Something very strange happens. Beethoven inserts musical material from the first movement. Emotionally for the listener, it feels as if one is reviewing and re-assimilating earlier life events. This innovative "cyclical" approach to symphonic composition would be used by later composers.
0:52	The bass recitative returns. It begins to feel as if the basses are taking us on a journey through life's tribulations.
1:13	Musical material from the second movement is introduced.
1:18	The bass recitative returns.
1:34	Musical material from the third movement is introduced.
1:44	The basses engage in dialogue with material from movement three.
2:05	A first brief sounding of the "Ode to Joy" in the winds. Bass interruptions continue.
2:37	Now the basses take up the "Ode." Beethoven writes three variations on the theme. The texture in each variation gets thicker as more instruments are added. Notice that the form of the "Ode" is ABB (subdivided as: aa¹ ba¹ ba¹).
3:19	Variation 1: theme in the viola section. Bassoon, cellos and basses play a countermelody.
4:03	Variation 2: theme in first violins. Second violins and basses provide a countermelody.
4:46	Variation 3: full orchestra. Theme is in the brass and woodwinds.
5:29	Transitional material based on "Ode" theme.
6:10	The "Fanfare of Terror" returns. It feels as if the movement has begun anew. This time, however, the string bass recitative is replaced by the human voice.
6:18	Beethoven's words introduce the poem:

Freunde, nicht diese Töne! / O friends, not these notes!
Sondern lasst uns angenehmere / Rather let us take up something more
Anstimmen, und freudenvollere. / Pleasant, and more joyful.
Freude! / Joy!

| 7:06 | The chorus echoes: |

Freude! / Joy!

| 7:10 | Baritone continues with the "Ode to Joy" theme. Winds add countermelodies. |

Freude, schöner Götterfunken / Joy, lovely divine light,
Tochter aus Elysium / Daughter of Elysium
Wir betreten feuertrunken, / We march, drunk with fire,
Himmlische, dein Heiligtum. / Holy One, to thy holy kingdom.
Deine Zauber binden wieder, / Thy magic binds together
Was die Mode streng geteilt; / What tradition has strongly parted,
Alle Menschen werden Brüder, / All men will be brothers
Wo dein sanfter Flügel weilt. / Dwelling under the safety of your wings.

| 7:37 | The chorus repeats the last four lines of the stanza. |
| 7:56 | Vocal quartet sings the "Ode" theme. |

Wem der grosse Wurf gelungen, / He who has had the great pleasure
Eines Freundes Freund zu sein / To be a true friend to a friend,
Wer ein holdes Weib errungen, / He who has a noble wife
Mische seinen Jubel ein! / Let him join our mighty song of rejoicing!
Ja – wer auch nur eine Seele / Yes, if there is a solitary soul
Sein nennt auf' dem Erdenrund! / In the entire world which claims him

continued

	Und wer's nie gekonnt, der stehle	If he rejects it, then let him steal away
	Weinend sich aus diesem Bund.	Weeping out of this comradeship.
8:22	Chorus, repeats the last four lines.	
8:42	Quartet sings:	
	Freude trinken alle Wesen	All beings drink in joy
	An den Brüsten der Natur;	From nature's breasts.
	Alle Guten, alle Bösen	All good and evil things
	Folgen ihrer Rosenspur.	Follow her rose-strewn path.
	Küsse gab sie uns und Reben	She gives us kisses and grapes,
	Einen Freund, geprüft im Tod;	A friend, tested unto death,
	Wollust ward dem Wurm gegeben,	Pleasure is given even to the worm
	Und der Cherub steht vor Gott.	And the cherubim stand before God.
9:09	Chorus repeats the last four lines of this section, emphasizing "vor Gott."	
9:49	Following a dramatic pause after the climax on the word "God," the bassoon plays single tones, then is joined by other woodwinds in yet another version of the "Ode." This section is known as the Turkish march, so termed because of the addition of percussion instruments associated with Turkish Janissary (military) bands: triangle, cymbals, and bass drum. Perhaps this was Beethoven's way of broadening the cultural palate of his musical testament of brotherly love.	
10: 18	(fade out)	

NY PHILHARMONIC IN NORTH KOREA, 2008

On February 26, 2008, the New York Philharmonic became the first major American orchestra to play in North Korea. The concert, which was broadcast to some 200 million listeners around the world, came during a stand-off in the nuclear negotiations taking place between North Korea and the United States. Concert proponents hoped the event would inspire a softening in diplomatic relationships. Opponents, meanwhile, felt it inappropriate for an American orchestra to play for an immoral regime.

The program bridged cultures East and West. Featured was music of American composer George Gershwin, the "New World" symphony by Czech composer Antonín Dvořák, and an arrangement of the Korean folksong "Arirang." Tears flowed at concert's end as audience and musicians, unwilling to leave their respective places, waved goodbye to one another.

QUESTIONS FOR THOUGHT

- How is it that Beethoven's Symphony No. 9 can appeal to such diverse political agendas? Might this pose a problem for listeners with different national allegiances?
- Some think that Beethoven's "Ode to Joy" theme sounds like a folksong. Why might this be so?

ACTIVITIES AND ASSIGNMENTS

- The formal structure of the last movement of Beethoven's Ninth has been debated; how might you describe or diagram the form of the excerpt above?
- Investigate how film director Stanley Kubrick (1928–1999) uses Beethoven's Ninth Symphony during the "aversion therapy" scene in *A Clockwork Orange* (1971). How does the particular performance that Kubrick chose affect the drama?
- Find other political or cultural references to Beethoven's Ninth.

THE ENIGMA OF SHOSTAKOVICH

Russian-born composer Dmitri Shostakovich (1906–1975) was recognized as a "true son of the Communist Party." His second symphony commemorates the tenth anniversary of the October 1917 Bolshevik Revolution; his eleventh (subtitled "The Year 1905") commemorates the Russian Revolution of that year. He wrote music for propaganda films and served on various Soviet committees. For his support, the Party gave him a summer home.

But his relationship with the Soviet authorities was often troubled. He was variously denounced as an ideologically unsuitable composer. The Soviet newspaper *Pravda* condemned his 1934 opera *Lady Macbeth of the Mtsensk District* as being immoral; it was temporarily withdrawn from the repertory. Other works were censored as well. Political friction also cost Shostakovich his teaching position at the Leningrad Conservatory.

Who was this man, a loyal Soviet or political dissident? The answer may be "both." While some aspects of Soviet ideology appealed to Shostakovich, others did not.

The Zapatista Movement

On January 1, 1994, the same day that the North American Free Trade Agreement (NAFTA) went into effect, the revolutionary Zapatista Army of National Liberation (EZLN) mobilized in Chiapas, one of Mexico's poorest states. The EZLN claimed that NAFTA would take from the poor and give to the rich, that NAFTA was little more than a "death certificate" to Mexico's indigenous peoples.

In protest, EZLN militia took over towns and produced demands for dialog with government leaders. They sought neither power nor independence, but equality in representation. Also, they sought payment to the Mayan people for the natural resources that NAFTA would take from their land.

The movement was led by Subcomandante Marcos, an articulate and cagey politician who used the media and internet to take EZLN's philosophy to the world. In Chiapas, Marcos worked for the needs of the Mayan underclass. His broader goal moved beyond ethnicity or national boundaries, however. Hoping to speak for all oppressed peoples, he once told a journalist:

The flag of the Zapatista Army of National Liberation (EZLN) in San Cristobal de las Casa, Chiapas state, Mexico, 2012.
AFP/Getty Images.

Marcos is gay in San Francisco, black in South Africa, an Asian in Europe, a Chicano in San Ysidro, an anarchist in Spain, a Palestinian in Israel, a Mayan in the streets of San Cristóbal, a Jew in Germany, a Gypsy in Poland, a Mohawk in Quebec, a pacifist in Bosnia, a single woman on the Metro at 10 p.m., a peasant without land, a gang member in the slums, an unemployed worker, an unhappy student and, of course, a Zapatista in the mountains.

The EZLN armed revolution was quickly subdued by the Mexican army. Politically, however, the movement remained active for about twenty years. Traditional Mayan clothing, food, and language became associated with political resistance and solidarity.

Music also played a role. Songbooks, not unlike those once used by political parties in the United States, were distributed. One-hundred-year-old songs about Emiliano Zapata (1879–1919), hero of the 1910 Mexican Revolution, returned to the **mariachi** repertoire. Mayan culture came to symbolize the struggle to maintain ethnic traditions in a globalizing world.

EZLN also inspired musical responses abroad. In France, the political singer Renaud recorded the song "Adios Zapata," which remembers the deeds of Zapata, Pancho Villa (1878–1923), and Che Guevara (1928–1967). In Los Angeles, the punk rock band Rage Against the Machine recorded "Zapata's Blood" (1997) and "People of the Sun" (1996), which seem to promote the idea of armed resistance.

But violence was not part of Subcomandante Marcos's vision. Marcos fought his revolution with ideas, not blood. He found unity in diversity. He fought for the freedom to be different.

EZLN's musical anthem is the *corrido* "El Himno Zapatista." Corridos are narrative songs (traditionally in triple meter) that are often sung in times of political upheaval. Many were written during the Emiliano Zapata-led Mexican Revolution (1910–1920). More were written in Chiapas in support of the Zapatista movement. @ 8.7

"El Himno Zapatista" neatly bridges the gap between the Mexican Revolution and the struggle in Chiapas. The song borrows its melody from "Con Mi 30 30," a corrido that inspired revolutionary soldiers in 1910. The lyrics are new so as to fit current times. Many versions of the song are currently circulating on the internet. Lyrics vary slightly from one performance to the next.

ACTIVITIES AND ASSIGNMENTS

- Investigate how music is currently used as a tool in political campaigns, social movements, and expressions of nationality.

- Research the music of various 20th-century North America political movements, such as suffrage, the labor movement, the Civil Rights Movement.

- Take a few minutes to reflect on the idea of nation. What would the ideal nation be like? How would its music sound?

Conclusion

"Man is by nature a political animal."
—Aristotle

In this chapter we focused on music in relation to the modern nation-state. One can define politics more broadly, however. Political action includes any competition for social power between distinct interest groups or individuals. Seen from this perspective, we can speak of ethnic politics, gender politics, religious politics, and so on. Often these categories are interwoven one with the other.

To the extent that musicians strive to engage and influence socially, their art is political by nature. Ultimately, however, music's meaning resides in the mind of the listener. The same sounds that bind and empower one group might work to alienate and disenfranchise another. Hendrix's performance of "The Star-Spangled Banner" can alternately be interpreted as unpatriotic or a quintessential expression of civil liberty. Beethoven intended his Ninth Symphony to help usher in an era of universal brotherhood, but the music has also been appropriated to forward the agendas of oppressive regimes around the world.

Whenever you listen, think about music's power to persuade. Musicians and audiences, the record industry and governments, indeed all individuals and institutions are motivated by ever-shifting combinations of self and social interest. Listen thoughtfully and you are sure to hear the political nuances.

Key Terms

- chou
- corrido
- Cultural Revolution
- dan
- folksong
- gu shi
- guban
- jing
- jinghu
- Jingju
- mariachi
- The Mighty Five
- nationalism
- pizzicato
- program music
- recitative
- sheng
- symphonic poem
- Yang Ban Xi

Essay Questions

- How might the performance of a national anthem simultaneously unify and divide?
- Is national music different from ethnic music?
- Can you sing three national anthems that were not discussed in this chapter? What does your answer suggest about your relationship with the world?

CHAPTER GOALS

- To explore the ways music supports, protests, mourns, and remembers war.
- To understand how music reflects human responses to war and/or conflict.

CHAPTER NINE

Music and War

QUESTIONS FOR THOUGHT
• How does music impact war? How does war impact music?
• How might music imitate the sounds of war?
• Call to mind a war-related song that you know. Does it present a particular point of view? Is it persuasive?

Released in 2005, the album *Live from Iraq* reveals war from the soldiers' standpoint. Songs are about survival and fear, sacrifice and loss. The group's music is Kevlar tough. Absent is the glossy sexuality and tough-guy posing of so much music produced stateside. Instead we hear about the trauma of war, real war. Production is basic; in-the-trenches authenticity trumps packaging.

A body of music has sprung up in response to the Iraq War. During the buildup and early months of the 2003 invasion, songwriters dug in their heels with hard and generally unnuanced positions either in support of, or opposition to, the conflict. Country music star Toby Keith's (b. 1961) "Courtesy of the Red, White and Blue (The Angry American)," for example, spoke for a public blindly lashing out for revenge in the aftermath of the September 11, 2001 attacks on the World Trade Center and elsewhere. A voice of restraint was British punk-rocker-turned-folksinger Billy Bragg (b. 1957). In "The Price of Oil," Bragg saw the opportunistic hand of global economics as the real incentive for war. @ 9.1

> "And there is no reimbursement for the price that we pay."
> —"Live from Iraq" by 4th25 (pronounced Fourth Quarter)

Music and War

For thousands of years, music and war have gone hand in hand. A reference in the Old Testament (Judges 7) cites Gideon's men blowing three hundred *shofarot* (rams' horns) as they marched into battle. Roman legions employed similar instruments. Centuries later, European armies would add drums and **natural trumpets** to their musical arsenal.

Always, military music has flowed back and forth between fields of combat and general culture. Beginning in 1095 and lasting for over 300 hundred years, European Christians undertook a series of crusades into the Middle East. The early ventures were designed to recapture the Holy Land from Muslim rule; later projects sought to halt the Ottoman (Turkish) Empire's encroachment into Europe. The wars inspired new repertories of music, including pilgrims'

You get more than he does
WHAT ARE YOU DOING WITH THE DIFFERENCE?
PAY OFF!
BUY
WAR SAVINGS CERTIFICATES
buy as many as you can afford

World War I poster, ca. 1917.
Courtesy of The Metropolitan Museum of Art, Gift of William C. Moore, 1972.

songs, **planctus** (laments), and rallying cries. One military-inspired melody from the 15th century, "L'homme armé" ("The Armed Man"), was embedded into more than forty settings of the Catholic Mass.

In the 16th century, composers cultivated a programmatic genre of vocal and instrumental battle works. These compositions typically included military fanfares. Singers were given onomatopoeic figures such as "ta-ri-ra-ri-ra-ri-ra-ri" or "pa-ti-pa-toc-pa-ti-pa-toc" to represent the chaos of combat.

The best known of these battle pieces was the **chanson** "La guerre" (1528) ("The War") by French composer Clement Janequin (ca.1485–after 1558). So popular was this piece that it inspired not only a series of instrumental battle compositions but even **battle masses.**

"La guerre" commemorates the French victory over the Swiss controlled Duchy of Milan (Italy) at the Battle of Marignano (1515). The battle marked a victory for modern warfare (artillery and cannons) over the Swiss pike (long spear) and sword. Casualties were high: twenty-eight hours of combat left over 16,000 dead.

"La guerre" includes the earliest known musical examples of military battle calls (trumpet and drum signals that instructed soldiers to advance, retreat, or perform maneuvers). Interspersed and sung within Janequin's text and melody are five calls:
@ 9.2

- *Alarm*: short–long, short–long (either a single pitch or "mi-sol, mi-sol")
- *To the Standard*: short–short–short–short–long ("fa–do–do–do–do")
- *Advance*: long–short–long–short–long (a single pitch)
- *Boots and Saddles*: even notes ("do–sol–sol–sol")
- *To the Horse*: short–short–long (a single pitch)

Late 17th-century natural trumpet.

Courtesy of The Metropolitan Museum of Art, The Crosby Brown Collection of Musical Instruments, 1889.

German side drum, 1694–1733.

Courtesy of The Metropolitan Museum of Art, Gift of William H. Riggs, 1913.

Standard Bearer and Drummer, Sebald Beham, 1544.

Courtesy of The Metropolitan Museum of Art, Gift of Felix M. Warburg and his family, 1941.

Thirty years after Janequin's original four-voice version of "La guerre," another Renaissance composer, Phillippe Verdelot (ca. 1480–ca. 1530) added a fifth voice. It is this five-voice version that is commonly performed today, and to which we now turn.

"La guerre," by Clement Janequin (Philippe Verdelot, fifth voice)

LISTENING 9.1 GUIDE

Texture: Polyphonic
Meter: Duple and triple
Form: Two parts, each through composed

Prima pars (First part)

Janequin calls his fellow Frenchmen to listen to the story of Marignano. As was typical of the period's style, most of the words are lost in the dense polyphonic tangle of voices. Nevertheless, one can clearly hear the initial exhortation, "Escoutez" (Listen).

Quickly repeating tones and syllables mimic the beating of drums and the chaos of combat. (Sung battle calls are indicated in bold type.)

0:00	Escoutez tous, gentilz Galloys, La victoire du noble roi Francoys	Listen, all gentlemen of France To the victory of the noble King Francis.
0:31	Et orrez, si bien escoutez, Des coups ruèz de touts costés. Phifres soufflez. Frappez tambours, Tournez, virez. Faittes vos tours, Phifres soufflez battez tousjours	You will hear, if you listen, Blows thudding on all sides. Fifes resound. Beat the drums, Turn and wheel. Perform your maneuvers, Fifes resound, continue to battle.

Here the meter changes from duple to triple meter to provide contrast. Composers of the time often employed metric and textural changes as a way to give their music a tangible sense of form. In the following century, composers would develop this device by writing distinct stand-alone movements.

1:03	Avanturiers, bons compagnons, Ensemble croisez vos bastons. Bendez soudain, gentils Gascons, Haquebusjers, faittes vos sons. Nobles, sautez dans les arçons, Armes bouclez, frisques et mignons.	Adventurers, good country men, Together cross your staves Bend the bow, noble Gascons Riflemen make your sound Noblemen leap into your saddles, Don your arms, gentlemen and servants.
1:24	La lance au poing hardis et promptz Donnez dedans, grincez les dents Soyez hardiz, en joye mis.	Lance in hand and ready Strike them, grit your teeth Be bold and joyful.
1:36	**Alarme, alarme.**	Alarm, alarm.

The chanson then returns to duple meter. The texture thins and we hear clearly, "Let each urge himself on," set to a gently descending motive that repeats several times.

1:40	Chascun s'assaisonne, La fleur de lys. Fleur de haut pris, Y est en personne.	Let each urge himself on, The fleurs de lys. The noble prize, Is there in person (i.e. the King of France).

Here both duple and triple meter sound against one another in different voices.

2:09	Poulsez faucons et gros canons Pour faire bresche aux compagnons Et mettre à mort ces Bourguignons, Sonnez trompettes et clairons.	Let small and great cannons thunder To make of the Brescians And put to death these Burgundians Sound trumpets and bugles.

The *prima pars* ends in triple meter on a strong cadence at 2:30.

continued

Secunda pars (Second part)

Onomatopoeic battle sounds, using both **vocables** and actual words, dominate the second part. Here the text is even harder to follow than before; battle sounds come and go, covering up actual phrases. The resulting musical chaos pictures the melee of battle.

Janequin initially writes a fanfare using **articulation syllables** (used when learning to play the trumpet), then four military calls. Due to the thick polyphonic texture, however, the calls are nearly impossible to hear. Perhaps Janequin is duplicating the confusion of battle; perhaps he simply preferred to obscure his clever references. It is worth noting that these same calls appear 100 years later in trumpet instruction manuals. The fact that Janequin incorporates them indicates the existence of remarkably similar calls long before existing written documentation.

2:37	Fan frere le le lan fan	(Trumpet articulation syllables)
	Boutez selle.	Mount your horses
	A l'estandart	To the standard
	Tost avant	Everyone advance
	Gens de'armes **á cheval**	Men of arms, to [your] mount
	Farirarirariron	(battle sounds)
	Tost **à l'estandart**	Everyone to the standard
	Frere le le lan fan	(Trumpet articulation syllables)

The meter changes from duple to triple; pairs of voices answer each other for "fire and thunder."

3:40	Bruyez, tonnez	Fire, thunder
	Bruyez bombardes et faucons	Fire the bombards and cannons

The meter then slips back to duple.

3:55	Pour entrer sur ces Bourguignons.	To destroy these Burgundians.
4:01	Teu teu teu pedou pedou . . .	(battle sounds)
4:13	Rendes-vous Bourguignons	Rendezvous Burgundians
	Sortez du lieu, sortez, vuidez.	Leave, get out and be gone.
	Ne vous faittes plus canonner,	No longer use the cannon,
4:21	La place fault abandoner	Abandon the place.
	Tarirarira . . . la la la . . . Pon pon pon . . .	(battle sounds)
4:53	Courage, France. Donnez des horions	Courage, France. Strike your blows
	Chippe choppe, torche lorgne!	Chip, chop, well done, look!
	Zin zin patipatac . . .	(battle sounds)
5:10	A mort à mort . . .	To the death, to the death
	Frappez, batez, ruez, tuez	Strike, beat, lash out, kill
	Serre, France, tarirarira . . .	Close ranks, France (battle sounds)
5:26	Courage.	Courage.
	Donnez dedans, grincez les dents	Strike them, grit your teeth
	Fers esmolus, choquez dessus,	Sharpened swords, strike [them] down
	France, courage, ils sont en fuyte,	Courage France, they are in flight
	Ils montrent les talons, courage compagnons	They show their heels, courage companion
	Donnez des horions,	Give blows,
	tuez ces Bourguignons.	Kill these Burgundians.
	Ils sont confus, ils sont perdus,	They are confused, they are lost
	Prenez courage, après, après suyvez de près,	Take courage, after them, after them, follow them closely.
6:07	Victoire au grand roy des Françoys.	Victory to the great King of the French.

JANISSARY BANDS

Turkish military bands (*Mehterân*, known in the West as Janissary bands) were known for their colorful uniforms and shrill, penetrating sound. They made their mark in Europe during the 17th and 18th centuries in Ottoman Empire wars. Western art music composers such as Haydn, Mozart, and Beethoven invoked the "exotic" by using Turkish sounding instruments (large drums, bells, cymbals) in their compositions.

European military bands greatly increased their ranks by adding Turkish percussion instruments. By the late 18th century, Western military bands were employing "Moorish" percussionists (in this context meaning dark-skinned) dressed in "Eastern" style clothing and using extravagant drumming gestures. A similar look and sounds would be in vogue in the United States at the time of the Civil War. The modern-day marching band, with its military style uniforms and precision drills, traces its origins directly to these Turkish-influenced military bands.

Sounds would continue to transfer from battlefield to concert hall. Three centuries later, in his Symphony No. 9 (Chapter 8: Music and Nation), Beethoven incorporated the cymbals and triangles of Turkish Janissary bands. Half a century after that, Tchaikovsky asked for real cannons in his rousing *1812 Overture* (1880).

America's most famous soldier/composer was "The March King," John Philip Sousa (1854–1932), who directed (and wrote for) the United States Marine Band from 1880 to 1892. Upon leaving the Marines, Sousa formed a civilian band that toured the nation and the world for thirty-nine years. The Sousa Band became an American institution.

Sousa's most popular composition is "The Stars and Stripes Forever," written on Christmas Day, 1896. From that day forward, the Sousa Band performed the piece at nearly every concert until the composer's death. A 1987 act of Congress made "The Stars and Stripes Forever" the National March of the United States.

In the pages that follow, we will study relationships between music and war in a variety of settings. We begin with the Vietnam War (1959–1975), then backtrack in time to the 1800s to study the American Civil War (1861–1865) and the Native American **Ghost Dance**. After the Ghost Dance, we investigate Eastern European Jewish culture enduring under the shadow of the Holocaust. Finally, we turn to the remembrance of war by studying a trio of 20th-century concert pieces, which in turn celebrate life, honor the dead, and represent war's inestimable horrors.

MUSIC AS A WEAPON

"Acoustic bombardment" is the term military officials now use for the practice of using music to disorient, traumatize, and psychologically wear down enemy combatants. The principle is simple—just like the horns at the gates of ancient Jericho, only a lot louder. In Iraq, in the days leading up to the 2004 invasion of Fallujah, soldiers strapped giant speakers to the roofs of their Humvees, then blasted heavy metal music into the city. The practice has been used time and again.

"Almost anything you do that demonstrates your omnipotence or lack of fear helps break the enemy down," Lt. Col. Dan Kuehl told the *St. Petersburg (FL) Times* in 2004. "Soldiers play the stuff they like, of course. Music that gets them pumped up, songs like AC/DC's 'Hell's Bells.'"

The battlefield is not the only use of musical weaponry. The BBC, *Time* magazine, the *New York Times*, and other sources reported instances of blaring music being used to "soften" prisoners held in Iraq and Guantanamo Bay. Often the music, which ranged from Metallica's "Enter Sandman" to Barney the Purple Dinosaur's "I Love You," was accompanied by sleep deprivation, solitary confinement, extremes of heat and cold, and other tactics.

The Vietnam War, 1959–1975

The 1960s was a time of great turbulence. The Berlin Wall, the most visible sign of the Cold War in Europe, was built in 1961; the following year, the United States was brought to the brink of nuclear war during the Cuban Missile Crisis. The Civil Rights Movement was in full swing at home while, on the far side of the world, war was devastating Vietnam.

Musicians expressed opinions about all of these events. Through their songs, they hoped to heighten awareness and influence others. Folk singer Joan Baez took an active role in both the Civil Rights Movement and the anti-war movement. Bob Dylan, who never wanted to be associated with any "movement," nevertheless recorded a number of socially provocative songs in 1963/64, including: "Blowin' in the Wind," "Masters of War," "A Hard Rain's a-Gonna Fall," "Talking World War III Blues," And "The Times They Are a-Changin'."

It was not until 1965, a year of dramatic American troop escalation, that rock 'n' roll musicians began to write about the Vietnam War. The first important endeavor was "Eve of Destruction," by the gravelly voiced Barry McGuire. The biblically nuanced folk-rock anthem blasted social injustice from Selma, Alabama to the jungles of Vietnam. So controversial was the song's political message that ABC-affiliate radio stations refused to play it. Even so, "Eve of Destruction," with its awkward five-line verse and clumsy rhyme schemes, went to No. 1 on the Billboard pop charts.

Despite his commercial success, McGuire did not speak for the majority of Americans, at least not in 1965. A musical skirmish of sorts ensued when The Spokesmen released "Dawn of Correction." The song borrowed McGuire's melody, added a bouncy country-and-western-style **Jew's harp** accompaniment, and tightened the song's formal structure. The lyrics of "Dawn of Correction" advanced the Domino Theory, which hypothesized that should South Vietnam fall to Communism, so would the rest of Asia and then the world, just like a neat line of tumbling dominoes.

"Dawn of Correction" was not commercially successful. Nor did it manage to engage the national consciousness. That, however, did not mean that pro-military music was out of step with the nation. In fact, the most formally disciplined and commercially successful of all the Vietnam War-related songs was Staff Sergeant Barry Sadler's 1966 "Ballad of the Green Berets," which featured a resolute drum cadence and taut orchestration. Sadler's voice had the simultaneously confident and humble tone of a man accustomed to giving and following orders. A male chorus singing behind Sadler suggested the strict code of military comradeship.

Adding to the song's appeal was Sadler's personal history. Not only was he himself a Green Beret, but he had served as a medic in Vietnam where he won the Purple Heart, an honor awarded to those wounded or killed in action. The song sold two million copies in just five weeks, nine million copies over all. It was the best-selling single of 1966, beating out everyone from The Beatles to Frank Sinatra. The song was subsequently featured in the 1968 movie *The Green Berets*, starring John Wayne (1907–1979).

Contrast Sadler's neatly polished ballad with a piece by singer/songwriter Joe McDonald, leader of the San Francisco-based band Country Joe and the Fish. The group's most memorable song was also the decade's most sardonic anti-war contribution, a taunting jug-band parody titled "I-Feel-Like-I'm-Fixin'-to-Die Rag" (1967). Cheery apocalyptic lyrics inviting young men to put down their books and pick up guns are supported by a tooting kazoo and a grab-bag of musical clichés.

THE VIETNAM WAR

The Vietnam War lasted from 1959 to April 30, 1975. Until that point, it was the longest military conflict in U.S. history. Officially, it was a civil war between Communist (the Vietcong) and non-Communist Vietnamese. Seen more broadly, however, it was a cold-war fight that indirectly pitted the United States against the Soviet Union and the People's Republic of China. In spite of the fact that some seven million people died, Congress never officially declared war on North Vietnam. The fighting remained a "police action" until the fall of Saigon and American withdrawal.

"Ballad of the Green Berets," by Robin Moore and Staff Sgt. Barry Sadler

Texture: Homophonic
Meter: Quadruple
Form: Strophic

Few ballads tell grander stories than this one of service, death, and figurative rebirth. At song's opening we are introduced to the "brave men of the Green Beret." Soon, a wife receives the news that her husband has died in combat. His last request? That the tradition continue. She must make sure that son follows father and becomes a Green Beret.

The song's production quality is unsophisticated but highly effective, a model of musical economy. A precise snare drum cadence, suitable for marching, highlights the soldierly ideals of austerity and resolve. Utilitarian harmonies sound in the background. The lyrics are set strophically in simple AABB rhymes and follow (with slight variations) the same rhythmic scheme: short, short, long . . . /short, short, short, long. Each stanza is eight measures in duration. Images are strong and direct: "fighting soldiers," "fearless men," "men who mean just what they say," "brave men," and of course, men who die serving their country.

0:00		Drum cadence and simple harmonies

0:07	Stanza A	"Fighting soldiers . . . "

Sadler enters with the first stanza. The melodic range is relatively wide (an octave and one-half), but there is a sense that Sadler is talking more than singing.

0:28	Stanza B	"Silver wings . . . "

With each stanza that follows, the orchestration gets thicker and louder as the music moves toward a final climax. Listen to the bass as it enters to provide a strong foundation.

0: 51	Stanza C	"Trained to live . . . "

A men's choir enters in this stanza singing a wordless countermelody. Perhaps they symbolize the anonymity of common soldiers supporting one another.

1:14	Stanza B	"Silver wings . . . "

Sadler continues his story. The choir continues its wordless countermelody.

1:37	Stanza D	"Back at home . . . "

The choir joins Sadler with the lyrics. An organ—an obvious symbol of death, church, and community—enters to support the harmony. Small trumpet fanfares punctuate the tale.

1:59	Stanza E	"Put silver wings . . . "

The fanfares become more prominent.

Despite young people's obvious stake in the war's progress, mainstream popular musicians produced comparatively little protest music. The Temptations recorded "Ball of Confusion" (1970) and Edwin Starr recorded "War" (1970), both for Motown Records. Jamaican reggae star Jimmy Cliff recorded "Viet Nam" (1971). That same year the Beach Boys somehow wedged "Student Demonstration Time" onto the album *Surf's Up* (1971). The era's darkest release, though not specifically addressing the Vietnam War, was The Doors' nihilistic **dirge** "The End" (1967), which was also featured in Francis Ford Coppola's 1979 film, *Apocalypse Now*.

QUESTIONS FOR THOUGHT

- We studied the text, rhythmic cadence, and chorus in "Ballad of the Green Berets." What are some of the song's other musical attributes? How do they support Sadler's aesthetic and political intent?

- Some listeners find "I-Feel-Like-I'm-Fixin'-to-Die-Rag" to be deeply offensive. Others enjoy its dark humor. What is your response? Why?

- Music is often used as a marketing device. Do you think war and peace can be marketed through music? Can musicians use war, or peace, for marketing themselves? Examples?

ACTIVITIES AND ASSIGNMENTS

- View the helicopter gunship attack in Francis Ford Coppola's *Apocalypse Now* (1979). Perhaps you recognize the music. What is it? What does it represent in its original context? Is this movie scene an example of using music as a weapon?

- Compare and contrast songs from the war in Iraq with those from the Vietnam War. Are there common themes? Has the musical language changed?

- Investigate how popular song reflected war sentiment during World War I and World War II. Were the songs hawkish or dovish, interventionist or isolationist? Did the music impact popular thought or government policy?

EMOTION IN MUSIC

Strange as it may seem to us today, sentimental songs of the 19th century were expected to bring listeners of either sex to tears. Men were expected not to show "feminine" emotions in response to their own trying circumstances, but they were free to do so in response to a moving song. A tearful response was acceptable because such feelings were experienced communally as human universals. Seen in this light, rather than compromising manhood, tears confirmed one's depth of humanity. President Lincoln was typical of his time. Although firm enough to push America's bloodiest war to its conclusion, he wept freely when moved by song.

LOWELL MASON (1782–1872)

As men struggled back to their line after General Pickett's failed assault at Gettysburg, a decisive moment in the Civil War was immortalized with music when a Confederate Band played Northerner Lowell Mason's hymn "Nearer My God to Thee." Mason was a Boston-based choir director and organist. He composed over 1600 hymns, wrote music instruction books, introduced music education into the public schools, and helped create the first Sunday school for African-American children. He also wrote the melody for "Mary Had a Little Lamb."

The American Civil War, 1861–1865

"I don't believe we can have an army without music," remarked Confederate General Robert E. Lee. In both the North and the South, the common soldiers agreed. As armies were mobilized, so was music. By the end of 1861, just eight months after the attack on Fort Sumter, the Union army supported 618 bands and nearly 28,000 instrumentalists.

In camp and on the battlefield, music was ubiquitous. In combat, field musicians—fifers, buglers, and drummers—were often stationed near commanding officers where they conveyed signals to the troops. Many musicians were just boys. Minimum enlistment age for musicians was officially 12, but the rule was often ignored. @ 9.3

Many boy soldiers were killed, their sacrifices memorialized in a variety of songs. The most famous of these, "The Drummer Boy of Shiloh," was tearfully sung in family parlors and army camps on both sides of the Mason–Dixon Line.

More than any other American armed conflict, the Civil War caught the public's musical imagination. Thousands of war-related songs were published as sheet music. Sometimes, songs attempted to sway public sentiment; more often, however, they reflected concerns of the moment. Upbeat songs of 1861 and 1862 roused civilians and soldiers alike to "rally 'round the flag" (as in George Root's "Battle Cry of Freedom," 1862). But as the war continued unabated and casualties soared, topics took a darker tone, such as the maudlin "Who Will Care for Mother Now?" This and similarly bathos-drenched songs were sometimes banned in military camps. Officers feared that listening to the music would weaken their men's fighting resolve, perhaps even contribute to desertion.

Popular in both the North and South was John Hewitt's (1801–1890) strophic setting of the poem "All Quiet Along the Potomac Tonight." Set for solo voice with a sparse piano accompaniment, the song is fragile and eerily moving. Part of the emotional effect derives from the meter. How discomforting it must have been to listen to this lonely song of death presented in the feel of a waltz, a genre normally associated with social dancing and romance.

"All Quiet Along the Potomac Tonight," by John Hewitt

LISTENING **9.3** GUIDE

Texture: Homophonic
Meter: Compound duple
Form: Strophic

Although the song sold briskly in Hewitt's strophic arrangement for voice and piano, in army camps it would often have been accompanied by guitar. The song's vocal range is narrow; the style is unadorned and direct. This makes sense. After all, this story about the lives and deaths of common soldiers was designed to be singable and appreciated by untutored musicians and listeners. Of course, simplicity of delivery also encourages a listener to focus on the lyrics, which is where the emotional power resides.

Verse 1:
All quiet along the Potomac, they say,
Except here and there a stray picket
Is shot, as he walks on his beat, to and fro,
By a rifleman hid in the thicket.
'Tis nothing! a private or two, now and then.
Will not count in the news of the battle;
Not an officer lost, only one of the men,
Moaning out, all alone, the death rattle.

THE CHORUS TO CHAS. CARROLL SAWYER'S "WHO WILL CARE FOR MOTHER NOW?" 1863

"Soon with angels I'll be marching,
With bright laurels on my brow.
I have for my country fallen,
Who will care for mother now?"

Sheet music, "Who Will Care for Mother Now?".
Courtesy of American Song Sheets, David M. Rubenstein Rare Book & Manuscript Library, Duke University.

Music and Resistance

How to stand firm when continued defiance is hopeless? The question has no answer, but people have often turned to music when all else has failed. We now study two examples of songs of resistance. First we look at the Ghost Dance, a millennial-like movement that sprang up in the American West in 1889. Then we look at the important role that music played during the Holocaust.

Ghost Dance

The Civil War briefly slowed down the nation's ongoing westward expansion. But with war's end, the focus again turned to Euro-American settlement of the Great Plains. By the mid-1880s, dwindling resources made the Plains Indians' traditional lifeways unsustainable. Military resistance was pointless, perhaps impossible. Most Native Americans were confined to reservations where food was scarce, shelter inadequate, and disease rampant. Those still free were on the run or had sought safe harbor in Canada.

The future looked worse still. It was in this period of desperation that the Plains Indians experienced a brief resurgence of hope. The source was Wovoka, a Nevada Territory-based medicine man of the Paiute ethnic group. Like Tävibo had before him, Wovoka prophesied an apocalypse in which the world would be devastated by natural disasters. As the event unfolded, the white man would be destroyed. Native Americans would regain their traditional lands and lifeways. Even the ancestors would return to life.

The future was set, but Wovoka told the people they could speed the great day's coming by turning their attention to song, dance, and prayer. There would be other rewards as well. Those who internalized the philosophy with sufficient power would become invulnerable to the soldiers' bullets.

Wovoka believed the spiritual power of song and dance could overcome the physical power of guns. His vision developed into the Ghost Dance, a religion that quickly spread outward from Nevada's Great Basin. Soon, believers were found all across the Plains, and from Arizona to Canada. Thus began the endgame in the struggle for control of the Great Plains.

Some made pilgrimages to the Great Basin so that they might receive the teaching directly from Wovoka. Converts passed on the religion's tenants. Songs, which were obtained through individual visions, were believed to hold great power.

Only self-sacrifice could bring about a true vision. Accordingly, believers prayed and even subjected themselves to a variety of physical deprivations that would make them more open to having a mystical experience. Every song received was unique. More importantly, it was believed to be a talisman, which when sung, empowered the receiver and prepared the planet for the new age.

Ghost Dance celebrations attracted practitioners by the thousands and the gatherings were peaceful. Even so, white officials feared the possibility of a new rebellion. Soon, the United States government banned both the religion and the singing of its songs. Gatherings were forcefully dispersed.

The Ghost Dance movement was short lived. It effectively ended on December 29, 1890 when 150 Lakota Sioux, mostly women and children, were shot down on a frozen plain in South Dakota by American soldiers. The event became known as the Battle of Wounded Knee. Many of the Lakota had been Ghost Dance practitioners. Some accounts suggest that the Ghost Dance itself might have helped raise tensions.

| Sioux Ghost Dance.

Arapaho and Comanche Ghost Dance songs

Texture: Monophonic
Form: Paired phrases
Recordings made in 1894 by James Mooney.

Ghost Dance songs are sung in a chant-like fashion with a small melodic range and steady metrical flow. Texts focus on deprivation or revelation. Song forms were modeled on the Great Basin format of short paired (repeated) phrases (AA BB CC, etc.), often with slight variations. "Father Have Pity on Me" (Arapaho) ends with a final repeat of the AA section. "Yellow Light from Sun is Streaming" (Comanche) has a brief tag ("Hey yo") at the beginning:

Arapaho Ghost Dance song (AA BB CC)

Meter: Duple

0:03	(A) Father, have pity on me.
	Father, have pity on me.
0:12	(B) I am crying for thirst.
	I am crying for thirst.
0:20	(C) All is gone, I have nothing to eat.
	All is gone, I have nothing to eat.

Repeat form plus AA.

Each phrase ends on the tonic, which is also the lowest tone in the piece. Thus, every phrase falls to its completion, which adds to the dirge-like feel. The range is narrow, just a perfect fifth from "do" to "sol," a range attainable by any voice. The Ghost Dance used a slow walking step, which can easily be imagined in the song's tempo. Notice that the song is performed by a single voice. Though sometimes thousands danced together, each sang his own individual song and heard his own inner music.

Comanche Ghost Dance song (AA BB B'B')

Meter: Non-Metric

0:04	(A) Light from sun is flowing.
	Light from sun is flowing.
0:10	(B) Yellow light from sun is streaming.
	Yellow light from sun is streaming.
0:17	(B') Yellow light from sun is streaming (sung at lower pitch level).
	Yellow light from sun is streaming (sung at lower pitch level).

Music of the Holocaust

The Nazi-driven genocide known as the Holocaust (1938–1945) resulted in the death of six million Jewish people, along with other oppressed minorities. Though mostly confined to urban ghettos or concentration camps, Jews occasionally were able to fight back. But without guns or mobility, uprisings were most likely to result in even greater death tolls, particularly because of vicious German reprisals on the populace at large. Tens of thousands were forced to dig their own graves, then shot.

Even when facing a hopeless future, life in the newly created ghettos stumbled forward. Schools met and children studied. That sort of resistance could not be stopped. Neither could music. Street singers sang of hunger and corruption, of freedom and rebellion. Inside their homes, families sang the songs of the Jewish faith: the "Kol Nidre" (Chapter 7: Music and Spirituality) on Yom Kippur, songs from the Haggadah on Passover, and songs of the Sabbath every Friday evening.

> "Looking at us, a stone would have burst out crying. Old people and children went like cattle to be sacrificed."
> —Rikle Glezer

ANITA LASKER-WALLFISCH (b. 1925)

Anita Lasker-Wallfisch was 17 years old when she was sent to Auschwitz, the most notorious of the Nazi Germany death camps. Upon arrival she was stripped naked. Her head was shaved and her arm tattooed. When interrogated about her background, Wallfisch said that she played the cello. The answer saved her life. Wallfisch was told to wait in a corner while the camp's orchestra director was summoned.

"So I stood there. Instead of being led to the gas chamber, I had a conversation about cello playing and music," Wallfisch recalled during a 1999 BBC World Service radio broadcast.

The orchestra director was Alma Boset, niece of famed composer and conductor Gustav Mahler. Like her uncle, Boset ran her orchestra to exacting standards. Such was the pressure to play well, said Wallfisch, that it helped her survive the horrors all around.

"If you looked out of the window, you saw the chimneys and the smoke of burning people. And we, in an almost crazy way, concentrated on playing music, [on playing] the right notes," she said.

Every day the orchestra played as the men marched to and from the factories. As the Russians advanced through Poland in 1944, the camp's orchestra was disbanded. The musicians assumed they would be sent to the gas chambers. Instead, they were transported to Bergen-Belsen. Wallfisch survived. After the war, she moved to England, where she performed as a member of the English Chamber Orchestra.

Anita Lasker-Wallfisch.

Courtesy of Giles de la Mare Publishers, from *Inherit the Truth 1939-1945: The Documented Experiences of a Survivor of Auschwitz and Belsen.*

Songs of partisan resistance were heard in the countryside where armed guerrillas fought throughout the war. The most famous of the resistance songs was "Zog Nit Keyn Mol" ("Never Say"). Set to a Russian melody, the song was sung in at least seven languages and known throughout Eastern Europe.

Even the death camps had music. At one point, Auschwitz-Birkenau supported six orchestras, the largest with over 100 musicians. Mozart symphonies were performed as men, women, and children were sent to the gas chambers. Over one million people died at Auschwitz.

Strangest of the ghettos was Theresienstadt, Czechoslovakia. The town had not supported a Jewish population before the war, but Germans used the idyllic location to create a "model" ghetto filled with Jewish intellectuals. The site was opened for a June 23, 1944 visit by the Red Cross, which toured the town and attended a performance of *Brundibár* (1938), a children's opera written by Hans Krása (1899–1944), then a prisoner there (but later transferred to Auschwitz where he died two days later). Hidden behind the tour's gloss, and not noticed by the Red Cross, were the horrendous living conditions and food shortages. To alleviate overcrowding, many had been sent to Auschwitz in the days before the Red Cross's arrival. In reality, Theresienstadt was a concentration camp. Of the 140,000 Jews brought there, fewer than 20,000 survived.

A Song from Vilna

Between July 4 and July 20, 1941 over 5,000 Jews were slaughtered by the German army and local volunteers at Ponar, a forest recreation center a few miles south of Vilna, Lithuania. A second wave of killings took place on August 31. Both massacres were in preparation for the opening of the two

Vilna ghettos on September 6. By the end of October, another 10,000 more Jews had been murdered, enough to close one of the ghettos. It was during this time that 18-year-old Rikle Glezer, herself imprisoned in the Vilna ghetto, wrote the poem "Es iz geven a zumer-tog" ("It was a Summer's Day").

Glezer's Yiddish words gave voice to the horrors of the Ponar massacre and subsequent life in the Vilna ghetto. She emphasized shared experience—"We are tortured . . . cut off from the world"—and drew on biblical language of sacrifice. Perhaps her words provided some small comfort to those who struggled to survive.

Shortly after writing this song, Glezer was deported to a death camp, presumably to be exterminated. Instead, she managed to escape and join a resistance group fighting in the Lithuanian forests. Glezer survived the war and eventually settled in Israel.

"Es iz geven a zumer-tog" ("It was a Summer's Day"), poem by Rikle Glezer

LISTENING 9.5 GUIDE

Texture: Homophonic
Meter: Duple
Form: Strophic

The lyrics of this strophic song are set to the tune "Papirosn" (Cigarettes), a popular Yiddish theater song. This recording uses an accordion and mandolin as accompaniment. The melody uses both the natural and the harmonic minor scales, with "ti" sometimes lowered to "te." The text is set syllabically. The arching melodic contour repeatedly reaches into the singer's upper range. The singer's melody is followed heterophonically by the mandolin.

The strophe is divided into two melodically similar parts, each with four phrases. The first phrase begins on the low tonic, moves up the octave, and extends to "me," in the next octave (the highest note in the piece). Then a quick descent to "sol."

0:00	Instrumental introduction	
0:27	Es iz geven a zumer-tog, Vi shtendik zunik-sheyn.	It was a summer's day, Sunny and lovely as always.

The second phrase begins where the last left off and leaps back up to "me." Then a slow descent to "fa."

Un di nature hot dan gehat In zukh azoyfil kyeyn.	And nature then Had so much charm.

The third phrase is a symmetrical arch moving from "fa" up to the next octave's "re" and back down to "fa."

Es hobn feygelekh gezungen, Freylekh zukh arumgeshpringen.	Birds sang, Hopped around cheerfully.

The last phrase, shorter than the others, resolves to the tonic.

In geto hot men undz geheysn geyn.	We were ordered to go into the ghetto.

The second half of the strophe proceeds in much the same way, though melodic changes here and there accommodate the different text. The general curve of each phrase remains the same.

0:53	Akh shtelt zikh for vos s'iz fun undz! Gevorn! Farshtanen hobn mir: s'iz alts farloyrn. S'hot nit geholfn undzer betn, Az s'zol emitser undz retn– Farlozn hobn mir dokh undzer heym	Oh, just imagine what happened to us! We understood: everything was lost. Of no use were our pleas That someone should save us— We still left our home.

QUESTIONS FOR THOUGHT

- Above you read that Mozart was performed in World War II concentration camps as victims were led to their death. What was the point of this? A small act of (perhaps calming) kindness preceding mass murder? A cruel final demonstration of "Aryan" superiority? Entertainment for the prison guards? Consider these multiple perspectives.
- If you had a story like "Es iz geven a zumer-tog" to tell, what kind of music would you use? How might using an already popular melody add to or take away from the telling?

ACTIVITIES AND ASSIGNMENTS

- The Library of Congress supports online a brief 1894 video of Ghost Dancing by members of the Buffalo Bill's Wild West Show. The film is silent so we cannot know the music to which they were dancing. Perhaps these were Ghost Dance movements, perhaps not. Watch the video (www.loc.gov/item/00694139/) and compare movements with the songs we studied. Do they fit?

Music and Remembrance: Three Responses to World War II

"We laughed, knowing that better men would come,

And greater wars; when each proud fighter brags

He wars on Death—for Life; not men—for flags."
—Wilfred Owen

Finally, we move to the concert hall and look at a trio of compositions written in response to, or in remembrance of, World War II. French composer Olivier Messiaen's *Quatuor pour la fin du temps* (1941) is an intimate and complex chamber music work written in a German prisoner of war camp. British composer Benjamin Britten's *War Requiem* (1962) commemorates the re-consecration of St. Michael's Cathedral in Coventry, England. Polish composer Krzysztof Penderecki's *Threnody for the Victims of Hiroshima* (1960) experiments with unusual sound textures to invoke the most destructive seconds in human history.

Olivier Messiaen (1908–1992): *Quatuor pour la fin du temps* (*Quartet for the End of Time*)

World War II began in Europe on September 1, 1939, with Germany's *blitzkrieg* invasion of Poland. Although a series of treaties were supposed to compel France, Great Britain, and other counties to protect Poland and declare war on Germany, none did so. Despite fierce resistance, Poland fell in just thirty-four days. A period of calm followed as Germany rested and repositioned its armies. Through the winter, the world anxiously waited. The inevitable came on May 10, 1940 when Germany sidestepped France's imposing Maginot Line and invaded through the Ardennes Forest. France surrendered in just six weeks.

Among the French army prisoners of war was medical corpsman Olivier Messiaen, who was shipped east to Stalag VIIIA in Silesia, Poland. It was there, on a snowy January evening in 1941 that Messiaen premiered his *Quartet for the End of Time*. The music was inspired by the description of the Apocalypse in the Book of Revelation.

Messiaen's audience consisted of fellow POWs and German guards. Many prisoners were sick; most were malnourished. The musical instruments available—clarinet, violin, cello, and piano—were substandard.

Despite the conditions, Messiaen's music transcended time and space. For a short time at least, these hardened men—prisoners and guards thrown together by the horrors of war—found inner shelter and shared common bonds. "Never before have I been listened to with such attention and understanding," Messiaen remembered years later.

For Messiaen, a devout Catholic, the music was a response to the suffering brought on by war. It was also a musical testament of spiritual faith. Across some forty minutes of "clock" time and eight individual movements, Messiaen's quartet portrays the end of the physical universe and suggests humankind's path to spiritual salvation.

First movement ("Liturgie de cristal") from *Quatuor pour la fin du temps*, by Olivier Messiaen

LISTENING
9.6
GUIDE

Texture: Homophonic
Meter: Triple
Form: Overlapping cycles

The four instruments are sorted into two groups, which are then juxtaposed one against the other. The clarinet and violin, representing the voices of the blackbird and nightingale respectively, symbolize nature. The cello and piano symbolize the impersonal eternal, what Messiaen calls "the harmonious silence of Heaven."

The songbirds' characters could hardly be more different. The blackbird sings out rambling melodies that float across octaves and metered time. Against this, the sprightly nightingale interjects high-pitched chirps. Each creature seems to live in its own world, each self-absorbed and blithely unaware of the other.

The vibrant life of birdsong is silhouetted against the screen of a cool and dispassionate musical eternity. How to create such an effect? Messiaen does so by juxtaposing mathematically derived cycles of melody, harmony, and rhythm. The piano part, for example, juxtaposes a repeating twenty-nine-chord sequence against a repeating seventeen-event rhythmic pattern. As the diagram below maps out, the rhythmic sequence repeats nearly twice before the chords complete a single cycle. Because of the two large prime numbers involved (29 and 17), it takes 493 events for the two patterns to realign to their original positions. The movement ends long before that happens.

Events:	1	2	3	...	17	18	19	...	28	29	30	31	32	...	492	493	494
Rhythmic sequence #:	1	2	3	...	17	1	2	...	11	12	13	14	15	...	16	17	1
Chordal sequence #:	1	2	3	...	17	18	19	...	28	29	1	2	3	...	28	29	1

The cello part is also built on asymmetrical cycles. Most striking, however, is the pentatonic melody featuring **glissandos** and **harmonics**, which create eerie tones atypical of the instrument's characteristic sound.

"Liturgie de cristal" is perhaps the most impenetrable of the quartet's eight movements. Its complexity derives from Messiaen's desire to represent and integrate the impersonal austerity of eternity with the freedom of nature.

How might one listen to this complicated piece? A strategy will help you to understand and appreciate. We suggest you listen several times, focusing your attention differently on each listening.

- On first listening, take in the entirety. Get a feel for the timbres and tempo at which events unfold.

- On second listening, follow the clarinet/blackbird, where the majority of the melodic material resides. Get a feel for the shape of the music and the creature's personality. You will probably notice how the other instruments occasionally intrude and interrupt your attention.

- On subsequent hearings, gradually expand your focus.

CYCLES AND MUSIC

To help understand the cyclical concept underlying the piano part of *Quatuor pour la fin du Temps*, visualize the orbital duration of planets in our solar system. To begin, choose a spot in the zodiac: say, 1 degree of Aries. Viewed outward from the Sun, Earth is in that position one time per year; Venus (because its solar orbit is smaller) returns after just 225 Earth days. Mars (because its solar orbit is larger) returns after 687 Earth days. Occasionally, two of the planets align at 1 degree Aries. Venus and Earth will do so every 82,125 Earth days. Earth and Mars will do so every 250,755 Earth days. All three planets align just once in every 56,419,875 Earth days. Then, of course, the cycle starts all over again.

Benjamin Britten (1913–1976): *War Requiem*

When commissioned to write a piece to mark the 1962 reopening of St. Michael's Cathedral, British composer and committed pacifist Benjamin Britten decided to write a **Requiem** Mass. The eighty-five-minute work requires army-sized forces: two orchestras, organ, adult chorus, boy choir, and three vocal soloists. Verses drawn from the Catholic Mass for the Dead (the Requiem) are sung in Latin. The remaining text comes from the poetry of World War I infantryman Wilfred Owen (1893–1918).

The character of the music ranges from anguish to joy, the dynamics from whisper soft to cannon loud. Sometimes bells toll and martial trumpets sound. Other times, a single fragile voice entreats for peace. The text juxtaposes images of violence and suffering with pleas for redemption. There are searing indictments of the political leaders who led the various nations into war. Always, however, Britten's message is one of peace.

Britten divided his musical forces into three symbolism-rich groups:

- The soprano soloist, adult chorus, and full orchestra represent tradition. They perform the Catholic Mass for the Dead and stand for the impersonal and universal ritual that the Mass signifies. The text is in Latin.

- The two male soloists represent British and German soldiers. They are supported by a small orchestra. The men sing of war's brutality and senselessness. The text is drawn from Owen's poetry.

- The delicate sounds of the boy choir and organ represent innocence and hope. The text is Latin.

COVENTRY CATHEDRAL

Situated in the city of Coventry (95 miles northwest of London), the skeletal ruins of St. Michael's (or Coventry) Cathedral stand today as a reminder of the horrors of war. The late 14th-century Gothic church (elevated to cathedral status in 1918) was bombed by the German Luftwaffe on the night of November 14, 1940. The attack lasted for more than ten hours, destroying over 4000 of the city's homes and three-quarters of its factories.

The people of Coventry rallied and the very next day agreed that the cathedral would be rebuilt. Ten years later, architect Basil Spence (1907–1976) was chosen from over 200 candidates to design the new cathedral, to which he adjoined the ruins. The new building was consecrated in May 1962.

Coventry is also known for its famous Christmas tune, the "Coventry Carol." The 16th-century song comes from a sacred play—likely mounted by the city's textile guilds—that portrays the Christmas story, including the Slaughter of the Innocents. The carol itself depicts a mother quieting her soon-to-be-murdered infant.

Prime Minister Winston Churchill walks with the Mayor of Coventry and a member of the Church of England clergy through the ruined nave of Coventry Cathedral after it was bombed by the German air force in November 1940.

War Office Official Photographer, Library of Congress Prints and Photographs Division.

The juxtapositions of the three groups can be simultaneously exhilarating, horrifying, and haunting. Time and again, glorious passages for trumpets and rattling drums portray the terrible grandeur of war, which the boy choir seems to notice not at all.

The music is set in six movements, each named after sections of the Mass liturgy: 1) Requiem aeternum, 2) Dies Irae, 3) Offertorium, 4) Sanctus, 5) Agnus Dei, and 6) Libera me. Each movement is unique in character; each combines Latin text with Owen's poetry. The Offertorium, for example, draws on the biblical story of Abraham and his son, Isaac (Genesis 22:1–24). In Owen's version, however, Abraham (who represents Europe's political leaders) ignores the angel's instruction. He slays the boy, "and half the seed of Europe, one by one." As the tenor and baritone soloists repeat this text, the celestial voices of the boy choir, which are apparently unaware of the horror that is unfolding in the bloody trenches below, sing of the rejuvenating power of sacrifice:

Hostias et preced tibi Domine
laudis offerimus; tu suscipe pro
animabus illis, quarum hodie
memoriam facimus: fac eas, Domine,
de morte transire ad vitam.
Quam olim Abrahae promisisti
en semini ejus.

Lord, in praise we offer to Thee
sacrifices and prayers, do Thou receive them
for the souls of those whom we remember
this day: Lord, make them pass
from death to life,
as Thou didst promise Abraham
and his seed.

Closing the Requiem is the paralyzing Libera Me (Free me), which takes place in the darkened land of the dead. There, the souls of soldiers once enemies and now comrades in death, remember how they killed one another. The boy choir, still oblivious to earthly suffering, sings of life everlasting. The baritone sings:

I am the enemy you killed, my friend.
I knew you in this dark; for so you frowned
Yesterday through me as you jabbed and killed.
I parried; but my hands were loath and cold.
Let us sleep now.

Agnus Dei from *War Requiem,* by Benjamin Britten

 LISTENING 9.7 GUIDE

Texture: Homophonic
Meter: Duple

The Agnus Dei juxtaposes the tenor soloist against the boy choir. The tenor darkly intones Owen's poem "At a Calvary Near the Ancre," which combines the story of Christ's crucifixion with fighting along the Ancre River, a part of the massive World War I Battle of the Somme. At Golgotha, says the Bible, soldiers guarded the crucifixion while Christ's disciples hid in fear and the scribes displayed their scorn. In the trenches near the Ancre, says Owen, the priests prayed in relative safety while soldiers bore the cross of death. The Beast of the poem is both the Devil and war itself. Owen's priests, with their renunciation of brotherly love in the interest of petty nationalism ("bawl allegiance to the state"), are in league with the Devil.

The scalar motion in the strings that opens the Agnus Dei runs like a string of pearls throughout the movement. Notice that the chorus intones this exact opening melody in each of its entrances.

0:13 *Tenor*

The tenor enters with a descending melody that, like a series of sighs, seems to rise only so that it might fall once again.

One ever hangs where shelled roads part.
In this war He too lost a limb,
But His disciples hide apart;
And now the Soldiers bear with Him.

1:09	*Chorus* Agnus Dei, qui tollis peccata mundi, dona eis requiem.	Lamb of God, that takest away the sins of the world, grant them rest.
1:32	*Tenor* Near Golgotha strolls many a priest, And in their faces there is pride That they were flesh-marked by the Beast By whom the gentle Christ's denied.	
1:58	*Chorus* Agnus Dei, qui tollis peccata mundi, dona eis requiem.	

Britten now quickens the pace of the entrances. With the line "The scribes on all the people shove," the statements are cut in half so the soloist and chorus interact more frequently.

2:18	The scribes on all the people shove And bawl allegiance to the state,	
2:30	*Chorus* Agnus Dei, qui tollis peccata mundi . . .	

The tenor returns to the opening gesture:

2:37	*Tenor* But they who love the greater love Lay down their life; they do not hate.	
3:05	*Chorus* Dona eis requiem.	

The text shifts from anguish to hope. Listen to the tenor's fragile upper range, as he shifts to Latin and intones his transcendent final plea, "Give us peace."

3:23	*Tenor* Dona nobis pacem.	Give us peace.

Krzysztof Penderecki (b. 1933): *Threnody for the Victims of Hiroshima*

A number of music's customary elements—melody, harmony, and meter—are eliminated in Penderecki's jarring *Threnody* (1960). Instead, walls of discordant tones grate one against another. *Threnody* offers no tune and no beat, just dissonance—often searing, occasionally brutal. Who would have imagined that such sounds could come from the same string ensemble of violins, violas, and cellos that composers from Bach to Britten used to create such beauty? As in a nightmare, the familiar has become alien and foreboding.

Penderecki achieved his effects by using clusters of pitches that are packed so closely together—sometimes just **microtones** apart—that individual pitches are lost in eddies of sound. The result is that instead of hearing melodic lines, one hears broad bands of texture that slide upwards and downwards in murky and dissonant streams.

Other techniques employed by Penderecki include "extended" techniques, such as playing the instruments' unspecified highest possible note, tapping on the instruments with fingers, and drawing the bow in unusual places (such as across the **bridge** and between the violin's bridge and **tailpiece**).

Threnody lacks rhythm in the usual sense. There is no beat or meter to follow with the tap of a foot or nod of the head. That does not mean that sonic events occur randomly, however. Penderecki mapped out his score according to clock time. Certain effects last for ten seconds, others for much longer. It is as if human time—as defined physically by heartbeat, bodily movement, or breath—has been replaced by impersonal time of machines, perhaps nuclear physics.

Hiroshima, Japan, shortly after August 6, 1945.
Everett Historical/Shutterstock.com.

Threnody for the Victims of Hiroshima, by Krzysztof Penderecki

LISTENING
9.8
GUIDE

Texture: Various
Meter: Non-metric
Form: ABA Each section is marked by a change in musical texture

0:00   **Section A**

The first section is the longest. Here the thick tones slide against one another. Sometimes they expand outward. Other times they seem to collapse in upon themselves.

6:25   **Section B**

The B section is in a **pointillistic** style in which the sounds appear as many separate, even disconnected, events, almost like a universe of slowly blinking stars existing in three-dimensional space. This section has a rhythmic quality to it, but it is one of bubbling activity rather than toe-tapping metric consistency.

7:25   **Section A**

The sustained sounds of the A section return and intermingle with those of section B.

What do all these sounds have to do with nuclear holocaust? That's for the listener to decide. In fact, when Penderecki wrote the piece, Hiroshima was not on his mind. Instead, he was using experimental sound textures, perhaps in an **expressionistic** fashion that attempted to explore the dark emotional reaches of the human mind. The music's original title was simply the descriptive *8'37"*, reflecting the music's length. It was only later that Penderecki connected the music to Hiroshima and changed the title.

THE EXORCIST AND MORE

Music by Penderecki was prominently featured in director William Friedkin's (b. 1935) *The Exorcist* (1973) and director Stanley Kubrick's (1928–1999) 1980 film adaptation of the Stephen King (b. 1947) novel *The Shining*. *Threnody* was also used in the 2008 Oscar-winning film *The Hurt Locker*, directed by Kathyrn Bigelow (b. 1951).

QUESTIONS FOR THOUGHT

- What do you think of *Threnody*? Does it fit your definition of music?
- What was your emotional response to *Threnody*? Try to understand why you felt the way you did.
- What does war sound like in music?
- Imagine you have just received a commission to write a piece commemorating a war. Describe what it might sound like. What instruments would you use and why? Would it be solemn? Religious? A rousing march? Would the melody be singable? The harmonies discordant?
- Messiaen combined sounds of nature with the abstract sounds of eternity. Britten contrasted sacred and secular understandings. Penderecki took the familiar (a string orchestra) and turned it into something forbidding and alien. What other sorts of juxtapositions might make for powerful listening experiences?

THE END OF WORLD WAR II

The United States Air Force dropped the atomic bomb "Little Boy" on Hiroshima on August 6, 1945. That event, in conjunction with another bomb dropped three days later on Nagasaki, effectively ended World War II. The combined death toll of the two explosions is estimated at nearly 250,000 people, almost all of whom were civilians.

ACTIVITIES AND ASSIGNMENTS

- Compare and contrast pro- or anti-war music from different wars. Did any of the compositions influence public opinion?
- Use the internet to examine music from various world conflicts. How are different points of view portrayed musically?

Epilogue: Syria

"Syria is our home
A home we love
Whose soil is our love
Your hell is our paradise."
—from "Janna" ("Paradise"),
a Syrian resistance song based
on an Iranian love song.
Lyrics by Abdul Baset al-Sarout.

Accompanied by an oud-playing colleague, a Syrian refugee sings about home and loss. The performance is brief. After just a few lines the man is overcome with emotion. He cannot continue.

Since the beginning of the Syrian Civil War in 2011, millions of refugees have fled the destruction of their towns, cities, and homes. Some travel just across the border to Jordan and the teeming Zaatari refugee camp (population 80,000, and where the above performance took place). More take their chances crossing the Mediterranean Sea in hope of finding asylum in Europe.

Syrian woman playing the oud in Palmyra, Syria, 2016.
LOUAI BESHARA/AFP/Getty Images.

Most Syrian refugees escape with little more than their lives. Too often they die trying. Perhaps it is a small consolation that musical heritage is carried in hearts and minds. Music helps refugees remain connected to people and places left behind.

Informal music making by refugees has been mostly undocumented, but some videos can be found on the internet. Relatively settled refugees have worked to develop large ensembles. Based in Germany is the Syrian Expat Philharmonic Orchestra, which made its debut in 2015. Mosaic, an Istanbul, Turkey-based refugee chorus, provides members with a community, a sense of belonging in a foreign city. "When we sing we feel strong; we feel proud," says Maisa Alhafez, Mosaic's conductor.

Key Terms

- acoustic bombardment
- articulation syllables
- bridge (on violin)
- chanson
- dirge
- expressionistic
- Ghost Dance
- glissando
- harmonics
- Jew's harp
- microtone
- natural trumpet
- pointillistic
- planctus
- Requiem Mass
- tailpiece
- vocable
- Wovoka

Essay Questions

- **Consider the pieces we studied in this chapter. If all the words were replaced with the syllable "la," which compositions, if any, would you identify as being war-related simply by listening? On what would you base your decisions?**

- **This chapter suggests there are important differences between music that embodies the sounds of war and music that reflects upon the experiences of war. Where do our examples fit?**

Chantons hur ledette
auer ta mulette
quelque note douille

Tuant eft de gxoe
elle a labour uet
mes ic fais le t

CHAPTER GOALS

- To examine the expression of love in musical settings from various time periods and genres.
- To hear how different aspects of love can be portrayed musically.

CHAPTER TEN

Music and Love

ACTIVITIES AND ASSIGNMENTS

- Ask your parents what love songs were popular when they met. Do they have any special feelings for those songs?
- What are your favorite love songs? Has your taste changed since you were in high school? Junior high? What aspects of love do the songs portray?
- Is there a typical love song "sound"?
- Investigate how courtship rituals differ across cultures. How do love songs in these cultures reflect different social norms?

Love is infinitely varied. On occasion, its realization inspires bold leaps of faith. Other times, it brings inner struggle and self-sacrifice. Sometimes, love just plain hurts. You might feel love for family or friends, for God or country, or for the beauty of nature. The ancient Greeks grouped love into four categories: philia (friendship), xenia (social hospitality), agape (idealized love), and eros (sensual love). Perhaps you can identify other groupings that better reflect our own times.

> "If music be the food of love, play on, give me excess of it."
> —William Shakespeare (1564–1616) *Twelfth Night*, Act I, scene 1

Love has always been a favorite topic for musicians. This chapter focuses on the many sides of romantic love. We begin with the blossoming of young love, then seduction, then journey into the dark corners of unrequited love and infidelity. We close with sounds as blissful as those with which we began, with French chanteuse Edith Piaf's classic love song "La Vie en Rose."

The Dawn of Love

The Walt Disney Company has been introducing children to the thrill of love's first blush ever since the 1937 release of *Snow White and the Seven Dwarfs*, the world's first full-length animated musical. That film's classic love song, "Someday My Prince Will Come," became a jazz standard and one of the most often performed songs of all time.

Think back to your own childhood. Perhaps you too watched Disney characters fall in love, perhaps those from the animated *Beauty and the Beast* (1991), winner of Academy Awards for Best Music/Original Score and Best Music/Song. The story, based on a French folk tale, tells of a young woman at the threshold of adulthood. @ 10.1 A selfish prince, cursed and turned into an ugly beast, holds her captive. To break the spell, the prince must learn humility and win the girl's love. After a series of misunderstandings, he succeeds. The moral is clear: true beauty resides within.

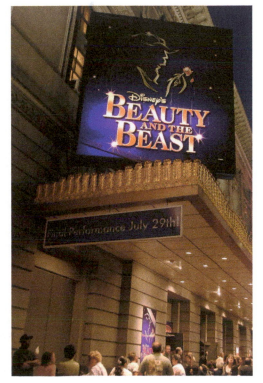

Beauty and the Beast at the Lunt-Fontanne Theatre, 2007.
Donna Ward/Getty Images Entertainment.

LISTENING 10.1 GUIDE
"Something There," lyrics by Howard Ashman, music by Alan Menken

Texture: Homophonic
Meter: Duple
Form: AABA

Listen to "Something There" from the film's soundtrack. Notice how melody and lyrics combine to portray unfolding love. Belle sings, "There's something." She pauses; then sings "almost kind." Pause again. She is hesitant, and we hear it in the fragmented start and stop quality of the melody. In the next line, Belle blurts out the reason for her uncertainty, "he was mean . . . and unrefined." No hesitancy here. Her mind is clear when it comes to the unpleasant stuff.

But the story is not yet over. We know this from the melody, which pauses on an unresolved harmony. Belle's music starts over, "And now he's dear." Belle says she is sure, but is she really? If so, why does she continue to hesitate? Why did not she see all these nice things before, she wonders. Still, the phrase ends on the tonic. Belle's thoughts are complete, even if Belle and Beast's relationship remains unresolved.

Now it is Beast's turn. Using the same melody, rhyme scheme, and phrase structure (all telling signs that the two are on the same wavelength), Beast reveals his own unsure steps toward loving Belle by singing "And when we touched." Whatever he may be feeling, he must wait. Belle is the one who will decide the fate of their suddenly deepening relationship.

Resolution arrives with the third stanza, when Belle changes the melody. Listen carefully with heart and mind. Is there any doubt that she has fallen in love? She moves into a higher vocal range, sustains and embraces the melody, and enjoys its luminous freedom.

The discovery of love is always fresh, of course. But this love—for a beast—is truly remarkable. As Belle drinks in its splendor, so do we. After all, neither she nor we anticipated that such a love could be so wonderful. So lovely was the "new and a bit alarming" phrase that the composer repeats the melody for us with "true . . . he's no Prince Charming." "New" and "True"—the words are raised in melody for our approval, like glasses held high in a wedding toast.

One cannot stay suspended in midair forever, though. So, the melody continues, gradually winding downward into familiar territory with, "there's something in him that I simply didn't see." Resolution has been achieved in the music, and—if the melody can be believed (it can)—in Belle's heart.

Clara Schumann at the piano, 1837.

Idealized Love

Love inspires. Clara Wieck Schumann (whom we met in Chapter 6: Music and Gender) and her husband Robert composed twelve Lieder from *Liebesfrühling* (*Dawn of Love*), a set of poems by German poet Friedrich Rückert (1788–1866). Clara's setting of the poem "Liebst du um Schönheit" ("If You Love for Beauty," 1841) was written in the first year of the couple's marriage, while she was pregnant with their first child.

The text eschews the trappings of physical beauty; youth and wealth are fleeting, the poem warns. Love itself is eternal, however. It is ever beautiful, young, and rich. Schumann confirms this idea with her song's unadorned simplicity, natural ease, and quiet radiance.

THE GERMAN *LIED*

Today, the term **Lied** (*Lieder*: pl.) generally refers to a German art song of the Romantic era (19th century), but the term, which simply means "song," has been used since the Middle Ages. The 19th-century Lied was written for a solo singer to be accompanied by a pianist, and was designed to be performed in the intimate setting of a private drawing room. Texts, generally about love, were borrowed from German poets, including Johann Wolfgang von Goethe (1749–1832), Friedrich Schiller (1759–1805), and Wilhelm Müller (1794–1827), among others. The greatest composers of Lieder were Franz Schubert (1797–1828), Robert Schumann (1810–1856), and Hugo Wolf (1860–1803).

"Liebst du um Schönheit" ("If You Love for Beauty"), by Clara Wieck Schumann

LISTENING
10.2
GUIDE

Texture: Homophonic
Meter: Duple
Form: Strophic

Listen to the song. It is easy to imagine that anyone could sing this song, just like everyone can give and receive love. The song is written in "modified" strophic form, with slight musical differences in each verse. Notice that while verses 1 and 3 are stable, verses 2 and 4 are more active, both rhythmically and melodically. The resolute melodic conclusion of verse 4 seems to confirm love's power.

Time	German	English
0:00	The piano introduces the song with two phrases that will be repeated in the first line of every strophe.	
0:07	Liebst du um Schönheit, / O nicht mich liebe! / Liebe die Sonne, / Sie trägt ein gold'nes Haar!	If you love for beauty, / Oh do not love me! / Love the sun, / It has gold hair!
0:34	Liebst du um Jugend, / O nicht mich liebe! / Liebe den Frühling, / Der jung ist jedes Jahr!	If you love for youth, / Oh do not love me! / Love the spring-time / That is young each year!
1:00	Liebst du um Schätze, / O nicht mich liebe. / Liebe die Meerfrau, / Sie hat viel Perlen klar.	If you love for wealth, / Oh do not love me! / Love the mermaid, / Who has many limpid pearls!
1:28	Liebst du um Liebe, / O ja, mich liebe! / Liebe mich immer, / Dich lieb' ich immerdar.	If you love for love, / Oh yes, love me! / Love me forever; / I will love you forevermore!

Humorous Seduction

Carmen (Chapter 6: Music and Gender) is perhaps opera's most dangerous seductress. The most irrepressible may be Serpina, the titillating take-charge servant girl from Italian composer Giovanni Battista Pergolesi's (1710–1736) comic opera *La serva padrona* (*The Servant Mistress*, 1733). Serpina's goal is to marry the hapless Uberto, her former guardian and present employer.

Is Serpina in love with Uberto or does she simply seek an improved social station? Perhaps both. Whatever the case, Serpina will not be denied. The characters and plot are stock, drawn from the Italian theatrical genre *commedia dell'arte*. @ 10.2

Pergolesi conceived *La serva padrona* as an **intermezzo**, a genre of light entertainment to be performed during the intermissions of more serious (and supposedly more important) operatic fare. On the opening night in Naples, Italy, however, *La serva padrona* out-shone the main event. The opera became popular across Europe.

In Paris, performances helped incite the **Querrelle des Bouffons** (or War of the Buffoons, 1752–1754), a vigorous literary debate about the relative virtues of French serious opera versus Italian comic opera. The controversy quickly expanded into a (half-disguised) political argument over the rightful power of government. That dam would eventually break with the French Revolution (1789).

La serva padrona.
Cammenina42/Wikimedia Commons/CC-BY-SA-3.0.

LISTENING 10.3 GUIDE

"Lo conosco" ("I Can See It"), by Giovanni Pergolesi

Texture: Homophonic
Meter: Duple
Form: Strophic

The highlight of Act I is the duet "Lo conosco," a comic portrayal of seduction. The duet begins with a full verse from Serpina followed by a response from Uberto.

0:00	A brief orchestral introduction features strings and harpsichord

0:15   Strophe A

Notice the shortness of each phrase. Serpina's speech is broken into bits. She is pushing her agenda, sometimes one word at a time.

Serpina

Lo conosco, lo conosco	I can see it, I can see it
a quegli occhietti,	in your eyes,
a quegli occhietti	in your eyes,
Furbi, ladri, ladri, malignetti.	You're a cunning, scheming, dirty old man.
Che sebben voi dite "no, no, no"	You keep saying "no, no, no,"
Pur m'accennano di "si, si, si, si, si."	But you really mean "yes, yes, yes, yes, yes."
Pur m'accennano di "si."	But you really mean "yes."

0:33   Strophe A

Flustered, Uberto responds similarly. Perhaps he is at a loss for words. Has Serpina hit upon the truth? (Notice, too, that they sing identical melodies, as did Belle and Beast. That is important.)

Uberto

Signorina, signorina,	Miss, miss,

v'ingannate, v'ingannate!	you're wrong, you're wrong!
Troppo, troppo, troppo, troppo	Too much, too much, too much
in alto vi volate!	Your ambitions fly too high!
Gli occhi ed io vi dicon "no, no, no"	Both my eyes and I say "no, no, no."
Ed è un sogno questo "si, si, si, si, si."	And you're dreaming if you hear "yes, yes, yes, yes, yes."
Ed è un sogno questo "si."	And you're dreaming if you hear "yes."

0:53 The musical tempo does not change, but Serpina slows things down by expanding the words, letting the vowels ring. She seems almost to embody the words "Che maestà!"

Serpina

Ma perché, ma perché?	But why, but why?
Non son grazïosa?	Am I not graceful?
Non son bella e spiritosa?	Am I not beautiful and spirited?
Su, mirate leggiadria, leggiadria.	Just look how elegant, how elegant!
Ve' che brio, che maestà, che maestà!	What panache! What dignity! What dignity!

1:17 More rattled still, Uberto sings (to himself) a slowly rising chromatic line. Is this a playful musical jest on sexual arousal? Can he resist? We'll see.

Uberto (aside)

Ah, costei mi va tentando quanto va che me la fa	(Ah, she must be testing me to see how long I can resist.)

1:24 Serpina and Uberto continue their sparring using bits and pieces of the strophe A, along with new material. Serpina, aware her plan seems to be working, pushes her advantage. But too soon.

Serpina (aside)

Ei mi par che va calando, va calando.	I think he's weakening, (aside)
Via, Signore!	Decide then, Sir!

Uberto

Eh, vanne via!	Get out!

Serpina

Risolvete!	Decide!

Uberto

Eh, matta sei!	You must be mad!

1:35 Confusion (and tension) rising, Serpina and Uberto start singing at the same time. "Che imbroglio." What a mess indeed. Messes are the foundation of comedy. And sometimes love.

Serpina

Son per voi gli affetti miei,	All my feelings are for you.
E dovrete sposar me,	You must marry me.
dovrete, dovrete, dovrete, sposar me!	You must, you must, you must, marry me!

Uberto

Oh, che imbroglio, ch'imbroglio,	Oh, what a mess, what a mess, what a mess
ch'imbroglio, egli è per me!	I've gotten into!

1:47 Now we get an instrumental interlude, which gives the characters a few moments to regain their composure and the audience to savor the characters' discomposure.

Back to the beginning with Serpina once again on the attack. Interaction is quicker; phrases shorter; gestures more exaggerated.

1:53 Strophe A material

Serpina

Lo conosco si, a quegli occhietti furbi,	I can see it in your eyes, you cunning,
ladri, malignetti.	scheming, naughty old man.

Uberto
Signorina, signorina, v'ingannate.

Miss, miss, you're wrong

Serpina
No, no, no, no,
che sebben, che sebben, che sebben voi dite
pur m'accennano di "si."

No, no, no, no,
You keep saying "no,"
When you mean to say "yes."

Uberto
V'ingannate!

You're wrong!

Serpina
Ma perché, ma perché?
Io son bella, grazïosa, spiritosa.

But why, but why?
I am beautiful, graceful, spirited.

Uberto (aside interrupts Serpina)
Ah, costei mi va tentando.

(She's testing me.)

Serpina (aside)
Va calando si, si.
Ve'che brio, che brio,
Che Maestà, che maestà!

(He's weakening, yes, yes.)
See what panache I have! What panache!
What dignity! What dignity!

Uberto (aside)
Quanto val, quanto val, Quanto val che me fa la.
Laralla, laralla, la la la la la la la.

She's just seeing how long I can resist.
Laralla, laralla, la la la la la la la.

2:53 Singers together.

Serpina
Via, signore, resolvete!

Decide then, Sir!

Uberto
Eh, vanne via. Eh matta sei!

Get out! You must be mad!

Serpina
Son per voi gl'affetti mei,

All my feelings are for you.

Uberto
Signorina, v'ingannate!

Miss, you're wrong!

Serpina
E dovrete si, si!

You must, yes, yes!

Uberto
Signorina, no, no!

Miss, no, no!

Serpina
E dovrete sposar me!

You must marry me!

Uberto (aside)
Oh, che imbroglio egli è per me!
Quanto va, quanto va, quanto va che me la fa!

Oh, what a mess I've gotten into!
She's just seeing how long I can resist!

Serpina
Io son bella, grazïosa, spiritosa

I am beautiful, graceful, spirited

Uberto
La ra la, la ra la.

La la la, la la la.

Serpina
Ve'che brio, ve che brio!

What panache I have! What panache!

Uberto
Oh, che imbroglio, oh, che imbroglio!

Oh, what a mess, oh, what a mess!

Signorina signorina	Miss, miss
Serpina	
Va calando, si, si.	He's weakening, yes, yes. (aside)
Son per voi, son per voi,	All for you, all for you,
Son per voi gl'affetti miei.	My feelings are all for you.
Uberto	
Signori-, signori-, signorina, matta sei!	Miss . . . miss . . . Miss, you must be mad!
Serpina	
E dovrete si, si.	You must, yes, yes.
Uberto	
Signorina, no, no!	Miss, no, no!
Serpina	
Si, si!	Yes, yes!
Uberto	
No, no!	No, no!
Singers together.	
Serpina	
Si, si dovrete, dovrete, dovrete sposar me, sposar me!	Yes, yes, you must, you must, you must marry me, marry me!
Uberto	
Oh, che imbroglio, ch'imbroglio, ch'imbroglio egli è per me, egli è per me!	Oh, what a mess, what a mess, what a mess I'm in, I'm in!

QUESTIONS FOR THOUGHT

- **Why is Uberto so resistant? Do you hope he gives in? Why or why not?**
- **How do the relationships differ between the couples Belle and Beast and Serpina and Uberto? Is this reflected in the music?**
- **Compare and contrast the songs we have examined so far. What things do they share? How are they different?**

Unattainable Love

Serpina eventually gets her man. More often, however, the would-be lover comes up short. For centuries, songwriters have turned spurned love's pain into artistic gain. Such was the case in medieval France, where poet/musicians called **troubadours** (female: trobairitz) and **trouvères** (female: trouveresses) developed an entire tradition of song and poetry cataloging love's many sides. In particular, they were fascinated with the unattainable romance of courtly love, also called *fin amours*.

According to the idealized rules of the time, a knight pledges his love and obedience to the lady of the court. @ 10.3 His love inspires great deeds and he strives always to be worthy of her affection. But because of her higher social status (not to mention that she is married to his sire), their love can never be consummated.

Luckily, there is a bright side to all this. Through his suffering, the knight is ennobled. And like the era's belief in alchemy, which sought to turn lead into gold, his erotic desires are reborn on a higher plane. He develops firm character and honorable bearing.

In an age when marriage was based on merging property rather than compatibility, the troubadours and trouvères did much to legitimize the notion of romantic attraction. In their vision we see the roots of our own society's ideals of romantic love.

THE DANGEROUS WORDS OF LOVE

In 1985, Tipper Gore co-founded the Parents Music Resource Center (PMRC), a group of Washington wives dedicated to educating parents about violent and sexually explicit lyrics in popular music. They believed that an increase in rape and other violent crimes, teen pregnancy, and drug use was due in part to inappropriate messages in the songs to which young people listened. As a result of PMRC efforts, "Parental Advisory Labels" were put on albums containing explicit lyrics. Some stores pulled "offensive" music from their shelves.

PMRC opponents worried that guidance labels would lead to censorship. They also predicted that labeling might encourage more record sales to curious buyers. In the end, labeling did little to curb buying habits. Nonetheless, cashiers are still required to check IDs of teens buying labeled CDs; online stores also include labels on digital listings.

Sexually explicit lyrics are not new to the recording industry. Consider the double entendres from Bessie Smith's 1928 recording "Empty Bed Blues" in which she variously describes her man's love-making skills.

Smith's spicy lyrics were in line with centuries of tradition. Four hundred years earlier the Renaissance composer Jacob Arcadelt (1507–1568) set the words "a thousand deaths per day I'd be content to die" in his Italian **madrigal** "Il bianco e dolce cigno" ("The White and Sweet Swan"). Dying, in the parlance of the day, was a metaphor for sexual intercourse.

THE MIDDLE AGES

Life in the Middle Ages (ca. 400–ca. 1430) was not easy. Common people lived in thatched or stone cottages near or on their lord's estate. Sharing the living quarters with livestock provided much-needed warmth in the winter. The church and the nobility controlled wealth and power. The social order of these two institutions was highly regulated. Almost every aspect of upper-class and religious life unfolded according to strict formulas of behavior. Rituals and ceremonies provided welcome routine in an age when nature's capriciousness, rulers' whims, and wandering armies could wreak havoc at any time.

Since commoners were not literate, music from the Middle Ages was written down by the clergy or nobility. Sacred monophonic chant constitutes the largest repertory from this period, but by the 13th and 14th centuries polyphonic genres such as the **motet** and chanson had been established.

Antoine Busnoys (ca. 1430–1492)

The creative era of the troubadours and trouvères came to an end around the time of the Black Death (1348), but the idea of unrequited love lingered on. Here we look at an example from the 15th century, a chanson (French for "song") by Antoine Busnoys (Boon-**wah**, or Boon-**way**). Little is known of Busnoys's professional life. Presumably, like other composers of the time, he moved from church to court as opportunities became available. One thing we know for certain is that he worked as a singer at the powerful Burgundian Court of Charles the Bold (1433–1477). We also know that Busnoys had a scandalous side. On at least five occasions he arranged to have "a certain priest" beaten. One consequence of those acts was excommunication (though he was later reprieved), no small penalty in those times.

Like most composers of the 15th century, Busnoys wrote polyphonic chansons, usually for three voices and usually in one of three *formes fixes* (fixed poetic forms). These works were mostly love songs intended for the entertainment of the court. As with the medieval tradition of courtly love, the topics often dealt with unrequited love, forced separation of lovers, or praise and devotion toward a noble lady. Quite often, the male in the song suffered extreme anguish over a lost or unattainable lover.

Shepherd and Shepherdess Making Music, South Netherlandish tapestry, ca. 1500–1530.

Courtesy of The Metropolitan Museum of Art, Bequest of Susan Vanderpoel Clark, 1967.

Busnoys was known for putting secret messages in his music. Sometimes he hid his name in the text; sometimes instead of musical notation he wrote cryptic poems to indicate the exact notes and rhythms of a line. The chanson we examine below contains an acrostic that spells out the name Jaqueljne D'Aqvevjle (j=i and v=u). (See the first letter of each line.) Only those few who looked at the manuscript would have noticed the reference. This is one of four Busnoys chansons that, in one way or another, refer to the mysterious Jacqueline.

There were two women named Jacqueline de Hacqueville whom we can identify during Busnoys's life. Either might be the chanson's subject. One was the wife of Jean Bouchart, a Parisian nobleman. There is some evidence that Busnoys had an affair with this Jacqueline in the 1460s. The other candidate was a lady-in-waiting, first for Princess Margaret Stuart (of Scotland) and later for Marie d'Anjou, wife of France's Charles VII. In either case, neither woman would have been openly available to Busnoys, a cleric bound to celibacy in the Catholic Church. Perhaps this is why Busnoys uses the formulaic voice of courtly love to further hide his real lover's identity.

"Je ne puis vivre" is in the form of a *bergerette* (one of the era's *formes fixes*). At the beginning and end of a bergerette there is a refrain, where the text and music are the same (notated as "A"). Following the first "A" is a pair of two-line stanzas sung to the same music (notated as "b, b"— lower case because the stanzas have different texts). Next comes a new seven-line verse sung to the same music as the "A" refrain (notated as "a"). Finally, the opening "A" section is repeated. Thus, the form of the bergerette is AbbaA (7 lines–2 lines–2 lines–7 lines–7 lines).

Two more of the song's characteristics exemplify the era's aesthetic values. First, the rhythmic quality of the melodies is ambiguous, alternating between duple and triple groupings. Second, Busnoys alternates between syllabic and melismatic text settings. In "Je ne puis vivre," each section of the form opens syllabically, with every tone given one syllable of text. The end of nearly every phrase ends melismatically, with a flurry of notes for each syllable.

Notice too, the relationship between the three voices. Using a technique called imitation, they sing almost the same melody, but each voice enters a bit later than the other (much like a round). As the piece develops, Busnoys changes the distance between the imitating voices. He also varies the order in which the voices enter. Composers in the latter half of the 15th century were just beginning to experiment with an imitative texture. Busnoys was among the first.

For early Renaissance composers, experimenting with texture, the interweaving of individual lines, and the subtleties of rhythmic play trumped the logical and neatly ordered expression of text.

Emotional tone painting of the sort we explored above with Belle was not part of the 15th-century aesthetic. That said, today's listeners might easily interpret the imitating (or "chasing") voices as mirroring the pursuit of unattainable love that occasioned the narrator's teary misery.

PERFORMING CHANSONS

Composers in the 15th century rarely specified performing forces. Most chansons were written for three voices, but as far as scholars can tell, they could have been performed by vocalists (male or female), instrumentalists, or a combination of singers and instruments.

LISTENING 10.4 GUIDE

"Je ne puis vivre ainsy toujours" ("I Cannot Live Like This Forever"), by Antoine Busnoys

Texture: Polyphonic
Meter: Duple and triple
Form: AbbaA (Bergerette)

Section A
The first voice to sing is the soprano, imitated quickly by the tenor (0:03). At 0:15 the alto enters and tenor drops out. All three voices cadence at 0:28. Notice that some words are pronounced differently from modern French.

0:00	Je ne puis vivre ainsy toujours	I cannot live like this forever
	Au mains que j'aye en mes dolours	Unless I have, in my misery

In this part, the tenor and soprano begin together, imitated by the alto at 0:32.

0:30	Quelque confort	Some comfort;
	Une seulle heure ou mains ou fort;	Only an hour—or less or more,
	Et tous les jours	And every day
	Léaument serviray Amours	I will serve you loyally, Love,
	Jusqu'a la mort.	Until death.

Section b (words and music different from above, meter changes)
Each b section begins homophonically for the first three words.

1:09	Noble femme de nom et d'armes,	Lady, noble in name and arms,
	Escript vous ay ce dittier cy.	I have written this song for you,

Section b (music the same as "b" above, but new words)

1:40	Des ieux plourant a chauldes larme	Weeping warm tears from my eyes
	Affin qu'ayés de moy merchy.	In order that you have mercy upon me.

Section a (music the same as "A" above, but new words)

2:15	Quant a moi, je me meurs bon cours,	As for me, I die slowly but surely,
	Vellant les nuytz, faisant cent tours,	Awake at night, walking back and forth a hundred times
2:43	En criant fort,	Crying loudly,
	"Vengeance!" a Dieu, car a grant tort	"Vengeance," to God, because most unfairly,
	Je noye en plours;	I'm drowning in tears;
	Lorsqu'au besoin me fault secours,	Just when I need help, I get none,
	Et Pitié dort.	And Pity sleeps.

Section A (words and music the same as "A" above)

3:19	Je ne puis vivre ainsy toujours (etc.)	I cannot live like this forever (etc.)

Obsessive Love

Franz Schubert (1797–1828): "Gretchen am Spinnrade" ("Gretchen at the Spinning Wheel")

Austrian composer Franz Schubert (1797–1828) composed approximately 600 Lieder. For him, love in all its varieties was a regular theme. For example, the Lied "Der Erlkönig" (1815) describes a desperate father riding for help as his beloved son is dying in his arms. *Die Winterreise* (*The Winter's Journey*, 1827) is a massive twenty-four-piece **song cycle** telling the story of a spurned lover wandering through the dead of winter. We will study "Gretchen am Spinnrade" (1814), which Schubert composed for solo voice and piano when he was only 17 years old.

The text for "Gretchen" is from Johann Wolfgang von Goethe's (1749–1832) *Faust* (1806), the story of the lonely intellectual who makes a pact with Mephistopheles (the devil). @ 10.4 Theirs was the usual one-sided bargain: a few years of earthly pleasure in exchange for eternal damnation.

Faust's pleasure quickly results in other people's misery. As the play unfolds, he meets the innocent Gretchen, whom he is determined to seduce. With the devil's help, he succeeds— but not without complications. Along the way, Faust poisons Gretchen's mother, then murders her brother. When Gretchen becomes pregnant, Faust deserts her. Forsaken, the despairing Gretchen murders her newborn child and is eventually condemned to death.

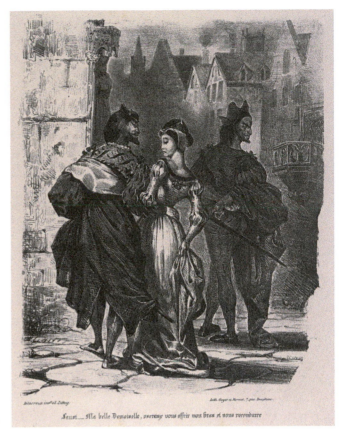

Faust Trying to Seduce Marguerite (Gretchen), Eugène Delacroix, 1825–1827.

Courtesy of The Metropolitan Museum of Art, Gift of David J. Impastato, 1962.

FRANZ SCHUBERT (1797–1828)

Franz Schubert showed extraordinary musical talent as a child, but he never became a virtuoso performer—a skill essential to making a decent living as a 19th-century musician. As a teenager, Schubert studied composition with Antonio Salieri (1750–1825), who was immortalized as Mozart's arch rival in the 1984 movie *Amadeus*. By the age of 16, Schubert had already composed numerous piano pieces, string quartets and his first symphony. Though he died at age 31, Schubert had time to write over 600 songs, nine symphonies, and a wealth of chamber music.

"Gretchen am Spinnrade" ("Gretchen at the Spinning Wheel"), by Franz Schubert

LISTENING
10.5
GUIDE

Texture: Homophonic
Meter: Compound duple
Form: Through-composed with refrain

Gretchen works her spinning wheel and obsesses over Faust, who has deserted her. Emotional balance destroyed, her mind runs in circles like the wheel which she turns. All this we infer before Gretchen sings even a word. The piano tells us this with the relentless melodic pattern that opens the composition.

continued

Except for the first verse, which Schubert uses as a refrain, each stanza is given new music, a technique that helps to portray Gretchen's restless mind. The refrain, in contrast, provides both an anchor of familiarity and reinforces the theme of circularity. Try as she might, life is going nowhere for Gretchen, just round-and-round. Schubert changes the harmonies throughout the piece, which, by shifting the floor upon which the melody stands, further contributes to the feeling of uneasiness.

The song's climax arrives on the words "sein Kuß!" ("his kiss"). As the moment approaches, the melody rises and harmonies intensify. The text becomes shorter, more breathless as Gretchen lists Faust's traits, each one fortifying the others—he is lofty, noble, kind, and strong. But his touch and kiss . . . beyond description. She is overwhelmed. The spinning stops. All is silent.

Then the obsession starts all over again. Round and round she goes. Escape is impossible.

0:00	*Refrain*	
	Meine Ruh' ist hin,	My peace is gone,
	Mein Herz ist schwer;	My heart is heavy;
	Ich finde sie nimmer	I'll never find peace,
	Und nimmermehr.	Never again.
0:24	Wo ist ihn nich hab'	When he is not with me
	Ist mir das Grab,	It's like a tomb.
	Die ganze Welt	The whole world
	Ist mir vergällt.	Is bitter.
0:38	Mien armer Kopf	My poor head
	Ist mir verrückt,	Is turned around.
	Mein armer Sinn	My poor senses
	Ist mir zerstückt.	Are torn apart.
0:57	*Refrain*	
	Meine Ruh' ist hin, . . .	My peace is gone, . . .
1:17	Nach ihm nur schau' ich	I look only for him
	Zum Fenster hinaus,	Out the window.
	Nach ihm nur geh' ich	For him only do I go
	Aus dem Haus.	Out of the house.
1:30	Sein hoher Gang	His lofty bearing.
	Sein' edle Gestalt	His noble form.
	Seines Mundes Lächeln	The smile on his lips.
	Seiner Augen Gewalt,	The power of his gaze.
1:43	Und seiner Rede	His speech's
	Zauberfluß	Magical flow.
	Seine Händedruck	The touch of his hand,
	Und ach, sein Kuß!	And then, his kiss!
2:16	*Refrain*	
	Meine Ruh' ist hin, . . .	My peace is gone, . . .
2:36	Mein Busen drängt sich	My heart pines
	nach ihm hin;	For him.
	Ach, dürft' ich fassen	Ah, if I could just touch him
	Und halten ihn	And hold him.
2:49	Und küssen ihn,	And kiss him
	So wie ich wollt',	As much as I want.
	An seinen Küssen	Beneath his kisses
	Vergehen sollt'!	I would melt away!
3:03	O konnt ich ihn kuessen	If I could just kiss him
	So wie ich wollt,	As much as I want,

	An seinen Kuessen		Beneath his kisses
	Vergehen sollt!		I would melt away!
	An seinen Kuessen		Beneath his kisses
	Vergehen sollt!		I would melt away!
3:27	[Meine Ruh' ist hin.]		My peace is gone.

Hector Berlioz (1803–1869): *Symphonie fantastique*

Like Schubert, French composer Hector Berlioz (1803–1869) was inspired by the tempest of unrequited love. For the 26-year-old Berlioz, however, the passion was of his own making. The object of his rapture, English actress Harriet Smithson (1800–54), did not even know of his existence. Perhaps the anguish was good for Berlioz. It inspired the most audacious concert music yet to be conceived in the Western art tradition. (The composition's program [story], written and distributed by the composer himself, includes opium use, murder, and a witch's orgy.)

Central to the construction of *Symphonie fantastique* is the ***idée fixe*** (fixed idea, or obsession motive) a rambling, constantly transforming melody that represents the object of his affection. Transformed to fit unfolding situations, the *idée fixe* is woven in throughout the composition. @ 10.5

Caricature of Berlioz conducting, Jean Ignace Isadore Gérard Grandville, from Louis Reybaud's *Jérome Paturot à la recherche d'une position sociale* (Paris, 1848).

We will study the symphony's fourth movement, "Marche au supplice." Berlioz's program reads:

Marche au supplice: Convinced that his love is unappreciated, the artist poisons himself with opium. The dose of the narcotic, too weak to kill, plunges him into a sleep accompanied by horrible visions. He dreams that he has killed his beloved, that he is condemned and led to the scaffold, and that he is witnessing his own execution. The procession moves forward to the sounds of a march that is now somber and fierce, now brilliant and solemn, in which the muffled noise of heavy steps gives way without transition to the noisiest clamor. At the end of the march the first four measures of the *idée fixe* reappear, like a last thought of love interrupted by the fatal blow.

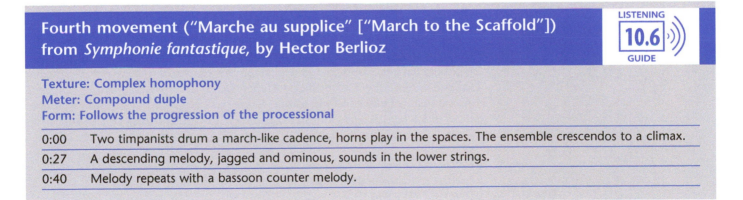

Fourth movement ("Marche au supplice" ["March to the Scaffold"]) from *Symphonie fantastique*, by Hector Berlioz

LISTENING 10.6 GUIDE

Texture: Complex homophony
Meter: Compound duple
Form: Follows the progression of the processional

0:00	Two timpanists drum a march-like cadence, horns play in the spaces. The ensemble crescendos to a climax.
0:27	A descending melody, jagged and ominous, sounds in the lower strings.
0:40	Melody repeats with a bassoon counter melody.

0:54	Full orchestra takes up the melody. Listen to the counter melodies. Do you hear a gossiping bloodthirsty crowd waiting for an execution? Anyone's execution? This sounds like a celebration. The mood is gay.
1:18	Pizzicato strings fragment the melody and turn it upside down. Bassoons chatter.
1:38	New march melody. Who would have thought an execution could be so festive?
2:20	After a pause, the march takes up again with renewed vigor.
4:08	Everything stops. Clarinet plays part of the idée fixe. Our lover's last thought? Suddenly, with a terrific crash, the guillotine comes down. Head, then drums roll. Brass fanfare. Tah-dah! The crowd cheers.

QUESTIONS FOR THOUGHT

- How do tempo and dynamics affect the emotional content of "Gretchen am Spinnrade"?
- How would you describe the texture of "Je ne puis vivre" compared to that of "Gretchen am Spinnrade"?
- We discussed the idea of obsession's circularity in "Gretchen am Spinnrade." Do you see any notion of circularity in the form of "Je ne puis vivre"?
- How does form affect the meaning of each song?
- In Schubert's work, how does the spacing of the stanzas affect the drama?
- Is "March to the Scaffold" tragic or comic, realistic or caricature? All of them?
- In the pieces we have discussed so far, which composer do you think was most concerned with creating music that mirrored the meaning of the text? How was this accomplished?

Love's Betrayals

Part of what makes Schubert's "Gretchen" so powerful is the fact that she is so unaware of her true relationship with Faust, a relationship that we on the outside can understand all too well. Could any real person be as foolish as poor Gretchen? Of course. It happens all the time.

In this section we meet a pair of spurned lovers—one innocent, the other quite worldly. On the one hand, a teenaged geisha, Cio-Cio-San, sings of rapturous love that she believes crosses cultural boundaries and will endure time and distance. She eventually learns that her husband has deserted her. On the other hand, country and western star Hank Williams has no such illusions. In song after song he looks betrayal straight in the eyes.

Madama Butterfly

Gazing seaward from the balcony of a small house in the hills above Japan's Nagasaki harbor, Cio-Cio-San waits for the return of U.S. Navy Lieutenant Pinkerton, her American husband. Three years have passed since the dashing American naval officer set out to sea. There has been no contact. Pinkerton does not even know that he is a father. Even so, Cio-Cio-San sings of her husband's

Female entertainer with Shamisen, Teisai Hokuba, early 19th century.

Courtesy of The Metropolitan Museum of Art, The Howard Mansfield Collection, Purchase, Rogers Fund, 1936.

fidelity. She sings of love's unshakeable power to bridge time and space, to navigate the abyss between cultures East and West.

Alas, Pinkerton has not been faithful. In fact, apparently he hardly thinks of her at all. He will soon return, however. When that happens, Cio-Cio-San's straw world of illusion comes crashing down.

Italian composer Giacomo Puccini's (1858–1924) *Madama Butterfly* (1904) is one of opera's most beloved stories. The music is emotionally penetrating; the plot is heartbreaking. *Butterfly*, a tale of an American sailor's hubris and a Japanese girl's innocence, reflects the ways in which Europeans perceived American and Japanese culture at the dawn of the 20th century. As for love betrayed, that theme is timeless.

As for the plot, not much happens externally. The important events are internal, played out in the players' hearts and minds. Below is a synopsis of the story.

ACT I Nagasaki, Japan. U.S. Navy Lieutenant B.F. Pinkerton inspects a house he has just leased from a marriage broker. Included in the deal is Cio-Cio-San (Madama Butterfly), a ready-made wife. For the foot-loose Pinkerton, the marriage is just a lark. Not for Cio-Cio-San. The 16-year-old girl plans to devote her life to her new husband. In renouncing her Buddhist faith to become Christian, she turns her back on both family and culture.

ACT II. Three years have passed. Cio-Cio-San awaits her husband's return. The money is almost gone; other suitors are asking for her hand. Cio-Cio-San insists that she has not been deserted. And even if she has, the point is moot. Pride will not allow her to return to her former life. A cannon blast in the harbor announces the arrival of an American ship, Pinkerton's. As dusk falls, Cio-Cio-San prepares for her husband's return.

ACT III. It is dawn and Cio-Cio-San has fallen asleep waiting. Pinkerton enters with Kate, his American wife. Cio-Cio-San awakens and realizes the terrible truth. She agrees to surrender her son to the couple but only if Pinkerton himself returns to fetch him. Alone again, Cio-Cio-San bows before a statue of the Buddha, then takes a dagger and prepares to commit *seppuku*, ritual suicide. As she dies, Pinkerton's voice can be heard calling to her from the distance.

"Un bel dì, vedremo" ("One Fine Day") from the opera *Madama Butterfly*, by Giacomo Puccini

LISTENING
10.7
GUIDE

Texture: Homophonic
Meter: Triple, quadruple and duple
Form: ABA[1]

In this Act II aria Cio-Cio-San sings of her lover's return. She tells her servant, Suzuki, how she will hide at his approach, both to tease him and so not to die from the excitement of reunion.

She will die, but not from love's ecstasy. We in the audience already know all this. But we are powerless observers and Cio-Cio-San cannot be saved. As Puccini understood, this makes listening to the aria all the more devastating.

The music begins with a soaring melody in the soprano's upper range. Gradually the melody relaxes its way downward. Notice the characteristic sound of the highly trained operatic vocal style: the smooth diction, the pure tone nuanced by the use of vibrato. Cio-Cio-San seems to pause and savor each word of the opening line—"One fine day, we will see . . . "

Anticipation, which kept her suspended in that lovely hopeful upper range, is eased as she describes the smoke of the ship entering the harbor. Think about the imagery. Is love strong like a great ship plowing the seas? Or is love fleeting, like smoke in the wind?

0:00	**Section A** (triple meter)
Un bel dì, vedremo	One fine, clear day, we shall see
Levarsi un fil di fumo	A thin trail of smoke arising,
Sull'estremo confin del mare.	On the distant horizon, far out to sea.
E poi la nave appare.	And then the ship appears.

0:40 Puccini moves the lyrics forward as he paints a sensuous picture of the ship—brave and powerful against the blue sea. Once again, he slows the action. "En . . . tra . . . nel porto," she sings, pausing on the word "enter," as if the ship will never arrive. An upward melody paints the stalwart power of the ship's canons. And again, the words slow as Cio-Cio-San savors Pinkerton's arrival.

Poi la nave bianca	Then the white ship
Entra nel porto,	Enters into the harbor,
Romba il suo saluto.	And thunders out its greeting.
Vedi? È venuto!	You see? He has arrived!

1:20 Now we learn about the inner life of this child/woman. Despite the years of waiting, she will continue to play love's seductive games. She will be coy. He must come to her.

Io non gli scendo incontro. Io no.	I'll not go down to meet him. Not I.

Section B

The key changes to minor and the meter is now duple. The orchestra plays long notes while Cio-Cio-San seems to "talk" to herself, using one syllable per note.

Mi metto là sul ciglio del colle e aspetto,	I shall stay on the hillside and wait,
E aspetto gran tempo	And wait for a long time,
E non mi pesa	And I'll not grow weary
La lunga attesa.	Of the long wait.

1:50

E uscito dalla folla cittadina,	Emerging from the city crowds,
un uomo, un picciol punto	A man is coming, a tiny speck
s'avvia per la collina.	Starts to climb the hill.

2:20

Chi sarà? chi sarà?	Who is he? Who?
E come sarà giunto	And when he arrives.
Che dirà? che dirà?	What will he say? What will he say?
Chiamerà Butterfly dalla lontana.	He will call "Butterfly" from the distance.
Io senza dar risposta	I, without answering,
Me ne starò nascosta	Will remain hidden.
Un po' per celia.	A little to tease him.

3:00 **Section A¹**

The opening melody reappears, giving balance and a sense of closing to the aria. The familiar melody is briefly interrupted by an almost frantic assertion to Suzuki that Pinkerton will return. The aria ends in an emotional frenzy, literally on a high note as Cio-Cio-San sings "l'aspetto" ("I will wait for him."). The orchestra sounds the last trace of the hopeful, poignant theme.

E un po' per non morire	And a little so as not to die,
Al primo incontro;	At our first meeting;
Ed egli alquanto in pena	And then rather worried
Chiamerà, chiamerà:	He will call, he will call:
"Piccina mogliettina,	"My little one, my tiny wife
Olezzo di verbena"	Perfumed Verbena"
I nomi che mi dava al suo venire.	The names he gave me when he came last.
[a Suzuki]	[to Suzuki)]
Tutto questo avverrà,	All this will happen,
Te lo prometto.	I promise you.
Tieni la tua paura,	Keep your fears to yourself,
Io con sicura fede l'aspetto.	I, with faithful trust will wait for him.

Country and Western Music and Hank Williams (1923–1953)

Puccini built his story on a matrix of innocence, deception, and revelation. Country and western love songs rarely bother with such complexity. Instead, the genre cuts right to the chase. Infidelity may hurt, but it is rarely a surprise.

Few figures in American popular life have inspired the public imagination as much as singer/songwriter Hank Williams. In a few short years, the once dirt-poor Alabama country boy helped transform country and western music from regional curiosity to national voice. Along the way, Williams brought new depth to the genre's principal song topic: love gone wrong.

Authenticity and hard living were the Williams trademarks. He grew up tough and fast, learned to smoke and drink before his teens, and was soon addicted to painkillers and women. His music drew from bitter personal experience—from the hurt of poverty, the hurt of a father rarely seen, the hurt of both domineering mother and wife, and from the dull pain of too many one-night stands.

Mostly hidden from the public was the rage. Williams was insecure and self-destructive, often violent. Fistfights were common; he carried a handgun. Williams burned his candle quickly and brightly. He would be a national star by age 25, dead from drink and drugs at age 29.

Williams never learned to read music. He learned to play guitar mostly by watching others. His only teacher, and perhaps his strongest adult role model, was Rufus Payne, a street singer. Payne taught Williams how to drink, how to survive on the streets, and how to play some guitar. Most importantly, he taught Williams how to entertain an audience.

Hank Williams: signed portrait, 1952.

By the seventh grade, the boy was featured twice weekly in fifteen-minute slots on Montgomery, Alabama's WSFA radio station. The airplay led to regional performances. Some were in schoolhouses; most were in roadhouses where Williams performed on stages protected by chicken wire to keep flying bottles at bay. Williams dropped out of school at age 19, still in the ninth grade.

The following summer Williams met Audrey Mae Sheppard Guy. She became his first wife and hoped to become his onstage partner as well. Short on musical talent, Guy never succeeded on stage. She does deserve some credit for her husband's career, however. She was the inspiration for some of his loneliest songs.

By 1946, Williams was a rising star. He headed to Nashville to audition for the publisher Acuff-Rose. A songwriting contract followed, then recordings. Even the early titles—such as "Wealth Won't Save Your Soul" and "Never Again (Will I Knock on Your Door)"—suggest the dark abyss that was the singer's private life. More upbeat in mood, but firmly within the country and western love genre was the songwriter's first big hit, "Honky Tonkin" (1947), a classic party song for the down and out.

Hank and Audrey lived the stories about which he sang. They fought often and violently. Infidelity was rampant on both sides. Audrey filed for divorce in early 1948, but the couple stayed together a while longer. (That fall they conceived Randall Hank Williams, country and western superstar Hank Williams Jr.)

Later that year Williams's career bumped upward when he was booked onto Shreveport's *Louisiana Hayride*, which was broadcast over the 50,000-watt radio station, KWKH. A contract at Nashville's Grand Ole Opry soon followed. The slump-shouldered 6'1," 140-pound singer/songwriter was on his way to becoming the genre's biggest star.

In 1948 he also recorded "The Lovesick Blues," Williams's first Billboard No. 1 country and western hit. The song, quaintly upbeat despite the desperation in the lyrics, is a study in contradictions.

One moment Williams's voice cracks, is if overcome by emotion. The next moment the hurt transforms into a playful yodel suggesting perhaps an "easy come/easy go" approach to relationships. Overall, Williams does not seem particularly upset by his loss.

Williams had found his mature compositional voice, which generally combined at least two perspectives on love. At the center was heartbreak. But the narratives were also aloof, as if one partner or the other was determined to keep love at a distance.

A series of hits followed this pattern, including in 1950 "Why Don't You Love Me" and "Long Gone Lonesome Blues," and in 1951 "Hey Good Lookin'" and "Cold, Cold Heart." Invariably, the songs' lyrics rang with autobiographical truths and the guilty hurt of infidelity. Most successful of all was "Your Cheatin' Heart," one of Williams's last compositions. A popular belief is that the song draws directly from his real-life marriage to Audrey. That may be so, but Williams never lacked for relationships capable of fulfilling this song's narrative.

As his reputation grew, Williams found himself imitated in musical areas far outside country and western. Italian-American crooner Tony Bennett (b. 1926) covered "Cold, Cold Heart." Others who recorded his music included pop singers Rosemary Clooney (1928–2002) (actor George Clooney's aunt) and the versatile singer/comedienne Jo Stafford (1917–2008). Almost single-handedly, Williams was giving country and western a national profile.

It is a curious reality that although country and western performers often project a hard-drinking and fast-loving persona, things tend to fall apart when that image is actually lived. This is especially true in the upper echelons of the entertainment industry where the financial consequences of canceled or compromised performances can be catastrophic. For Williams, fame and fortune did nothing to slow his self-destructive behavior. The drinking binges worsened, sometimes lasted for weeks. His career quickly disintegrated.

Yet even as his life descended into chaos, Williams's songs remained studies in fragile contradictions. He lived a life of too much alcohol and too many women, of failed promises and broken hopes. He never wrote as if any of these attributes were desirable. The songs throb with hurt.

Williams was inside all of his best songs. The personality that emerges from the music is of a sensitive, fractured, and easily wounded mercurial loner. Often he is aloof, sometimes just beaten down. But—in stark contrast to his real life—the Williams of song is never heartless, never hurtful.

LISTENING
10.8
GUIDE

"Your Cheatin' Heart," by Hank Williams

Texture: Homophonic
Meter: Duple
Form: Strophic, modified 32-bar song form (Intro–AABA– BA (interlude)–AABA)

The melody and lyrics have a natural and untutored feel. Each eight-bar section is built on two-bar melodic groupings. These aspects combine to give the song the quality of inevitability. There are no surprises to be found here.

The lyrics tell of a love affair gone wrong and the pain of infidelity. Even though she has left him, she too is going to suffer. Maybe not now, but soon enough.

But this is more than a revenge song. Listen to Williams's voice and how he uses vocal timbre to elicit our sympathy. Notice the tightness in his throat, how the voice is on the verge of cracking. Is he about to cry?

In case his own suffering is not already clear enough, Williams says it outright. "You'll walk the floor/The way I do," he sings. But "someday" (presumably when it's too late for reconciliation), that cheatin' heart of yours is going to "tell on you."

Notice the arrangement as well. While Williams sings over a simple bass line, the other melodic interest comes from the pedal steel guitar and the violin, which comment at the ends of vocal phrases. The steel guitar, which was still a relatively new sound to country music in the early 1950s, gets the first half of the interlude. Then the violin takes over.

THE PEDAL STEEL GUITAR

Though perhaps the most iconic of all country and western music sounds, the steel guitar has its roots not in Nashville or Memphis, but Hawaii. The term "steel" comes not from the instrument itself, which originally was an ordinary guitar, but from the metal slide the performer would use with his left hand. A similar technique, known as bottleneck guitar, was developed in early blues styles. The biggest difference between the two styles was that steel guitars were played horizontally, with the strings facing upward. Perhaps because the instrument traveled quickly with sailors, Hawaiian steel guitars soon became popular worldwide, from Nigeria (where they were heard in the pop music style *juju*) to Nashville. In the United States, innovators quickly dropped the acoustic body, which was replaced by electric pick-ups, a development that also helped to spur innovations in the electric guitar. Today, musicians like Robert Randolph are creating sounds never imagined by the instrument's early innovators.

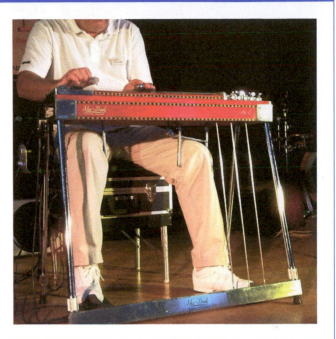

Steel guitar.

Patlaff/Wikimedia Commons/CC-BY-SA-3.0.

QUESTIONS FOR THOUGHT

- Think about the orchestral accompaniment of "Un bel dì vedremo." What instruments are used? How does the accompaniment contribute to the overall feeling of the aria?
- A Puccini trait is to double the vocalist's melody in the orchestra. Notice when he does this. Does he always double with the same instruments?
- Listen to Williams's "Honky Tonkin'." The singer invites "Miss Sad and Lonely" over to party, but expects her to pay. And when is she to come over? When she is down and out. Some party this is going to be. Notice also how he repeats "honky tonkin'." Why might he do this?
- How do the vocal qualities of Belle vs. Cio-Cio-San vs. Hank Williams affect the emotional content of each piece?
- Belle, Gretchen, and Cio-Cio-San are all in their teens. Do their vocal styles reflect their youth? How so or why not?

ACTIVITIES AND ASSIGNMENTS

- Compare the plots of *Madama Butterfly* and the musical *Miss Saigon*.
- Find additional songs about betrayal. How do the composers/performers communicate meaning?
- Compare Hank Williams's performance of "Lovesick Blues" with other performers, such as Patsy Cline, Charley Pride, or LeAnn Rimes. How do they differ, both musically and emotionally?
- Plan out a love song. What kind of poem would you use? What form? What instruments? How would your music portray meaning?

The Last Word: "La Vie en Rose"

Having surveyed budding love, idealized love, seduction, unobtainable love, obsessive, and unfaithful love, we close the chapter with an example of love's unquenchable spirit as portrayed in French chanteuse Edith Piaf's "La Vie en Rose" (1945). Piaf, whose own life was filled with the hurt of love gone awry, performs the song with an edge that convinces even the most hardened cynic that love cures all.

Piaf's American legacy is rich. Since 1990 over fifty-seven CDs of her music have been reissued. "La Vie en Rose" has been featured in dozens of movies, including *Bull Durham* (1988), *Saving Private Ryan* (1998), and *Something's Gotta Give* (2003). Performers who have recently covered the song include Grace Jones (b. 1948), Cyndi Lauper (b. 1953), and Celine Dion (b. 1968).

Edith Piaf, 1962.
Eric Koch/Nationaal Archief/
Wikimedia Commons/
CC-BY-SA-3.0-NL.

EDITH PIAF (1915–1963)

Edith Piaf remains one of France's most celebrated cultural icons. Her rags-to-riches story began with a broken family. Abandoned by her parents, she lived with her grandmother, who ran a brothel. Prostitutes helped raise her. Piaf had a child of her own by 17. Love life went from bad to worse when she took up with a pimp who forced her to hand over singing wages—that or sell her body as a prostitute.

At age 20, Piaf was discovered by Louis Leplée, a successful nightclub owner. With Leplée's help, Piaf received her first recording contracts. The good luck did not hold, however. Leplée was murdered the following year. Piaf was initially a suspect.

Despite a string of lovers, failed marriages, and scandals, Piaf's career continued to grow. She would perform eight times on American television's Sunday night variety-show *The Ed Sullivan Show* (broadcast 1948–1971), sing twice in Carnegie Hall, and appear in ten films. Her discography fills ten CDs. Piaf's last years were riddled with tragedy, including the death of a lover in a plane crash, a series of car accidents, alcohol abuse, and drug dependence. She died of liver cancer at age 47.

LISTENING 10.9 GUIDE

"La Vie en Rose" (1945), lyrics by Édith Piaf, music by Louis Guglielmi

Texture: Homophonic
Meter: Quadruple
Form: Strophic (A A¹A² B A³)

0:00	Orchestral introduction presents the song's main tune.
0:13	Piaf begins with a short recitative-like introduction.

0:26	**Phrase A**
	The melody begins at the top of the scale and relaxes gently downward, with the ease of the embrace that it describes. The tune ends on the inconclusive dominant harmony, telling us that there is more to come. Brass instruments seem to respond to her sentiments.
	Quand il me prend dans ses bras... When he takes me in his arms . . .

0:38	**Phrase A¹**
	Not only is there more to come, but better things as well. We move from embrace to words of love. As emotions move a notch higher, so does the lovely melody, which begins on "re" instead of "do" and then follows a similar downward trajectory.
	Il me dit des mots d'amour . . . He tells me words of love . . .

0:50	**A² phrase**
	Piaf returns to the opening pitch of phrase A, then sings a variation on the opening melody. Graceful and fresh, the melody, like love itself, seems to hold infinite possibilities for change and development.

1:02	**Phrase B**
	Here comes the confident—"we are destined for each other"—conclusion to all those A variations. On the highest pitches of the song, Piaf sings, "for life."
	C'est lui pour moi... It's him for me . . .

1:17	**Phrase A³**
	Very similar to the first A phase but ends conclusively on the tonic.

| 1:30 | Another recitative commentary |

| 1:47 | Quand il me prend dans ses bras . . .   When he takes me in his arms . . . |

Conclusion

In the movie *La Vie en Rose* (2008), an American journalist asks Piaf, "If you were to give advice to a woman, what would it be?" Piaf answers, "LOVE. To a young girl? LOVE. To a child? LOVE." Piaf understood that lives are shaped by love's grace, as well as its denial. Such is the human condition. Busnoys may have expressed his love in the musical language of the distant past, but the emotional experiences to which he gave voice may be ours as well. So too, we might share the distress of Schubert's Gretchen and Puccini's Cio-Cio San. Though separated by time and place, culture and language, perhaps we are not so different after all.

Key Terms

- *fin amours*
- idée fixe
- intermezzo
- Lieder
- *Querrelle des Bouffons*
- strophic

Essay Questions

- **Many people experience in music the power to enhance feelings of love. Why might this be?**
- **What types of love did we not discuss in this chapter? Can you think of musical examples?**

MUSICAL
NARRATIVES

CHAPTER GOALS

- To demonstrate how social issues are reflected in musical theater.
- To provide an overview of 20th-century American musical theater.
- To explore three groundbreaking 20th-century musicals.

CHAPTER ELEVEN

American Musical Theater

QUESTIONS FOR THOUGHT

- Do you have a favorite musical? Why does it appeal to you? Is it the music? The plot? The message? A combination of all of these?
- What are the characteristics of musicals you have seen or know about?

The lights are bright on Broadway—especially around Times Square, the heart of New York City's theater district. Today's tourists look skyward to gawk at giant computerized billboards; earlier generations were dazzled by the millions of electric lights that illuminated theater marquees. It was not for nothing that in 1902, just twenty years after the building of New York City's first electric power plant, the district earned the moniker "The Great White Way."

For actors, the theater district is a land where dreams are realized, but sometimes crushed. Generations of the nation's most talented thespians have flocked to New York in hopes of seeing their names on a theater marquee. Some succeed.

For audiences, the spotlighted stages of darkened theaters are sites where imagination becomes reality. Days are lived in minutes; lives are lived in hours. Love is often right around the corner, perhaps as close as a well-crafted song.

This chapter provides an overview of American musical theater. @ 11.1 We discuss and study examples from a variety of shows, but focus on three seminal productions covering a sixty-year period: *Show Boat* (1927), *West Side Story* (1957), and *Into the Woods* (1987). The three share five specific characteristics:

- All are "book musicals," that is, music and dance are integrated into the story.
- All are based on earlier literary sources.
- Each was subsequently made into a movie.
- All feature romantic love while highlighting vexing issues regarding social class or ethnicity.
- Each brought important innovations to Broadway.

The works are connected by "creative" heritage as well. Oscar Hammerstein II (1895–1960), who wrote the book and lyrics for *Show Boat*, was a mentor to Stephen Sondheim (b. 1930). @ 11.2 Sondheim's first Broadway assignment was as lyricist for *West Side Story*. Thirty years later, Sondheim wrote both music and lyrics for *Into the Woods*, the work we consider first.

> "There's no business like show business, like no business I know."
>
> —Irving Berlin (1888–1989)

Broadway show billboards at the corner of 7th Avenue and West 47th Street in Times Square, New York City. MattWade/Wikimedia Commons/CC-BY-SA-3.0.

Into the Woods (1987)

"Anything can happen in the woods," sings Cinderella's prince. He's right. In the woods, confusion reigns. A witch may be foiled, an angry giant slain.

Imagine all the Brothers Grimm stories you learned as a child all jumbled together as if ingredients in a single fairytale stew. Stir in some music and you have Stephen Sondheim's *Into the Woods*. Cinderella, Rapunzel, Little Red Riding Hood, Prince Charming, and Jack of beanstalk fame are all there. Each lives within her or his storybook world. But each also plays a role in the lives of the others.

There is plenty to engage the audience in the story itself. But underneath the surface world of the fairytale characters, *Into the Woods* is a theatrical parable about personal responsibility and the real lives we live—from the opportunities we encounter (but often fail to recognize) to the consequences we reap. Like real people, the show's characters are complex. Conflicted and unsure, they are alternately brave and cowardly, morally true or false. Often they are lost in a dangerous forest of their own making.

Evening in the Woods, Worthington Whittredge, 1876
Courtesy of The Metropolitan Museum of Art, Bequest of Henry H. Cook, 1905.

Into the Woods overflows with wonderful music, but we will look at only one song from a single scene, which features a meeting between the Baker and his long-missing father. The situation echoes Sondheim's own life. Sondheim's parents divorced when he was 10 years old. After that, Sondheim's father disappeared from his life. Fortuitously, the boy was then getting to know a neighborhood friend's father, Oscar Hammerstein. When, a few years later, the teenaged Sondheim sought some musical advice, Hammerstein was there to help. He taught him how to build a theatrical character, structure a song, and develop a story. For Hammerstein, a song not only needed to be complete in itself, it also had to enhance character and forward plot. It was a lesson Sondheim took to heart. He follows that formula in "No More."

The meeting takes place shortly after the "beanstalk" Giant has killed the Baker's wife. The Baker's inclination is to give up, desert his infant child and friends, and run away. Instead, as he wanders through the woods the Baker encounters the Mysterious Man (his father) who deserted his own family many years ago. Will son be like father? Maybe.

> "Careful the wish you make. Wishes are children."
> —Stephen Sondheim

"No More" from *Into the Woods*, music and lyrics by Stephen Sondheim

LISTENING 11.1 GUIDE

Texture: Homophonic
Meter: Duple and quadruple
Form: Strophic

"I thought you were dead," begins the Baker. They talk. The father admits he ran from his obligations. Then he accuses his son of planning to do the same. Harsh words, but true.

0:00	The song is introduced. The Baker, clearly blaming his father for his own troubles, sings that he will ask "no more questions" about being abandoned.
0:20	The Mysterious Man responds that children, not just parents, will disappoint. Then he adds, "forgive though they won't."
0:32	The Baker sings, "No more riddles . . . "
0:49	The Baker wants to shut down his emotional world. He continues, "No more feelings . . . " He is on the brink of true defeat.
1:09	Briefly courageous, the Mysterious Man will reach back into his son's life—just long enough to save him. Imitating his son's folly, the Mysterious Man sings, "Running away, let's do it . . . "
1:56	"Running away, we'll do it," he continues. He does not mean those words. He wisely adds, "The farther you run, the more you feel undefined."
2:35	As understanding briefly dawns, the two men sing together, "Like father, like son." The Mysterious Man runs away into the woods.
2:50	Singing to no one, and everyone, the Baker finishes the song on the otherwise empty stage. "No more giants . . . " Whatever comes, the Baker, unlike his father, will stand firm. We have resolution.

QUESTIONS FOR THOUGHT

- The Baker's father appears to live in the woods. Perhaps he never leaves. How does this square with his statement, "The farther you run, the more you feel undefined"?

ACTIVITIES AND ASSIGNMENTS

- Compare the film version of *Into the Woods* (2014, directed Rob Marshal) with a video of the 1987 Broadway production. Which do you prefer? Why?
- How does the music reflect (or perhaps not reflect) the father/son conversation? Do you learn anything about the two men through the music?

American Musical Theater: The Early Years

Historians tend to mark the beginning of American musical theater with the 1866 premiere of *The Black Crook*, a five-and-one-half-hour extravaganza that featured an inane plot and forgettable music. No matter. Audiences flocked to see the remarkable stage sets, and especially the scantily clad 100-woman "Amazon" chorus. The show ran for over a year at Niblo's Garden, a 3200-seat auditorium located at the corner of Broadway and Prince Street in Lower Manhattan. *Crook* set the bar for a series of similar extravaganzas that followed.

Also popular at the time were two other musical genres: **burlesque** and **blackface minstrelsy**. The former were not girlie shows as the word would imply today, but comic musical spoofs of serious plays, operas, or dance. A number of works by William Shakespeare were reconceived as burlesques.

Minstrel shows featured skits, songs, and dance in which white entertainers—their faces blackened with burnt-cork—parodied African-American culture. The genre's origin is attributed to New York City comedian Thomas Dartmouth Rice (1808–1860), who created the character Jim Crow. Rice's song "Jump Jim Crow" (we know the melody today as "Turkey in the Straw") achieved popularity nationwide. Imitators developed a series of "black" characters, including the urban dandy Zip Coon and the exuberant musician Mr. Tambo. The song "Dixie's Land," probably written in 1859 by Ohio-native Daniel Decatur Emmett (1815–1904), was popular on the New York City minstrel stage

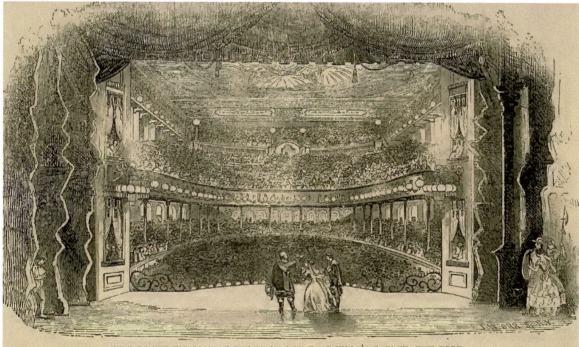

VIEW OF THE INTERIOR OF THE OPERA HOUSE, AT NIBLO'S GARDEN, NEW YORK.

Opera House at Niblo's Garden, New York City, 1853, from Gleason's *Pictorial Drawing-Room Companion,* vol. 4 no. 20 (Saturday, May 14, 1853), Boston, Engraved by J. W. Orr.

AFRICAN AMERICANS AND THE MINSTREL STAGE

After the Civil War, African Americans also composed for, and performed on, the minstrel stage. The idea of black actors imitating white actors imitating black culture seems absurd until one realizes that this was an effective (and complicated) strategy for people of color to break into the segregated entertainment industry. Black musicians who worked in the minstrel style included James A. Bland (1854–1911), who composed "Carry Me Back to Ole Virginny"; Will Marion Cook (1869–1944), whose show *In Dahomey* (1903) played on Broadway and received a command performance at Buckingham Palace; and Ernest Hogan (1865–1909), who is credited with helping to create the genre "ragtime."

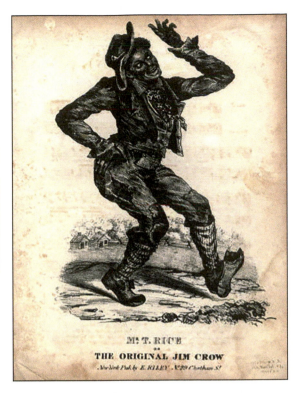

Cover to early edition of "Jump Jim Crow" sheet music with Thomas D. Rice pictured in his blackface role, 1832.

Courtesy of the Robert Cushman Butler Collection of Theatrical Illustrations, Washington State University Libraries.

before it became associated with the Confederacy during the American Civil War. Minstrelsy remained popular into the 20th century. Jack Robin, the protagonist in *The Jazz Singer* (1927), cinema's first "talkie," performed in blackface (Chapter 12: Music and Film).

European **operettas**, popular in the United States throughout the 19th century, also helped shape the earliest Broadway productions. Operettas were light-hearted, comic, and contained catchy tunes and spoken dialog. Hugely popular was the British team of W.S. Gilbert (1836–1911) and Arthur Sullivan (1842–1900), whose operettas include *H.M.S. Pinafore* (1878), *The Pirates of Penzance* (1879), and *The Mikado* (1885). A generation later, immigrant composers such as Irishman Victor Herbert (1859–1924) (*Babes in Toyland* [1903] and *Naughty Marietta* [1910]) and the Czech Rudolf Friml (1879–1972) (*Rose Marie* [1924] and *Vagabond King* [1925]) would write for both Broadway and Hollywood.

George M. Cohan (1878–1942) gets credit for "inventing" American musical theater as we know it today. The child of traveling **vaudeville** performers, Cohan, grew up on stage. @ 11.3 He wrote and performed his own material before reaching his teens. Cohen's shows were feel-good celebrations of American life. Storylines featured ordinary people experiencing extraordinary moments in their everyday lives. His characters spoke in the vernacular language of the time; music and dance numbers drew from the latest fads in popular culture. Classic Cohan songs include "Give My Regards to Broadway" and "Yankee Doodle Boy," both from his 1904 musical *Little Johnny Jones*.

Variety was central to the approach of the great impresario Florenz Ziegfeld (1867–1932) whose annual *Follies* show was a Broadway fixture from 1907 to 1932. Ziegfeld himself had no training in any of the theatrical arts, but he knew how to deliver what people liked. Regular stars of the Follies included W.C. Fields, Will Rogers, Anna Held, Fanny Brice (portrayed later by Barbra Streisand [b. 1942] in the Jule Styne [1905–1994] musical *Funny Girl* [1964]), and many others. Always, Ziegfeld featured bevies of beautiful women in various states of undress. Productions were a mishmash of stand-up comedy, skits, and song and dance. Teams of composers supplied the music.

Cover to English sheet music edition of "Give My Regards to Broadway," from *Little Johnny Jones*, 1904.

Courtesy of the Museum of the City of New York.

Irving Berlin at the piano and the stars of the film, *Alexander's Ragtime Band* (*Boston Globe*, 1938).

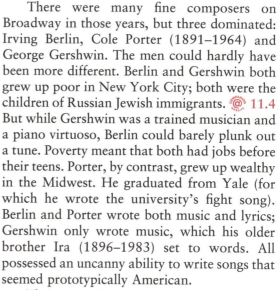

Cole Porter, Yale College, 1913.
Courtesy of Yale University Manuscripts & Archives Digital Images Database.

There were many fine composers on Broadway in those years, but three dominated: Irving Berlin, Cole Porter (1891–1964) and George Gershwin. The men could hardly have been more different. Berlin and Gershwin both grew up poor in New York City; both were the children of Russian Jewish immigrants. @ 11.4 But while Gershwin was a trained musician and a piano virtuoso, Berlin could barely plunk out a tune. Poverty meant that both had jobs before their teens. Porter, by contrast, grew up wealthy in the Midwest. He graduated from Yale (for which he wrote the university's fight song). Berlin and Porter wrote both music and lyrics; Gershwin only wrote music, which his older brother Ira (1896–1983) set to words. All possessed an uncanny ability to write songs that seemed prototypically American.

Their creative range was remarkable. Berlin, who wrote at least a song a day for his entire professional life, composed "God Bless America" and "White Christmas." His first hit, "Alexander's Ragtime Band" (1911), helped bring the broken syncopations of early jazz into popular song. "There's No Business Like Show Business," from his last hit Broadway show, *Annie Get Your Gun* (1946), would become Broadway's unofficial anthem.

Porter was the most elegant, and often the most eloquent, of the Tin Pan Alley composers. The gay Episcopalian millionaire Indiana farm-boy's secret to songwriting success? "I'll write Jewish tunes," he told Richard Rodgers in 1926. Around that time Porter's melodies grew longer and more chromatic; he began to favor the brooding minor keys.

Porter frequently wrote of love, but usually from a cool, detached perspective. His lyrics for songs like "Let's Do It" wink at the distinction between having sex and being in love. Adolescents learn about the birds and bees, but who, besides perhaps a biologist, ever thinks about the bees "doing it"? *Fleas* rhymes fine with *bees*, but why are they educated? Porter's juxtapositions become even more absurd as the song unfolds, bringing in sponges, oysters, clams, and jellyfish to the catalog of amorous creatures.

Porter—a worldly Indiana farm-boy Ivy League graduate, gay in a closeted world—knew a thing or two about incongruous juxtapositions. He excelled in making the distinguished appear mundane, the mundane appear distinguished. Often contrasts of high and low culture are presented side by side in comedic production-line style, as in "You're the Top" (1934) where Porter pairs a Shakespeare sonnet with Mickey Mouse.

Perhaps Porter's most charming juxtaposition came in his 1948 musical *Kiss Me Kate*, based on Shakespeare's *The Taming of the Shrew*. Both Shakespeare's and Porter's plots are too involved to detail here. Suffice to say, Baltimore replaces Shakespeare's Padua, Italy setting. *Kate* involves "real-life" American lovers fighting as they play parallel roles in a production of *Shrew*. Porter's finest comic moment comes when two thuggish gangsters give a lesson on how to win a girl in the duet, "Brush Up Your Shakespeare."

The most versatile of our three composers was George Gershwin. While groomed in Tin Pan Alley, Gershwin also had ambitions in the world of classical music. His jazz-inflected scores *Rhapsody in Blue* (1924) and *An American in Paris* (1928) both have secure positions in the orchestral repertoire.

Gershwin's first hit song was the minstrel-inflected "Swanee" (1919), which became a vehicle for a blackfaced Al Jolson (1886–1950). Gershwin and lyricist brother Ira had their first Broadway hit with the show *Lady Be Good* (1924), which featured the songs "Fascinating Rhythm" and "The Man I Love," both jazz standards today. A string of musicals followed, including *Funny Face* (1927), *Strike Up the Band* (1927), and *Of Thee I Sing* (1931), which won a Pulitzer Prize, and the "American folk opera" *Porgy and Bess* (1935) ("Summertime," Chapter 2, Listening to Music).

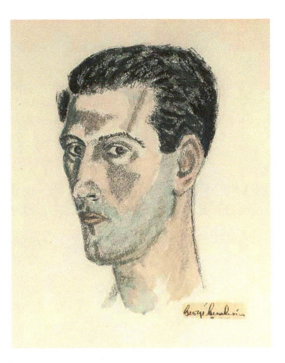

George Gershwin, self-portrait, charcoal and watercolor on paper.

Show Boat (1927)

American musical theater came of age in New York City on the evening of December 27, 1927. The occasion was the Broadway premiere of *Show Boat*, a wide-ranging story of life on a Mississippi riverboat. Written by composer Jerome Kern (1885–1945) with a book and lyrics by Oscar Hammerstein II, the musical went to the heart of the American social experience. The ingredients that had traditionally dominated American musical theater—plot-free revues, light romantic comedy, blackface minstrelsy, and young women in titillating costumes—were pushed to the background. Brought forward were moral confrontations over social class and race. The lives portrayed on *Show Boat*'s stage were beaten down, and sometimes broken, by social injustice, alcoholism, and marital infidelity.

The musical is drawn from a 1926 novel of the same title by Pulitzer Prize-winning author Edna Ferber (1885–1968). Action unfolds along America's geographic spine, the Mississippi River. There, along the mighty waterway that divides East and West and connects North and South—the artery that provided passage south for early explorers and passage north for the blues and jazz—Kern and Hammerstein tell the American tale of racial prejudice and social oppression. It is also the story of ordinary individuals working out their daily lives in relatively insignificant ways as they attempt to navigate life's eddies and shoals. Along the way, some of these people do great things.

Kern and Hammerstein sought to write a new sort of American musical, one in which music and drama were richly integrated. But they also worried about moving too far away from audience expectations. Thus, *Show Boat* unfolds at two levels. First and foremost, *Show Boat* is a powerful drama about the best and worst of American culture. Characters are richly developed, by both dialog and adept use of music. Second, *Show Boat*'s plot—which conveniently takes place on a "show" boat, after all—allows for the insertion of conventional theatrical entertainments. Thus positioned, Kern and Hammerstein were able to satisfy their audience's hunger for light-hearted music and dance while infusing an unprecedented level of social realism.

Show Boat is a lumbering giant, nearly four hours in its uncut form. Musical styles are drawn from an eclectic mix of spirituals, blues, and jazz; popular musical theater; and even soaring melodies of late 19th-century European opera.

Show Boat's storylines are labyrinthine. First and foremost, *Show Boat* tells the story of Magnolia Hawks, daughter of the showboat's captain. We first meet her as an innocent 17-year-old girl on the cusp of first love. By show's end, Magnolia has suffered a broken marriage and raised a daughter on her own. A self-made woman, she has also become worldly wise.

A secondary storyline revolves around Miss Julie Laverne, the showboat's leading lady, who is also Magnolia's childhood mentor. Miss Julie has African-American ancestry, but is fair-skinned and passes for white. Only a few people know her secret. One of these is her white husband Steve, the showboat's leading man. Because of **miscegenation** laws, their inter-racial marriage is illegal. Midway through the first act their secret is disclosed. To save Julie from arrest, Steve cuts her finger and

MISCEGENATION

Miscegenation refers to the mixing of races (from the Latin *miscere* "to mix" and *genus* "type"). Though a term of science, it was used in the United States as early as the pre-Civil War era to stir up fears of inter-racial marriage should slavery be abolished. Sixteen states still had anti-miscegenation laws in 1967, the year that the United States Supreme Court, in the case of Loving v. Virginia, ruled them unconstitutional.

PAUL ROBESON (1898–1976)

Paul Robeson, the son of a minister and former slave, was born in Princeton, New Jersey. In 1915, he matriculated at Rutgers University, only the third African American to do so. He earned letters in four sports, was twice elected to the All-American football team, and graduated as class valedictorian. Robeson studied law at Columbia University, but racial prejudice soured him to the profession. He eventually returned to his boyhood loves of singing and acting.

Robeson's most famous role was in *Show Boat* as Joe, who sings "Old Man River." Robeson's sympathy for the Soviet Union, a place he considered less racially prejudiced than the United States, led to a 1947 indictment by the House Committee on Un-American Activities. The State Department denied Robeson a passport until 1958.

Paul Robeson, June 1942.
Photo by Gordon Parks, Office of War Information, Library of Congress Prints and Photographs Division.

"To be free to walk the good American earth as equal citizens, to live without fear, to enjoy the fruits of our toil to give our children every opportunity in life—that dream which we have held so long in our hearts is today the destiny that we hold in our hands."

—Paul Robeson

swallows some of her blood. Steve proclaims his "blackness." He too has "more than a drop of Negro blood" in him, he tells the sheriff (and his stunned 1927 all-white audience).

Show Boat offers a goldmine of wonderful songs, including the operatic "Make Believe," during the singing of which Magnolia falls in "love at first song" with the riverboat gambler Gaylord Ravenol. We also hear "Can't Help Lovin' Dat Man of Mine" and "Bill" (both of which became jazz standards), and "Old Man River," which served as an anthem of the Civil Rights Era.

The Curtain Rises

In musical theater, first impressions are everything. So getting the opening scene right is essential. It is there we meet the characters, learn the issues, and get a feel for the musical language.

We will study *Show Boat*'s opening minutes, perhaps the most provocative minutes in the history of American musical theater. In order to set the mood, turn back the clock ninety years. Imagine that many of New York's social luminaries are in the Ziegfeld Theatre for opening night. The musical's title suggests a light-hearted evening of song and dance, all situated on a Mississippi riverboat. The idea sounds delightfully quaint to these Euro-American urban sophisticates.

Opening scene from *Show Boat*, music by Jerome Kern; book and lyrics by Oscar Hammerstein II

LISTENING
11.2
GUIDE

Texture: Homophonic
Meter: Duple and quadruple

0:00	The orchestra's low brass sounds represent Sheriff Vallon. It is a foreboding chromatic minor-keyed motive. Although you cannot possibly know this yet, the phrase will come to represent the brutal fist of the law. The curtain rises on a group of African-American stevedores loading cotton at a dock in Natchez, Mississippi. The year is 1880. Though slavery is abolished, life for these men has hardly changed. Bales across their shoulders, they sing in a ragged jazz-inflected rhythm, "Niggers all work on the Mississippi . . . while the white folks play."

Are you outraged by these opening words? Hammerstein hoped so. *Show Boat* brought to Broadway the bitter taste of American social realism. The words were calculated to shock, embarrass, and anger. Yet, almost immediately, productions found alternatives to "Niggers," including "colored folks," "darkies," and even the color-blind "Here we all." For historical reasons and to reintroduce the shock that Kern and Hammerstein intended, conductor John McGlinn insisted on using "Nigger" for the 1988 EMI *Show Boat* recording. The choice was controversial. Rather than sing the word, baritone Willard White and an all-black British chorus resigned from the project. They were replaced by baritone Bruce Hubbard (who is black) and London's Ambrosian Chorus. Hubbard agreed only after seeking council with colleagues and friends. Said Mr. Hubbard, "The way the word was once used is not fiction but fact. Blacks today may want to forget the past and build on the future, but we should never lose our sense of history" (*New York Times*, September 25, 1988).

0:44	The stevedores move to a supporting role as a chorus of African-American women takes up singing a song of their own. Underneath the women's melody, the men sing a bass riff.
0:56	The women join the men in a final repetition of the opening verse. Then comes new material.
1:09	"Cotton blossom" they sing. There is a lot going on here. Cotton Blossom is the name of the showboat, but here the words are tied to the land, to hard labor, and to the industry that once made slavery so lucrative. See how Hammerstein's lyrics are setting up connections.

Kern is busy making musical connections as well. Here is how:

- Sing the words "cotton blossom."
- Now hum just the melody.
- Now slow it down and hum it backwards with the same rhythm (long-long-short-short) and singing the first pitch twice.

Do you recognize the melody, hear the implied words? It is *Show Boat*'s most famous song, "Old Man River."

The chorus ends as the clarinet introduces a lovely new melody, a snippet from the song "Can't Help Lovin' Dat Man of Mine." A brief dramatic interlude unfolds. Queenie the cook and Steve greet each other. Queenie is then confronted by Pete, the ship's engineer, who wants to know where she got the brooch she is wearing. Queenie answers that Miss Julie gave it to her.

That means trouble. Pete, who is white, had given the brooch as a present to Miss Julie, who passes for white, but he knows is legally black.

2:24	Attention again focuses on the stevedores who reprise the show's opening lines. Tension is rising. We are still only half way through the scene.
2:53	Now the focus shifts to white America. The music becomes less syncopated and more playful, even a bit juvenile. Groups of well-dressed socialites come on stage. ("Mincing Minces" and "Beaux" is how Hammerstein identifies them.) Two young women look at a poster of Miss Julie and comment on her beauty.
3:13	The men break into song. They sing "What a pretty bevy" to new melody, but the harmonic background is essentially the same as that of the original black chorus.
	The stevedores sang of hard labor; the beaux sing of pretty girls:

continued

3:21	The Minces flirt back.
3:32	Beaux and Minces sing together.
3:44	Beaux sing, "See the show boat."
4:14	Finally, the music returns to the "Cotton blossom" melody first introduced by the stevedores. The chorus ends with Captain Andy's arrival on stage.

Kern and Hammerstein have used the show's opening minutes to set up sharply contrasted social worlds: one of hard labor, the other of frivolous indulgence. In real life, the Deep South worlds of 19th-century black and upper-class-white culture were just as divided. But they were also symbiotically connected by generations of social interaction and acculturation. In theatrical life, Kern and Hammerstein show these connections metaphorically by putting blacks and whites on the same stage (in itself a remarkable occurrence in 1927). They even sing together (though the words are wildly different).

This brings us to an axiom of well-written dramatic musical theater. When people sing together it is to show their connections, perhaps even to reveal relationships that the characters themselves do not understand. Seen from this perspective, the implication of this opening scene is that the fate of black and white Americans (and by implication, Americans of every heritage) is intertwined.

Show Boat shined light on the best and worst of the American social experience. In 1927, it provided an uncompromising mirror into which Americans might view the national soul. It continues to do so today.

QUESTIONS FOR THOUGHT

- Race is a central focus in *Show Boat*. It also casts its lens on gender. The two leading characters, Magnolia and Miss Julie, must make their way through life on their own. What other marginalized groups existed in 1920s America? What about today? Have other composers addressed these issues?
- Kern and Hammerstein romanticized African-American culture. We see, for example, Joe's nature-informed wisdom when he sings "Old Man River." What do you think of this perspective?
- In the first act, Queenie says that she is surprised that Miss Julie knows "Can't Help Lovin' Dat Man" because it is a "colored person's song." Might that have been a reasonable inference in 1880? What about today?
- If you were staging *Show Boat*, would you use the original opening lines or change them? Why or why not?

Moving Forward

Oscar Hammerstein would eventually team up with composer Richard Rodgers (1902–1979). Together, they would complete the integration of music and story begun in *Show Boat*. Theirs would be the most influential musical theater lyricist/composer team of the 20th century.

Before joining Hammerstein, Rodgers worked with lyricist Lorenz Hart (1895–1943). They wrote wonderful songs together, including "Blue Moon" (1934), as well as "The Lady Is a Tramp" and "My Funny Valentine" for the 1937 Broadway show *Babes in Arms*. Both became jazz standards. If not for Hart's failed struggle with alcoholism, the partnership might have produced much more.

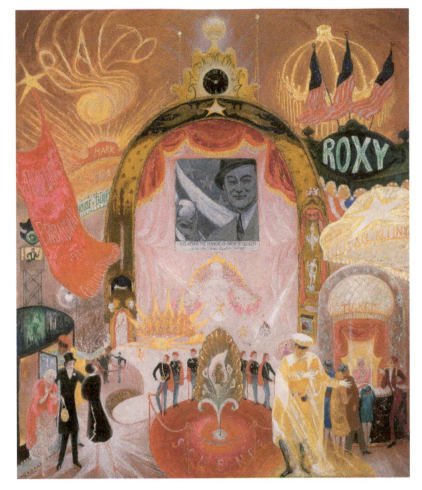

Cathedrals of Broadway, Florine Stettheimer, 1929.

Courtesy of The Metropolitan Museum of Art, Gift of Ettie Stettheimer, 1953.

Hart was a master lyricist, as we can see in the song "Bewitched, Bothered and Bewildered" (from the 1940 musical *Pal Joey*). Listen to the song online and notice the multiple-syllable rhymes ("wild again," "beguiled again," and "child again"), the inner rhymes ("simpering" and "whimpering"), the alliteration ("bewitched, bothered and bewildered"), and the inversion of the stanza's opening "I'm" with the closing "am I."

And what about the breakdown of resistance? Have the inner conflicts of seduction ever been told in song with more clarity? The narrator's emotional anchor, such as it is, seems to be no more than the consistent confusion of "bewitched, bothered and bewildered."

Despite their jewel-like songs, Rodgers and Hart never found the dramatic formula to fully integrate words and music into the unified narrative style Kern and Hammerstein began in *Show Boat*. That would be achieved in 1943 with Rodgers and Hammerstein's *Oklahoma!*, the first of numerous collaborations that also produced *Carousel* (1945), *South Pacific* (1949), *The King and I* (1951), and *The Sound of Music* (1959), among others.

In many ways, all of these shows borrowed and expanded on the ideas brought forth in *Show Boat*. Central was a concern with the American experience, either at home or abroad. Also depicted— and subsumed under a larger heading we might call "doing the right thing"—were the tensions related to social class and freedom, women's rights and sexual autonomy, racial prejudice, and violence. In these musicals people make mistakes and suffer for them. Sometimes they die violently. Always there is a moral.

Rodgers and Hammerstein shows were invariably life embracing, even as they fearlessly explored their era's most difficult social issues. In *South Pacific*, race was once again at issue when two American characters fall in love, U.S. Navy nurse Nellie Forbush with a French expatriate widower who is raising his half-Polynesian children, and Marine Lieutenant Joe Cable with a young Asian woman. Both are stymied by their prejudice ("You Have to be Carefully Taught").

In fact, Broadway, the theatrical voice of a nation of immigrants, has often concerned itself with issues of identity, be it ethnicity, religion, social class, or assimilation. Rodgers and Hammerstein may have set shows in the South Pacific and Siam (*The King and I*, 1956), but we see those faraway places through American eyes. Even *The Sound of Music*, located in Austria, has a real-life American ending with the Von Trapp family immigrating to the United States in 1942.

An exception to this formula was *Threepenny Opera* (premiered in Berlin as *Die Dreigroschenoper*, 1928) by composer Kurt Weill (1900–1950), who immigrated to the United States in 1935 and Marxist playwright Bertolt Brecht (1898–1956), both German. The show has seen many revivals since its 1933 Broadway premiere, most recently in 2006 with Allan Cumming and Cyndi Lauper.

Dreigroschenoper is a scathing portrayal of social corruption. Brecht depicts a vicious world populated by thieves and beggars, pimps and prostitutes, and corrupt authorities. Weill's music is fittingly dissonant and coarse. Sometimes it lurches as if performed by an intoxicated Salvation Army band.

The show's most famous song is "Mack the Knife," which became a jazz standard as well as a vehicle for gravel-voiced trumpeter Louis Armstrong (1901–1971). Most of the music has a brutal edge. In the song "Pirate Jenny," newlywed Polly rattles off a fantasy-revenge song cruel enough to shock even the hardened criminals for whom she sings. "Pimp's Ballad" (or "Tango Ballad") is a mesmerizing duet featuring Macheath and his prostitute girlfriend.

THE BEGGAR'S OPERA

Two hundred years before *Dreigroschenoper*, John Gay's *The Beggar's Opera* (1728) was a mainstay on the London stage. Although titled an opera, the work is actually a spoken play augmented with well-known tunes set to new words. Characters came from the underbelly of society: thieves, convicts, whores. The plot ridiculed the city's public figures and satirized Italian opera, which was hugely popular in London at the time. *The Beggar's Opera* spawned a new genre (the ballad opera) and paved the way for English operetta. Weill and Brecht used a darker version of Gay's plot for their *Threepenny Opera*.

The Beggar's Opera, anonymous, British, 18th century.

Courtesy of The Metropolitan Museum of Art, Harris Brisbane Dick Fund, 1932.

ACTIVITIES AND ASSIGNMENTS

- Select a well-known song by Berlin, Porter, or Gershwin and investigate its history. Who recorded it? In what genres? Does the song appear in any movies? On stage? Is the song still performed today?

West Side Story (1957)

Moving to the rhythmic inflections of jazz and Latin America, members of two rival gangs prowl the reaches of Manhattan's West Side. They keep their center of gravity low, as if drawing in sustenance from the earth. Occasionally, frustrations seem to boil over as figures leap upward in liberating, gravity-defying balletic movements. Sometimes the gangs' paths intersect. The foes posture and threaten; violence is imminent.

West Side Story begins not with a song or clarifying dialog. The voice of reason is silent. Instead, we are confronted by the angular and feral muscularity of movement. Two street gangs—one Anglo, the other Latino—are strangely bound. They seem to hate each other, but they move to the same music. They also share the same mean streets and derelict playgrounds. Lost in parallel cycles of poverty and hopelessness, it seems as if these street toughs hate for no better reason than the invigorating power of hatred itself.

The Russian playwright Anton Chekhov (1860–1904) noted that if you include a gun at the beginning of a story, someone has to get shot. Applying Chekhov's axiom to the opening scene of *West Side Story*, we know this for certain: blood will flow; people will die. This being Broadway, some will also fall in love.

Perhaps the storyline sounds familiar. *West Side Story* is an updating of Shakespeare's *Romeo and Juliet*. Gangs of Jets and Sharks replace families of Montagues and Capulets. Tony is our Romeo; Maria is our Juliet. When they meet at a gym dance, love is instantaneous.

As originally conceived in 1949 by playwright Arthur Laurents (1918–2011) and director/choreographer Jerome Robbins (1918–1998), the show was to be set in Manhattan's Lower East Side. The love interest paired an Irish Catholic with a Jew, a classic Broadway formula for socially problematic interaction.

But while religion provided the explosive chemistry of earlier American times, its power to alienate had lessened by the mid-20th century. It was decided to move the setting across town and north where social tensions were on the rise as a result of the recent influx of Puerto Rican immigrants.

TABLE 11.1 Side-by-side plot comparison between *West Side Story* and *Romeo and Juliet*

WEST SIDE STORY	ROMEO AND JULIET
• New York City streets.	• Verona, Italy.
• Officer Krupke breaks up a gang fight.	• The Duke stops inter-family fight.
• A back alley. Tony sings "Something's Coming."	• Party preparation at the Capulet home; Juliet is introduced to Paris.
• Bridal Shop. Maria and Anita.	• Capulet home.
• Dance at the gym. Tony and Maria meet.	• Capulet's party. Romeo and Juliet meet.
• A fire escape.	• Balcony scene.
• Drugstore.	• Friar Lawrence's cell
• Tony's buddy Riff is killed by Bernardo, Maria's brother.	• Romeo's friend Mercutio is killed by Tybalt, Juliet's cousin.
• Tony kills Bernardo.	• Romeo kills Tybalt.
• Tony spends the night with Maria.	• Romeo sleeps with Juliet.
• Tony is told that Maria is dead.	• Juliet takes sleeping potion.
• Tony roams the streets hoping for death. Chino kills him.	• Romeo arrives at Juliet's tomb. Thinking her dead, he poisons himself.
• Maria chooses life.	• Juliet awakens and stabs herself.

Playbill, *West Side Story*.

Not only did the stereotype of hot-blooded Latinos seem to offer a more compelling storyline, but it also invited a musical score filled with the rhythmic inflections of Latin jazz, so popular at the time. Leonard Bernstein composed the music @ 11.5; Stephen Sondheim wrote the lyrics.

Dramatically, the show is tightly knit. In this sense, it is perhaps even more dramatically effective than Shakespeare's original. Here is how:

- It's more concise. The entire story—first love to death—unfolds in less than forty-eight hours.

- At story's opening, Tony has broken free of the Jets, his old gang. He is on the way to becoming his own man. Tony is drawn back in as a favor to old comrades, and just for a night. Fidelity to a false ideal leads to his destruction.

- The Jets are responsible for the confusion that leads to Tony's death.

- Unlike Juliet, Maria rises above the hatred that surrounds her. She chooses to live.

ENSEMBLE FINALE

Bernstein borrowed the ensemble finale from a convention that developed in early 18th-century comic opera and which was exploited with great success by Wolfgang Amadeus Mozart. Librettists would devise scenarios that required all the main characters to be on stage together. The composer would then take the opportunity to 1) show his skill in manipulating multiple sets of music simultaneously, and 2) provide a rousing conclusion to the act.

We will study the Quintet that forms the second section of the three-part **ensemble finale** to Act I. Part one of the finale begins intimately. Tony and Maria are alone together and make wedding vows during which they sing "One Hand, One Heart." Part three is all action. A rumble unfolds during which Bernardo kills Tony's friend Riff and Tony kills Bernardo, Maria's brother.

Sandwiched in between is the Quintet, which pits Sharks against Jets, allows Tony and Maria to sing of their unfolding love, and spotlights the icy Anita anticipating a hot-love rendezvous with Bernardo. All sing about what they most desire. The Sharks and Jets sing of revenge. Tony and Maria sing of their love. Anita sings of carnal bliss. Tying the various actors together is the element of immediacy. All want satisfaction *tonight*.

Quintet, finale to Act I from *West Side Story*, music by Leonard Bernstein, lyrics by Stephen Sondheim

LISTENING
11.3
GUIDE

Texture: Homophonic
Meter: Duple and quadruple
Form: A A¹ B A C (B, A, A¹ together)

0:00	**Section A** The Quintet opens with the instrumental sounds of a world in disorder. Brass and percussion riffs explode in flashes of dissonance and belligerence. Aggression rules. In the bass line we hear a three-tone ostinato. These triple groupings jar against a duple feel in the brass and percussion. Adding to the tension, the brass instruments and bass play in different keys.
0:06	*Jets* "The Jets are gonna have" Notice the alliteration with the growling "r" repetitions.
0:22	*Sharks* "gonna hand 'em a surprise . . . Tonight!" The word, "Tonight," both closes the first section and opens the door for the Jets to begin a new section that is both shorter (three lines instead of eight/nine) and more exuberant.
0:39	Sondheim's word play: the Jets "rock it" and the hungry Sharks "get it."
0:51	The interaction builds as the two gangs shout accusations, oblivious of each other. Finally, they shout in unison, "Tonight!"
0:58	**Section A¹** The musical texture is similar to the opening, but the orchestration is lighter and sounds less aggressive. Tones slide sensually up and down. Whereas the opening was street-gang tough, this section sounds more like tough love. Now we hear Anita. Looking forward to getting some sexual "kicks" of her own tonight, she maintains the nine-line format of the Sharks. Presumably, she does this for two reasons. First, Anita is Bernardo's lover, a Shark. Second, "tonight" again serves as a hand-off, this time to Tony and Maria.
1:19	**Section B** Tony and Maria reprise their song from earlier in the act. Now "tonight" reveals the possibilities of first love, first passion. Yet there is trouble hidden in the words. The morning star is Venus, the planet of love. But Tony will not live to see the dawn. Sondheim also plays with the concept of time. Tony longs for a magical night in which time will stop; Maria begs the endless day to hurry up and finish. Contrast Tony's melody line with Maria's. His is grounded in strong scale degrees; the melodic intervals are relatively wide. Perhaps this is indicative of his masculinity.
2:10	**Section A** Following Maria's verse, Bernstein writes an orchestral climax of brass and pounding timpani. The romantic reverie is interrupted by the return of the Quintet's percussive opening. Perhaps this material felt exciting on first hearing. Now, however, juxtaposed against Maria's dreams, it has explosive nastiness.
2:27	**Section C** (B, A, and A¹ together) Maria sings of love as the Jets posture in the background. (Notice that the character "Ice" sounds a lot less confident than the guys ready to stand *behind* him.) Bernstein is starting to lay contrasting sections on top of another. We can enjoy this layering in two ways. First, we see it from "inside" the play. Bernstein is showing us important relationships within the story, reminding us how everything is interwoven. Second, we can enjoy it from "outside" the play, that is, from a technical point of view. Bernstein is about to show off his compositional skill. He adds lines and complexities like a juggler who, although he already has an impossible number of balls in the air, keeps adding more.

LINCOLN CENTER: ANOTHER WEST SIDE STORY

Bernstein's Sharks and Jets are fictional, but the rough West Side neighborhood they inhabited was real. Once a working-class African-American community, by the 1950s Manhattan's "San Juan Hill/Lincoln Square area" consisted of crowded, run-down tenements. Its residents dealt with ever-present ethnic tensions. When NYC officials declared the neighborhood a slum, extensive urban renewal ensued. Now situated on 16 acres of old San Juan Hill is one of the most important performance complexes in the world: The Lincoln Center for the Performing Arts. Twelve theaters, concert halls, opera houses and lecture halls provide space for the New York Philharmonic, Metropolitan Opera, New York City Ballet, The Julliard School, and more. Ground was broken in 1959. The last concert hall was completed ten years later. Construction halted briefly to accommodate the filming of *West Side Story*.

Metropolitan Opera, New York City.
Lechhansl/Wikimedia Commons/CC-BY-SA-3.0.

QUESTION FOR THOUGHT

- Gang violence is far more prevalent today than in 1957. It is also far more deadly. How would a musical about today's gangs differ from *West Side Story*? What kind of music might be used?

Stephen Sondheim

Following *West Side Story*, Sondheim received an appointment as lyricist for composer Jule Styne's *Gypsy* (1959), which featured Ethel Merman (1908–1984) in the role of Mama Rose Lee, show business's most fanatical stage mother and arguably American musical theater's greatest female role. Perhaps Sondheim drew from his own childhood when writing for Rose, the first of many overbearing women to populate Sondheim musicals. Search the internet for the lyrics from "Everything's Coming up Roses," the rousing finale of *Gypsy*'s first act. Mama Rose may want her daughter to succeed, but even more (as the final line confirms), Rose seeks vindication for herself.

With *A Funny Thing Happened on the Way to the Forum* (1962) Sondheim made his debut as both lyricist and composer. Thus began a string of more than a dozen musicals, each of which broke new ground in terms of style and content. The theme of love—most often quick trysts and infidelities—runs through Sondheim's work. Lacking a storyline altogether (perhaps Sondheim's theatrical metaphor for the one-night stand) is *Company* (1970, revived in 2006). *Company* explores the superficial love life of the confirmed bachelor Bobby, as witnessed through the eyes of his not very helpful married friends. Marriage has never looked so uninviting.

A Little Night Music (1973) is a modern take on 19th-century European operetta. It is written almost completely in triple meter and features a cast involved in tangled and misguided love affairs across generations and social classes. Only the innocent pre-pubescents and the aged wise are spared love's foibles.

Other major Sondheim shows include *Pacific Overtures* (1976), the gruesome thriller *Sweeney Todd: The Demon Barber of Fleet Street* (1979), *Sunday in the Park with George* (1984), and *Passion* (1994).

More Stories to Tell

As it turned out, *West Side Story*'s Maria and *Gypsy*'s Mama Rose were just the first of a decade's worth of strong women to populate the Broadway stage. Soon to follow were the entrepreneurial Dolly Levy (*Hello Dolly!*, 1964), the willful Fanny Brice (*Funny Girl*, 1964), Tevye's strong-minded daughters (*Fiddler on the Roof*, 1964), and the flamboyant Mame (*Mame*, 1966).

In addition to the theatrical rise of women (which paralleled the emerging women's movement in real life) the social upheavals of the 1960s also had their effect on Broadway. As the turbulent decade unfolded, producers wondered what kinds of music and stories would bring the next generation of patrons into the theaters. Some thought the answer might be hippies and rock 'n' roll. In 1968 came the opening of *Hair: The American Tribal Love-Rock Musical*, in which the show's characters let their hair hang out while searching for their identities. The off-Broadway nude musical show *Oh, Calcutta* (1969) let it *all* hang out. Skits were provided by John Lennon (1940–1980) and other pop music icons.

All in all, however, rock musicals have been pretty tame affairs. Andrew Lloyd Webber (b. 1948) had his first hit with *Jesus Christ Superstar* (1971), which helped usher rock music into the Christian church. Webber followed the success of *Superstar* with another biblical rock musical, *Joseph and the Amazing Technicolor Dreamcoat* (1973). Opening around the same time were *Grease* (1972) and *The Wiz* (1975), a funky retelling of *The Wizard of Oz*.

Gypsy Rose Lee, 1956.
Photo by Fred Palumbo, Library of Photographs Division.

The 1980s were powered by a pair of blockbuster productions. Claude-Michel Schönberg's (b. 1944) *Les Misérables* (1980, adapted from a novel by Victor Hugo [1802–1885]) and Andrew Lloyd Webber's *The Phantom of the Opera* (1986, adapted from a novel by Gaston Leroux [1868–1927]). Both shows continue to fill theaters worldwide.

A trio of rock musicals had major successes in the late 1990s: *Rent* (1996), *Hedwig and the Angry Inch* (1998), and *Mamma Mia!* (1999), which featured music by the Swedish group ABBA. *Rent* drew inspiration from *La bohème*, an 1896 opera by Italian composer Giacomo Puccini. *La bohème* told the story of young Parisian artists living hand-to-mouth as they struggled to find their way in a world plagued by tuberculosis. *Rent* picks up the same themes but sets the story in New York City's East Village, where lives are being destroyed by AIDS. Composer Jonathan Larson (1960–1996), who lived in Greenwich Village and wrote *Rent* while earning his living as a waiter, drew his inspiration from a world he knew intimately. He died of an aortic aneurysm while the show was still in previews.

The Next Act

What will be Broadway's future? Because the expense of mounting a show is so great, the recent trend has been to go with productions that appeal to tourists and families, either revivals or adaptations of hit movies, including a number from Disney: *Beauty and the Beast* (1994), *The Lion King* (1997), *Tarzan* (2006), *The Little Mermaid* (2007), *Aladdin* (2011), and *Frozen* (2018).

Broadway, however, will always surprise. Consider the music and dance review *FELA!* (2009). One has to assume that never in his wildest spliff-inspired dreams did Nigerian pop superstar Fela Anikulapo Kuti (1938–1997) expect his life and art to be the stuff of Broadway theater. The iconoclast creator of the funk-inflected Afro-beat style, gadfly to Nigeria's corrupt politicians, and polygamist (he married twenty-seven women in a single ceremony), spent his life rebelling against the constricting bonds of social norms.

Lin-Manuel Miranda and the cast of *Hamilton*, 2016.
Bruce Glikas/FilmMagic/Getty Images.

Finally, we briefly consider composer/lyricist Lin-Manuel Miranda (b. 1980), whose first Broadway production, *In the Heights* (2008), presented a musical collage of life in New York City's ethnically diverse Washington Heights neighborhood. Winner of four Tony Awards, the show was a return to New York's early theatrical days when narratives often featured the vibrant lives of the city's heterogeneous cultural mix.

Miranda expanded his focus from neighborhood to incipient nation when he conceived the hip-hop-inflected *Hamilton* (2015), a quasi-historical musical about Alexander Hamilton (ca. 1755–1804). @ 11.6 Miranda's Hamilton (the role was originally played by the composer himself)—immigrant statesman, Revolutionary War officer, lawyer, Founding Father, Federalist, and first Secretary of the Treasury—resides in time present and past. He fights in the 18th century to give birth to a nation, but sings rap, the contemporary language of resistance. Characters also represent today's ethnic mix; Euro-American historical figures are played by African-American and Hispanic actresses and actors. For careful listeners, webs of meaning are further enhanced by Miranda's many references to founding fathers of another sort—Gilbert and Sullivan, Rodgers and Hammerstein, Stephen Sondheim, Notorious B.I.G. (1972–1997), and Mobb Deep's Prodigy (1974–2017), to name just a few.

Key Terms

- blackface minstrelsy
- book musical
- Broadway
- burlesque
- ensemble finale
- lyricist
- minstrel show
- miscegenation laws
- Niblo's Garden
- operetta
- Times Square
- vaudeville

Essay Questions

- A number of pieces written for the musical stage have been produced as movies. What is gained? What is lost?

- Intuitively, one might assume that a theatrical production's musical style should fit the social setting being staged. Lin-Manuel Miranda's rap musical *Hamilton* belies that idea. If you wrote a musical, what would it be about? What type of music would you use? Why? Would your choice affect the audience's perception of the characters?

CHAPTER GOALS

- To explore ways that music defines cinematic characters and communicates action, mood, and emotion.
- To provide a brief overview of the history of music in film.

CHAPTER TWELVE

Music and Film

QUESTIONS FOR THOUGHT

- Think of a favorite movie. Can you remember the musical score? Why or why not?

- Watch a movie scene with the sound turned off. Now watch it again with sound. How is the experience different? What do you experience if you listen to the soundtrack without visuals? Do you "see" the movie in your mind?

- What kind of music would you use in a movie about your life? Would you use any specific styles or songs?

- You are a film composer assigned to write a score for a love scene. What style of music will you compose? What instruments will you use? What type of music would you compose for a car chase?

- Choose two friends and assign them musical themes. What influenced your choices?

Come summertime, the Hatch Shell on the Boston Esplanade is a busy place for music. The annual Fourth of July celebration with the Boston Pops can attract 400,000 people. Millions more watch the event on television. Along the shell's stone façade are inscribed the names of the luminaries of Western art music: Bach and Beethoven, Mozart and Haydn, Copland and Williams.

That's John Williams (b. 1932). For Bostonians, the film composer extraordinaire and former conductor of the Boston Pops has earned a place among music's immortals.

Most film composers live their creative lives in relative anonymity. Their music is widely heard, but few theatergoers know their names. @ 12.1 In this chapter, we move cinema music from background to foreground and explore the complex relationships between music and film. In particular, we study the ways in which film music is specifically designed to represent, enhance, and clarify the social experience unfolding on screen. We begin by studying the flying scene from Williams's *E.T.: The Extra-Terrestrial* (1982), then gradually weave our way forward chronologically from early film to the recent past. Along the way we investigate other musical scenes from select iconic features, including: *Metropolis* (1927), *Cabin in the Sky* (1943), *The Day the Earth Stood Still* (1951), *The Hidden Fortress* (1957), and the *Star Wars* movies. Each example offers insights into the social times in which it was created.

> "I've always tried to subordinate myself to the picture."
> —Max Steiner (1888–1971)

E.T.: The Extra-Terrestrial (1982)

With police vehicles blocking the road, the boys' frantic escape attempt appears to have failed. But then the bicycles gently lift into the sky and we know E.T. is going home after all. It is an inspired moment. As the kids take flight, especially if you watch the scene with a child's sense of wonder, you may even feel yourself inhale at lift-off, as if to soar along with them.

The scene is magical. Credit the visual conjuring to film director Steven Spielberg (b. 1946). But if you watch with ears wide open, it feels as if the power of flight is provided by the swirling, leaping string melodies of John Williams. Such is music's command.

The Boston Pops Esplanade Orchestra performing at the Hatch Shell, Boston, July 4, 2005.
Garrett A. Wollman/Wikimedia Commons/CC-BY-SA-2.0.

JOHN WILLIAMS (b. 1932)

Born in New York City, Williams spent his youth in Los Angeles where he eventually attended UCLA. After serving in the Air Force, Williams returned to New York to attend The Julliard School. In the 1950s, Williams began writing music for television, earning four Emmy Awards. His film scores include, among many others, music for *The Poseidon Adventure* (1972), *The Towering Inferno* (1974), *Jaws* (1975), the *Star Wars* series (1977–2017), the *Indiana Jones* series (1981–2008), the first three *Harry Potter* movies (2001–2004), *The BFG* (2016), and many others. Williams has composed music for over 100 films. He has won five Oscar awards, twenty-four Grammy awards, and four Golden Globe awards. Commissions include themes for four Olympic Games as well as the NBC Nightly News. Williams served as music director of the Boston Pops Orchestra from 1980 to 1993. He holds honorary degrees from twenty-one American universities.

John Williams and Steven Spielberg.
Featureflash Photo Agency/Shutterstock.com.

Music is an essential part of the cinematic experience. Soundtracks intensify emotion, provide structure, and help viewers make connections. But soundtracks do this work furtively. Often, we are only dimly conscious of music's presence.

The *E.T.* chase scene pits boys on bikes against men in cars. Outgunned and out-horse powered, the kids furiously pedal up neighborhood streets and barrel down hills. Their getaway is accompanied by the sounds of squealing tires, racing engines, clattering bikes, and choppy dialog. These are the film's **diegetic** sounds, that is, the sounds of the world inhabited by the film's characters.

Inaudible to those characters, however, is the non-diegetic music of Williams's orchestral score. The music is irregular and peripatetic, like the chase scene it enhances. Short brass fanfares echo the children's noble desire to save E.T.; propulsive rhythms keep the tension high. As events become more desperate, the boys split up. Musical ideas seem to break apart as well. They crystallize and disintegrate with virtually every camera change.

Midway through the chase, E.T.'s face momentarily fills the screen. Williams's music follows the visual. Sounds seem to slow down, then expand. The shift provides a momentary reduction in musical tension, a chance to catch our breath. But it also foreshadows the escape to come. The melody, with its opening octave leap upward, tells us a secret the desperate boys cannot fathom: E.T. has a plan.

The chase continues. Momentarily, the boys have dodged the police. They think they have escaped. Suddenly, however, the road is blocked, capture imminent. Once again, the camera presents a close-up of E.T.; the music holds a drawn-out chord. Action is suspended. Is E.T. doomed?

As the "flying" theme sounds, the bikes lift skyward. Tension is replaced with relief, restraint with freedom. The film's diegetic world is mostly silent. Even the boys seem to live in the magic of Williams's soundscape. We listen and watch, and marvel.

E.T.: The Extra-Terrestrial, bike scene.
Archive Photos/Moviepix/Getty Images.

LISTENING 12.1 GUIDE
Flying scene from *E.T.: The Extra-Terrestrial*, music by John Williams

Texture: Complex homophony
Meter: Frequently changing

0:00	Search for the scene on the internet or cue the movie to 1:40:00. Our listening guide is timed to when the boys begin their escape. In the score, rhythmic string figures are punctuated by a series of repeated fanfare-like motives in the brass instruments. (Notice how neatly the police siren fits in between the brass themes.)
0:38	The boys go off-road and glide downhill. Choppy figures in the brass. Musical ideas shift quickly.
1:02	The boys ride over the police car. Rhythmic ostinati in the high strings.
1:18	Brass fanfares return.
1:25	The camera focuses on E.T.'s face. The "flying" theme is heard.
1:40	More chasing. We hear new brass figures, which will later form a secondary thematic idea in the flying section.
2:23	A drawn-out chord. E.T.'s future hangs in the balance.
2:28	The boys and bicycles lift off. Strings move to the foreground as the flying theme sounds.
3:20	The boys return to earth. Listen as Williams "lands" the children with his descending major scale: do-ti-la-sol-fa-mi-re-do.

QUESTIONS FOR THOUGHT

- Does listening to the flying theme trigger any other emotional cues for you? We hear the same octave leap we heard in the opening of Harold Arlen's "Over the Rainbow." Any connection?

- Think about the following musical sounds: a harp, a marching band, a jazz solo. What might each of these sounds represent in our culture? How might a film composer use them to communicate characters, moods, or settings?

- What does the *E.T.* story suggest about our social order and values? How does Williams's music for the chase scene reflect the movie's moral stand?

ACTIVITIES AND ASSIGNMENTS

- Once Williams's soaring melody is connected with flight, the link is super-glue inseparable. Think of other film music that inspires strong imagery.

- Have someone play short clips of well-known movie scores or television theme songs. Can you identify the movie or show? Possibly even a specific scene? How does music reflect and enhance the movie's or show's social character? Can you identify the music's composer?

- Listen to the orchestral suite *The Planets* (1916) by British composer Gustav Holst (1874–1934). Compare Holst's early 20th-century symphonic portrayal of outer space with Williams's score for *E.T.* Keep Holst and Williams in mind when later in the chapter we discuss Bernard Herrmann's (1911–1975), iconic score for *The Day the Earth Stood Still*.

- Watch the opening sequence of *The Terminator* (1984) and listen for the terminator's "heartbeat" in Brad Fiedel's soundtrack. Are these sounds diegetic or non-diegetic? Why do you think so? The heartbeat appears numerous times throughout the movie. How does it affect your viewing experience?

Early Film

The first publicly screened motion pictures appeared at the end of the 19th century. Silent and short, the films were novelties offered as part of bigger theatrical entertainment packages featuring live comedy routines, music, and dance. Theater managers soon discovered they could use music to mask the distracting noise made by primitive projection systems. Music also seemed to add emotional warmth to the ghostly black-and-white on-screen images. @ 12.2 Curiously, music seemed to make film more "real," perhaps through music's power to engage emotions.

Of course, it was also helpful if the musical emotions fit the film's narrative. Accordingly, silent films were soon released with musical cue sheets. These earliest "soundtracks" drew freely from a standard repertory of melodies that audiences were sure to recognize. Sometimes the score was written out; often it was improvised on organ or piano. The first major American movie to be fitted with a full orchestral score was director D.W. Griffith's racially incendiary saga *The Birth of a Nation* (1916). Much of the music, composed by Joseph Carl Breil (1870–1926), was original.

The Jazz Singer (1927)

Music itself was the focus of *The Jazz Singer*, cinema's first feature-length "talkie." The film was adapted from a successful Broadway stage show and starred the popular blackface-entertainer Al Jolson (1886–1950). The score was a musical grab bag that included popular songs, traditional Jewish sacred melodies, and classical music.

The film's protagonist is Jack Robin. Born and raised on New York City's Lower East Side, Jack is the son of a Jewish cantor. His father wants him to follow the family tradition and sing in temple. But Jack dreams of a life on Broadway. The two argue and Jack runs away. Over the succeeding years, Jack breaks from his ethnic and cultural heritage and experiments with new ones. He changes his name (from Jakie Rabinowitz to Jack Robin), falls in love with a gentile woman, and becomes a "jazz" singer. In spite of all, father and son ultimately reconcile. The movie concludes with Jack forsaking his Broadway debut to sing "Kol Nidre" (Chapter 7: Music and Spirituality) in his dying father's place for Yom Kippur, the most sacred of the Jewish High Holy Days.

Similar stories portraying the complex issues surrounding ethnic identity and the conflicting pressures of cultural retention and assimilation had long been popular on the American stage. *The Jazz Singer* struck a pressure point. The film was remade three times. A 1952 version starred Danny Thomas (1912–1991); a 1959 made-for-television version featured Jerry Lewis (1926–2017); a 1980

Crowd gathering to see *The Jazz Singer* outside the Warners' Theater, NYC.

John Spring Collection/Corbis Historical/Getty Images.

version cast Neil Diamond (b. 1941). Other movies that follow a similar storyline of a musician from an ethnic minority assimilating into mainstream American culture include *The Benny Goodman Story* (1955) and *La Bamba* (1987), the story of teen idol singer Ritchie Valens (1941–1959).

COMPOSING A FILM SCORE, STEP BY STEP

The composer's job is to serve and enhance the film's narrative. After initially "screening" the film, the composer, along with the director and perhaps others, begin the "spotting" process in which initial decisions are made about where music should be included. Each such musical insertion is called a "cue." A cue might last just seconds, or minutes. Generally, the composer and director will work together to develop a general concept for the entire score. Often stylistically appropriate models, called "temp tracks," are borrowed from preexisting music and used as musical placeholders to establish a feeling for the scene. As the composing gets underway, particular ideas, actions, or characters are often linked with specific melodies, rhythms, or instrumental textures. These leitmotifs, or leading motives, as they are called (Chapter 6: Music and Gender), are used to tie the film's narrative together.

Composers today often write only the piano score, then rely on a team of orchestrators to arrange the music for additional instruments. Because musical timings must be exact, recording is often done with the conductor leading the instrumentalists while watching the actual film footage. In a process called ADR (automated dialog replacement), basic dialog is often dubbed in after the filming is completed. This process is particularly common when singing is involved.

Director and composer work closely together, often forming strong relationships that continue beyond the initial film project. Long-term director–composer teams include Alfred Hitchcock (1899–1980) and Bernard Herrmann (1911–1975), Steven Spielberg and John Williams, and Tim Burton (b. 1958) and Danny Elfman (b. 1953).

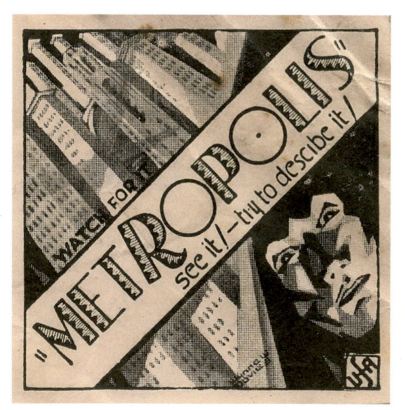

Advertisement for the film *Metropolis* (1927).
Archives New Zealand/Wikimedia Commons/CC-BY-SA-2.0.

Metropolis (1927)

In 1927 came the release of German director Fritz Lang's silent-film classic *Metropolis*. The film presents a dystopian urban future that pits poor against rich, humanity against machine.

The story takes place in 2026. Deep beneath the city's skyscrapers live the numbed laborers who endlessly maintain the giant engines that run the city. Living high above in their pleasure gardens are the elite few who benefit from the workers below. Added to the mix is a maniacal *Machinenmensch* (human machine, or robot). Human in appearance, the robot wreaks destruction across all levels of society.

The mostly original score was conceived by German composer Gottfried Huppertz (1887–1937), who conducted a live orchestra at the Berlin premiere. Huppertz called for thick sound textures heavy with brass instruments. Rhythms drive; harmonies grate. We examine the first few minutes of the score, which begins near the conclusion of the film's opening credits.

Huppertz's score also used previously composed music carefully chosen to stir strong emotions. "La Marseillaise," the French national anthem (Chapter 8: Music and Nation), is used during the workers' revolt. The Catholic funeral chant "Dies Irae" is heard when Death dances with the statues of the Seven Deadly Sins.

Opening of *Metropolis*, music by Gottfried Huppertz

LISTENING
12.2
GUIDE

Texture: Complex homophony
Meter: Quadruple

1:40	The music commences in grandiose style, with the ascending brass tones of a gigantic fanfare. Timpani sound as the music begins a long cadence coinciding with the geometric on-screen presentation of the film's title. As the title dissolves into a vast city skyline, humanity's glorious technological future is implied in both sight and sound.
2:27	Then we see the gears and wheels, driving pistons and billowing steam of the enormous machines that allow the city to run. Their visual power is seductive, a seeming testament to humankind's ingenuity. What to make of all this mechanical muscle? The music tells us. Contrasting rhythms and textures agitate one against the other, like bullies restlessly pushing their way down a sidewalk. Each melody is displaced by another as the camera pans across the mechanical images.
2:52	Listen to the ominous pulsing of clarinet and bell. The sound is tied to the seconds ticking away on a ten-hour clock, the duration of the workers' shifts. This is a world tied to machines, not the natural cycles of nature. The rhythmic energy gradually breaks apart. As the whistle blows, we see rows of deflated workers changing shifts.
3:18	Brutalized by the machines they serve, the workers stand zombie-like. Heads down, they trudge to and from the elevators that connect their underground quarters to the machines above. Now we hear a group of themes, all of which signify the dull misery of the laborers' underground existence.

Theme 1	3:26:	A dreary string melody
Theme 2	3:45:	A pair of descending scales.
Theme 3	4:10:	A simple melody sounded in the brass and echoed in the strings.

Time and again these various leitmotifs reappear in the movie. Each repetition intensifies the film's emotional content while helping to connect scenes separated by time and place.

ANOTHER SOUNDTRACK FOR *METROPOLIS*

In 1984, Italian record producer Giorgio Moroder created an eighty-minute version of *Metropolis* using music by Pat Benatar, Adam Ant, Freddy Mercury, and others. The internet features a number of *Metropolis* clips refitted with contemporary soundtracks.

MUSIC AND MACHINE

Composers have long been fascinated by the possibilities of representing machines through music. In the early 20th century, some attempted to wed music to the sounds of industrialization. Music of the future would be "the music of noise," claimed Italian composer Luigi Russolo (1885–1947). Russolo and other Futurists encouraged colleagues to fill their scores with sounds of pots and pans, rattling sheets of metal, typewriters and car horns. In the 1950s and 1960s composers experimented with electronically produced sounds to portray futuristic worlds. The visionary soundtrack for the sci-fi classic *Forbidden Planet* (1956), composed by Louis Barron (1920–1989) and Bebe Barron (1925–2008), features a score filled with electronic bleeps, whirs, and a variety of other-worldly sounds.

Hollywood's Golden Era

Many thought "talkies" would mark the end of music for film. After all, what need for musical filler now that pictures spoke? For a brief period, music was mostly abandoned. The exceptions were opening credits (where music functioned like an overture) and when musicians were performing diegetically within the film's narrative. Between 1927 and 1930 over 22,000 theater musicians across the country lost their jobs.

It soon became clear, however, that movie audiences wanted music. Academy Award winner *The Broadway Melody* (1929) was the first feature-length movie to fully integrate music, dance, and plot. It also heralded an exodus of artists from the stages of New York City to more lucrative opportunities in Hollywood, California. Thus began the "Golden Age" of movie musicals, which lasted from the 1930s to the early 1950s. @ 12.3 Its stars were many and ranged from the ever-boyish Mickey Rooney (1920–2014) to the hipster Frank Sinatra (1915–1998), from the sexy comedienne Marilyn Monroe (1926–1962) to the elegant dance team of Fred Astaire (1899–1987) and Ginger Rogers (1911–1995) to swimmer Esther Williams (1921–2013). Williams performed many of her "dance" routines underwater.

NEW YORK TO HOLLYWOOD

Three of the greatest Golden Age film composers were Max Steiner, Dimitri Tiomkin (1894–1979), and Alfred Newman (1900–1970). All three left New York City for Hollywood.

Steiner, an Austrian who studied piano with German composer Johannes Brahms (1833–1897), came to the United States in 1914 and worked on Broadway as an arranger and conductor. He moved to Hollywood in 1929 and worked primarily for Warner Brothers. A gifted melodist, Steiner pioneered the use of original music in film. He scored over 300 films, including *King Kong* (1933) and *Gone with the Wind* (1939). Steiner received twenty-six Academy Award nominations and won three Oscar awards.

Tiomkin began his career in St. Petersburg, Russia as a silent-film pianist. He came to New York City in 1925 and four years later moved to Hollywood, where he wrote music for about 125 films. Tiomkin is remembered for his scores to *Lost Horizon* (1937) and his long association with Frank Capra, which included the films *Mr. Smith Goes to Washington* (1939) and *It's a Wonderful Life* (1946). Tiomkin won four Oscar awards.

Newman, an American from Connecticut, began his performing career in vaudeville at the age of 13. Five years later he was conducting Broadway shows. In 1930 Newman moved to Hollywood where for twenty-one years he served as general music director at Twentieth Century Fox. Newman scored over 200 films and won nine Oscar awards. He also wrote the theme music for the popular television show *Rawhide* (1959–1966).

Then as now, audiences loved spectacle. The choreography of Busby Berkeley (1895–1976) added titillation to the cinematic mix. His dance routines featured phalanxes of scantily clad women moving with drill-team precision. Berkeley's film *Whoopee!* (1930) helped launch the dance musical. Hard-pressed Depression-era patrons flocked to the choreographer's upbeat films, including *42nd Street*, *Footlight Parade*, and *Gold Diggers of 1933*—all released with domino inevitability in a single year.

Equally well received was the work of dance legend Fred Astaire (1899–1987). Astaire teamed up with Ginger Rogers (1911–1995) in ten films, including *The Gay Divorcee* (1934) and *Top Hat* (1935). The duo attracted the period's finest songwriters, including Irving Berlin, Cole Porter, and George Gershwin.

The end of the decade saw the release of *The Wizard of Oz* (1939), one of Hollywood's most enduring movie musicals (Chapter 3: Three Listening Examples).

Fred Astaire and Ginger Rogers in *The Barkleys of Broadway*, 1949.

QUESTIONS FOR THOUGHT

- Are there musical movie stars today whose careers might compare to Fred Astaire, Marilyn Monroe, or Judy Garland?
- Are there movies today that incorporate music, dance, plot, and spectacle in the same way as those of Hollywood's Golden Age?

Race Film: *Cabin in the Sky* (1943)

Up through World War II, American film had parallel industries. One was marketed to whites, the other to African Americans. The latter were known as "race films." @ 12.4 A great many race films featured African-American musicians in leading roles.

One such film was *Cabin in the Sky*, a Broadway musical made into a movie directed by Vincente Minnelle (1903–1986). Along with comedian Eddie Anderson (1905–1977), *Cabin* featured some of the era's greatest musical entertainers, including vocalists Ethel Waters (1896–1977) and Lena Horne (1917–2010), trumpeter Louis Armstrong, band leader Duke Ellington, and dancers John "Bubbles" Sublett (1902–1986) and Bill Bailey (1912–1978).

Cabin tells the story of "Little Joe" Jackson (Anderson), a gentle-spirited backslider who, having strayed one time too many from the straight and narrow, is mortally wounded during a fight. Though slated for an afterlife in hell, the prayers of his loving wife Petunia (Waters) reach the gates of heaven. Joe is given a second chance at life and redemption.

Ethel Waters, Kenneth Spencer, Eddie Anderson, Lena Horne, and Rex Ingram in the film *Cabin in the Sky*, 1943.

Cabin was filmed during World War II (1939–1945), an important time in American race relations. Overseas, African-American regiments in the segregated American armed forces were distinguishing themselves in combat. Here at home, both the Roosevelt Administration and the NAACP were pressuring Hollywood to create more substantial roles for black actors. *Cabin in the Sky* was supposed to help break black/white barriers.

That was the idea, anyhow. In fact, the film was a stew of the usual racial stereotypes. The story was set within a hodge-podge of clumsy oppositions: rural versus urban, virtue versus vice, fidelity versus infidelity, folk music versus jazz. Heaven's forces wear white, Satan's minions wear black. Scenes alternated between minstrel-era plantation-style locations on the one hand and highly sexualized nightclub life on the other. Presumably, sticking to the former gets one to heaven; the latter earns a ticket to hell.

The film's many musical numbers generally accentuate these stereotypes, such as when dancers strut and swing to the Ellington orchestra's pulsing rendition of "Things Ain't What They Used to Be." But when the band switches to the strikingly named tune "Goin' Up," stereotypes briefly falter. The mood feels like a religious revival. Dancers stand transfixed as trombonist Lawrence Brown (1907–1988) plays like the angel Gabriel himself. When the dancing continues, the mood combines secular frenzy with quasi-religious ecstasy.

We examine an earlier moment in the film, when Waters is featured in the song "Taking a Chance on Love" by Vernon Duke (1903–1969). Little Joe has just given Petunia a washing machine for her birthday. When Petunia starts to cry from joy, Little Joe picks up a guitar, whistles an introduction, and Petunia starts to sing. The non-diegetic sounds of a jazz big band mysteriously appear in the background.

The song is set in a straightforward 32-bar song form. Neatly symmetrical, the performance goes through the 32-bar cycle four times. Half the performance is devoted to song, half to dance. Waters takes the first sixty-four bars. Her lyrics are clever, full of inner rhymes and one-line refrains. Bailey adds physicality as he riffs and even moonwalks his way through the next thirty-two bars. Anderson calms things down with a comedic soft-shoe routine that includes carelessly sitting on the stove and then jumping into the sink to cool off.

Near the end of Anderson's routine, Waters begins to vocalize a lovely counter melody. At first, her tone is sweet and gentle. Then it becomes rough, sensual, and jazz inflected. It is a sound well within the real Waters's stylistic range, but not the churchy Petunia's. Little Joe is shocked, maybe even a little intimidated by his wife's suddenly lusty display. He interrupts her. The song ends.

QUESTIONS FOR THOUGHT

- How does film create and maintain the distinction between character and actor? What role does music play in this?
- What conditions are necessary for an actor to reside invisibly with his character? Does Elvis Presley or Eddie Murphy ever disappear completely within their characters? What about Madonna?
- Does music in film still portray race in such stark contrasts?

Post-World War II

War's end brought America a new worldliness and confidence. This can be seen in a variety of post-war films. *On the Town* (1949), with music by Leonard Bernstein and Roger Edens (1905–1970), combined Frank Sinatra, Gene Kelly (1912–1996), and Jules Munshin (1915–1975) as three irrepressible sailors on shore leave in New York City.

Kelly went on to star in two more dance musical classics: *An American in Paris* (1951) and the invariably sunny *Singin' in the Rain* (1952). In the first of these Kelly plays a young artist abroad. In the second he is a silent-movie star trying to make the transition to "talkies."

Gene Kelly in *Singin' in the Rain*, 1952.
Michael Ochs Archive/Moxiepix/Getty Images.

PLAYBACK SINGERS: WHO IS REALLY SINGING?

In some films, playback singers are used to pre-record the songs for on-screen personalities who then lip sync in front of the camera. The American soprano Marni Nixon (1930–2016) sang for Deborah Kerr (1921–2007) in *The King and I*, Audrey Hepburn (1929–1993) in *My Fair Lady*, and Natalie Wood (1938–1981) in *West Side Story*. She dubbed for so many famous actresses she was nicknamed "The Ghostess with the Mostess."

One of the most convoluted uses of playback singers occurs in *Singin' in the Rain*, whose plot revolves around the very idea of vocal dubbing in the early days of sound films. Here we watch the film's ingénue, Kathy Sheldon (played by Debbie Reynolds, 1932–2016), dubbing on screen the unfortunately shrill voice of Lina Lamont (played by Jean Hagen, 1923–1977), a silent movie star trying to make the transition to "talkies." But in reality, it is Reynolds herself who is being dubbed by Hagen's real-life voice in their scenes together. Furthermore, in the songs "Would You?" and "You are My Lucky Star," the never-credited Betty Noyes (1912–1987) sings in place of Reynolds. Such substitution, though studios did their best to keep their secrets, were quite common.

The Day the Earth Stood Still (1951)

Despite the initial post-World War II exuberance, the emerging Cold War with the Soviet Union stirred considerable anxiety. In 1947, the House Un-American Activities Committee (HUAC) singled out Hollywood as a source of Communist propaganda. Subsequent hearings led to the blacklisting of many within the industry, including: composer Aaron Copland (1900–1990), singer Paul Robeson and E.Y. "Yip" Harburg (1896–1981), whose contributions included song lyrics to both *The Wizard of Oz* and *Cabin in the Sky*. The Korean War (1950–1953), the first of two American wars fought to contain Communism, would claim some 54,000 American lives. It was in this climate of fear that author Harry Bates's (1900–1981) short story "Farewell to the Master" (1940) was adapted into the film *The Day the Earth Stood Still* (1951).

Directed by Robert Wise (1914–2005) with a musical score by Bernard Herrmann, *The Day the Earth Stood Still* presents Klaatu, the interplanetary traveler who lands his flying saucer in Washington,

BERNARD HERRMANN (1911–1975)

Born in New York City, Herrmann's early musical career was centered at the Columbia Broadcast System (CBS). He was hired to compose and conduct for educational radio programs, but eventually became the staff conductor of the CBS Orchestra. It was at CBS that Herrmann met Orson Welles (1915–1985) and provided music for Wells's infamous 1938 *War of the Worlds* radio broadcast. Three years later, Herrmann wrote the soundtrack to Wells's cinematic masterpiece *Citizen Kane* (1941). In 1955, Herrmann began an eight-film and ten-year collaboration with the director Alfred Hitchcock. Herrmann died in his sleep after a long recording session of his score for Martin Scorsese's (b. 1942) *Taxi Driver* (1976). It is said that the composer, who had been in poor health, died of exhaustion.

Films in which Herrmann collaborated with Alfred Hitchcock:

1955	*The Trouble with Harry*	1958	*Vertigo*	1963	*The Birds*
1956	*The Man Who Knew Too Much*	1959	*North by Northwest*	1964	*Marnie*
1956	*The Wrong Man*	1960	*Psycho*		

Klaatu and Gort in *The Day the Earth Stood Still*, 1951.

D.C. Klaatu's mission is to warn Earth's governments that they must mend their warlike ways before venturing into space. Disobeying this command will result in humankind's annihilation. Backing up Klaatu is Gort, an invincible robot.

How does one capture the sounds of outer space? Herrmann invented new tone combinations. His orchestra used a combination of thirty brass instruments, groups of pianos and harps, as well as a vibraphone, an electric violin, and two **theremins**. In order to add to the otherworldliness, some of the music was inserted into the soundtrack backwards.

We will analyze the film's opening sequence, which unfolds as the title captions are rolling. The music sounds strange to our ears, but the overall form is straightforward. The credits begin traditionally, with a picture of the 20th Century Fox marquee accompanied by the company's drum-roll-to-brass fanfare. Then the screen goes dark.

THEREMIN

Imagine making music just by waving your arms. You can if you have a theremin, an electronic instrument invented in 1919 by the Russian physicist Leon Theremin (1896–1993). The theremin is a favorite in science fiction, but is also used in popular music. The Beach Boys' "Good Vibrations" (1966) features a variation on the instrument. So do recordings by Led Zeppelin, Mötley Crüe, and Phish.

The theremin works by sensing electromagnetic waves in the human body. The instrument has two antennae. One controls pitch; the other controls amplitude (dynamics). A musician performs by adjusting the distance between her hands and the antennae, thereby controlling pitch and volume.

Lew [Leon] Theremin demonstrating the theremin, December 1927.

Opening sequence from *The Day the Earth Stood Still*, music by Bernard Herrmann

LISTENING
12.3
GUIDE

Texture: Complex homophony
Meter: Quadruple
Form: Introduction, A B C B A B C

0:14	**Introduction** The movie begins with Herrmann's score. What a contrast from the heroic Fox fanfare. An eerie downward-moving glissando sounds like a missile falling to earth. There is a cymbal roll crescendo. As the screen lights up, stars race toward the viewer. We are traveling through outer space. Out of the starry void, the film's title appears in plain block letters.
0:21	**Section A** The full musical ensemble makes its appearance. Low brass tones tumble downward in four gestures. The more brilliant and high-pitched sounds of trumpets move in parallel and alternating directions. The effect of all this is an uncomfortable stretching and seething. As the tones repeat they are joined first by the weirdly seductive sounds of the theremins, then by rhythmic punctuation from the harps. This movie, the score tells us, will be serious and thought provoking. It will be slow-paced and far outside our everyday experience.
0:39	**Section B** Now we hear the high brass instruments play a fanfare, one almost reminiscent of the 20th Century Fox theme. But as these heroic tones fade, the music seems to open up, like the deep space that fills the screen. Harps and pianos pluck and hammer. It seems that musical outer space is not only vast and full of mysterious forces, but also endlessly active. Listen to the theremins. Do they remind you of singing? Perhaps Herrmann is presenting us with an irresistible Siren-like call to explore outer space.
0:47	The fanfare is echoed by the lower brass.
0:56	**Section C** Sounds of ostinati and theremins move more toward the front as the brass instruments softly repeat their initial motives.
1:15	**Section B** Brass fanfare and low echo.
1:31	**Section A** The original "stretching" gesture returns as we see two planets on screen. Is one Earth? Is the other Klaatu's? Do the planets move in tandem? Do they resist each other like the accompanying tones in the brass section?
1:47	**Section B** There is time for one last brass fanfare as the clouds of Earth appear on screen. We seem to have moved through space to our destination; perhaps we see through the eyes of Klaatu. Have you also noticed how the music has forced you to slow down emotionally, as if you really were traveling through the vastness of space? How different that feeling is from the frantic activity we are about to witness on the planet below.
1:56	**Section C** There is a cadence of sorts and a view of water. This signals the end of the credits section and the beginning of the movie proper.
2:00	Nervous pulsing ostinati sound as the water fades into radar screens revealing the presence of a UFO.

QUESTIONS FOR THOUGHT

- Do you think the music for *The Day the Earth Stood Still* sounds as strange today as it did to audiences in the 1950s? Why or why not?
- Search the internet for music associated with Gort. What does the music tell us about the robot?

Beyond Hollywood: *The Hidden Fortress* (*Kakushi toride no san-akunin*) (1958)

Poster for *The Hidden Fortress*, 1958.
Movie Poster Image Art/Moviepix/Getty Images.

While the West looked fearfully into the future, the great Japanese film director Akiro Kurosawa (1910–1998) explored the social values developed during his country's feudal past. Prominent in Kurosawa films are themes of honor and duty, self-control and loyalty. Kurosawa was a master of spectacle who generally reserved his biggest set pieces for battles. But not always. *The Hidden Fortress*, with music by Masaru Sato (1928–1999), offers instead a traditional dance that is seamlessly integrated into the overall narrative.

The action takes place in 16th-century Japan. As war rages, 16-year-old Princess Yuki (Misa Uehara, 1937–2003) must cross enemy lines to reach the safety of her clan. Adding to her burden is the fact that she must bring with her 400 ingots of gold, money needed to ensure her clan's survival. Guarding Yuki is her general, Rokurota Makabe (Toshiro Mifune, 1920–1997). Tagging along are the untrustworthy and hopelessly inept soldier/farmers Tahei and Matakishi.

All along the escape route, the company moves from one harrowing experience to another. The fugitives survive detection by Makabe's wits, but time and again are nearly undone by the foolishness of Tahei and Matakishi. With each new adventure, the haughty princess has new experiences. Yuki moves toward wisdom as she gradually learns the ways of the world.

All of these notions come into play during the fire festival scene. Yuki and Makabe (with the ingots carefully hidden within sticks of wood) join a procession to the festival site. The event seems the perfect disguise. Since everyone is carrying wood, princess and company can simply evaporate into the crowd.

A FAMILIAR PAIR?

The bumbling peasants Tahei and Matakishi—one tall and gaunt, the other short and round—may seem familiar. They were the inspiration for George Lucas's (b. 1944) C-3PO and R2D2. The opening scene of *The Hidden Fortress*—with the battle-weary peasants stumbling across an open landscape—is echoed in an early scene from the original *Star Wars* movie (1977).

QUESTIONS FOR THOUGHT

- Yuki holds the hand of the peasant woman. Why not General Makabe's?
- Do you think the music of this scene communicates the same ideas to Western and Japanese audiences?

> ## *The Hidden Fortress,* fire festival scene, music by Masaru Sato
>
> **LISTENING 12.4 GUIDE**
>
> (Excerpt begins at 1:43:48 on the DVD) @ 12.5
> **Texture: Heterophonic**
> **Meter: Quadruple**
>
> The scene opens with the fugitives' arrival at the festival. They push their cart to the edge of the fire circle. The princess, distant as always, looks on from the perimeter as the fervent peasants chant:
>
> > The life of a man
> > Burn it with the fire
> > The life of an insect
> > Throw it into the fire
> > Ponder and you'll see
> > The world is dark
> > And this floating world is a dream
> > Burn with abandon
>
> The chanting is accompanied by a shakuhachi (Chapter 3: Three Listening Examples) playing softly in the background. A drum punctuates the end of each line. A ritualistic dance ensues as the peasants throw burning brands into the fire; **taiko** drummers beat out pulsing rhythms.
>
> All goes smoothly until the revelers see the cart of sticks. To the horror of Tahei and Matakishi, the crowd attempts to push the entire cart into the flames. A struggle ensues and soldiers arrive. Fearing discovery, Makabe takes charge. He rolls the cart, gold and all, into the fire. Everyone dances.
>
> It is a wonderful scene. Tahei and Matakishi stumble through the choreography unable to take their eyes off the burning cart. Yuki and Makabe dance as well. Yuki, embracing the expectations of separate worlds, holds the hand of the peasant to her left. To her right is her general and protector. They do not touch.

Diversification

As the 1950s progressed, production companies diversified their output. A series of successful Broadway stage musicals were adapted for film. The racially incisive 1927 musical *Show Boat* (Chapter 11: American Musical Theater) was adapted into a socially softened 1950 film. The same year also saw the film release of composer Irving Berlin's 1946 Broadway hit, *Annie Get Your Gun.*

"Bigger is better" marked the Hollywood approach. Stages were abandoned for grandiose outdoor sets; marquee film stars often replaced lesser-known stage actors. The 1955 film adaptation of Frank Loesser's (1910–1969) *Guys and Dolls* (1950), for example, featured superstars Frank Sinatra and Marlon Brando (1924–2004). The adaptation of *The Sound of Music* (1965), shot in Austria and Germany, remains the most financially successful American film musical of all time.

The same period saw the rise of the pop music film. One of the genre's biggest stars was Elvis Presley (1935–1977), who between 1956 and 1970 starred in thirty-one movies. His first, *Love Me Tender*, pitted brother against brother in the post-Civil War South. Future movies cast Presley as convict (*Jailhouse Rock*, 1957), boxer (*Kid Galahad*, 1962), soldier (*GI Blues*, 1960), and trapeze artist (*Fun in Acapulco*, 1963), among myriad other professions. Always, Elvis found reasons to sing and dance.

Pop music of all sorts lit up movie screens. Beginning in 1963, co-stars Annette Funicello (1942–2013) and Frankie Avalon (b. 1939) starred in a series of "beach party" movies. Innocence was the rule of thumb. Probably never before nor since have teens in love acted with such restraint. The Beatles were featured in three movies: *A Hard Day's Night* (1964), *Help* (1965), and *Yellow Submarine* (1968). Rock documentaries included Bob Dylan's (b. 1941) *Don't Look Back* (1967),

BOLLYWOOD

The world's largest film industry resides in India. Bollywood is the nickname given to that portion of the industry that emanates from Mumbai (formerly Bombay). Though the primary language is Hindi, films often incorporate two or three languages, including English. Bollywood films generally feature comedy, spectacle, formulaic characters, and actors and actresses whose star status rivals that of any Hollywood idol. Song and dance are essential. Many Bollywood clips (and full movies) are available on the internet.

Woodstock (1970), and The Band's *The Last Waltz* (1978). Rock parodies include Rob Reiner's (b. 1947) *This Is Spinal Tap* (1984) and Jack Black's (b. 1969) *School of Rock* (2003).

Animated film musicals have had a long and successful run. Walt Disney's (1901–1966) *Snow White and the Seven Dwarfs* was the first full-length animated musical. Jiminy Cricket's "When You Wish Upon a Star" from *Pinocchio* (1940) became the Disney theme song. That same year Disney released *Fantasia* (1940), which featured cartoon animation set to music by J.S. Bach, Ludwig van Beethoven, Igor Stravinsky (1882–1971), and others. Disney has continued to produce animated musicals. A string of successes came in the early 1990s with *Beauty and the Beast* (1991) (Chapter 10: Music and Love), *Aladdin* (1992), and *The Lion King* (1994). *Frozen* (2013) became the highest grossing animated film of all time.

New Explorations

Composer Philip Glass (b. 1937) has made a point of using contemporary musical styles to celebrate the cinematic past. He wrote scores to accompany two early film classics, director Tod Browning's (1880–1962) *Dracula* (1931/1999) featuring Bela Lugosi (1882–1956), and French director Jean

Philip Glass Ensemble performing *Powaqqatsi* (*Life in Transformation*).
Hiroyuki Ito/Hulton Archive/Getty Images.

Cocteau's (1889–1963) *La Belle et la Bête* (*Beauty and the Beast*) 1946/1995. The latter he transformed into a film/opera (vocalists sing from behind the screen).

Also important has been Glass's work with director Godfrey Reggio (b. 1940). Together they created the QATSI trilogy of *Koyaanisqatsi* (*Life Out of Balance*, 1982), *Powaqqatsi* (*Life in Transformation*, 1987), and *Nagoyqatsi* (*Life as War*, 2002). Think of these films as portraits in motion. Reggio says that he sought to "rip out all the foreground of a traditional film" (actors, plot, story) and bring background imagery forward. The subsequent emptiness is both thrilling and emotionally challenging. In *Koyaanisqatsi*, Glass supports the unfolding scenes with **minimalist** music of slowly fluctuating harmonic patterns. Insistent pulsating rhythms grow as the visual imagery gradually shifts from natural to urbanized settings.

In *Decasia: The State of Decay* (2002), director Bill Morrison (b.1965) draws material from deteriorated black-and-white nitrate film stock. Disembodied characters seem to move through a world coming apart. Images bubble with the destructive energy of decomposition. The effects are surreal: sometimes beautiful, other times horrifying. A boxer bobs and weaves as he punches into decayed oblivion. Machine gears spin toward their own destruction.

Michael Gordon (b. 1956), who scored the film, says that his compositional idea was to make the music sound as broken as the images look, as if the music was "covered in cobwebs." The film opens with the grinding sounds of percussionists scraping metal sticks in circles around the rims of old automobile brake drums. The orchestra, which is literally "broken," is divided into two halves, each intentionally out of tune with the other. Rhythms pulse with feverish energy. Pitches grate and waver as if the musical machine is too decrepit to hold a solid center. Dissonance is constant and jarring.

ACTIVITIES AND ASSIGNMENTS

- **Watch a clip from *Decasia: The State of Decay*. Can you discover thematic narratives or messages imbedded in the decay?**
- **Get together in a group and create your own short film using video clips or photos. Using the same visual materials create two different sound tracks that portray contrasting moods, emotions, or plots.**

Dissecting an Epic: *Star Wars*

Since cinema's beginning, filmmakers have reveled in filling the screen with themes of epic proportion. Among the most famous attempts are *Gone with the Wind* (1939), *Ben Hur* (1959), *Doctor Zhivago* (1965), *Apocalypse Now* (1979), *Saving Private Ryan* (1998), *The Lord of the Rings* (2001–2003), and *Avatar* (2009), all of which portray struggling individuals caught within a broader clash of cultures.

Now we briefly consider perhaps cinema's grandest epic—the still-unfolding triple-trilogy *Star Wars* saga (1977–), with musical scores by John Williams. Beginning with the very first movie (*Episode IV*, 1977), Williams's task was to create a musical soundscape that would link the films to each other. Williams used leitmotifs to accomplish this.

In *Episode IV*, Luke Skywalker, Princess Leia, Darth Vader, the rebel resistance, the Force, and the Death Star all received leitmotifs. Luke Skywalker's theme, which plays through the opening crawl ("a long time ago in a galaxy far, far away"), is the most prominent music of the entire series. Indeed, in its march form, you might already simply associate it with *Star Wars* as a whole. In contrast, Leia's theme is slow and dreamy. The rebel resistance theme is martial like Luke's, but it is more plucky than domineering, more like a fox than a lion. The Death Star receives no melody at all, just dissonant harmonies. The same themes, or variations on them, can be heard in *The Force Awakens* (2016), along with new themes for Rey, Kylo Ren, and even BB-8, the droid.

ACTIVITIES AND ASSIGNMENTS

- Find and listen to *Star Wars* leitmotifs (or search "musical themes") on the internet. Does the music's quality fit the character or thing?
- Learn to recognize the themes, then watch one of the movies. Does this change your viewing experience? If so, how?

A Final Scene

We began the chapter with a quote from Max Steiner, who throughout the 1930s and 1940s was arguably Hollywood's most important composer. Now we return to him. Steiner's music was ingenious, filled with leitmotifs, innovative textures, and psychological depth. Quite simply, Steiner opened the path on which subsequent film composers would follow.

To demonstrate this, we examine a snippet of Steiner's work, the fog scene of the original *King Kong* (1933). Armed with our new understandings, we can easily detect the way in which Steiner guides, even coerces, us into the psychological drama. @ 12.6

King Kong: Fog scene

If you can, begin your listening with the first tones of the film's credits (0:15), a descending three-tone motive. At 1:33 it sounds again, this time accompanied by the on-screen words, "And lo, the beast looked upon the face of beauty." Now skip forward to 20:40. We are aboard ship at night

King Kong under attack, 1933.

John Kobal Foundation/ Moviepix/Getty Images.

cruising through a foggy veil toward Skull Island. Echoing the visual effect of the fog, the music soundtrack opens mysteriously with disembodied tones set up by stagnant strings, plucking harp, and distant-sounding woodwinds. Adding to the effect is the lack of rhythmic direction, which produces a suspended, timeless feeling. From this texture gradually emerges a clarinet (21:20) again sounding the three-tone downward-moving motive already familiar from the film's opening credits. In sight and sound we sit at the boundary between worlds as we drift blindly between the modern and the primitive, between the conscious and unconscious, and between the known and unknowable.

Perhaps our intuition has already told us the meaning of the descending three-tone motive. It is Kong. And Kong, Steiner's music tells us, is more than a brutal, sky-scraper-scaling, chest-thumping monster. He is an enigma, perhaps even a symbol of our own primal nature, of the destructive and noble drives that make us human.

Steiner's score binds us to the action, disturbs our inner tranquility. Curiously, however, the musical themes themselves are not particularly memorable. One cannot sing the fog music, for example; Kong's doleful three-tone motive has no independent melodic life. That was the way Steiner wanted it. He preferred that audiences focus on the film's images, while he worked musical magic surreptitiously in the background.

Future composers, such as John Williams and Howard Shore (*Lord of the Rings* 2001–2003), would take a different approach. For them, the central musical themes would often be placed in the foreground where they would become essential parts of the remembrance package that we take home from the theater. Who can forget the jolly can-do march theme that binds the various Indiana Jones movies, the booming drums of Saruman's Isengard from *The Two Towers*? How about the five-tone "Call of the Mother Ship" from *Close Encounters of the Third Kind* (1977)?

Take a moment to hear in your mind E.T.'s flying theme. Did the scene's images and emotional quality come along in tandem? As the music unfolded in your head, did the weighty troubles of the world seem a bit lighter, if just for a moment? If so, you have witnessed—and inwardly manifested—music's power to spur imagination, to expand breadth of experience, and to sustain and enhance emotional worlds.

Key Terms

- diegetic sounds
- leitmotif
- minimalism (minimalist)
- non-diegetic sounds
- ostinato (pl. ostinati)
- race film
- score
- taiko
- theremin

Essay Questions

- Think of a movie you recently watched. Did you notice (perhaps even focus on) the music? Why or why not? Can you remember it?
- Watch a movie scene with the sound turned off. What do you hear in your mind?
- Replace the soundtrack of a movie scene with other music. Does the switch impact your understanding or empathy for the scene?

CHAPTER GOALS

- To examine dance genres in different cultures and times.
- To see how dance reflects regional/national histories and identities.
- To understand the relationship between music and movement.

CHAPTER THIRTEEN

Music and Dance

QUESTIONS FOR THOUGHT

- **Do you like to dance? Why or why not?**
- **What kind of music makes the best dance music?**
- **How many different kinds of dance cultures are there on your campus?**

In the minimalist video *Hotline Bling* (2015, with music sampled from Timmy Thomas's 1972 song "Why Can't We Live Together?"), Canadian rapper Drake's rejected lover sings and dances, mostly alone in front of empty computer-generated backgrounds. Less is more. There is not much to the dancing either. Most anyone could do it. But Drake being Drake, that was more than enough to satisfy fans. And inspire them.

> "Dance is a song of the body."
> —Martha Graham (1894–1991)

Perhaps like no other art form, dance invites participation. How to participate with a video? Fans chose to edit and redistribute. Fan-created superimposed soundtracks have Drake dancing to merengue, to vocalist Tom Jones, to reggae master Bob Marley, and to pianist Vince Guaraldi's "Linus and Lucy," to name just a few. Video images were also manipulated. Drake dribbles a basketball, swings a tennis racquet, fights with a light saber, chops vegetables, and even exterminates roaches. *Saturday Night Live* used the song/video in a skit. One video has Barack Obama singing and dancing.

Dance is endlessly adaptable; it can be utilized to express any emotion. Like music, dance is found in all cultures and appears to be essential to the human condition. In this chapter we explore dance in a few of its many contexts, from South America to West Africa, and from Europe to the United States. We begin with tango. Then we move to Brazil where we study the Afro-Brazilian dance/martial art *capoeira*. From capoeira we go to Ghana, West Africa to study *baamaaya*, a colorful dance of the Dagbamba ethnic group. Next we go back in time to learn about dance during the European Renaissance. Then we follow European dance forward for an overview of the development of classical ballet. The chapter closes in the United States with a brief discussion of modern and popular dance traditions.

Tango: Argentina

Tango began in the smoky bars and dancehalls of the 1890s immigrant-infused *arrabales* (slums) of Buenos Aires, Argentina. There, *compadritos*—savvy young men tough and poor, but slickly dressed—created a dance that echoed the codes of urban street life. Even today, tango recalls the machismo of 1890s compadrito identity.

Shiva as Lord of the Dance (Nataraja), ca. 11th century.

Courtesy of The Metropolitan Museum of Art, Gift of R.H. Ellsworth Ltd., in honor of Susan Dillon, 1987.

From Buenos Aires the dance spread quickly, probably transmitted by sailors who took it across the Atlantic Ocean. By 1912, tango was a sensation in Paris and became established as one of the world's most popular dances. It remains so today. @ 13.1

Tango is about the heat of romance. Song lyrics tell of loves gained and lost—of jealousies and rivalries, broken hearts and wounded pride. A tangoist's pain does not heal. Instead, it becomes a source of creative expression (Chapter 10: Music and Love). Such emotions are captured in countless tango songs. Lyricist Pascual Contursi (1888–1932) used slang-drenched language in "Mi noche triste" ("My Sad Night," 1916) to describe his broken heart. Baritone vocalist Carlos Gardel's (1890–1935) iconic recording helped make the song one of tango's early classics.

The earliest tango ensembles were small and portable; their instrumental heritage was European. *Tercetos* (trios) usually consisted of violin, flute, and either guitar or accordion. By the early 1900s, the ensemble had grown in size and standardized into the *orquesta típica criolla*, a quartet that included violin, flute, guitar, and *bandoneón*, a small German-made button-style accordion. Later ensembles would grow to the size of small orchestras, with string bass, piano, cello, expanded string sections, and as many as four bandoneóns.

The most important tango musician of the second half of the 20th century was bandoneón player, composer, and band leader Astor Piazzolla (1921–1992). Although born in Argentina, Piazzolla spent much of his childhood in New York City, where he heard both jazz and classical music. Piazzolla began playing the bandoneón at age 9, was a virtuoso by age 13. When his family returned to Argentina in 1937, the 16-year-old Piazzolla left home. He rented an apartment in Buenos Aires and began his performing career.

Piazzolla's musical interests were broad. When not on the bandstand, he studied classical composition in Paris and later orchestral conducting. Piazzolla eventually returned to Buenos Aires, where in 1955 he formed his own tango orchestra. Piazzolla's approach drew from the full breadth of his musical experience. He revolutionized the tango sound.

"Libertango," by Astor Piazzolla, from *The Tango Lesson*

LISTENING 13.1 GUIDE

Texture: Complex homophony
Meter: Quadruple
Form: 32- and 16-bar sections

0:00	A male dancer moves alone. We hear clapping and violin glissandi in the background. He bursts through the double doors (literally *la salida*) into the open space of the loft. As he does so, the music's 32-bar form begins.
0:06	Potter and her partner move quickly across the loft in *caminata* steps. As their motion slows, Potter seems to draw lines across the floor with her toes (*el lapiz*).
0:32	Potter takes a new partner as another 32-bar section begins. Notice the *boleos* and *ganchos*.
0:58	Again, Potter changes partners. Dance flow changes as well.
1:24	Potter picks up the visual pacing by having the entire quartet appear as the 32-bar section begins. One woman; three men. All three men act simultaneously as partners to Potter.
1:51	The musical pacing quickens as the form shifts to 16-bar cycles. As the form shortens, so do the dance partnerships. Potter changes partners every few bars.
2:04	Quick partner changes continue.
2:17	Quick partner changes continue. The camera pans away. The men start to emphasize lifts as the dance contour becomes increasingly vertical.
2:30	Lifts continue to be emphasized. At the end of the dance, Potter settles with Veron, who began the dance as a soloist.
2:43	Veron spins Potter as the scene fades out.

Dance Steps

Tango is a dance for couples. It is led by the man, who holds his partner in the *abrazo* (embrace) position. Dancers move in strong, broad steps. The body is erect, though slightly forward. Except for flourishes, feet generally stay close to the floor.

Improvisation is the key to great tango dancing, but improvisation is built on standardized movements. These include the *caminata* (forward walking step), its reverse direction (*el retroceso*), the *salida* (the "exit," actually the step that often begins the dance), and *giros* (turns and rotations). More complex movements include *el lapis* ("the pencil," in which a dancer seems to draw figures on the floor with the foot), *ochos* (steps and pivots that outline figure-eights), *ganchos* (in which the dancer hooks his or her leg around a partner's leg), and whip-like leg movements called *boleos*.

Tango has been featured in many films. Italian heart-throb Rudolf Valentino (1895–1926) danced to "La Cumparsita" (1917, composed by Gerardo Matos Rodríguez [1897–1948]) in *The Four Horsemen of the Apocalypse* (1921). Half a century later, Marlon Brando (1924–2004) and Maria Schneider (b. 1952) lay drunken waste to a tango contest in *Last Tango in Paris* (1972). Two films of the 1990s—*Scent of the Woman* (1992), with Al Pacino (b. 1940), and *Evita* (1996), with Madonna (b. 1958) and Antonio Banderas (b. 1960)—featured the classic song "Por una Cabeza" ("By a Head," 1935), written by Gardel and Alfredo le Pera (ca. 1900–1935).

Real-life experience inspired director Sally Potter's film *The Tango Lesson* (1997). The story, which unfolds in Paris and Buenos Aires, is quasi-autobiographical. Potter, playing herself, is having trouble writing a screen play. To relax, she decides to take tango lessons with Argentine tango master Pablo Veron. The two strike a deal. If he can teach her to dance like a professional, she will give him

ASTOR PIAZZOLLA

Remembering a composition lesson with Parisian pedagogue Nadia Boulanger (1887–1979), Piazzolla said, "When I met her, I showed her my kilos of symphonies and sonatas. She started to read them and suddenly came out with a horrible sentence: 'It's very well written.' And stopped, with a big period, round like a soccer ball. After a long while, she said: 'Here you are like Stravinsky, like Bartók, like Ravel, but you know what happens? I can't find Piazzolla in this.' And she began to investigate my private life: what I did, what I did and did not play, if I was single, married, or living with someone, she was like an FBI agent! And I was very ashamed to tell her that I was a tango musician. Finally I said, 'I play in a

Astor Piazzolla with the tango singer Roberto Goyeneche, April 1982.

night club.' I didn't want to say cabaret. And she answered, 'Night club, *mais oui*, but that is a cabaret, isn't it?' 'Yes,' I answered . . . It wasn't easy to lie to her.

She kept asking: 'You say that you are not a pianist. What instrument do you play, then?' And I didn't want to tell her that I was a bandoneón player. . . . Finally, I confessed and she asked me to play some bars of a tango of my own. She suddenly opened her eyes, took my hand and told me: 'You idiot, that's Piazzolla!' And I took all the music I composed, ten years of my life, and sent it to hell in two seconds."

Saavedra, Gonzalo. "Interview with Piazzolla." www.piazzolla.org/interv/#english.

the leading role in her next film. Both events come to pass. The romantic rub is that Veron the dancer expects to lead. But when it comes to making the film, he must follow.

The dance scenes are inspirational. We will look at just one, a quartet with Potter, Veron, and two additional men. The scene is shot in an empty loft—the space is ample, but stark, like tango itself. The choreography is set to Piazzolla's "Libertango" (1974).

"Libertango" is simple in form—a 32-bar sequence repeated again and again with ever changing orchestration. After five repetitions the form is shortened to sixteen bars, a device that has the effect of quickening dramatic pace and intensifying the emotional impact. Search out Veron and Potter's "Libertango" performance on the internet. Notice how the choreography follows the form, how Potter uses the loft's architecture—first the doorway leading into the hall, then the pillars—as markers to signify the breaks between musical sections and dance partners.

QUESTIONS FOR THOUGHT

- Dance, says film director Sally Potter, "is essentially about stillness." What might she mean by this?
- How does Piazzolla's music in the listening example help to portray the sensuality of the dance?

ACTIVITIES AND ASSIGNMENTS

- Investigate the history and evolution of another contemporary dance genre.

Capoeira: Brazil

In tango, men and women play a game of seduction. Perhaps the dance takes place in a steamy nightclub where seduction is truly the objective. In ballroom dancing, and every choreographed and staged performance—the seduction is simply a façade, play acting designed to project the aesthetics of the dance. In this sense, dance is closely related to theater. Performers take on personae, which are acted out for themselves, their partners, and those looking on.

Traveling north from Argentina to Brazil one encounters a different sort of dance theater. Tangoists play at seduction; Brazil's practitioners of *capoeira* play with the idea of combat. And just as tango's seduction can be real, so too, the kicks and spins of capoeira offer its practitioners real-life skills that can be used in self-defense. @ 13.2

Let's construct a scene. Two capoeiristas eye each other warily as they "dance" the *ginga*, a back-and-forth-step pattern designed to facilitate quick movements and sudden changes in direction. Suddenly, one opponent breaks the pattern. He spins and kicks in the other's direction. The blow falls short as the would-be victim cartwheels out of range. A moment later, a counterstrike is launched.

Throughout, the combatants have moved to the percussive rhythms of the *berimbau*, a one-stringed musical bow. They are surrounded by a *roda* (ring) of fellow capoeiristas singing songs, playing percussion instruments, and clapping. Each awaits his or her own opportunity to step inside the roda and play the *jogo* ("game") of capoeira. The jogo is exhausting. When the players tire, they are quickly replaced. And so it goes. Competition and camaraderie mix and mingle as the afternoon wears on.

Capoeira is lightning quick and exciting to watch. It can also be deadly. A century ago, capoeiristas who had honed their skills within the roda fought for real on the streets of Rio de Janeiro. They fought barefoot, sometimes holding straight-edged razors between their toes. Legs, you see, reach further than arms.

Capoeira's roots are unclear. Folklore holds that capoeira originated during Brazil's slavery era and that African slaves used it as a vehicle for resistance and escape. The fight, according to oral

Capoeira roda, Porto Alegre, Brasil, 2007.
Tetraktys/Wikimedia Commons/CC-BY-SA-3.0.

tradition, was hidden within dance. Thus, slaves were able to hone their martial skills on the master's plantation, right under the noses of their oppressors.

While there is no hard evidence to back up this scenario, it is certainly true that slaves did escape frequently enough to found a number of free communities in the Brazilian forests. These *quilombos*, as they were known, varied in size and permanence. The largest was the multi-settlement area of Palmares, with a population perhaps as large as 20,000 and a governance system based on African political conventions. Palmares survived as an independent community for more than half a century, until its destruction in 1695.

At the very least, Brazilian slavery and capoeira are intertwined. Slavery was abolished in 1888. In 1890, legislation was enacted that made it illegal to practice capoeira. The practice continued nonetheless.

Whatever role capoeira may have had in Brazil's early history, it is clear that the ideas embodied in the above stories are central to the dance/sport's affective power. The jogo is about learning to stand strong for one's rights, about showing tenacity under adversity. Capoeira is also about building a community of support, about finding people who will stand with you in times of need.

The father of modern capoeira was Mestre Bimba (Manuel dos Reis Machado [1900–1974]). Bimba added new techniques to the jogo, thereby making it a more efficient fighting art. Perhaps more importantly, he advocated for capoeira's cultural value as a marker of Afro-Brazilian heritage. Due in large part to Bimba's efforts, capoeira was legalized in the early 1930s. Under Bimba's guidance, capoeira, which had previously been confined to the lower social classes, became a national sport. No longer simply a fight against oppression, it also became part of a cooperative initiative for racial understanding and national identity.

Music is central to the jogo. Players must move in accordance with the musical tempo as provided by the berimbau, the instrument that leads the ensemble. Percussion instruments—which might include the *pandeiro* (tambourine), *agogo* (iron bell), *atabaque* (hand drum), *reco-reco* (rasp), and hand clapping—add rhythmic support.

Songs are sung in Portuguese in a call-and-response style typical of African communal singing. The melodies are short and easy to sing; response sections are usually just a few words long. As a sign of solidarity, everyone in the roda sings. Texts may have to do with everyday life, but generally concern some aspect of capoeira.

"My woman will tell you that capoeira conquered me," says one song. "The capoeirista may stumble, but does not fall," says another. Frequently heard is the song, "No nêgo você não dá" (Don't Give Him a Thing" [meaning, "Don't let your guard down"]) which exhorts the players to play the game hard. As the song progresses, the solo leader may create an endless variety of lyrics. Always, however, the choral response will be "Dá, dá, dá, dá no nêgo" (Give, give, give it to him" [meaning, "Defeat your opponent"]).

THE BERIMBAU

The berimbau is a musical bow, probably of African origin. A hollowed-out gourd is attached to the bow and serves as a resonating chamber. To play, the bow string is struck with a stick. Different sounds can be achieved by pressing against the string with a coin or flat stone. In the stick hand, the player also holds a small rattle (*caxixi*), which thickens the music's texture and provides a rhythmic counterpoint. In capoeira, some berimbau rhythms have names and are associated with specific movements.

Three berimbau players playing the rhythm for a capoeira in Baltimore, MA, featuring Mestre Cobra Mansa, 2003.

Sam Fentress/Wikimedia Commons/CC-BY-SA-2.0.

ACTIVITIES AND ASSIGNMENTS

- There are many video examples of capoeira on the internet. Compare and contrast two styles: Angola and Regional.
- Compare capoeira to other martial arts traditions. What are the similarities and differences?
- Many colleges and universities have capoeira groups. Does yours?

Baamaaya: Ghana, West Africa

In Africa, where there is music, there is dance. In urban nightclubs, lithe dancers move to the seamless grooves of Congolese *soukous*, Nigerian *jùjú*, Zimbabwean *chimurenga*, Senegalese *mbalax*, and other popular music styles. In traditional contexts, adolescents dance to signify their coming into adulthood; adults dance to celebrate the dead and honor the gods. Here we study baamaaya, a colorful traditional dance of the Dagbamba, an ethnic group residing in Ghana's Northern Region.

Baamaaya's roots are unclear. Elders in the community sometimes refer to the dance as *tubankpele*. The word recalls the custom of dancers performing with corn husks stuffed into their belts. There are conflicting stories about tubankpele's origin. One account says it was danced at night because the movements kept mosquitoes away. Another account says the dance, with its twisting hip motions, was done to tease women. Yet another account says that tubankpele refers to *tubani*, a popular dish made of beans wrapped in leaves.

A separate origin tale is attached to the name baamaaya, which translates to English as "the fields are wet." According to some stories passed down by oral tradition, many years ago there was a drought in the region, causing much hunger. The village priests learned through divination that the drought was punishment for a crime a man committed against a woman. To appease the gods, the men were told to wear women's clothing and to dance. They were expected to dance until rain began to fall. So the men dressed up and danced. After some time, clouds appeared in the sky. Eventually, it began to rain. To be certain that the entire region was receiving rain, a boy was sent out to investigate. When he returned, he called out the words *"baa maaya"* ("the fields are wet"). Or so the story tells us, anyway.

Whatever the tale's factual truth, its moral imperative is plain enough: the entire community is responsible for the actions of the individual. A bad deed committed by one, results in suffering for all.

Today, baamaaya is performed for many occasions, but is most closely associated with funerals, which can take months to prepare and days to conduct. At large funerals, it is common to have performances by multiple music and dance ensembles. Baamaaya generally takes place in the pre-dawn hours, beginning sometime after midnight and continuing until dawn.

A baamaaya performance has multiple sections, each associated with specific rhythms and steps. The first section is called baamaaya *sochendi*, or baamaaya "procession." This is the music that the dancers move to as they walk from the place in which they prepared for the performance (the "backstage dressing room," if you will) to the actual performance location. Some musicians say the drum rhythm (a repeated pattern of short–short–short–long) speaks the word *tu-ban-kpe-le*. Others attach the rhythm to the words *naa daa wariba* (Naa Daa dancers [are coming]). Baamaaya sochendi is associated with the section of the story when the men, after having been instructed by the priests, made their way to the dance grounds.

A baamaaya performance's main section is called baamaaya *mangli*, or "principal" baamaaya. This section reenacts the way the men danced to appease the gods and bring the rain. As the dancers move in a circle, their hips swivel back and forth in a shimmy motion, like a high-speed version of the 1960s teen dance craze, "the twist." Baamaaya mangli may continue for a number of hours. Several shorter sections follow, each related to subsequent parts of the story.

The dancers' costumes imitate (or parody) women's dress. To accentuate their hips, dancers wear belts from which hang yarn pom-pom balls. Under the belt is a short skirt. Costumes often include a hat made of monkey skin. Dancers may carry a goat-tail switch or fan. On their ankles they wear metal jingles, which add an additional rhythmic layer to the music. In addition to the dancer's jingles, the instrumental ensemble consists of drums, *sayalsa* (rattle), and *calamboo* (a small wooden flute). Some performances also include praise singers.

Two types of drums are played—the hourglass-shaped variable-pitched *luŋa* and the *guŋgoŋ*, which has a single snare on each drumhead. Dagbamba musicians are renowned for their luŋa drums, which, like the dùndún drums of the Yoruba, speak by imitating the pitch and rhythmic inflections of speech (Chapter 7: Music and Spirituality).

Throughout a baamaaya performance, the luŋa drummer beats out proverbs that comment on community events, recall family histories, and encourage the dancers to "give their all" to the performance. The proverbs are often aimed at social pressure points. Many appeal to notions of individual virtue or the importance of community. Consider the lessons embodied in the following luŋa phrases:

"Nubliyini nubliyini kupi kogli." ("One finger can never pick up a stone.")
"Dakoli kutoiko." ("The bachelor cannot be a good farmer.")

DANGEROUS MOVES

Dancing skill is highly valued in Dagbamba culture. But because dance tends to focus attention on highly skilled individuals, it can also be a source of social tension. It is common practice for baamaaya dancers to protect themselves by wearing protective amulets sewn into their belts or armbands, hung from necklaces, or attached to their goat-tail switches.

 **LISTENING 13.2 GUIDE** **Baamaaya**

Meter: Quadruple and duple

This video is from the village of Kapalibe, in Ghana's Northern Region, and features a May 2002 performance by the Suglo N'mali Dang Ensemble (Patience Maintains Family Ensemble). In this folkloric performance there are no praise singers. Even so, the event is language rich. The following drum language and calamboo flute melodies are performed all within the first two minutes of the performance:

Luŋa phrases:

> *Jarigu ziem bin barigu.*
> *Ka bin barigu gbago.*
> [A foolish person underestimates a trap and becomes caught himself.]

> *Yam ni yam kutoi kpe.*
> *Jarigu mini yam dan be.*
> [Two wise people cannot live together.
> One must be foolish, the other must be wise.]

> *Jerigu ziem peto.*
> *So di bori lala o daa bi nya.*
> [A foolish person refuses pants.
> Another wants them and cannot have them.]

> *Biegu ni n'sa nya chugu.*
> *Kadi sagm ka ŋubi nimdi.*
> [Tommorow is Chugu (a festival day).
> We will eat lots of cornmeal and meat.]

Calamboo phrases:

> *A dinbei. A dinbei ayiŋa.*
> [Your bad deeds will end in your home.]

> *Ay lag paga ko ti lanjaa,*
> *Nimi tuba naa lanjo.*
> [If you fall in love with a woman and she proves fickle,
> You should never go back to her.]

0:00	As the video begins, we do not see the musicians, but hear them approaching. Drummers play the rhythm baamaaya sochendi.
0:17	The first musician to enter the dance circle is the sayalsa player. Behind him come the luŋa player and two guŋgoŋ players.
0:46	We get a first glimpse of the calamboo player.
1:15	Immediately behind the last drummer we see two dancing men. Their presence is tolerated, but they are not part of the planned performance.

1:20	We get our first unobstructed view of the dancers. Some are wearing monkey-skin hats. All are wearing pom-pon belts and white skirts.
1:50	Here is another surprise. A woman is dancing.
2:50	The drummers switch to the baamaaya mangli rhythm. The dancers start "twisting." While the general style of the motion is set, each dancer performs the movements in his or her own fashion. The calamboo player (followed by one of the guŋgoŋ players) squats down and directs his music to encourage one particular dancer.

QUESTIONS FOR THOUGHT

- Baamaaya developed in Dagbamba villages. Today it is performed by folkloric ensembles across Ghana and throughout the world. Imagine ways in which outsiders might experience baamaaya as compared to the Dagbamba themselves. What is lost? What might be gained?

- Some Dagbamba believe that the dance's twist-like motion was brought to Dagbon from the country of Gabon in Central Africa. If this is true, does this fact make the dance less authentic? What might it suggest about traditional dance?

- Read the following drum phrase. How do you interpret it?

    Jankuno makpeme cheng kuliga ka jangbarisi ya tori tora. (Literally: Cat/matrilineal aunt travels to draw water, mice dance tora.)

ACTIVITIES AND ASSIGNMENTS

- Imagine that you can understand the drum language and recognize the song melodies. The musical texture becomes relatively transparent as rhythmic complexity gives way to language and melody supports song. How does this change your listening experience?

Dancing Baamaaya in Ghana, West Africa, 2004.

Photo courtesy of Allison Eckardt.

European Dance

From the West African present, we now travel back in time to the European Renaissance (ca. 1430–1600). The term (from "re-naissance" or "rebirth") refers to a time in European history when artists, writers, and musicians looked back to ancient Greece and Rome for intellectual and artistic inspiration. It was a time of extraordinary development in the arts and sciences, when scholars used their growing understanding of the past as a springboard into the future. Those centuries produced some of Western civilization's greatest thinkers and artists, including Brunelleschi (1377–1446), Leonardo da Vinci (1452–1519), Machiavelli (1469–1527), Copernicus (1473–1543), Michelangelo (1475–1564), Raphael (1483–1520), and William Shakespeare (1564–1616). The technological and scientific advances of the Renaissance—among them the printing press in 1439—changed the course of history.

Renaissance Dance

Well-bred ladies and gentlemen of the 16th century were required to master certain skills. For the woman, sewing and embroidery were essential. Men had more vigorous obligations, such as jousting, falconry, or archery. Both sexes were taught to dance—social standing and the ability to catch a mate depended on it. Witness the following account from a 1589 dance manual:

"The Washerwomen's Branle," page from Thoinot Arbeau's *Orchesography*.

CAPRIOL (the student): I much enjoyed fencing and tennis, and this placed me upon friendly terms with young men. But, without knowledge of dancing, I could not please the damsels, upon whom, it seems to me, the entire reputation of an eligible young man depends.

ARBEAU (the teacher): You are quite right, as naturally the male and female seek one another and nothing does more to stimulate a man to acts of courtesy, honor, and generosity than love. And if you desire to marry you must realize that a mistress is won by the good temper and grace displayed while dancing . . . And there is more to it than this, for dancing is practiced to reveal whether lovers are in good health and sound of limb, after which they are permitted to kiss their mistresses in order that they may touch and savor one another thus to ascertain if they are shapely or emit an unpleasant odor as of bad meat. Therefore, from this standpoint, quite apart from the many other advantages to be derived from dancing, it becomes an essential in a well-ordered society.

(Excerpt from *Orchesography*, Thoinot Arbeau, Dover ed., 1967, pp. 11–12)

The author, Thoinot Arbeau (1519–1595) was a French cleric and dancing master. His *Orchesography* is the best-known and most detailed dance treatise of the Renaissance period. From this work we learn much about the role of dance in the 16th century. Perhaps most important for posterity, Arbeau devised a method for notating dance steps in coordination with the music. Without this system, many period dances would have been lost.

A master of contemporary etiquette, Arbeau also suggested how to behave in polite society. A gentleman must "spit and blow [his] nose sparingly" and if such actions prove unavoidable, he should turn his head away and "use a fair white handkerchief." Good advice still today.

What did Renaissance dance look like? First and foremost, proper posture was essential. The torso was erect, but relaxed; the head held high. As for movement, the emphasis was on fancy footwork. This was especially true for the male, who was unconstrained by the long skirts and heavy undergarments worn by women. Men's movements included skips, leaps, and turns. All these movements were designed to demonstrate virility, to allow the man the opportunity to exhibit his athletic prowess before the fairer sex.

Some dances resembled modern-day circle or line dances. Any number of dancers could participate. One such dance was the *branle* (pronounced "brawl")—a simple dance with peasant origins. Dancers held hands and moved from side to side in a circle or line. Arbeau mentions many kinds of branles, but perhaps the most fun are those he calls "mimed" branles—ones that mimic sounds or actions of animals or people at work or play.

We will look at an old favorite, the "Branle des lavandieres," or "Washerwomen's Branle." The dance was so named because the clapping of the dancers sounded like the noise of women beating clothes as they did laundry along the banks of Paris's Seine River.

Let's examine the piece as presented in Arbeau's treatise. First, notice the musical notation is read top to bottom. Do not be confused—this is not the norm for Renaissance notation, which, like today, was read horizontally left to right. Arbeau uses this format so that the notes line up one-to-one with the dance steps (*piedi*), which are written in the middle column. Typical of dance music notation of the time, Arbeau notates only a melody. Renaissance musicians, like today's jazz musicians, would have improvised accompanying harmonies on the instruments they had available.

"Branle des lavandieres"

LISTENING **13.3**))) GUIDE

Texture: Monophonic and Homophonic
Meter: Quadruple
Form: Strophic (each strophe AABBCC)

0:00	Strophe 1 First you will hear the soprano recorder play the unaccompanied melody as notated in Arbeau. The phrase structure is: AABBCC
0:25	Strophe 2 Next a bass recorder and lute harmonize the melody as the dancers begin the steps. Eventually the entire ensemble joins in.
0:50	Strophe 3
1:15	Strophe 4 The dance is done in a circle with dancers facing in toward the center (in this case, three couples). Men and women alternate places. The basic movements are simple:

Phrase A
    Step to the left, right foot closes.
    Repeat.
    Step to the right, left foot closes.
    Repeat.
Repeat Phrase A
    Phrase B (Now the pattern shortens. Dancers face each other.)
    Step left, right foot closes.
    Step right, left foot closes.
Repeat Phrase B
    Phrase C (notice that the directional symmetry is broken)
    Step left, right foot closes.
    Repeat.
Repeat Phrase C

The more complicated choreography, as listed in Arbeau's far-right column, has the women putting their hands on their hips in phrase B as the men scold them with a menacing finger. On the repetition, the movements are reversed—the women scold. In the last section, Arbeau instructs the dancers to clap their hands. The choreography can change according to the number of repetitions of the various melodic lines. Rather than the basic steps to the left to close the movement, dancers might choose to turn in a circle and hop, as shown here.

QUESTIONS FOR THOUGHT

- Arbeau connects dance with good etiquette and courtship. Are there any vestiges of this today?
- How do the social functions of the four dance traditions described so far (tango, capoeira, baamaaya, and Renaissance dance) differ? How are they the same?

ACTIVITIES AND ASSIGNMENTS

- The steps to the "Branle des lavandieres" are quite simple. Form a circle with your classmates and give the dance a try.

Classical Ballet

Not all of Europe's dance traditions are as easy to perform as the "Branle des lavandieres," of course. Classical ballet, which also has its roots in the Renaissance, is one of the world's most technically difficult styles. @ 13.3

Historians generally cite the year 1661 as the beginning of Europe's formally schooled theatrical dance tradition. That was the year the *Académie Royale de Danse* was founded in Paris. Housed inside what is now the Louvre Museum, the school was sponsored by King Louis XIV (1638–1715) who hoped to "reestablish the dance in its true perfection." The "Sun King" (he earned the moniker as a boy when he danced the role of the Greek god Apollo) was a great lover of music, dance, and theater. In ballet, the three art forms would be combined.

At first, ballet was presented in between movements of plays. Over the next century, ballet would also be incorporated into opera. Sometimes an opera's ballet would forward the storyline, other times it was simply to be enjoyed in its own right. By the mid-18th century, three principal ballet character types had developed:

- the noble, or *sérieux* character (gods and kings)
- the *demi-caractère* (noblemen, fauns and other lesser gods)
- the *comique*, or *grotesque* character (woodsmen, buffoons, and other colorful commoners).

By the mid-19th century, ballet had developed into its own full-blown entertainment genre, the **story ballet.**

Strongly influenced by the era's Romanticist bent, story ballets tell tales of love and deceit, magic and mayhem. Typical of the genre is *Giselle* (1841, music by Adolphe Adam [1803–1856]), a tale thickly wrapped in 19th-century Romantic symbolism. Here, the innocent peasant girl Giselle is wooed by Albrecht, a nobleman whose father is forcing him to marry a noblewoman he does not love. When Giselle discovers Albrecht's deceit, she dies of a broken heart. The distraught Albrecht then wanders off into the forest. As darkness descends, he is attacked by the vampire-like *wilis* (the ghosts of girls who died after their lovers betrayed them). The *wilis* dance as they slowly steal away Albrecht's life essence. Luckily for him, Giselle comes to the rescue. She protects Albrecht until the rising sun dispels the spirits. As the final curtain falls, the lovers separate.

The Rehearsal of the Ballet Onstage, Edgar Degas, ca. 1874.
Courtesy of The Metropolitan Museum of Art, H.O. Havemeyer Collection, Gift of Horace Havemeyer, 1929.

By the mid-19th century, ballet's creative center had moved from Paris to Russia. There, French émigré ballet-master Marius Petipa (1818–1910) would expand ballet's technical and expressive range. Revered for his artistry and feared for his obsessive and controlling personality, Petipa choreographed over fifty different ballets. Petipa's choreography is still remembered and duplicated today. Nineteenth-century Russia also produced the century's greatest ballet composer, Pyotr Tchaikovsky, who wrote *Swan Lake* (1877), *The Sleeping Beauty* (1890), and the perennial holiday favorite *The Nutcracker* (1892).

BASIC BALLET TERMS TO TAKE TO THE THEATER

Arabesque (in Arabic fashion): The dancer places weight on a single leg while the other is extended behind.

Ballerina: A female dancer

Corps de ballet: The full dance ensemble, minus soloists

Danseur: A male dancer

Fouetté: A whipping motion of the leg used to change direction or propel the body in circles.

Grand pas (Grand step): A suite of dances within the story of the ballet. The dances are to display artistry and do not contribute to the storyline.

Pas de deux (Step of two): A duet, usually performed by female and male leads.

Pirouette: A spinning turn on one leg.

Plié: A bending of the knees outward. The back remains straight.

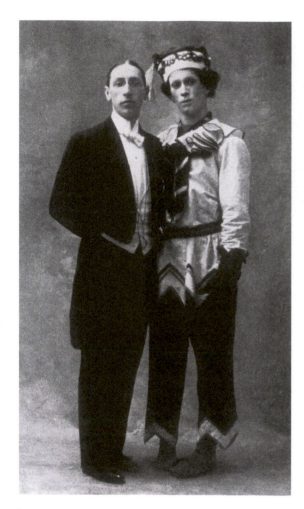

Igor Stravinsky with dancer Vaslav Nijinski as Petrouchka, 1911.

Apic/Hulton Archive/Getty Images.

The Early 20th Century

The Russians would revolutionize 20th-century ballet, but in Paris, not Russia. There, in 1909, impresario Sergey Diaghilev (1872–1929) formed the *Ballet Russes* (Russian Ballet). The company featured two of Russia's greatest dance artists, ballerina Anna Pavlova (1881–1931) and danseur/choreographer Vaslav Nijinsky (1890–1950). Over the next four years, Diaghilev commissioned and premiered ballets by Europe's finest composers, including Maurice Ravel's *Daphnis et Chloé* (1912), Claude Debussy's (1862–1918) *Jeux* (1913), and three ballets by the Russian Igor Stravinsky (1882–1971): *L'Oiseau de feu* (*The Firebird*, 1910), *Petrushka* (1911), and *Le sacre du printemps* (*The Rite of Spring*, 1913).

Historically, the most important of Stravinsky's ballets is *Le sacre du printemps*. *Le sacre*'s story unfolds in pagan Russia at the arrival of spring. In order to assure the season's fecundity, a virgin girl is forced to dance herself to death. The ballet is divided into two parts, "The Adoration of the Earth" and "The Sacrifice." @ 13.4

It is safe to say that the world had never heard sounds like those conceived by Stravinsky for this ballet. Nor had ballet ever employed movements like those choreographed by Nijinsky. Stravinsky's harmonies were intensely dissonant; the rhythms were driving and unrelenting. Nijinsky's feral choreography mirrored the music.

Nijinsky turned ballet upside down. Whereas classical ballet emphasized graceful leaps and vertical lift, Nijinsky's choreography for *Le sacre* kept dancers close to the earth. Whereas classical ballet emphasized the beauty of the human torso, Nijinsky buried his dancers under heavy costumes. His movements often had a brutal quality. There was no place for the Romanticism of earlier times. Nijinsky's poor virgin quivered with fear.

At the premiere, the audience probably did not know what to make of the production. They were opinionated nonetheless. Shouting, even fist fights, broke out between supporters and detractors; items were thrown on stage and into the orchestra pit. A near riot ensued.

LISTENING 13.4 GUIDE

"The Augers of Spring" ("Dances of the Young Girls") from *Le sacre du printemps* (*The Rite of Spring*), by Igor Stravinsky

Texture: Complex homophony
Meter: Changing

Le sacre is scored for an unusually large orchestra—quintuple winds—meaning five of each woodwind instrument, eight horns, five trumpets, three trombones, two tubas, nine timpani plus numerous other percussion instruments, and a larger than normal string section. Stravinsky also has the instruments playing in atypical and sometimes difficult registers. The result is an orchestral timbre that was as shocking as the choreography.

The entire ballet lasts about thirty minutes. We listen to the second scene, where the dancers first appear. They celebrate the advent of spring.

0:00	Strings play a loud, dissonant chord with irregular accents, punctuated by horns.
0:09	English horn and bassoon interrupt with an ostinato.
0:14	Strings and horns enter again, as above, now with piccolos, trumpets, and oboes commenting.
0:29	Bassoon trill introduces trumpet interjections and piccolo twittering.

0:39	Strings and horns repeat the opening figure.
0:48	Bassoons join in with melody fragments. At 0:53 other instruments participate with the bassoon.
1:19	Pizzicato string chord followed by a long tones in the horn. Bass and percussion interrupt.
1:23	A descending trumpet call trills dissolves into bassoon with English horn trill.
1:30	Violins enter with glissando chords. At 1:29 strings play with the wooden part of the bow (*col legno*, with wood) producing a clicking sound.
1:43	The horn, then flute, plays a soaring legato melody. Other instruments comment percussively at 1:45.
2:04	While winds and strings continue playing ostinati, the low-pitched alto flute plays a quiet, lyrical melody in the background, answered by flute.
2:15	The orchestra gets louder as more instruments are added. Timpani plays a broken-chord ostinato. Clarinet adds shrill comments.
2:36	Strings play ostinati with syncopated pizzicato chords. As more instruments join in, the texture gets increasingly dense. Instruments sound melodic fragments above the ostinati. Tension builds to the end.

Despite the opening night chaos, Stravinsky's score would go on to become one of the most influential orchestral compositions of the century. Nijinsky's choreography had a less auspicious fate. The ballet had only eight performances in Paris. Shortly afterwards, composer and choreographer quarreled. After Nijinsky developed a mental illness, the choreography was lost.

In the 1980s, dance scholars recreated the Nijinsky choreography by piecing together scraps of information taken from reviews, dancers' recollections, and instructions written into the rehearsal score. The Joffrey Ballet "premiered" the reconstruction in 1987. Appraising the reconstructed "original," dance historians now see Nijinsky's choreography as an uncompromising endeavor to break free of the strict regimen of movement and expression that had both guided and confined classical dance.

IGOR STRAVINSKY

Stravinsky wrote in nearly every compositional style of the 20th century. His early works reflect Russian nationalism. This was followed by a period of Neoclassicism in which the composer embraced the styles and forms of the 18th century—though with a modern compositional language. In the 1950s, Stravinsky experimented with the 12-tone system formulated by Arnold Schoenberg (Chapter 14: Music in Concert). Stravinsky was born in Russia. He lived in Switzerland and France before immigrating to the United States in 1939.

STRAVINSKY by Picasso

Drawing of Igor Stravinsky by Pablo Picasso (1920s–1930s). Library of Congress Prints and Photographs Division.

American dancer and choreographer, Martha Graham, performs *Lamentation*, 1935.

UCLA Library/Masters/Getty Images.

Modern Dance

The incentive for new, more natural movements was in the air before *Le sacre*. American dancer Isadora Duncan (1877–1927), who had moved to Paris in 1900, had already abandoned ballet's restrictions. Dancing barefoot while dressed in flowing robes reminiscent of ancient Greece, Duncan moved in an improvisatory style that sought new freedoms in movement and new ways to liberate the female body from the restrictive confines of Western social norms. Thus, even as Duncan looked backwards to Greek models she was creating a springboard for the emerging ideas and ideals of artistic modernism. In this sense, Duncan is the founder of the modern dance movement.

Duncan initiated the modern dance movement, but it was American Martha Graham (1894–1991) who most profoundly developed and shaped it. Consider Graham's *Lamentation* (1930, music by Zoltán Kodály [1882–1967]), a sparse and emotionally unsettling work created as America fell deep into the hurt of the Great Depression. @ 13.6 There is little dance movement in the traditional sense. Instead, the performer—who is confined within a tube of stretchy fabric that, like skin, extends from feet to head—seems to struggle for freedom. She grieves, begs, even writhes, but solace is denied. There is no catharsis, no resolution.

Graham choreographed nearly 100 works. Perhaps best known outside dance circles is the vibrant *Appalachian Spring* (1944), set to music by Aaron Copland (1900–1990). Important choreographers who spent formative years in Graham's company include Erick Hawkins (1909–1994) and Merce Cunningham (1919–2009). Graham students included a variety of actors as well as pop star Madonna (b. 1958).

ACTIVITIES AND ASSIGNMENTS

- Investigate the Joffrey Ballet's 1987 reconstruction of *Le sacre du printemps*. How accurate do you think the performance was? On what do you base your judgement?
- Watch other productions online. How do they differ from Joffrey's?

Popular Dance

While American choreographers were exploring the abstractions of modern dance, new popular styles were evolving in the dance halls. Swing dance—known in various times and styles as Lindy Hop, Jitterbug, and other names—drew from African-American dance movements and soon gained popularity across all strata of American society.

With the rise of rock 'n' roll, swing gave way to new dance styles, including the Twist, the Latin-inflected Boogaloo, and a variety of short-lived dances with names like the Swim, Monkey, and Mashed Potato. Important in disseminating the new dances were the popular television shows *American Bandstand* (1952–1989) and *Soul Train* (1971–2006), hosted by Dick Clark (1929–2012) and Don Cornelius (1936–2012) respectively. Virtually every popular music star and ensemble from rockabilly idol Jerry Lee Lewis (b. 1935) to Run-D.M.C. appeared on the shows. Teens danced the latest steps as the celebrities performed.

Jitterbugging in a Negro juke joint, Saturday evening, outside Clarksdale, Mississippi November 1939.
Photo by Marion Post Walcott, Library of Congress Prints and Photographs Division.

QUESTIONS FOR THOUGHT

- How does dance function in our society? How different are the dance experiences of North Americans from those of Ghanaians or South Americans?
- Who dances in our culture? Is dance associated with any gender, sexual orientation, age, or ethnic background? How so?
- Do you enjoy dancing? Why or why not?

Conclusion

We have seen that dance is about much more than physicality. Dance is a vehicle for personal expression and a corporeal repository for social values. Baamaaya, for example, combines dance, music, and theater to give voice to cultural ideas about justice and social balance. Capoeira's mock fight keeps alive memories of those who fought for real in a centuries-long battle against slavery and racial oppression.

Athletic brilliance alone will never satisfy the rich expressive possibilities of dance. The mind and heart must lead. Nijinsky's choreography in *Le sacre de printemps* may have been ground-breaking in terms of movement, but novelty in itself is not enough to make for a compelling performance. It is only when we see terror in the eyes of the innocent girl chosen to die that we in the audience are inescapably drawn in, even become accomplices. Then we also begin to understand the power of society to order our lives, even decide who lives and who dies. Such is the powerful lens of dance.

Key Terms

- abrazo
- baamaaya
- ballet
- Ballet Russes
- bandoneon
- berimbau
- branle
- caminata
- compadrito
- capoeira
- choreographer
- ginga
- giros
- guŋgoŋ
- impresario
- jinga
- jogo
- luŋa
- orquesta típica criolla
- piedi
- roda
- salida
- story ballet
- tango

Essay Questions

- Express different types of music through bodily movement (it need not be conventional "dance"). Describe your experience.
- Is all music "dance" music? If not, which is not. Why?

CHAPTER GOALS

- To examine concert traditions of different genres and cultures.
- To learn about different performing forces and styles of music.
- To examine significant works from three concert traditions.

CHAPTER FOURTEEN

Music in Concert

ACTIVITIES AND ASSIGNMENTS

- Share your concert experiences with others in the class. What are the commonalities? The differences?
- Attend a variety of concerts and observe the customs and behaviors of performers and attendees. How does musical style relate to concert ritual?

In October of 2004, singer Ashlee Simpson (b. 1984) stood ready to perform as the *Saturday Night Live* cameras rolled. The band started and the audience heard Simpson's voice. But her lips hadn't moved. SN was missing the L. Something had gone terribly wrong.

> "What we play is life."
>
> —Louis Armstrong (1901–1971)

The idea had been for the band to play live along with a pre-recorded rhythm track while Simpson sang or lip-synched along with a pre-recorded vocal track. Because the band was live, the audience would never know that Simpson was not. That was the idea, anyhow. The pre-recorded tracks started as planned, but played the wrong song—the same song the band had performed earlier in the show.

It was a convulsive moment, one not unlike the little dog Toto pulling open the curtain to reveal the not-so-great-after-all Wizard of Oz. Simpson did not even pretend to sing. She bounced around for a few moments—she later called it a "hoe-down"—then got off stage. As the band played on, the show's director cut to a commercial.

Live performance is not for the faint of heart. Consider the case of tenor Jerry Hadley (1952–2007), who in 1979 made his New York City Opera debut as a last-minute replacement. Not having had a chance to rehearse on stage, Hadley's first gaffe occurred when he caught his sword in the rungs of a chair. Moments later Hadley got too close to a candle that turned the long plume of his hat into a torch. Every performer hopes to "catch fire," especially in a debut performance, but not like that.

While things do go horribly wrong, they can also go wondrously right, such as when a speaker captures the heart of a crowd or a band finds the perfect groove. When a great performer is "on," witnessing the event can be transformational.

In this chapter, we focus on performance and present music as it might be heard in concert, that is, in musical events where the music itself is the focus and in which the audience sits and listens rather than actively participates. We begin with a mock program by a symphony orchestra. Next we downsize and look at chamber music, that is, programs by soloists or small ensembles. From there we travel to India to study a Hindustani improvisatory musical form called *gat-tora*. Finally we explore a selection from a mock jazz concert, Dizzy Gillespie's (1917–1993) "A Night in Tunisia" (1942).

As you work though this material, keep in mind the concepts you have learned in previous chapters. Issues of identity—whether seen through the lenses of ethnicity, nation, gender or spirituality—are invariably playing in the background. Remember, even events in the concert hall are about more than musical tones. Concerts reflect attitudes about the way people expect society to function. Paying close attention to these actions and attitudes can tell us important things about who we are.

QUESTIONS FOR THOUGHT

- Rock bands rarely play "live" on television. Singers sometimes lip-sync "live" performances, especially when their acts include high-energy dance routines. Does this information make a difference in your appreciation of the artist's performance?
- How does your familiarity with a band's recordings affect your live performance expectations?
- Why bother to see a band live? After all, the recordings will present a more polished sound. And they are error free.
- The band Milli Vanilli achieved infamy when it was revealed that Fab Morvan (b. 1966) and Robert Pilatus (1965–1998) did not actually sing on their recording. Their 1990 Grammy Award for Best New Artist was revoked and the band's popularity went into a tailspin. Were these consequences fair?
- Think back to a concert that you particularly enjoyed. What elements made the event so special? Think about a concert that you did not enjoy. Why did it disappoint?

A Symphony Orchestra Concert

As the lights dim, the well-dressed audience in Los Angeles's Walt Disney Concert Hall becomes quiet. A disembodied voice requests that cell phones be turned off, perhaps also tells patrons how to find the nearest exits in case of emergency. Moments later, the **concertmaster** (the principal violinist), walks on stage to polite applause. He bows to the audience, then turns and looks at the oboist, who sounds the pitch **A440**. The orchestra tunes—first the woodwinds and brass, then the strings. More silence and waiting. @ 14.1

Finally, the conductor enters. She bows to the audience, steps onto the podium, and raises a baton. Motion ceases and time seems to stop. With the wave of an arm the concert begins.

It is a selection from Aaron Copland's ballet *Rodeo* (1942). You probably recognize some of the melodies—perhaps from a movie soundtrack or a television commercial. Maybe you are wondering about the musical context. Why perform a ballet without dancers? What is "cowboy music" doing in an elegant concert hall? @ 14.2

There are no hard-and-fast rules about how an orchestral concert should be put together. There are, however, general models. Pops concerts, for example, usually open with a selection of light classical pieces. After intermission, the stage is turned over to a well-known pop or jazz soloist. "Serious" orchestral concerts also have standardized programming. The most common format features three works: a light introductory piece (often an **overture**), a **concerto**, and a symphony.

The overture serves two main purposes. First, it allows audience members a chance to settle in and warm up their ears for the more complex music to follow. Second, it allows latecomers to be seated relatively early in the concert. (There is a significant difference between classical music concerts and rock, pop, or jazz concerts. In classical music performances, late patrons are only allowed into the hall between pieces, or occasionally between movements, or at intermission.)

The second piece on a formal concert program is usually a concerto, a composition featuring a solo instrumentalist with orchestra. Then comes intermission—a chance for the audience to stretch, renew social and business connections, and, if the soloist was sufficiently inspiring, perhaps even order a subscription for the upcoming season. Following intermission, the orchestra offers the most serious and expansive composition of the evening, generally a symphony.

Our mock concert follows the standard model outlined above. We feature three well-known compositions, each from a different historical period. Aaron Copland's *Rodeo* is from the mid-20th century. Antonio Vivaldi's Concerto in E major is from the Baroque era. Wolfgang Amadeus Mozart's Symphony No. 40 in G minor is from the Classical era. Our concert opener, the high-spirited *Rodeo*, would fit equally well in a pops or classical concert. We will study a single movement from each of our sample compositions.

Frank Gehry's Walt Disney Concert Hall, Los Angeles, California.
Photo by Carol M. Highsmith, Library of Congress Prints and Photographs Division.

THE PROGRAM

Four Episodes from *Rodeo* (1942) .... Aaron Copland (1900–1990)
    Buckaroo Holiday
    Corral Nocturne
    Saturday Night Waltz
    Hoe-Down

Concerto No. 1 in E major (*La Primavera*) (1725) .... Antonio Vivaldi (1678–1741)
    Allegro
    Largo
    Allegro

INTERMISSION

Symphony No. 40 in G minor K. 550 (1788) .... W.A. Mozart (1756–1791)
    Molto allegro
    Andante
    Menuetto
    Allegro assai

Aaron Copland at the piano.

Aaron Copland

Brooklyn, NY-born Aaron Copland composed in many styles during his long career. He is best remembered for the earthy "everyman" style of music that he wrote during the years just prior to, during, and following World War II. As titles of that time period suggest—the ballets *Billy the Kid* (1938), *Rodeo* (1942), and *Appalachian Spring* (1944); the opera *The Tender Land* (1954); and orchestral works *El Salon Mexico* (1936), *An Outdoor Overture* (1938), *Fanfare for the Common Man* (1942), and *Lincoln Portrait* (1942)—these were years in which Copland (like many of his colleagues) celebrated the hopes and freedoms of American life. Copland's work occasionally drew from authentic folk music themes. More often, however, the melodies were original, just folk-like in character.

"Hoe-Down" from *Rodeo*, by Aaron Copland

LISTENING 14.1 GUIDE

Texture: Complex homophony
Meter: Duple
Form: Introduction ABA

Introduction

0:00	Welcome to the hoedown! A percussive cymbal crash and swirling string pattern opens the music. The music portrays a cowgirl/cowboy party, but the sounds make it easy to imagine spinning lariats, bucking broncos, and lots of whirling dust.
0:04	Just moments into the music the trumpets play an angular theme that is echoed in the woodwinds and strings. Notice how impatient those trumpets are—full of youthful energy. They play and the strings echo. Before the echo is even completed, the trumpets jump in again.
0:19	Listen to the clippity-clop of the horses and how the rhythm jumps around. Are you beginning to wonder about these cowboys' riding skills? Or are they just teasing us tenderfoots, like clowns at a rodeo?

Section A

0:40	Another cymbal crash and the strings (embellished with winds and xylophone) play a catchy country fiddle-like melody.
0:48	Dance groove.
0:56	The fiddle theme returns. Then it breaks into smaller fragments and expands throughout the orchestra.
1:20	Fiddles again.
1:35	String flourish, just like the opening measures of the introduction. This return to the opening music serves as both an exit from Section A and an entrance into Section B.

Section B

1:39	A trumpet solo initiates the B section. Notice the colorful sound made by a snare drum. Is that a gun? A whip? Some cowboy strutting his stuff?
1:48	Oboe, followed by clarinet and violin, takes up the trumpet melody. Notice how the instruments share the melody and play off each other's ideas. It sounds like these instrumentalists are great friends, just like the happy-go-lucky cowboys.

1:55	Return to the music that opened the B Section.
2:04	Here begins a syncopated figure in the winds and piano that alternates four times with the strings. After the fourth wind entrance, the strings can no longer be contained. They take off in real hoe-down style.
2:25	A flourish leads to this closing section. The horse clip-clops return, but everyone seems much too tired to care.
Section A	
2:50	Back to the fiddle melody for a couple go-rounds. Then a rousing finale.

ALAN LOMAX (1915–2002)

Ethnomusicologist and folklorist Alan Lomax spent much of his life collecting music from around the world, particularly the American South. Among the many musicians he and his father recorded and helped popularize were blues artists Huddie ("Lead Belly") Ledbetter (1888–1949) and McKinley (Muddy Waters) Morganfield (1913–1983). Lomax's complete recordings add up to some 150 hours of music and interviews. His recordings and videos are available online at http://research.culturalequity.org/home-audio.jsp.

Alan Lomax playing guitar on stage at the Mountain Music Festival, Asheville, North Carolina. @ **14.3**
Alan Lomax Collection at the American Folklife Center, Library of Congress.

Copland's music has been woven into American culture. *Fanfare for the Common Man* was used during television broadcasts of the 1996 Olympics in Atlanta, GA. The soundtrack to Spike Lee's film *He Got Game* (1998) uses Copland's music extensively. A tune from "Hoe-Down" was featured in a series of television advertisements promoting the American Beef Association.

It might seem odd to take music from a ballet and turn it into a commercial, but similar musical transformations happen all the time. In fact, Copland was borrowing as well. He took his "Hoe-Down" melody from the book *Our Singing Country*, which he found in the New York Public Library. Contained within were folksongs collected in the 1930s by the father and son team of John (1867–1948) and Alan (1915–2002) Lomax. The tune, which has its roots in England, was also popular in the Appalachian fiddling repertoire, where it was known by the title "Bonyparte" or "Bonyparte's Retreat."

Choreographer/dancer Agnes de Mille and Frederic Franklin in *Rodeo*, 1942.
Constance Bannister Corp/Hulton Archive/Getty Images.

QUESTIONS FOR THOUGHT

- Listen again to "Hoe-Down" and imagine a story. Create choreography. What might your dance look like?

- Copland wrote this music for dance. Yet, it is very successful heard all by itself. Why?

- Do you think it was appropriate to use "Hoe-Down" in a beef commercial? Why or why not? Can you think of contexts in which musical borrowing would not be appropriate?

Antonio Vivaldi

Venice, Italy is situated in a saltwater lagoon at the edge of the Adriatic Sea. Today, just as 300 years ago when Vivaldi lived there, people travel the city's narrow pavements by foot and its canals by gondola or water taxi.

Besides its waterways, Vivaldi's Venice was known for its four *ospedale*, charitable institutions that cared for orphaned girls and young women. For those who showed talent in music, these institutions provided exceptional training, even professional opportunities. On the faculty was Vivaldi, who wrote nearly half of his more than 500 concertos for the girls in his charge.

You have probably heard his Concerto in E major, titled "La Primavera" ("Spring"). Like Copland's "Hoe-Down," this music has earned a central place in contemporary culture through commercials, film scores, and even as background music in shopping malls. "Spring" is from a collection of four concertos for violin soloist and orchestra called collectively *The Four Seasons* (1725). Each three-movement concerto depicts a different season. Every movement musically depicts a poem apparently written by Vivaldi himself. The poem for the first movement of "Spring" is full of opportunities for musical descriptions of nature—birds, breezes, and thunderstorms.

Venice: The Rialto, workshop of Francesco Guardi, 18th century.
Courtesy of The Metropolitan Museum of Art, The Jack and Belle Linsky Collection, 1982.

CONCERTO

A concerto is a large-scale work, usually in three movements (fast, slow, fast) that features an instrumental soloist (or a small group of instrumentalists) with orchestra. Vivaldi was highly influential in the genre's early development. Generally, a concerto alternates musical passages featuring a soloist with passages featuring the orchestra. Both soloist and orchestra share thematic material but the soloist often has virtuosic sections that stretch the technical capabilities of the instrument. Important later composers of the concerto include Mozart, Beethoven, Brahms, and Tchaikovsky.

First movement (Allegro) from Concerto No. 1 in E major, op. 8, "La Primavera" ("Spring"), by Antonio Vivaldi

LISTENING 14.2 GUIDE

Texture: Complex homophony
Meter: Duple
Form: Ritornello—orchestral refrain (ritornello) alternates with solo passages

0:00	Orchestral introduction. The piece begins with a lively, bouncy violin theme played over a steady pulse in the cellos and basses.
0:10	Orchestra repeats same phrase more softly.
0:18	Violins play a slightly different theme, in the same character as the introduction. This theme will be repeated many times throughout the movement and is called a *ritornello*. Low strings continue pulsing as before.
0:27	Repeat ritornello more softly.
0:35	Now the violin soloist enters, accompanied by the orchestra. Listen to the violin trills, as well as the short descending scales and repeated tones. What do these sounds characterize from the poem?
1:01	The orchestral ritornello is transformed into a new, smoother idea portraying murmuring streams and caressing breezes.
1:42	Orchestral ritornello.
1:50	String tremolo (agitated, fast repeated notes) depicting the impending thunderstorm.
1:57	Virtuoso solo passages and orchestral tremolo alternate.
2:19	Orchestral ritornello.
2:27	Solo with repeated notes answered by orchestral violins.
2:47	Orchestra.
2:59	Solo.
3:15	Orchestral ritornello.
3:21	Orchestra repeats ritornello more softly.

Springtime is upon us.
The birds celebrate her return with festive song,
And murmuring streams are softly caressed by the breezes.
Thunderstorms, those heralds of spring, roar,
Casting their dark mantle over heaven,
Then they die away to silence,
And the birds take up their charming songs once more.

Now it is intermission. It is time to relax and refresh, perhaps to compare with friends your reactions to the concert's first half. So, take a break yourself. When you come back we will tackle the evening's most challenging work, Mozart's Symphony No. 40 in G minor, K. 550 (1788).

SYMPHONY: A PIECE OR AN ENSEMBLE?

In earlier chapters, we learned that the word "symphony" refers to a large performing ensemble, which includes strings, and usually winds, brass, and percussion instruments. But the term also refers to a multi-movement composition performed by that ensemble. The genre developed in the mid-18th century when Haydn, Mozart, and others established its importance in the concert repertory. Beethoven (see Chapter 8: Music and Nation) greatly expanded the form, in both length and complexity.

Symphonic compositions continue to spark the imagination. In 2009, American conductor Michael Tilson Thomas (b. 1944) led the YouTube Symphony Orchestra in the world premiere of Chinese composer Tan Dun's (b. 1957) *The Internet Symphony*. The orchestra was made up of young musicians from around the world, all of whom auditioned by uploading their performances to YouTube. @ 14.4

Wolfgang Amadeus Mozart

Mozart wrote over 600 works including symphonies, operas, concertos, sacred works, string quartets and other chamber pieces. In 1862, Ludwig Ritter von Köchel (1800–1877) published a chronologically arranged catalog of Mozart's compositions. To this day, "K" numbers are used to identify this body of work. @ 14.5

The last three years of Mozart's life were difficult. With Vienna at war, the performing arts suffered. As Mozart's performing opportunities decreased and his income dropped, he was forced to move his family to less expensive lodgings and even borrow money from friends. Despite his troubles, this was a remarkably fertile period for composition. Mozart wrote his last three symphonies (nos. 39, 40, 41) during the summer of 1788.

The Last Moments of Mozart, Armand Mathey-Doret, 1888.

Courtesy of The Metropolitan Museum of Art, Gift of Charles Sedelmeyer, 1888.

The four-movement structure of Symphony No. 40 is typical of the 18th-century symphony:

- Molto allegro. Fast tempo; first movements are usually in sonata form.
- Andante. Slow or moderate tempo; second movements are usually lyrical.
- Menuetto. Quick or moderate tempo; based on the triple-meter dance.
- Allegro assai. Fast tempo; in sonata form.

We will study the fourth movement, which is in sonata form. As we learned in Chapter 5, sonata form has three main sections: exposition, development, and recapitulation. In the exposition, the composer presents two tonal (key) areas, which usually contain contrasting melodic themes. In the development section, the composer deconstructs the exposition materials and explores new tonal areas, which increases musical instability and psychological tension. In the recapitulation, the two sections presented in the exposition return, except now the second key area sounds in the home key. Harmonic resolution is achieved.

Fourth movement from Symphony No. 40 in G minor, by Wolfgang Amadeus Mozart

LISTENING 14.3 GUIDE

Texture: Complex homophony
Meter: Duple
Form: Sonata

Exposition

0:00	Within the first theme of the exposition you will hear four very short motives in different combinations:

	1. A quickly rising melody	(a and a')
	2. A turning melody	(b and b')
	3. A single high "shout" sounded twice, short /long	(c)
	4. An "echoing" phrase an octave lower.	(d)

Each idea lasts just a second or so. We can combine the motives to get Theme 1 (AABB) in the tonic (home) key of G minor.

0:00	A (a and b followed by a' and b')
0:07	A repeats
0:14	B (c and d, repeat of c and d, then a' and b'
0:21	B repeats
0:29	Transition music takes us from Theme 1 to Theme 2. This music is less memorable, and non-repetitive. The section begins with echoes of b', then moves to new material. A big cadence brings the music to a stop. We have arrived at our destination: Theme 2.
1:03	Theme 2. Notice the contrast from Theme 1. Notes are longer; emotional affect is more inward. The theme is played twice, first by the violins (1:03), then by wind instruments (1:18).
1:31	Sudden exuberance signals the end of Theme 2 and the beginning of the exposition's closing section.

Development

1:57	Here Mozart breaks apart his musical ideas and "develops" them. The music is fragmented and harmonically unstable. The entire orchestra seems to be calling out the "a" motive from Theme 1. Try to notice and count all its occurrences.

Recapitulation

3:08	The music is like the beginning, although abbreviated. First (at 3:08) and second themes (at 3:45) are played again.

VOCALESE

Vocalese is the act of setting lyrics to pre-existing instrumental solos. Although the practice was probably first developed by jazz singer Eddie Jefferson (1918–79), the name was likely coined by jazz critic Leonard Feather (1914–94). Vocalist Jon Hendricks was the most prolific vocalese lyricist. The Grammy Award-winning trio Lambert, Hendricks & Ross recorded classic vocalese albums drawn from recordings of the Duke Ellington and Count Basie big bands. In Hendricks's lyrics to Ellington's "Cottontail," a hipster Peter Rabbit risks ending up as rabbit stew just to get his carrot "fix" from the farmer's garden. Hendricks's lyrics to "Birdland" (1977) as recorded by the jazz/rock super-group Weather Report, helped the vocal group Manhattan Transfer win a Grammy Award (1980).

Generations of students have applied vocalese techniques to the first theme of the last movement of Mozart 40. Try singing along with these goofy, but almost operatic, words:

Oh Mozart's in the closet. [a]
Let him out. Let him out. Let him out. [b]
They locked him in the closet. [a']
Let him out. Let him out. Let him out. [b']

[repeat]

"Help! Help! [c] It's dark in here." [d] [2X]
They locked him in the closet. [a']
Let him out. Let him out. Let him out. [b']

[repeat]

Dave Lambert, Annie Ross, and John Hendricks.
Bill Wagg/Redferns/Getty Images.

Chamber Music

Far more intimate than orchestral concerts are recitals, which feature soloists or small chamber ensembles. During the 18th and 19th centuries, much of this music was written for the pleasure of amateur musicians who performed for one another and friends in the parlors of private homes. Today, because relatively few people are skilled performers, recitals are usually given by professionals in public venues.

The most popular chamber music combinations were (and still are) the string quartet (two violins, viola, and cello) and the piano trio (violin, cello, and piano). Solo piano recitals were enormously popular as well, especially during the 19th century when many middle-class families owned a piano.

There is a large body of chamber music literature, far more than for orchestra. We will look at compositions by Franz Joseph Haydn (1732–1809), Niccolò Paganini (1782–1840), and Arnold Schoenberg (1874–1951). Historians consider Haydn to be the "father" of both the string quartet and the symphony. Even though he did not invent either genre, he brought them to a high level of artistry and established their long-term importance. Paganini is remembered as one of the most charismatic and accomplished virtuosos in the 19th-century Western art music tradition. Even today, performing Paganini's fiendishly difficult music represents a rite of passage for every serious classical violinist. Schoenberg's **expressionist** *Pierrot lunaire* (1912) perhaps sounds as hallucinatory today as it did at its premiere.

Franz Joseph Haydn, String Quartet in E flat major, op. 33, no. 2, "The Joke" (1781)

Haydn had a keen wit. Often, his humor shone in his music. A prime example is the last movement of "The Joke" quartet. Of course, in order to "get" a joke, one has to understand its context. Humor

FRANZ JOSEPH HAYDN (1732–1809)

Haydn's parents recognized their child's musical talents early. Because they could not afford to give him proper training, they sent the 6-year-old boy to live with a musical relative. When Haydn was eight he became a choirboy at St. Stephen's Cathedral in Vienna, where he received extensive musical training.

Haydn spent most of his adult life working for the Esterházy family, fabulously wealthy Hungarian royalty. As their employee, Haydn was required to wear a servant's uniform and follow the family to various estates. One of these was Esterhaza, a magnificent, if mosquito-infested, palace in rural Hungary. There Haydn was in charge of running the orchestra, playing chamber music for important guests, producing operas, and composing music. Although Haydn often felt isolated, separation from his peers seems to have inspired him to creative heights.

In the last years of his life, Haydn became a free agent. He journeyed to London where his music was wildly popular. There it was performed in some of Europe's earliest public concerts.

Inside view of St. Stephen's Cathedral, Franz Alt, 1849.

functions by setting up expectations, and then breaking them. Getting the humor in "The Joke" quartet requires that we understand the expectations of **rondo** form.

A classic rondo presents initial thematic material (A), which is followed by an "episode" of new material (B). The music then returns to original A refrain before setting off in another episode (C). This process of alternating new and old continues throughout. Thus, a rondo form with three episodes would be: ABACADA.

Fourth movement (Presto) from String Quartet in E flat major, op. 33, no. 2, "The Joke," by Franz Joseph Haydn

LISTENING 14.4 GUIDE

Texture: Complex homophony
Meter: Duple
Form: Rondo

0:00   **A (refrain)**
        The A section has two ideas; "a" and "b" arranged as follows:
        a (0:00)
        a (0:08)
        b (0:14)
        a (0:32)

continued

	b (0:39)	
	a (0:56)	
1:03	**B (episode)**	
	This section modulates away from the home key	
1:33	**A (refrain)**	
	The refrain is back in the home key of E flat. Notice that the "a" and "b" ideas do not repeat.	
	a (1:33)	
	b (1:40)	
	a (1:59)	
2:05	**C (episode)**	
	This episode stays in the home key. Another joke—Haydn's audience would have expected it to change keys.	
2:38	**A (refrain)**	
	Very short refrain—uses only one iteration of "a."	
2:47	**Coda**	
	The coda begins with a slow tempo—an adagio. Haydn then teases his audience by playing the "a" phrase again but interrupting it. Each interruption gets longer until the audience wonders when the piece will actually end. When he finally ends the phrase we are relieved. But stay tuned. The best joke is yet to come.	

Paganini, lithograph by Hetty Krist.
Hetty Krist/Wikimedia Commons/CC-BY-SA-3.0.

The rondo in this quartet has two episodes, so Haydn's audience would have expected the basic form to be ABACA, which it is, sort of. Once the audience knew what A sounded like, they would have felt confident in predicting how the movement would end. That's where Haydn decided to have a little fun. After the first phrase of the final A section, he inserts a coda, a closing section. The coda begins as an adagio. Soon, we hear a bit of the A material. Then a pause. Then a little more of A. Another pause. Still more of A. Pause. Finally, the end of A. And so the movement ends. Or so one would assume . . .

Niccolò Paganini, Caprice in A minor, op. 1, no. 24 (ca. 1805)

Public concerts for a middle-class audience had only recently become the norm when violinist, guitarist, and composer Niccolò Paganini came of age. Music's first "box office superstar," Paganini concertized throughout Europe. In one year alone, he gave 151 concerts and traveled over 5000 miles by carriage.

Tall, gaunt, and pale, with unruly shoulder-length black hair, the violinist gave a wraith-like appearance on stage. He also dazzled. Women wept when he played. Critics, perhaps jealous of the great performer's charisma, remarked on the demonic quality of his appearance, but acknowledged his unprecedented technical facility.

Paganini's offstage life added to his mystique. He earned a fortune performing, but lost much of it gambling. A notorious womanizer of "hot Genovese blood" (a self-portrayal), intrigues followed his every move. Unfounded rumors dogged his reputation,

Caprice in A minor, op. 1, no. 24, by Niccolò Paganini

LISTENING 14.5 GUIDE

Texture: Varied
Meter: Varied
Form: Theme plus eleven variations and finale

The *24 Caprices for Solo Violin*—short, fanciful, and virtuosic—were perfect vehicles for Paganini. Though originally intended for his own performances, today they are standard recital pieces. Caprice 24 begins with a theme based on a snappy and angular rhythmic motive: long—short-short-short-short-short-short.

Eleven variations follow, each demonstrates a different technical feat. The work ends with a bravura finale.

0:00	Theme:	0:00	A
		0:03	A
		0:07	B

Notice the contrast between conjunct motion and the octave leaps. As you listen to the variations, try to keep this theme in mind. Although the melodies change, the harmonic and formal structures remain the same.

| 0:15 | Variation 1 |
| | Beats are divided into groups of three with grace-note flourishes. The range expands up an octave |

| 0:30 | Variation 2 |
| | The melodic material returns to the original range; the rhythmic density increases. An outline of the original melody can be heard behind undulating chromatic passages. |

| 0:48 | Variation 3 |
| | A plaintive variation using octave "double stops" (playing on two strings at once). Notice that some of the melodic material is inverted and **retrograde**. The rhythm is reduced to half speed. |

| 1:20 | Variation 4 |
| | This is played one to two octaves above the original theme. Much of this variation consists of descending chromatic scales. |

| 1:37 | Variation 5 |
| | Notice the disjunct motion and wide range of this variation as the violinist breaks the theme into octaves. The underlying harmonies are emphasized in the accented low notes. |

| 1:58 | Variation 6 |
| | Again we hear double stops, this time with scales at the interval of a third in the A phrases and in tenths in the B phrase. |

| 2:24 | Variation 7 |
| | The rhythm returns to triplets similar to those of Variation 1. |

| 2:45 | Variation 8 |
| | Chords are played by drawing the bow over three of the strings. |

| 3:06 | Variation 9 |
| | The technique used here is called "left-hand pizzicato"; instead of plucking with the right hand, as usual, the violinist must keep the bow in the right hand in order to play alternating bowed and plucked notes, executed by the left hand. This was a technique that Paganini made famous. |

| 3:25 | Variation 10 |
| | Played in the very top of the violin's range, this variation's delicacy and soft dynamics contrast with the more exuberant sections that surround it. |

| 3:54 | Variation 11 |
| | This variation uses double stops, sudden leaps from low to high, and melodically ascending flourishes. |

| 4:18 | Finale |
| | Extends the last variation for a flashy finish. |

but added to his box-office appeal. It was said that a "crime of jealousy" had sent him to jail for fifteen years (during which time, conveniently enough, he learned to play the violin so well).

With long fingers and remarkable flexibility, Paganini's violin playing astounded audiences. To show off, he played entire works on only one string, fingers crawling up and down the violin's neck with spider-like dexterity. Paganini rarely published his compositions, thus ensuring he would be their only performer. That worry was mostly unfounded. He was probably one of few violinists at the time who *could* perform them.

Arnold Schoenberg, *Pierrot lunaire* (*Moonstruck Pierrot*, 1912)

Composers often create expectations, only to defy them. Haydn did so by humorously breaking up a rondo structure, one of music's most predictable forms. Paganini defied expectations in a theme and variations format by amazing his audience with jaw-dropping virtuosity, like a juggling unicyclist continually adding balls to an already seemingly impossible routine.

Just over a century later in Vienna, Austria, Arnold Schoenberg would defy preconceptions about the nature of music itself. Schoenberg's tones explored uncharted psychological experience, especially the symbolic cacophony of the unconscious mind as had recently been outlined by Austrian psychologist Sigmund Freud (1856–1939). Schoenberg's *Pierrot lunaire* set to music a song cycle of twenty-one poems by Belgian **symbolist** poet Albert Giraud (1860–1929). Schoenberg composed for a female vocalist and an ensemble of five musicians playing eight different instruments.

ARNOLD SCHOENBERG (1874–1951)

Schoenberg is one of the most influential composers of the 20th century. His work is associated with **Expressionism**, an artistic movement that focused on portraying the dark turbulence of the human psyche. Schoenberg was the leader of the Second Viennese School of composition, which included Anton Webern (1883–1945) and Alban Berg (1885–1935). Mostly self-taught, early in his career Schoenberg wrote in the Romantic style of the late 19th century. His music became increasingly chromatic and dissonant as the 20th century unfolded. Schoenberg was central to the development of modern music, particularly in the area of atonality, that is, music that lacks a tonal foundation, or key center.

The remarkable *Pierrot lunaire* remains the canonic example of atonal Expressionism. After World War I, Schoenberg and his students developed the **12-tone system**, a formula that, in principle at least, requires the composer to use all twelve pitches of the Western octave before repeating any. The 12-tone method became the bedrock for many of the most innovative and experimental Western art music compositions of the first three-quarters of the 20th century.

Like his music, Schoenberg's life was one of transition and instability. Though raised Jewish, he converted to Lutheranism in 1898. In 1933 Schoenberg was forced to flee Nazi Germany. He went first to Paris (where he returned to the Jewish faith), then to the United States, eventually moving to Los Angeles where he taught at the University of Southern California and UCLA.

The Scream, lithograph by Expressionist artist, Edvard Munch, 1895.
Courtesy of The Metropolitan Museum of Art, Bequest of Scofield Thayer, 1982.

The poems' chimerical imagery is presented in **sprechstimme** (spoken singing), a weird-sounding vocal technique that resides somewhere between speech and song. The "neither this nor that" quality of the voice is matched by the music's dissonant pitch relationships and the absence of tonality (no "home" key, or tonic). Even today, for a listener not familiar with early 20th-century sounds and topics, *Pierrot* may sound like a trip to the looney (i.e. lunar or *lunaire*) bin. Perhaps accentuating the music's alien quality is its ephemeral quality; none of the twenty-one settings lasts much more than two minutes.

In adopting a 14th-century verse form called *rondel* (ABba abAB abbaA), Giraud mixed an old poetic structure with modern eccentricities. Each of Giraud's poems has three **stanzas** (two **quatrains** and a **quintrain**). Each poem's first two lines (AB) serve as a refrain. Both lines return at the end of the second stanza; the poem's first line closes the quintrain. Giraud's French lines rhyme accordingly: ABba abAB abbaA. (Neither Schoenberg's German setting nor our English translation found below follows the French rhyme scheme. Both follow the refrain organization, however.)

Pierrot Laughing, Adrian Tournachon, 1855.
Courtesy of The Metropolitan Museum of Art, Purchase, The Horace W. Goldsmith Foundation Gift, through Joyce and Robert Menschel, 1998.

First song from *Pierrot lunaire*, op. 21,"Mondestrunken," by Arnold Schoenberg

LISTENING **14.6** GUIDE

Texture: Polyphonic
Meter: Duple
Instrumentation: Flute, viola, cello, piano, voice

| | Den Wein, den man mit Augen trinkt, (lines 1, 7, 13) | The wine that one drinks with the eyes |
| | Gießt Nachts der Mond in Wogen nieder, (lines 2 and 8) | The moon spills nights into the waves, |

0:00	Piano begins with a quirky ostinato played four times. (You will hear this pattern, or variations on it, throughout the movement.) Voice, then flute, enter with counter melodies.
0:14	Notice the word painting. First, the leap to *eine Springflut* (a spring flood) and the lack of movement at *stillen Horizont* (silent horizon).
0:23	Instrumental interlude. Flute takes up piano's opening ostinato.
0:41	Voice re-enters. Schoenberg emphasizes the words' characteristics. The singer seems almost to "taste" desire *schauerlich und süß* (visible and sweet). The early refrain (A) moves quickly past, almost like an afterthought, though Schoenberg holds onto the word *Wogen* (waves) in part B.
0:59	Brief instrumental interlude.
1:03	A jump in energy as the voice returns and tells us of the rapturous experience of devotion. Pierrot is drunk on moonlight. He is looney: enraptured, ecstatic, and reeling. Is this devotion or insanity?
1:31	Closing. Piano plays the ostinato one last time.

QUESTIONS FOR THOUGHT

- How did Mozart use musical form to create audience expectations? What happens to the musical experience if the audience does not understand the musical language?

- If told well, a good joke can be funnier on second or third hearing. How might musicians "retell" Haydn's joke to an audience already in the know?

- Some people say that attending a Western art music concert is a passive experience. Do you agree? Why or why not?

- Imagine your favorite musician performing in the living room of your home and without the assistance of amplification. How would your experience of this "chamber" concert differ from an amplified event in an outdoor stadium? Which would you rather attend? Why?

ACTIVITIES AND ASSIGNMENTS

- Compare the forms of the compositions outlined above. Can you find similar structures in art, literature, or architecture?

- Write a poem that parallels rondo or sonata form.

- Listen to the first movement of Mozart's Symphony No. 40 in G minor. Can you identify the form and its different sections? Add words?

- Does your town or school have a symphony orchestra? Investigate its history or document its repertory. How does this compare to other American orchestras? See the League of American Orchestras for comparative data (www.americanorchestras.org/).

A Hindustani Recital

The gentle smell of incense wafts through the San Francisco concert hall as audience members find their seats. Some are dressed in colorful traditional clothing of the Indian subcontinent; others are dressed casually, in jeans. There are no chairs on stage. Instead, there is a large oriental rug upon which the musicians will sit. Floor-level microphones are in place to amplify the instruments. @ 14.6

There are also no programs to be distributed. The audience knows who will play but not what music they will hear. It is quite possible that the musicians do not know either. That decision might not be made until the artists are seated onstage, with instruments tuned and ready to go.

Our concert continues the performance we began in Chapter 2: Listening to Music, with sitarist Ravi Shankar and sarod player Ali Akbar Khan. Shankar was widely introduced to the West in the late 1960s through his association with the rock group The Beatles. Long before that, however, Indian audiences knew him as one of the master musicians of Hindustani music. Five-time Grammy Award-nominee Ali Akbar Khan was based in Northern California for the last forty years of his life. In 1967, he founded the Ali Akbar College of Music in Berkeley, CA. Khan and Shankar were lifelong musical collaborators and friends.

In contrast to the very formal behavior expected at Western art music concerts, audiences at a North Indian concert may come and go while the musicians perform. Many listeners will keep count of the **tala** (rhythmic meter) with their fingers. They might even exclaim out loud at exciting points in the music. A concert may last two to three hours without intermission.

The musical texture of a Hindustani performance can be divided into three basic elements: drone, melody/tonal palette (raga), and rhythm/meter (tala). Traditionally, the tambura sounds a drone on the pitches sa and pa (do and sol in a Western scale). This provides a stable pitch center for the soloists. Sometimes a small hand-pumped (or electric) organ (*śruti* **box**) replaces the tambura. In our performance, melody is shared between two Indian lutes: the sitar and sarod (supported by tambura drone). The sitar's timbre is bright and shimmering; the sarod's timbre is relatively dark and austere.

After the non-metrical alap section is completed, during which the musicians introduce the pitches and emotional color of the raga (Chapter 2: Listening to Music), a percussionist enters playing two small hand drums called *tabla* (*dahina* and *bayan* respectively). The higher sounding dahina is tuned to a specific pitch, usually the raga's sa, or home tone. The tabla player is responsible for marking tala.

Chatuttal Manj-Khamaj raga, performed by Ravi Shankar (sitar) and Ali Akbar Khan (sarod)

LISTENING **14.7** GUIDE

Texture: Biphonic and heterophonic
Meter: nonmetric in alap; a 16-beat cycle in gat-tora

0:00–3:37	Alap (for listening guide, see Chapter 2: Listening to Music)
3:37	**Gat-tora** (theme and improvisation)
	As the alap comes to an end, listen for the *mukhra*, a short phrase that begins the gat (main melody) and leads to *sam* (beat 1) at 3:37. Although there is no meter at its first appearance, the mukhra begins on (hypothetical) beat 12 and resolves on sam. (To help you identify this, the mukhra's tones are
	A♯ B A♯ . . . F♯ F♯ E♯(D♯)E♯ E♯ G♯ (F♯.)
	So begins the section featuring a recurring melody (gat) that alternates with sections of improvisation (tora). (You might think of this as a type of rondo, Hindustani style.)
	This performance uses a 16-beat tala (metric cycle). After you learn to recognize the gat, it will be easy to find *sam* (beat one) throughout the performance. The 16-beat cycle takes about fourteen seconds to complete (the next three sams fall at 3:51, 4:04, and 4:19).
	Try following the tala. You can do this by marking the beats with your thumb touching forefinger tip (sam), outside joint (beat 2), middle joint (beat 3) inner joint (beat 4). Repeat the process on the middle finger (beats 5–8), ring finger (beats 8–12), and pinky (beats 13–16).
5:11	A strong cadence is felt. Melodic conversations continue to unfold between sitar and sarod.
6:02	After a number of cycles, another mukhra cadence on sam at 6:02. Notice the musicians have returned to the gat melody. Have you also noticed that the tempo is gradually increasing?
6:15	Mukhra to sam at 6:15. Improvisations follow over multiple 16-beat cycles.
7:32	Increasing rhythmic density and virtuosic display. Sitar glissandos followed by a **tehai** (a phrase played three times) that signals the return to gat.
7:45	Gat. Tempo increases again.
7:57	Mukhra to sam at 7:57.
8:55	Tehai to sam.
9:58	Tehai to sam. Ever-increasing tempo.
13:32	A tehai to sam brings the performance to a close

QUESTIONS FOR THOUGHT

- We introduced our orchestra concert with the music to be performed. We introduced our Hindustani concert not with the repertoire, but with the artists who were performing. Why the different approach? What does that tell you about what is valued in each tradition?

- How do the concepts of rhythm and melody differ between Western art music and Hindustani music? What concepts do they share?

- What do the concert traditions of Western Europe and North India have in common? What are the differences?

ACTIVITIES AND ASSIGNMENTS

- Investigate how North Indian musicians are trained. How does it differ from music students in the West?

- Listen to the fusion group Shakti, featuring British jazz guitarist John McLaughlin, Hindustani tabla virtuoso Zakir Hussain, Karnatic violinist L. Shankar, and others. Each musician represents a different heritage, yet their music seems to fit well together. Why is this so?

Jazz

From its roots in turn-of-the-20th-century New Orleans, the story of jazz has been one of synthesis, innovation, and adaptation. Jazz began when musicians from this culturally diverse city found ways to combine African and European traditions. Rhythms were freed up; scales were given new shapes and colors. As jazz spread, first up the Mississippi River, then east and west, and eventually across the oceans, new influences were assimilated. Jazz found worldwide appeal. @ 14.7

But what exactly is jazz? First of all, it is music that is improvised. Musicians are expected to create and develop new ideas in the moment, with the same ease as two people having a spontaneous conversation. Second, jazz swings. The rhythmic groove is expected to flow and feel loose. Third, jazz performance is passed down from one musician to the next by oral tradition. Still today, and even in college settings, musicians primarily learn through a three-step process of listening, assimilating and imitating (re-creating), and ultimately coming up with original ideas.

Additional characteristics define jazz. Some argue that it is fundamentally an African-American genre. As evidence, they cite the music's African and Creole roots in New Orleans dance and the fact that the majority of jazz's greatest exponents and innovators have been black. Others argue that jazz is a state of mind. They say jazz is a way of thinking about and making music. In support of this idea they might point to the emphasis on musical individuality and creativity, or the emphasis on learning by ear rather than by musical notation. Or they might argue that jazz reflects a certain urban life style, an attitude of social resistance to the status quo, and even resistance to authority in general.

Still others will say that jazz is about life, that it is a visceral in-the-moment response to the world in which we live. For them, performance is about the evolving and ever-deepening relationship between musician and music, among musical colleagues, and between musicians and their audiences. Communication is everything.

Early on, there was a strong connection between jazz and dance. The big bands of Fletcher Henderson (1897–1952), Duke Ellington, Count Basie (1904–1984), and many others powered the swing dance crazes of the 1920s through 1940s. With the advent of the rhythmically complex bebop style and the rise of rock 'n' roll, jazz moved away from dance and toward an aesthetic based on listening.

Filling concert halls was the next step. This first happened in 1938, when clarinetist Benny Goodman (1909–1986) and his racially integrated band sold out America's most famous elite venue, New York City's Carnegie Hall. Today, jazz festivals in Newport, Rhode Island, Monterey, California, New Orleans, and Detroit provide the genre some of its broadest visibility.

Dividing the jazz century more or less in half, we will study the 1946 recording of the jazz standard "A Night in Tunisia," composed in 1941 or 1942 by trumpeter Dizzy Gillespie (1917–1993). This recording features trumpeter Miles Davis (1926–1991) and alto saxophonist Charlie Parker (1920–1955). The piece is a modified version of AABA 32-bar song form (Chapter 3: Three Listening Examples).

MINTON'S PLAYHOUSE

Henry Minton's jazz club in Harlem, NYC, was a primary destination for late-night jazz in the 1940s. It was Minton's Playhouse where jazz's most innovative artists came to play, challenge each other, and share ideas. It was in these heated sessions that modern jazz was forged. According to trumpeter Miles Davis, just 18 years old when he arrived in New York to go to school in 1944, "you brought your horn and hoped that Bird [Charlie Parker] and Dizzy would invite you to play with them up on stage. And when this happened you'd better not blow it." Davis didn't.

Portrait of Thelonious Monk, Howard McGhee, Roy Eldridge, and Teddy Hill, Minton's Playhouse, New York City, ca. September, 1947.

Photo by William P. Gottlieb/Library of Congress Prints and Photographs Division.

"A Night in Tunisia," by Dizzy Gillespie

LISTENING
14.8
GUIDE

A 1946 recording featuring Charlie Parker (alto sax), Miles Davis (trumpet), Lucky Thompson (tenor sax), and Arvin Garrison (guitar).
Texture: Complex homophony
Meter: Quadruple
Form: AABA 32-bar song form with introduction and interlude

0:00   **Introduction, 12 bars**
A two-bar-long riff played by piano and guitar sounds twice before bass and drums join in (0:05) for four more bars. Notice the rhythmic vitality as the riff surges forward, then relaxes. Saxophone joins in with a counter riff (0:11). The pitch centers of these lines move in opposite directions.

continued

0:16	**A section, 8 bars**
	As the introduction's riffs seethe underneath, Miles Davis plays an angular rising and falling melody with muted trumpet. In stark contrast to the riffing behind him, Davis's centered playing exhibits "eye-of-the-storm" tranquility. Curiously, this contrast seems to increase the overall energy to pressure-cooker level. We get a moment of relaxation at bars 7–8 when the riff patterns break.
0:28	**A section repeats, 8 bars**
0:39	**B section, 8 bars**
	Rhythmic tension relaxes as the band shifts into a loose swing groove. Melody, now played by Charlie Parker on saxophone, is rounder as well. Also notice that while the A section melody moved quickly upward, the B section melody moves gracefully downward.
0:50	**A section, 8 bars**
	Riff returns; so does the trumpet.
1:01	**16-bar interlude**
	For the first twelve bars of the interlude saxophones present a single repeated rhythmic figure. Then the band drops out and saxophonist Charlie Parker fills in the space. Wow. The pressure cooker just exploded.
1:23	**A/A sections, 16 bars**
	Parker continues to improvise. Keep track of the form, either by counting bars or singing the song's composed melody.
1:45	**B/A sections**
	Davis takes over the improvisation. Davis implies the original A section melody (1:56).
2:07	**A/A sections, 16 bars**
	Tenor saxophonist Lucky Thompson plays sixteen hard-swinging bars. Notice the darker texture of the tenor saxophone.
2:28	**B section**
	Guitarist Arvin Garrison takes over.
2:39	**A section**
	Davis returns to the song's composed melody. Original texture returns.
2:50	**Coda**
	The piece ends as it began.

QUESTIONS FOR THOUGHT

- Extended improvisatory solos are the norm in jazz clubs, but this recording lasts just over three minutes. Why so short? (Think about 1940s recording technology.)
- "A Night in Tunisia" has been *sampled* for recordings by Gang Starr ("Manifest," 1989) and other rap musicians. Does knowledge of the music's 1940s source change how you experience this song? ("Manifest" also samples James Brown, Wilson Pickett, and others.)

ACTIVITIES AND ASSIGNMENTS

- Research two or three of the many jazz types and compare their histories and musical styles.
- "A Night in Tunisia" has been recorded many times. Compare and contrast different versions.

Coda

In this chapter we looked at typical concert pieces from three different traditions: Western art music, Hindustani art music, and jazz. We have seen variations in musical styles, performance space, and expectations of behavior. These variables only increase when you consider the many other concert traditions around the world.

What makes a concert? It is far more than the music. A concert is a social phenomenon that brings people together to experience and express shared values. Attending a musical event helps people feel like they are part of a group. It reaffirms their social history and legitimizes interests and beliefs. The kinds of concerts one enjoys can be just as clear a marker of identity as political, religious, ethnic, and gender identifications. In fact, all of these things contribute to, and reflect, the types of music we enjoy. Just as our identities evolve and grow in accord with ever-broadening life experiences, so too do our musical tastes.

Three Performances

Consider the following scenarios:

1. On stage in Seattle a group of Mbuti pygmy hunters from Central Africa moves stealthily through the haze of dry-ice fog and the brownish hues of carefully designed stage lighting. They enact the successful hunt of imaginary game, then celebrate with song and dance. At intermission, the audience strolls past sale tables of CDs and African art.
2. In Darmstadt, Germany a large metal box sits alone on stage. The audience waits. This being the city's international biennial new music festival, it is anyone's guess as to what will happen next. The performance begins with taps and clanks coming from inside the box. Eventually— with the help of sledge hammers, metal sheers, and a blow torch—the performers bang, slice, and melt their way out. One of them, a saxophonist, blows for a couple minutes. Then the piece is over.
3. In Pengosekan, a village on the Indonesian island of Bali, American university students file nervously into a courtyard. They sit down among the bronze gamelan instruments and adjust their traditional batik-cloth wraps. Just a few weeks ago, some them had never heard a gamelan orchestra. Today they will perform for the Balinese community.

What to make of these performances? The first example, which might be termed folkloric, invites the audience to imagine a strange and primal world in which the lives of man and nature are interwoven, perhaps as they were at the dawn of humankind. The Darmstadt example also apparently focuses on humankind's relationship to the world. Perhaps the message is about freeing oneself from the unfeeling metal of modern industrial life. Or perhaps the piece is a call to "tune in" to the sounds of our modern environment. The Bali example suggests broadened horizons, a journey of social expansion, musical initiation and inclusion.

Any performance can be read in an endless variety of ways. The interpretations above focus on broad cultural ideas. In what other ways might we look at these performances? What might a focus on the performers and audience reveal? What might we learn by focusing on just the sound of the music?

Would you like to know what was going through the Mbutis' minds as they "hunted" on that Seattle stage? When the performance was over, did they head backstage for a real meal? Perhaps Chinese takeout? And what about the audience? Did they feel closer to the Mbuti or more alienated than ever? What was the difference between this performance and "human zoos" of the 19th and early 20th centuries (Chapter 5, Music and Ethnicity)?

The college students performing in Bali (a mixed ensemble of women and men) might have felt as if they too were exhibits in a human zoo. Here, however, the centuries-old imbalance of power between cultures West and East was inverted. This time it was the "exotic" West on display as the East watched on.

As for the Darmstadt performance, what was it like inside of the box? Hot? Smoky? Were the musicians worried about fire from the blowtorch? Were they banging and cutting in a consciously "musical" way or just trying to get the heck out? We know something about the audience's response—they hooted and whistled (a derisive act in Europe), and even threw coins at the stage.

How else might we analyze these three performances? Do you see gendered scripts being played out? What about scripts demonstrating ethnicity or nation, politics or spirituality? What about love or war? What was the relationship between Mbuti music and dance? Was the Darmstadt banging and cutting a kind of musical theater? What are the rules of performance when jungle meets stage, blow torch frees saxophonist, or when West travels East?

We have not talked about the musical sound in any of these performances. But those too are based on culture-bound codes of understanding. Certainly the Mbuti understood the music they were singing. They knew how the sounds should fit and when to start and stop. Presumably, few in the audience possessed this knowledge. In contrast, the Balinese audience knew better than the students what the music should sound like, though enjoying the performance's cultural novelty almost certainly outweighed the performers' technical shortcomings.

Harder to figure out is the Darmstadt concert. Clearly the audience did not think highly of the piece, but whose fault was that? The composer's? The performers'? To what was the audience reacting? To the sounds alone—perhaps as combinations of tones that failed to be meaningful? Or were listeners reacting to the absurdity of the performance itself? (And finally, in their noisy reaction was the audience "performing" as well?)

What makes music (or any art form) "good?" How do we judge excellence? Why do we like the music we like? It is never as simple as appreciating sequences of well-constructed tones. Culture is central.

We began this book with the story of Mrs. Campbell, the 93-year-old Alzheimer's patient who upon hearing the music of her childhood threw off two years of silence and began to sing. Then, when the music stopped, she once again slipped away.

What did Mrs. Campbell "hear" in those old tunes? Did she remember back ninety years to when, sitting atop her father's shoulders, she was the tallest kid in the room? Maybe she smelled the sweetness of a homemade pie or re-shared a secret with a childhood friend. Perhaps she even felt the tentative touch of love's first kiss. We cannot know, of course. But these sorts of memories seem more than possible. After all, musical experience connects us to the present and the past, prepares us for the future. Quite simply, music helps light the way as we live our lives.

Key Terms

- A440
- alap
- big band music
- concertmaster
- concerto
- double-stops
- expressionist
- gat-tora
- Hindustani music
- jazz
- Köchel numbers
- movement
- mukhra
- *ospedale*
- overture
- raga
- retrograde
- ritornello
- rondel
- rondo form
- sam
- sampled
- sonata form (exposition, development, recapitulation)
- sprechstimme
- śruti box
- stanza (quatrain and quintrain)
- string quartet
- symbolist
- symphony (two definitions)
- tabla
- tala
- tehai

Essay Questions

- How is live music different from recorded music? Which do you prefer? Why?
- A live music concert involves many more elements than music. What are they? How might they affect your experience?

- To examine technology's role in music past and present.
- To think about technology's potential future impact.

CHAPTER FIFTEEN

Music and Technology

ACTIVITIES AND ASSIGNMENTS

- Imagine a world without electricity. How often would you hear music?
- Ask your grandparents or elderly neighbors about their musical experiences when young. How are they different from your own?

Shanghai, China

Bathed in laser lights and surrounded by a glow-stick-wielding audience numbering in the tens of thousands, Hatsune Miku, the world's first anime **vocaloid** software superstar, rocks the stage. For the next two hours, as her flesh-and-blood band plays at mind-numbing volumes, Hatsune's 3D holographic image—with its green body-length pony-tails—sings, dances, and intrigues. Never before has pop music, alternately despised and embraced for its lack of authenticity, been so unapologetically artificial. Fans dance and sing along as they revel in the spectacle. Some may even fall in love.

Hatsune Miku is just one of a growing number of anime vocaloid pop stars. Of course, other not-so-musical software companions are already a part of everyday life: Alexa, Siri, and more. Still others fill our imaginations (R2-D2 and BB-8, as well as the T-800).

Today's music industry is dominated by electronic technologies: software, sound sampling, and digital recording/playback. But music has always been influenced by technology (the science, or theory, of techniques). In this chapter we explore the impact of technology, past and present. We divide the discussion into two broad overviews. First, discovery and invention; second, preservation, reproduction, and dissemination. All these topics are closely related.

> "We live in a society exquisitely dependent on science and technology, in which hardly anyone knows anything about science and technology."
> —Carl Sagan (1936–1996)

VOCALOID

Vocaloid is a voice synthesizer that uses sound samples from human singers. Users can input any melody, then attach words to each tone. Timbre, vibrato, dynamics, and other sound characteristics can be adjusted at any point. Sound samples are available for a number of different singers and languages, including English, Japanese, Chinese, Spanish, Korean, and more.

Hatsune's program was first released in 2007 by Crypton Future Media, a Japanese software company. Japanese anime voice actress Saki Fujita provided the vocal samples from which Hatsune's voice is created. Undergoing constant refinement and software development, the potentially forever-young Hatsune Miko is improving with age (and more sophisticated code).

QUESTIONS FOR THOUGHT

- Find on the internet a music video of Hatsune Miko or that of another vocaloid. What is your reaction? Why? Could you become a fan? Why or why not?
- What impact might vocaloids have on flesh-and-blood musicians?
- Most of today's pop singers use Auto-Tune, a processor that corrects out-of-tune pitches. Is this good for music? Is Auto-Tune like steroids for athletes?

Discovery and Invention

Defining Sound

If a tree falls in the forest and no one is there to hear it, does it make a sound? Consider two possibilities. First, we might define sound as a subjective auditory experience. In that case, the falling tree made no sound. Second, we might define sound mechanically, as a wave form moving through a medium (gas, liquid, or solid). In this case, our falling tree generated plenty of sound.

The acoustical sciences are in action all around us. An acoustician helped design your earphones and music system, had a say in your car's design, and also the lecture halls at your school.

Let's build a definition. Acoustics is the study of mechanical waves, whether found in gases (everyday speech or a jet's sonic boom), liquids (an ocean or a pregnant woman's uterus), and solids (from vibrating engines to solid earth). Our focus will be on the sounds humans hear.

AUDITORY RANGES

Humans with normal hearing can perceive sound ranging from 20 Hertz (Hz) or cycles per second (cps) to 20,000 Hz. Standard pianos range from 27.5 Hz to 4186 Hz.

An increasingly higher amplitude is required to recognize sound at the upper and lower extremes. This partially explains why many listeners like their music loud. Increased volume allows them to perceive more sounds at the edge of their hearing range. (Unfortunately, there may be a price to pay: permanent damage to the auditory nerves.)

Dogs cannot hear as low as humans, but they hear much higher frequencies (67 Hz to 45,000 Hz). A cat's hearing range is higher still. Some species of bats can hear sounds as high as 200,000 Hz (or 200 kHz)

QUESTIONS FOR THOUGHT

- What if we use our imagination to hear a tree fall? Is that sound? To either stimulus—real tree or imagined—the aural centers of the brain respond similarly.
- Can a deaf person experience music? How? Investigate the role of music in the world of hearing or deaf culture. How does this relate to definitions of sound?
- Investigate the band Beethoven's Nightmare.

Properties of Mechanical Waves

There are three basic mechanical wave forms: longitudinal (or compressional), transverse, and surface. Sound waves are longitudinal. That is, as the wave moves outward from its source through a medium (air, liquids, solids), the medium's molecules are pushed (compressed) in the direction of the wave's outward flowing pressure. Because the pressure comes in waves, the pushing flows and ebbs. This causes compression and decompression that unsettles the medium's equilibrium. It is these vibratory disruptions that we hear as sound.

Transverse waves, however, are ones in which the particles pushed by the wave move perpendicular to the wave itself. Transverse waves require resistance, so they do not exist in air. A good example of transverse waves are the concentric ripples in water caused by dropping a stone into a pond. Another is the back-and-forth motion of a slinky.

Surface waves only occur at the boundaries between two different substances. Our water ripples are also surface waves. So is the shaking ground felt even hundreds of miles away from an earthquake.

A pregnancy ultrasound (around 3.5 MHz) makes use of longitudinal waves. Therefore, it is an acoustical phenomenon, even though these sounds are far above the range of hearing. Infrasonic seismic waves caused by an earthquake are also acoustical, even though the sounds are below the range of human hearing.

Acoustics of a String

To find the roots of acoustical science, we need to go back all the way to Pythagoras (ca. 570–495 BCE). You will remember him from the Pythagorean Theorem ($a^2 + b^2 = c^2$) you learned in high school math class. In addition to being a mathematician, Pythagoras was a philosopher, mystic, scientist, and acoustician. It was he who first explored the mechanics of a vibrating string, and thus provided a mathematical explanation for pitch.

Even 2500 years ago, every musician knew that plucking a taut string would give a specific pitch (which we now call the fundamental, or 1st harmonic). In his acoustical experiments, Pythagoras sought to learn more. He discovered that if a string is divided exactly in half, the pitch it produces is exactly one octave higher than the original. So, he realized, the geometrical relationship of a fundamental tone to its octave is 1:2. The octave tone above the fundamental is called the 1st overtone or 2nd harmonic.

Pythagoras proceeded to divide the string into smaller segments: thirds and fourths. Here he discovered two additional intervals respectively. Dividing the string into three equal parts produced a sound that was an octave and a fifth (2nd overtone or 3rd harmonic) above the original string. Dividing the string into four equal parts produced a sound two octaves higher (3rd overtone or 4th harmonic) than the fundamental.

From bottom to top, these relationships can be expressed mathematically. From a fundamental to the 2nd harmonic is the relationship of 1:2. From the first octave (2nd harmonic) to the fifth above (3rd harmonic) is the relationship of 2:3. From the fifth (3rd harmonic) up to the next octave (4th harmonic) is the relationship of 3:4. Pythagoras stopped there. But we can continue to divide the string and hear more overtones. With each subsequent equidistant string division, the pitch will get higher and the interval between subsequent pitches will get smaller.

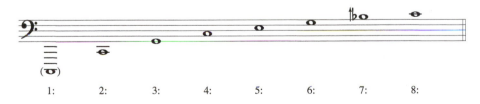

FIGURE 15.1 Overtone series with "C" as fundamental.

Pitch and Vibration

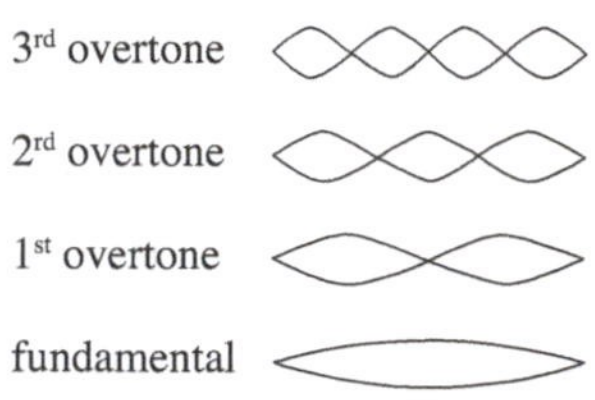

FIGURE 15.2
String fundamental vibrations.

(labels: 3rd overtone, 2nd overtone, 1st overtone, fundamental)

It was not until the 19th century that scientists were able to measure pitch in terms of vibratory speed. The person who accomplished that was French scientist Felix Savart (1791–1841). Savart built a brass wheel with 720 "teeth." When the wheel was spun, the teeth plucked a card (an effect like a child putting a playing card against the spokes of her bicycle). When Savart spun the wheel quickly enough, the vibrating card began to emit a distinct pitch, which would rise or fall according to the speed with which the wheel was turning (and the plucked card vibrating). By measuring the wheel's rotation speed, Savart was able to assign specific vibratory frequencies to pitch.

When the card was plucked 110 times each second (causing it to vibrate back and forth at 110 cycles per second [cps]) the card produced the pitch A. When Savart doubled the vibration rate to 220 cps, another A (one octave higher) was heard. When Savart sped the wheel up to strike the card 330 times per second, he heard the pitch E (a 5th higher). Speeding up the wheel still further, the teeth striking the card 440 times per second, the pitch returned to A, two octaves higher than the original tone (and the pitch to which modern orchestras tune). Notice that Savart's vibratory relationships are exactly the same as Pythagoras' geometric relationships (1:2, 2:3, 3:4).

Harmonics

There is another important thing to observe about the mechanics of a vibrating string. When a string is set into vibration it produces the fundamental tone produced from the full length of the vibrating string. But a vibrating string also automatically (and simultaneously) divides itself into equally divided segments. This division produces the same series of harmonics (or overtones) Pythagoras discovered. One can hear them with careful listening. Theoretically, this tendency to divide (and produce ever-higher, and closer, overtones) could continue forever. But in practice it continues only as long as the string's structural integrity is maintained.

Harmonics are easy to hear on a piano. If possible, do some actual listening. Choose a key in the lower half of the instrument. Push it down hard and hold it. Listen not just to the main tone but also for the fainter harmonics produced above it. You will hear the octave relationship between the fundamental and the second harmonic (**do**–re–mi–fa–sol–la–ti–**do**). Listen higher and you will hear the third harmonic (**do**–re–mi–fa–sol–la–ti–do–re–mi–fa–**sol**). If you listen higher still you will hear the fourth harmonic, two octaves above the fundamental (**do**–re–mi–fa–sol–la–ti–do–re–mi–fa–sol–la–ti–**do**). Listen for even higher harmonics. There are plenty of tones still to be heard.

OVERTONES VS. HARMONICS

The words "overtones" and "harmonics" are sometimes used interchangeably, but they are not necessarily the same. The term "harmonic" refers to a vibratory rate that has an integer (whole number) multiple to the fundamental (1:2, 1:3, 1:4 etc.). The term "overtone" refers to any vibratory frequency occurring above the fundamental. Harmonics result in the experience of pitch. An overtone may or may not be a harmonic, but a preponderance of non-harmonic overtones results in the experience of non-pitched sound. Strings and wind instruments create harmonics, resulting in pitch; most drums and many idiophones (rattles, chalk boards, jack hammers) create a preponderance of non-harmonic overtones, resulting in non-pitched timbres.

We demonstrated overtones on the piano because they are easy to hear on this instrument. But every instrument has an overtone structure. Strings vibrate differently from air columns in wind instruments, which vibrate differently from drum heads. Even strings vibrate differently one from another. That is because some are made of metal while others are made of silk or animal matter. And because all strings have structural flaws, even "identical" strings will vibrate slightly differently one from another.

Wind Instruments: Open and Closed Pipes

Now that we have a good idea of how string acoustics work, let's investigate a small sample of wind instruments. We begin with the shakuhachi, a Japanese end-blown bamboo flute (Chapter 3: Three Listening Examples). Because the shakuhachi is open at both ends, acousticians call it an "open pipe."

A shakuhachi player produces sound by blowing a narrow stream of air across (not into) the *utaguchi* (or song mouth), a small indentation at instrument's end. Proper blowing across the utaguchi causes the air column throughout the tube to vibrate and form a sound wave. (The tube also acts as an amplifier.) As with a string, the longer the tube (and therefore the length of the sound wave), the lower the pitch. Also like a string, an air column can be coaxed into different vibratory rates. With increased energy, the air column in an open pipe will divide in half, producing an octave leap from the first to the second harmonic.

There are also important differences between sound waves occurring in an open pipe and a string. Unlike a string (which once in motion briefly continues to vibrate on its own), a shakuhachi's air column needs a continual input of energy. Stop blowing and the sound ceases almost instantaneously.

A shakuhachi's acoustics are fundamentally different from a string's in another important way. In Figure 15.2 you perhaps noticed that a string does not vibrate at its end points. These points of non-vibration are called **nodes**. (Dividing a string in half creates a node in the string's midpoint.) In contrast to Figure 15.2, Figure 15.3 shows that a shakuhachi wave has its maximum vibration (anti-node) at its ends. The shakuhachi's fundamental frequency wave has its node in the middle of the instrument.

Now let's briefly consider a clarinet, which is a "closed pipe." It is "closed" because the air-constricting mouthpiece through which air flow is blown into the pipe creates a node at that end. Figure 15.4 shows waves in a closed pipe. Notice that a closed pipe only produces odd-numbered harmonics. Why? Because a closed pipe must have a node at the blowing end and an anti-node at the other.

What does this mean for performers? Over-blowing the closed-pipe fundamental will produce the third harmonic, an octave and a fifth above the fundamental tone. Of course, a clarinetist (like a shakuhachi player) creates melodies by opening and closing tone holes, which (to the air column, at least) effectively changes the instrument's length.

Shakuhachi, 18th century.
Courtesy of The Metropolitan Museum of Art, Gift of Mrs. Howard Mansfield, 1948.

FIGURE 15.3
Shakuhachi: open pipe.

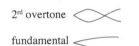

FIGURE 15.4
Clarinet: closed pipe.

Innovations in Brass Instruments

Curiously, many "brass instruments" are not made of brass. Conversely, some instruments made of brass—for example, the saxophone—are considered to be woodwinds. How come? The answer lies in the fact that scholars place instruments in this category according to the way sound is produced rather than the material from which the instrument is made.

Brass instruments are closed-pipe aerophones, like the clarinet. But rather than blowing air through a reed-covered mouthpiece, in a "brass" instrument the air column is sent into the pipe through a natural opening or mouthpiece against which the instrumentalist blows through buzzing lips. According to our buzzing-equals-brass definition, each of the following instruments are brass instruments: animal horns (a shofar, for example), conch shells, and the Australian aboriginal digeridoo, which is made from wood hollowed out by termites.

One early trumpet-like instrument was the salpinx, used by the ancient Greeks on the battlefield. Basically a long tube, the salpinx was constructed of either bronze or bone. During the Middle Ages, advances in metalworking allowed makers to create more elegant, and better-sounding instruments that were consistent one with another in size, shape, and thickness.

Keyed Bugle in E, American, 1830–1850.

Courtesy of The Metropolitan Museum of Art, The Crosby Brown Collection of Musical Instruments, 1889.

Yet, even though sound quality and consistency were improving, brass players were still limited to playing only the tones within their instruments' natural harmonic series. This limitation was overcome in 1810 when Irish bugle-maker Joseph Haliday invented the keyed bugle, which imitated the system of keys employed on woodwind instruments. By opening and closing tone-holes along the length of the instrument, brass players suddenly had a wide range of fundamental and overtone pitches from which to choose. Virtuosos were soon performing melodies previously reserved for woodwinds or stringed instruments. So revolutionary was the change that by the mid-1830s American military bands were eliminating woodwinds altogether and converting to all brass.

Soon after the invention of keyed brass instruments, manufacturers in Germany came up with an even better idea. Into their instruments they embedded vacuum piston and rotary valve mechanisms, which when engaged would seamlessly redirect the flow of air down different lengths of tubing, again changing the instrument's fundamental tone, but more efficiently than Haliday's keys. By the 1860s, the use of interchangeable parts allowed these instruments to be mass produced.

Developments in Keyboard Instruments

Clavichord, German, 1763.

Courtesy of The Metropolitan Museum of Art, Purchase, The Crosby Brown Collection of Musical Instruments, by exchange; Rogers Fund; The Barrington Foundation Inc. gift; gifts of Risa and David Bernstein, Carroll C., Beverly and Garry S. Bratman, Miss Alice Getty, and Erica D. White, by exchange; and funds from various donors, by exchange, 1986.

The earliest known "keyboard" instrument is the **hydraulis,** a type of organ invented around the year 300 BCE in Alexandria (in present-day Egypt). These instruments had as many as sixteen pipes, each of which had a lever that when depressed (by a hand, not fingers) allowed air to blow through the pipe. Similar instruments were still used in the court of Charlemagne (748–814).

The modern keyboard was invented around the year 1400, probably with the **clavichord,** which had 3.5 to 5 octaves. Sound is produced on a clavichord by depressing a long key set atop a fulcrum. As the front of the key is depressed, the back of the key (which is attached to a tangent, a small brass blade) rises and strikes the string. The clavichord is capable of generating only small levels of sound.

More versatile, and somewhat louder, is the harpsichord, which was perhaps invented about the same time or a little later. Rather than striking the string with a blade, harpsichord strings are usually plucked with a quill. The harpsichord is considerably larger than the clavichord and it has a large soundboard, which provides greater resonance.

The harpsichord's louder volume was helpful in concert settings, but a limitation was that the instrument is not capable of varying dynamics. Even so, the harpsichord was the most popular concert keyboard until the mid-18th century, when the piano gradually replaced it.

The piano was invented around the year 1700 by Bartolomeo Cristofori (1655–1731), a long-time employee of the Medici court in Florence, Italy. Unlike the harpsichord, Cristofori's instrument

Harpsichord, Italian, late 17th century.
Courtesy of The Metropolitan Museum of Art, Gift of Susan Dwight Bliss, 1945.

Bartolomeo Cristofori Piano, Florence, Italy, 1729.
Courtesy of The Metropolitan Museum of Art, The Crosby Brown Collection of Musical Instruments, 1889.

struck the strings with wooden hammers. Not only was the instrument louder, it was more versatile. It would soon come to be called a *gravicembalo col piano e forte* (harpsichord with soft and loud). That name would be shortened to pianoforte, and eventually to piano. Compared with the modern piano, these early instruments were delicate of frame and relatively modest in sound. During the 19th century, however, pianos began to be built with cast-iron frames, which allowed for much greater levels of string tension and the use of thicker, stronger strings. This produced a much wider dynamic range.

Electric pianos were developed in the 1920s. These instruments initially had strings, like a regular piano, but the strings (sometimes replaced by metal tines) were amplified not by a soundboard but by electronic pickups, like those on an electric guitar. Perhaps the most popular electric piano was the Fender Rhodes, brought to prominence in the 1970s especially through Chick Corea (b. 1941), Joe Zawinul (1932–2007), Stevie Wonder (b. 1950), and others.

Another iconic electronic keyboard was the Hammond B-3 organ. In the Hammond B-3, sound is produced electronically rather than by air driven through pipes. Classic Hammond B-3 recordings include "Gimme Some Lovin'" (1966) and "A Whiter Shade of Pale" (1967). Bands that made extensive use of the instrument were Emerson, Lake & Palmer, the Allman Brothers Band, and Deep Purple.

QUESTIONS FOR THOUGHT

- **Where do sound waves travel fastest: solids, liquids, or gasses? Why?**
- **Is the Hammond B-3 actually an organ?**

ACTIVITIES AND ASSIGNMENTS

- Strike a tuning fork and then place it in water. What do you see? What types of waves are these?
- Can you get more than one pitch by blowing in a bottle (containing the same amount of water for each pitch)? Why or why not?
- Search the internet for videos of vibrating strings.
- Search the internet for videos on "sound energy."

Music Preservation, Reproduction, and Dissemination

Notation

The earliest surviving example of music notation is a fragment of a composition for **lyre** preserved on a 4000-year-old etched clay tablet from Sumer (present-day Iraq). The oldest complete surviving composition is the Seikilos epitaph, which was engraved on a tombstone sometime between 200 BCE and 100 CE in the Hellenistic town of Tralles, located in present-day Turkey.

In Europe, beginning around 800, a system of notation was developed using *neumes*, figures that represented either single tones or groups of tones. Early neumes did not necessarily indicate exact pitches, but offered an outline of how the music might unfold. It was Guido of Arezzo (ca. 991–1033) who devised a staff system of lines and spaces that allowed for exact pitch representation.

Introduced around 1200 was a system of rhythmic representation, which was codified by Franco of Cologne (fl. mid-13th century). Bar lines—which initially were used only as visual aids for reading, but eventually came to indicate rhythmic meter—became increasingly common during the 16th century. Accidentals, most commonly flats, first appeared in the Medieval period, but modern key signatures were not standardized until the 18th century.

Music notation evolved to meet changing demands for accurate preservation and reproduction. But what happens when the music changes radically? That was the case in the 1950s when composers began to experiment with new textures and new timbres. Remember back to Penderecki's *Threnody for the Victims of Hiroshima*. The representation of exact pitch, meter, and harmony were irrelevant in *Threnody*, and so, therefore, was traditional notation. Accordingly, new systems had to be devised. Most common was graphic notation. Rather than indicating tones or rhythms, scores looked more like abstract art than music.

NOTATION: DESCRIPTIVE OR PRESCRIPTIVE

Musical notation is both prescriptive and descriptive. Prescriptive notation provides a map by which one can attempt to reproduce a composer's intentions, even if the performer has never heard the composition before. A transcription is descriptive, a map of exactly what was heard in a particular performance, mistakes and all. A transcription is not necessarily how the music *should* go, but how a particular performance *did* go.

If you think about it, even Beethoven's notation offers only guidelines. While showing pitches, tempo, and meter, there is plenty of room for interpretation. Jazz lead sheets are far less detailed. Lead sheets offer only broad guidelines for the performer, who is expected to expand on and improvise upon the composer's ideas.

ACTIVITIES AND ASSIGNMENTS

- Imagine a short melody, then try to notate it. Can your neighbor reproduce it as you intended? If not, try something different.

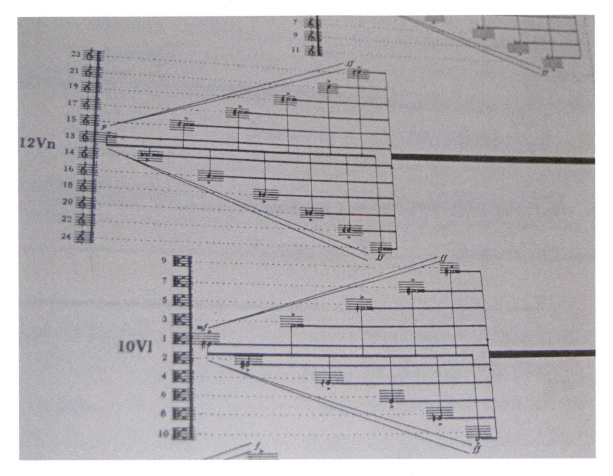

FIGURE 15.5 Graphic notation; excerpt from *Threnody for the Victims of Hiroshima*.

Audio Recording

Phonograph

The first working phonograph was designed in 1877 by Thomas Edison. The idea came from his attempt to invent a device capable of transcribing telegraphic messages. Edison's machine worked by attaching a stylus to a diaphragm attached to the end of a "sound tube." The stylus was then placed in contact with a soft material (first paraffin paper, soon thereafter tin foil) that had been wrapped around a spinning metal cylinder. As sound was sent into the sound tube, the diaphragm would vibrate and push the stylus against the tinfoil. When the soft tinfoil received impressions beneath the stylus, the sound's "shape" would be engraved.

Playback occurred when the stylus was once again run over the engraving. This time, the stylus vibrated according to the tinfoil sound impressions. (This is what happens with a contemporary record player.) Initially, playback quality was poor and engravings would lose integrity after just a few playbacks. Improvements came sporadically, but by the late 1890s Edison was recording on durable wax cylinders, and marketing playback machines for home use.

The next big advance came in 1901, when a system for mass producing recordings was devised. Within three years the retail cost of a cylinder dropped from $4 to 35 cents. Playback length doubled, from two to four minutes. Nevertheless, by 1912 it was clear that the cylinder was on its way out. Cylinders would be replaced with flat shellac discs (which were more convenient for storage).

In 1945, just in time for the post-World War II baby-boomer generation, vinyl records became commercially available. A decade later, and as the boomers approached their teen years and driving age, three additional culture-changing presents were bestowed: the world's first commercial transistor radio (the Regency TR-1), car radios, and portable 45rpm record players. All this was coincident

Frances Densmore at the Smithsonian Institution during a recording session with Mountain Chief of the Montana Blackfeet, 1916.

with the advent of rock 'n' roll. The period's car songs ranged in mood from Mark Dinning's maudlin death song, "Teen Angel" (1959) to Jan & Dean's lead-footed granny protagonist in "Little Old Lady (from Pasadena)" (1964).

Magnetic Recording

Magnetic recording has a history almost as long as the phonograph. The first commercially produced magnetic recorder was the telegraphone, invented around 1898 by Danish engineer Valdemar Poulson. The machine worked by magnetizing a thin wire as it was drawn across a magnetic head that was responding to the intensity and polarity of an electric audio signal. To convert the information back into sound, the magnetized wire was passed again over the (now passive) head, which responded to the information on the wire and converted that data back into sound. The beauty of magnetic recording was twofold. The recordings were highly accurate and the wire's magnetic field could be reset. That is, the wire's information could be erased and reapplied.

Originally, magnetic tape recording—done on steel tape or oxide-coated paper—was confined to dictation and telephone recording. It was not until after World War II that magnetic tape had developed to the point that it would be used for music production. The technology was very good. When broadcast over the radio, live performances and taped performances were virtually indistinguishable, a fact that golden-voiced crooner Bing Crosby (1903–1977) demonstrated by pre-recording a 1947 national broadcast. Magnetic tape would revolutionize the radio and recording industry. In the 1960s, overdubbing and multi-track (also called multi-channel) recordings became the industry norm.

Digital Formats

The next major leap forward in recording technology came in 1982 with the commercial introduction of the compact disc (CD). Not only were CDs smaller and more durable than vinyl records, they

RADIO

By 1947, approximately 1400 licensed radio stations were capable of reaching 98 percent of the population in the United States. But while radio bound large geographic areas with common information and voice, the nuances and idiosyncrasies of local community life were often underserved. Some 5600 towns and small cities did not have a single local station. Introduced in 1948 was the idea of licensing low power FM stations with a broadcast distance of ten miles or less. Due to increasing bandwidth congestion, however, in the late 1970s the FCC decided that any low-power station interfering with an existing or newly created larger station had to change its broadcast frequency, move its antenna location, or upgrade to 100 watts. As legal broadcast opportunities disappeared, "pirate" stations (unlicensed broadcasters) spread across the bandwidth. By the late 1990s, the FCC was shutting down an average of a dozen stations monthly. Nevertheless, many stations continue to operate, some reaching no further than just a city block or two.

SGT. PEPPER'S LONELY HEARTS CLUB BAND

The Beatles's *Sgt. Pepper's Lonely Hearts Club Band* (1967) represents a landmark use of audio technology. Then groundbreaking four-track technology was exploited in ways altogether new for popular music. Sounds were layered, juxtaposed and spliced in unexpected ways. In the album's title track, distorted guitar riffs keep step with the sounds of a military brass band. "A Day in the Life," the album's enigmatic and magisterial final track, looks toward an uncertain future while delivering a sobering eulogy for a receding past. As the song comes to a close, a huge orchestral crescendo expands into *Threnody*-like sonic cacophony only to be replaced by a massive E major chord simultaneously struck on three pianos. Overtones swirling, the sound rings for over forty seconds.

held considerably more music, up to eighty minutes on a single disc. The CD also introduced digital recording technology at the consumer level.

Until the CD, sound recording and playback technology was analog by construction, that is, the recording medium was *analogous* to the sound being preserved. For example, Edison's cylinder recordings were analog because they were produced by the direct impact of a stylus responding to sound vibrations in the atmosphere while being drawn across the cylinder. The weight of gravity allowed the stylus to then etch those movements into the cylinder's soft surface, thereby generating an analogous version, and three-dimensional picture, of the original sound. Analog playback works in the opposite direction. As previously noted, during a vinyl record playback, the stylus is drawn through previously etched grooves, which causes the stylus to vibrate and recreate the original sound, which is then amplified.

Digital sound recording differs from analog recording in fundamental ways. First, digital sound information is stored in binary code on a CD or hard drive. Second, while analog technology records sound in an unbroken and unified flow, digital recording preserves discrete moments in time, a technique that creates information gaps. Since these gaps are extremely brief, we experience a constant flow of sound. (Some listeners find digital sound to be less "rich," or "warm," than analog sound.) Third, cylinders, vinyl records, and magnetic tapes wear out over repeated playback. Sound quality diminishes accordingly. Because digital storage is code, which can be accessed passively, the sound quality is undiminished, even after the 10,000th playback.

Sampling

"You don't have to do no soloing, brother, just keep what you got. Don't turn it loose, 'cause it's a mother." Those were the instructions of soul/funk icon James Brown (1933–2006) for Clyde Stubblefield (1943–2017), his virtuoso drummer. The occasion was the 1970 recording of "Funky Drummer." Taken as a whole, the band's nine-plus minute track presents in-the-moment funk grooving and riffing at its very best—spontaneous, but grounded; rhythmically taut, but seemingly effortless; contained, but unfettered.

Nearly twenty years later, Stubblefield's eight-bar drum break, just seconds long, would be extracted from the recording and become the rhythmic backbone of rap music. Sound samples of Stubblefield's solo appear in more than 1400 commercially released rap songs, including Public Enemy's iconic "Fight the Power" (1989), as well as songs by LL Cool J, N.W.A, Nikki Minaj, Dr. Dre, Beastie Boys, and Sublime.

So what is sampling? And how does an eight-second drum break become the foundation for a song that lasts for minutes? Sampling is the process of taking a sound from one recorded medium and inserting it into a new one. Today, sampling is generally done by digitally extracting a selection from a pre-existing recording, modifying the sample to fit new requirements (perhaps adjusting tempo and timbre), and then inserting the sample into the new environment. A sample can easily be "looped" so that it repeats over and over, turning seconds of material into minutes on end (as has so often been the case for Stubblefield's solo).

DJ Kool Herc with James Brown single, 1999.
Mika Väisänen/Wikimedia Commons/CC-BY-SA-4.0.

Originally, looping was low tech. It was done by switching between two vinyl records with a technique called "the merry-go-round," invented in the early 1970s by Jamaican native/NYC transplant DJ Kool Herc (Clive Campbell [b. 1955]). As a teenager Herc spun records for dance parties in New York City's South Bronx. So how did Herc create his musical merry-go-round?

The process began with two identical vinyl records spinning on separate turntables. To start, Herc cued the first recording to the drum break's beginning, then let it play. While that was playing he cued the second recording to the same break's beginning. When the break was nearly completed on the first recording, he used a device called a cross fader to switch the sound system to the second recording. As that played, he cued recording number one. Herc "played" the turntables. By going back and forth between recordings, he could maintain the break as long as he wanted. **Turntablism** became an art in itself.

Perhaps the most iconic turntablist sound of the 1980s was **scratching**. Rhythmic noise was created by placing slip mats between the record and the turntable platter. Spinning the record forward and backwards created the scratch sound. The technique was made practical by the stability of the Technics DL-1200 direct-drive turntable (a turntablist's Stradivarius).

A virtuosic example of scratching by GrandMixer D.ST. (Derek Showard) can be heard on jazz keyboardist Herbie Hancock's (b. 1940) crossover recording "Rockit" (1983). Providing the foundation for the rhythmic texture was an Oberheim DMX drum machine and Cuban percussionist Daniel Ponce, who played bàtá drums (Chapter 7: Music and Spirituality).

Once the rhythms were laid down, Hancock added melodic layers with keyboard synthesizers and synthesized speech through a vocoder speech synthesizer. The result was a futuristic composition that ended up being performed live at the 1984 Grammy Awards. The band shared the

"RAPPER'S DELIGHT"

Although rap developed in the violent 1970s streets, parks, and apartment complexes of New York City's then dilapidated South Bronx, rap's first commercial hit was recorded by The Sugarhill Gang, three aspiring rappers from New Jersey. The men were brought together through auditions held by Sugar Hill Records co-owner and producer Sylvia Robinson, who in the 1950s had a moderately successful career as a singer with the duo Mickey and Sylvia. The beat for "Rapper's Delight," was built upon a looped sample of Chic's 1979 disco hit song "Good Times."

stage with four breakdancing/moonwalking human mannequins. Other scratching turntablists went on to develop a number of distinctive techniques and styles, including chirps, flares, stabs, beat juggling, and others.

QUESTION FOR THOUGHT

- Might technological advancements in sound production negatively affect how we make and consume music?

ACTIVITIES AND ASSIGNMENTS

- Listen to Mark Ronson's 2014 TED Talk on sampling.
- Search the internet for *The Avid Listener* blog, "DJ Kool Herc: The Man with the Master Plan."

Electronic Art Music

On May 39, 1956, Karlheinz Stockhausen's remarkable electronic music composition *Gesang der Jünglinge* (Song of the Youths) was premiered in the *Westdeutscher Rundfunk Köln* (West German Broadcasting Cologne) auditorium. Although a child's voice would be featured, there were no human performers, just five sets of speakers dispersed around the hall. As sounds floated and migrated from one space to the next through a five-track recording, the possibilities of surround sound audio systems (first used commercially in the 1940 Disney movie *Fantasia*) were exploited.

Stockhausen, a devout Catholic, originally conceived the composition as part of a Mass, but it was never performed as such. For text, Stockhausen drew from the Old Testament Book of Daniel, in which King Nebuchadnezzar orders three men thrown into a blazing furnace. Their crime? Failure to show proper deference. In a testament to the power of their faith, the men walk through the furnace unhurt.

KARLHEINZ STOCKHAUSEN (1928–2007)

Stockhausen was born in Germany on the brink of self-destruction, just five years before Hitler's rise to power and eleven before the outbreak of World War II. Stockhausen's mother, who had been institutionalized for mental instability, was "euthanized" by the Nazis in 1941. In 1944, the 16-year-old boy was conscripted into the German army as a stretcher bearer. His father, who fought in the German army, was killed in Hungary in 1945.

After the war, Stockhausen enrolled at the Cologne Conservatory of Music, where he studied until 1951. From there he went to Paris to study with Olivier Messiaen. Later, he studied linguistics, work that would pay off in *Gesang der Jünglinge*, one of his first experiments with electronic music, and considered by many to be the genre's first masterpiece.

Karlheinz Stockhausen October 1994 in the Studio for Electronic Music of WDR Cologne.

Kathinka Pasveer/Wikimedia Commons/CC-BY-SA-3.0.

To produce the composition, Stockhausen recorded a 12-year-old boy reading the Old Testament passages. Then the composer reduced the text to a few essential words (mostly focusing on "preiset den Herrn" ["praise ye the Lord"] and "jubelt" ["exult"]), which he then spliced, transposed, stretched, doubled, and enhanced as he added and merged them with electronic textures that imitated vowels and consonants. Stockhausen expanded vowels into long tones and turned consonants into noise. He also went in the opposite direction, manipulating synthesized sounds by turning white noise (what we think of as static) into consonants, and turning sine tones into vowels. With almost eerie prescience, perhaps foreboding, child and machine seem to merge. At times it is impossible to know which is which. Relatively little of *Gesang der Jünglinge* can be understood as language, just enough to reference the biblical passage (Daniel 3: 57–59):

Preiset (Jubelt) den(m) Herrn, ihr Werke alle des Hernn
lobt ihn und über alles erhebt ihn in Ewigkeit.
Preiset den Herrn, ihr Engel des Herrn
preiset den Herrn, ihr Himmel droben.

O all ye works of the Lord, praise (exult in) the Lord
Laud Him and exalt Him above all forever.
O ye angels of the Lord, praise ye the Lord
O ye heavens, praise ye the Lord.

Earlier in the century, composers had developed the 12-tone system (also known as serial technique), an organizational method by which (in theory at least) all twelve pitches of the Western octave would be used in a series before any tone was repeated. The idea was to eliminate the sense of a "home" tone (or tonic) toward which melodies generally find resolution, or rest. This was rootless music for an increasingly uprooted civilization.

In *Gesang der Jünglinge*, Stockhausen took the 12-tone effect of displacement to its logical conclusion. He treated *all* sonic aspects serially: not just pitch, but phonetic sounds (vowels and types of consonants), duration, texture, dynamics, even the directions from which the sounds came through the loudspeakers. One might expect meaningless cacophony from such an approach, but the music is both idiosyncratic and highly dramatic.

In addition to the boy's recitation, Stockhausen's sound sources included the cutting edge of the 1950s-era electronic music arsenal. His instruments included a sine- and square-wave generator, a low-frequency pulse generator, a 1/3 octave band-pass filter, a sine-wave beat-frequency oscillator, and a frequency amplifier/feedback filter. The boy's recorded words were chopped apart and passed (forwards or backwards) through filters.

TECHNICAL TERMS

- *Sine, square, and sawtooth waves*: this is a physical description of the wave shape each sound type produces in space. Each type is a single frequency (or pitch) without overtones. Each has a different timbre. At lower frequencies the sine wave sounds the smoothest, but differences between the three waves seem to lessen as pitch rises.

- *Band-pass filters* allow specific pitches to be heard while eliminating others.

- *Beats* occur when two pitches that are slightly different are sounded together. Because the waves have slightly different lengths, through time they have different peaks and troughs. This affects amplitude, causing beats.

QUESTION FOR THOUGHT

- Imagine hearing Stockhausen's *Gesang der Jünglinge* in 1956. Might audiences today react any differently? Why or why not?

Gesang der Jünglinge, by Karlheinz Stockhausen

LISTENING 15.1 GUIDE

Texture: Varied
Meter: Unmetered

According to Stockhausen, the composition is organized into six sections of increasing complexity. Divisions are not obvious.

0:00–1:02 Section 1
- An explosion of sound, then rising tones, as if life (or sacrificial smoke?) is floating upward toward the heavens.
- Ten seconds into the piece, we seem to have arrived. A boy sings, "Jubelt" ("Exult")
- We hear a chorus of children. Singing? Calling? Playing?
- We hear a series of synthesized sounds.
- Momentary quiet.

1:02–2:52 Section 2
- A chorus of children. Singing or playing? Teasing or worshipping?
- Then a single boy. Shifts between "Den Herrn jubelt" and "Preiset den Herrn." We hear voices juxtaposed with synthesized sounds.
- Silence seems to shout from moments of unnatural emptiness.

2:52–5:15 Section 3
- Solo voice . . . den Herrn . . . Sonne . . . und Mond. (Lord . . . Sun . . . Moon)
- Individual words (or syllables) are separated in time and dropped into electronic soundspace. Some words are intelligible. Others are not.

5:15–6:22 Section 4
- A choir of voices (all created from the single child, of course). Here the human dominates, though the sounds are sometimes quite unnatural.
- Tones simplify and disintegrate in single, lightly processed syllables.

6:22–8:40 Section 5
- The section begins with (playful?) isolated electronic punctuations, then maraca-like sounds. At 6:53, distant voices enter juxtaposed with electronics. The section closes with the maraca. (Do not be fooled. There are no conventional instruments being used.)

8:40–13:00 Section 6
- Increasing complexity. Electronic and human are often indistinguishable.
- Do you hear a "cough" (and its echo?) at 9:13? At 10:34, singing in the background?
- Sound fades to silence at 11:34, followed by a chorus of disembodied voices.
- Return to silence at 12:54, then a final electronic flourish.

ACTIVITIES AND ASSIGNMENTS

- Explore other electronic works by Stockhausen or works by Edgar Varese, Milton Babbitt, Iannis Xenakis, Laurie Anderson, Brian Eno, and others.
- Compare Thomas Morley's late 17th-century madrigal "Though Philomela Lost Her Love" to Milton Babbitt's *Philomel* (1964). Then read the Greek myth "The Rape of Philomela" (Ovid's *Metamorphosis*, Book VI). Does knowing the story affect your response to either of the two works?
- What is *musique concrète? Acousmatic music? Spectral Music?* IRCAM? STEIM?

Conclusion

For centuries, instrument makers used just their ears to develop instruments that had distinctive and resonant timbres. Today's producers strive for the same results when they mix a recording, as do acousticians when designing speakers or concert halls. Now, however, they are assisted by computer technology.

It's worth pointing out that virtually all of today's listening experience is electronically mediated, whether through stadium-rattling sound systems for audiences in the tens of thousands, or through the privacy of headphones or earbuds. An unamplified voice or acoustic guitar is a rarity, even in places of worship.

Imagine this future: sampling is so widespread and computer mediated sounds so versatile that traditional acoustic musical instruments become obsolete. Singing is always in tune. Diction is always perfect. There is never a mistake.

Imagine this future: artificial intelligence technology detects a market niche for another song from 75-year-old Beyoncé. The song is written, produced, and distributed in less than twenty-three seconds, while she is taking a nap with her fourteenth grandson. Distribution occurs during a thirty-second timeout of a Toronto Raptors game, when Drake habitually checks his news feed. Determined to keep up, Drake downloads the latest Digital Schubert app. His new "Lied" about rejected love is distributed before the in-bounds pass. (It is offered in all three official planetary languages, but available in 1234 others for a small surcharge.)

Imagine this future: digital Mozart and digital Hendrix team up with a younger-than-ever Hatsune Miko for a gig on the holodeck. You write yourself in as the band's virtuoso drummer.

ON THE BEAT

There is a good chance you know someone who makes rap beats or mixes audio tracks. Although commercial success is rare, it is easy to become involved in music production. Beginners can download free software capable of creating publishable tracks. Spend a few hundred dollars and one has the beginnings of a high-quality music workstation.

Key Terms

- acoustics
- aerophone
- clavichord
- closed pipe
- fundamental
- harmonic
- hydraulis
- longitudinal waves

- lyre
- neume
- node
- open pipe
- overtone
- phonograph
- Pythagorean Theorem
- sampling

- scratching
- sound waves
- surface waves
- total serialization
- transverse waves
- turntablism
- vocaloid

Essay Questions

- **Imagine a world without electronic technology. What would happen to music?**
- **Computer programs can already defeat chess masters. Imagine a computer program that can create music in a style indistinguishable from any master composer. Does that idea make you uncomfortable? Why or why not?**
- **What makes for "good" music?**
- **Has music improved over time?**

1/4 tone (quarter tone) A pitch that splits the difference between two half steps, such as the pitch midway between F and F sharp or B flat and B.

12-bar blues A form of the blues that divides phrases into three equal sections of four measures each (equaling twelve measures, or bars). The lyrics generally follow an AAB format. The harmonies proceed in a fixed pattern of tonic, subdominant, and dominant chords.

12-tone system (also called serialism or dodecaphony) A compositional method developed in the 1920s by Arnold Schoenberg.

32-bar song form A song that consists of four equal-sized sections of 8 measures each, with a melodic sequence of AABA.

A440 The musical pitch A above middle C. It has the frequency of 440 Hz, that is, a vibratory rate of 440 cycles per second. A440 is the standard tuning pitch in Western art music.

Aavartanam One complete cycle of a tala. Each cycle consists of a set number of pulses indicated by hand signals. (Karnatic music)

A cappella Literally "in the style of the chapel," indicating a vocal performance without instrumental accompaniment.

Acoustics The study of sound, specifically of mechanical waves: in gases, liquids, or solids.

Adhan (Arabic) Call to Prayer. Recited five times a day to call Muslims to worship.

Aerophones Instruments whose sound is produced by columns of vibrating air. Examples include the flute, oboe, trumpet, bagpipe, whistle, and so on.

Agogic An accent or emphasis produced by lengthening a note.

Alapana (Alap) In Indian classical music, an improvisatory, rhythmically free section that introduces and explores the melodic characteristics of a raga.

Alto Low female or very high male voice.

American Song Book (or Great American Song Book) A conceptual collection of popular songs composed for the music industry primarily between 1920 and 1960. The collection draws from Broadway show tunes, Hollywood film, and popular culture in general. Many of these songs are known as "jazz standards."

Arabesque A ballet position in which the dancer places weight on one leg while the other is extended behind.

Aria A song for a vocal soloist in genres such as opera or oratorio that usually portrays emotions or ideas. The aria contrasts with recitative, a speech-like style of singing that conveys the dialogue.

Atonality Refers to music that lacks a tonal foundation or key center. Atonal music was developed in the early 20th century as an alternative to the lush harmonic structures of late Romanticism.

Avant-garde An experimental or radical style in the arts. Often pushing boundaries, the avant-garde is associated with Modernism, which lasted from the late 19th to the mid-20th centuries.

Baamaaya A dance of the Dagbamba ethnic group of Ghana, West Africa.

Balafon A xylophone from West Africa.

Ballad A sung poem or verse that tells a story.

Ballerina A female ballet dancer. The term was once exclusively used to designate the principal female dancer in a professional dance company.

Bass Lowest male voice.

Basso continuo In Baroque music, the continuous bass line played throughout a piece, usually played on harpsichord or organ plus a cello, viola da gamba, or bassoon.

Bàtá Double-headed hourglass-shaped drum of the Yoruba ethnic group of West Africa.

Battle Mass A polyphonic setting of the Ordinary sections of the Catholic Mass in which the music replicated battle sounds.

Bayan The larger drum of the pair of Hindustani drums called tabla.

Beat A steady rhythmic pulse, usually organized into measures (or bars).

Beijing opera The most influential style of Chinese opera; includes singing, dialogue, acrobatics, and martial arts.

Bhakti Selfless devotion and love (Hindu).

Big band A jazz ensemble of ten to fifteen instruments performing the music of the Swing Era, the period from the 1930s through World War II.

Binary form A common musical form consisting of two sections (AB). When a portion of the material from the beginning of the piece returns at the end, the form is known as rounded binary (ABa).

Birimintingo A soloistic style of kora playing that features melodic improvisation.

Blackface Theatrical make-up used by white performers to portray African Americans in minstrel shows and vaudeville. Also used by black minstrel performers.

Blackface minstrelsy see Minstrel show.

Blues A music genre that grew out of the African-American experience in the Mississippi Delta.

Bocet (plural: bocete) A Transylvanian funeral lament.

Bodhisattva In Buddhism, a person who has achieved Enlightenment or Buddhahood but who vows to stay in the world to help others.

Bollywood Refers to India's Hindu language film industry; based in Mumbai. One of the largest film industries in the world.

Bolon An arched harp from West Africa.

Brahma The creator god in Hinduism. The supreme god who along with Brahma and Shiva, form the trimurti (trinity) of Hindu belief.

Brahmacharya In Hinduism, the first of four stages of life; up to age 25, focusing on education and celibacy.

Branle A Renaissance dance in which participants move from side-to-side in a circle or line.

Brass An instrumental section of the symphony orchestra, which generally includes trumpet, horn, trombone, and tuba.

Breeches role see Pants role.

Bridge On a stringed instrument, a small piece of wood that supports the strings and conducts their vibrations into the body of the instrument.

Burlesque Comic parodies of serious genres such as plays, operas, or dance.

Cacagan A pulsing and jagged vocal vibrato used in Java, Indonesia.

Cadence The ending point of a musical phrase, which often consists of a formulaic harmonic pattern.

Call and Response A performance style of singing in which a line is sung by one singer and responded to by one or more singers.

Cantor The person who sings liturgical music and leads the prayers in either Christian or Jewish religious traditions.

Cantus firmus An existing melody (often chant) used as the basis for a new polyphonic genre; used in motets or Mass Ordinary settings.

Capoeira Dance/martial art with roots in Afro-Brazilian slave communities.

Castrato (plural: castrati) An adult male vocalist castrated before puberty so as to prevent the change of voice. Castrati were used in church choirs and in opera. The practice was prevalent in the 17th and 18th centuries.

Cello (or violoncello) A low-pitched string instrument played between the knees.

Chamber music In Western art music, music for a small ensemble of musicians with one performer per musical part.

Chanson The French word for song, which often pertains to French songs of the 13th to 16th centuries.

Chant Genre of vocal music used by the Catholic Church from the Middle Ages to Vatican II. Chant is sung in Latin, is monophonic, and uses free, non-metered rhythms. It is also known as plainchant.

Chest voice In singing, the sound that resonates in the chest (rather than the head, as in falsetto). The speaking voice is considered to resonate from the chest.

Chorale Sacred songs written for the early Lutheran Church.

Chord Three or more pitches sounding at the same time.

Chordophones Instruments whose sound is produced by vibrating strings. Examples include the violin, guitar, piano, and kora.

Chromatic notes Tones other than those of the prescribed key.

Chromatic scale A scale of half-step (semitone) pitches that contains all twelve tones within the Western octave.

Church modes A melodic system consisting of eight "scales" or modes used in music of the Medieval period: dorian/hypodorian, phrygian/hypophrygian, lydian/ hypolydian, mixolydian/ hypomixolydian.

Cimbalom An Eastern European hammered dulcimer.

Classical music see Western art music.

Cleric In the Catholic Church, a person who is a member of the clergy.

Coda An optional section added to the end of a musical composition (literally: tail).

Coloratura An intricate vocal melody in 18th- and 19th-century Western art music; it is also a soprano voice-type characterized by the singer's ability to execute highly elaborate melodies.

Commedia dell'arte A theatrical form originally from Italy. Flourished in Europe from the 16th to the 18th centuries. Features stock characters and improvisation.

Composition A musical work.

Concertmaster/concertmistress The principal violinist in an orchestra who tunes the orchestra, helps make decisions regarding bowings and fingerings, and leads the first violin section.

Concerto A three-movement (usually) work for a soloist(s) and orchestra (or band).

Conjunct motion The stepwise progression of pitches in a melody.

Consonance Sounds that please the ear. Notions of consonance are socially defined and vary according to time and place.

Consort music Music written for a small number of instruments, particularly in the Renaissance period.

Corps de ballet The dancers in a ballet company, not including the soloists.

Corrido A popular Mexican narrative ballad in triple meter. Lyrics often detail social ills and feature heroes or villains.

Countermelody A contrasting melody played with a main melody.

Countertenor A male singer with a well-developed falsetto who sings in the alto range.

Dahina The smaller drum of the pair of Hindustani drums called tabla.

Danseur A male ballet dancer. It generally refers to a company's principal male dancer.

Deus ex machina Means "god from the machine" and refers to a plot device in opera and drama whereby insurmountable problems are solved by outside intervention (often divine).

Development The middle section of a sonata form where the musical materials from the exposition are manipulated rhythmically and harmonically.

Diatonic Tones contained within the key or tonality.

Didgeridoo An Australian aboriginal wind instrument that produces deep and varied drones.

Diegetic In film, music that is part of the narrative action; music that can be heard by the characters in the film.

Dirge A slow-paced mournful piece associated with death and/or funerals.

Discant organum In the Medieval period, a style of music with more than one voice, with each voice moving at a similar pace (i.e. note against note).

Disjunct motion Angular melodic motion that moves in leaps.

Dissonance Sounds that clash or harmonies that are not pleasing to the ear. Notions of dissonance are socially defined and vary according to time and place.

Dominant The fifth tone (or the chord built on the fifth tone) in a major or minor key.

Donkilo The basic tune of a jali's song.

Downbeat The first beat of a measure.

Drone A continuously sounding pitch; the instrument that sounds the drone pitch.

Electrophones Instruments whose sound is produced electronically.

Enlightenment The philosophical movement in the 18th century that emphasized reason and individualism.

Ensemble finale A convention of 18th-century comic opera (especially those by Mozart) whereby all characters assemble on stage at the end of an act, sing in their own musical styles, and comment on or resolve the action.

Exposition The initial section of a sonata form where the musical themes are introduced, which usually consists of two distinct themes in contrasting keys.

Expressionism A late 19th- and early 20th-century artistic movement originating in Germany concerned with expressing subjective and emotional meaning. Emphasizes (often disturbing or distorted) subjective experience

Ezan (Turkish) Call to prayer. Recited five times a day to call Muslims to worship.

Falsetto A method of vocal production that allows males to sing naturally in the alto or soprano ranges.

Fin amours French term meaning "chivalric" or "courtly love"; a formalized tradition of love between a knight and a married noblewoman. It is associated with troubadour and trouvère songs of the Medieval period.

Fin de siècle French for "end of the century." Usually refers to the end of the 19th century and the changes in European art and culture at that time.

Florid organum In the Medieval period, a style of music with more than one voice, where the bottom voice holds long notes while the upper voice/s sing many notes to each held note.

Folksongs Songs that are usually transmitted by oral tradition and associated with the ordinary "folk" in a particular country.

Form The overall shape or structure of a piece of music.

Formes fixes French term referring to the three "fixed forms" used in songs of the troubadours and trouvères.

Fouetté In ballet, a quick turning motion of the leg used to change direction or propel the body in circles.

Fugue A polyphonic musical composition in which a short melody or phrase, called the subject, is used imitatively in alternation with new musical material.

Fundamental The lowest frequency of any vibrating object. Also called the first harmonic.

Gamelan An instrumental ensemble of Indonesia; generally includes bronze xylophone-like instruments and gongs.

Gat-tora In Hindustani (North Indian) music in which sections of a composed melody (Gat) alternate with improvisation (tora).

Genre A category, usually of artistic output. Genres may be classified according to styles, eras, forms, subject matter, and so on.

Ghina' In Islam, secular vocal music.

Ghost Dance A late 19th-century Native American religious movement initiated by Wovoka.

Ginga Back-and-forth-step pattern designed to facilitate quick movements and sudden changes in direction in Brazilian capoeira.

Glissando An ascending or descending slide between two tones.

Grace note A quick, non-metered tone used as an embellishment to the tone it precedes.

Grand pas (Grand step) In ballet, a suite of individual dances within the story of the ballet. The suite serves as a showpiece for lead dancers and does not contribute to the storyline.

Grihastha In Hinduism, the second of four stages of life; focuses on marriage and family.

Guban Drum and clapper (Chinese).

Güçlü A shared pitch between two tetrachords in maqam.

Gu shi In Chinese opera, the master drummer.

Habanera An Afro-Cuban dance with a distinguishing rhythmic ostinato, which is also used as the basis of numerous Western art music compositions to denote exoticism or ethnicity.

Half step (semitone) The smallest pitch interval commonly used in Western music (example F to F sharp).

Harmonic singing (or chanting) A vocal technique whereby a singer simultaneously produces a fundamental pitch and its overtones; also called overtone singing.

Harmonics Generally refers to the resonant tones (overtones) sympathetically produced above a fundamental tone.

Harmony The combination of simultaneously sounding tones that produce chords or chord progressions.

Harpsichord Keyboard instrument with strings plucked by quills, or leather. Used most often in the Baroque period.

Hazzan A Jewish cantor (a person who leads the congregation in sung prayers).

Head The pre-composed part of a jazz piece.

Heterophony Musical texture in which slightly different versions of a melody are performed simultaneously by two or more performers. Heterophony is used more commonly in Asian, Middle Eastern, and Native American traditions than in Western music.

Hindustani music North Indian classical music.

Homophony A chordal texture; melody plus chordal accompaniment.

Hymn A religious song, usually sung by the congregation during worship services.

Idée fixe (fixed idea) A recurring, obsessive melodic motive.

Idiophones Instruments that produce sound by shaking or striking the body of the instrument. Examples include cymbals, woodblocks, and sleigh bells.

Impressionism A late 19-century French movement in painting concerned with shifting light and color. It also refers to some of the music of Debussy and Ravel, whose instrumental timbres are said to resemble the shimmering color palettes of their counterparts in the visual arts.

Improvisation The act of creating or performing music spontaneously.

Intermezzo A composition inserted between acts or movements of other works (plays or other pieces of music); or a title of a movement or independent composition.

Jali (or griot) (plural: jalolu) A bard of the Mandinka ethnic group of West Africa.

Jazz An improvisational musical genre that emphasizes improvisation, syncopation, and rhythmic swing. Its roots are in African-American culture.

Jews harp (or jaw harp) A small musical instrument of ancient origin that is held against the teeth or lips and plucked with the fingers.

Jinghu A small, high-pitched, bowed, spike fiddle with two strings. Used primarily in Beijing opera.

Jingju see Beijing opera.

Juke joint (barrel house) An African American informal social establishment that featured music, dancing, drinking, and gambling.

Kabuki Japanese dramatic genre using stylized songs and gestures.

Kacapi indung A zither-like Sundanese musical instrument that sets the tempo, provides interludes, and bridges in Tembang Sunda.

Kanun Turkish zither.

Karar A maqam's home tone, or tonic.

Karnatic (or Carnatic) music The classical music of South India.

Kemençe Turkish three-stringed bowed fiddle.

Klezmer An instrumental musical tradition of the Ashkenazi Jews of Eastern Europe.

Kol Nidre Aramaic for "all vows"; a prayer sung at the first service of Yom Kippur.

Komibuki Pulsing breath. A shakuhachi breathing technique used to focus the mind.

Kora A plucked twenty-one-stringed harp-lute from West Africa.

Kotekan Interlocking rhythmic parts that form the foundation of the Balinese rhythmic system.

Kriti In Karnatic music, a musical form that consists of three sections: pallavi, anupallavi, and charanam.

Kumbengo A repetitive melodic style played on the kora.

Kudüm Paired kettle drums used by the Mevlevi Order of Sufism.

Lament A song that expresses grief at a person's death.

Leitmotif A recurrent musical theme that represents people, places, things, ideas, or emotions.

Libretto The text of an opera.

Lied German term meaning "art song." Lieder (plural) were especially popular in the 19th century.

Lining out A way of performing hymns or psalms whereby a leader sings each line of the hymn slightly ahead of the congregation to cue the melody and lyrics.

Liturgy A fixed set of texts, prayers, and music that forms the basis for worship services.

Longitudinal wave One of three types of wave forms; sound waves are longitudinal. Also called compression waves.

Lute A pear-shaped, plucked stringed instrument popular in the Renaissance and Baroque periods.

Lyre A string instrument played with a plectrum (pick) used in Ancient Greece.

Madrigal An Italian Renaissance vocal composition, usually written for several voices and often polyphonic.

Magnus Liber Literally "great" or "large" book that contained new polyphonic genres that were composed in Paris in the 12th and 13th centuries. The book is not extant.

Major scale A collection of stepwise pitches, ascending and descending, that comprise the syllables do, re, mi, fa, sol, la, ti (do).

Mandala A work of visual art that symbolically represents the universe.

Maqam (plural: maqamat) Melodic modes used in traditional Arabic music.

Mariachi A folk music tradition of Mexico. Mariachi bands usually consist of violins, trumpets, guitar, and guitarrón (a large acoustic bass guitar).

Mass The daily Catholic Church service that features Holy Communion. It can also refer to a composition that sets to music the Ordinary sections of the Mass (see Mass Ordinary).

Mass Ordinary Sections of the Catholic Mass where the texts remain the same from day to day, including the Kyrie, Gloria, Credo, Sanctus, and Agnus Dei.

Mass Proper Sections of the Catholic Mass where the texts are different from day to day.

Mazurka One of many Romantic period "character" pieces for solo piano. The mazurka derived from Polish folk dances and was usually in triple meter.

Measure A unit of rhythmic time in Western music that contains a designated number of beats. (It is also called a "bar.")

Melisma When multiple pitches are sung to one syllable of text.

Melody Distinct pitches sounding one after another through time; the "tune" of a piece of music.

Membranophones Instruments whose sound is produced through vibrating membranes. Examples include most drums.

Meter The number and accentuation pattern of beats in a measure.

Mevlevi Order A suborder of Sufism, the mystical sect of Islam. In the West, the Mevlevi are commonly known as the Whirling Dervishes.

Microtone An interval smaller than a half step (or semitone).

Middle Ages (or Medieval Period) A European historical period that lasted from ca. 500 to the early 15th century.

Minimalism A style of music originating in the 1960s associated with composers Steve Reich, Philip Glass, and others. Distinctive features include repetitive, but slowly developing, melodies, harmonies, and rhythms.

Minstrel show Musical comedies popular in the 19th century in which white performers wore blackface and satirized African-American culture.

Miscegenation The mixing of "races" through marriage, cohabitation, sexual relations, or procreation. Usually referred to marriages between "whites" and persons of color.

Modal Music that is based on a melodic system of modes (see Church modes) rather than major or minor keys.

Modes see Church modes.

Mohra In Karnatic music, a thrice-repeated rhythmic cadential formula.

Monophony A musical texture in which a unison, single melody is sounded, no matter the number of performers.

Motet A sacred, polyphonic composition, usually for voices alone. It is one of the main genres of the Medieval and Renaissance periods.

Movement In music, a self-contained portion of a larger work. (A symphony, for example, generally contains four movements.)

Mridangam A double-headed drum used in Karnatic music.

Mukhra (or mukhda) In Hindustani music, a short phrase that leads to the first beat (see sam) of the rhythmic cycle (tala).

Musiqa In Islam, secular instrumental music.

Nationalism A mid- to late 19th-century compositional trend that used musical ideas identified with particular nations, regions, or ethnicities.

Natural trumpet A valveless trumpet.

Natya Shastra A Sanskrit Hundi treatise written between 200 BCE and 200 CE that describes in detail theater, music, dance, poetics, and aesthetics.

Ney A Middle Eastern end-blown flute.

Ngoni A West African five-stringed lute.

Node A point along a vibrating string that does not vibrate. For instance, a guitar string's end point, or where the finger touches a fret.

Noh A Japanese drama that uses masks, dance, and song.

Non-diegetic music Film music that does not exist in the world of the on-screen characters; also called the underscore.

Octave The relationship between one pitch and another with exactly twice the vibration speed. The consonance of the octave is recognized in all world cultures.

Opera A staged and sung dramatic work with instrumental accompaniment.

Operetta A short, lighthearted opera that includes spoken dialogue and song.

Oral tradition The passing of music from one generation to another by speech or song without written notation.

Oratorio Large-scale work for chorus, orchestra, and vocal soloists. Usually tells a story but is not staged.

Orchestration The way in which instruments are used in a piece of music, or the practice of arranging a composition for multiple instruments.

Ordinary see Mass Ordinary.

Organ Keyboard instrument which sounds via air through pipes. There are many varieties of organ from very small portable organs used in the Middle Ages to large, multi-keyboard organs installed in churches and palaces from the Baroque period to the present.

Organum In Western art music, the name given to the earliest works for more than once voice from the late 9th to 13th centuries. Usually consists of a chant with one or more added voices.

Organum quadruplum Organum for four voices; bottom voice is a chant fragment. Attributed to Perotin during the Notre Dame Period (late 12th–13th century).

Oríkì Praise poems from the Yoruba tradition.

Orìsà Sacred entities of the Yoruba religion.

Ornamentation Melodic embellishment.

Ornaments Individual melodic decorations or embellishments (often not notated) on notes, such as trills, turns, and glissandos.

Ostinato A repetitive melodic or rhythmic phrase.

Oud A pear-shaped lute used in Persian, Middle Eastern, North African, Arabic, Greek and other musical traditions.

Pants role An operatic role in which a woman plays a male character, generally an adolescent or young man. It is also called a "breeches role" or "trouser role."

Pas de deux A ballet duet, usually performed by female and male leads.

Pastiche An artistic work that makes use of pieces taken from a variety of sources.

Pentatonic scale A five-tone scale.

Percussion A classification of instruments that generate sound by being struck. This classification includes most membranophones and idiophones.

Peşrev An instrumental pre-composed piece with roots in the Ottoman court.

Phrase A group of pitches that form a conceptual unit.

Pickup A beat that occurs immediately before the beginning of a measure; also called an upbeat.

Pirouette In ballet, a spinning turn on one leg.

Pitch The highness or lowness of a sound; also called a "note" or "tone."

Pitch bending The modification of a tone by slightly raising or lowering its pitch.

Pizzicato The technique of plucking the strings of bowed string instruments.

Plainchant see Chant.

Planctus A lament (in song or poetry) that expresses grief or mourning.

Plié A dance position with knees bent outward while the back remains straight.

Pointillistic style In 20th-century music, when sounds appear as many separate, even disconnected, events.

Polyphony A musical texture in which multiple independent melodic lines sound simultaneously.

Popular (pop) music A category of music closely associated with the music industry, distributed through the mass media, and designed to appeal to a wide audience.

Power chords Loud, often electronically distorted chords that use the first and fifth degrees of the chord, which are a feature of many rock genres.

Powwow A gathering that celebrates Native American culture. Music and dance play a prominent role.

Primitivism An artistic and literary movement that celebrated nature, instinct, and non-Western "native" or "tribal" subjects.

Program music Music based on written or non-musical artistic works. Also known as "program music."

Proper see Mass Proper.

Protestant Reformation Sixteenth-century movement to rid the Catholic Church of abuses. German Reformation lead by Martin Luther resulted in the establishment of the Lutheran Church.

Qira'ah The method of reciting the Qur'an (Koran).

Quatrain A poetic stanza of four lines.

Querrelle des Bouffons (War of the Buffoons [comic actors]) A vigorous literary debate about the relative merits of French serious opera versus Italian comic opera. Took place in Paris during the Enlightenment.

Quintrain A poetic stanza of five lines.

Qur'an (Koran) The sacred book of Islam.

Race film American films marketed to African-Americans; lasted into the late 1940s.

Race records Sound recordings marketed to African Americans in the 1920s–1940s.

Raga In Indian music, a collection of pitches with characteristic intervals and embellishments used as the basis for melodic content. In Karnatic music there are seventy-two melakarta (parent) ragas and hundreds of janya (derived) ragas.

Ramayana (Rama's Journey) An epic Sanskrit poem that tells the story of Rama, an incarnation of the Hindu deity Vishnu.

Range The distance between highest and lowest pitches in a melody.

Recapitulation The final section of a sonata form in which the musical themes from the exposition are heard again, this time in the tonic (home) key.

Recitative Speech-like vocal style used in opera or oratorio that uses regular speech rhythms to carry the dialogue and forward the plot line.

Reclamation history The restoration of minority and women's contributions to the historical narrative.

Refrain A repeated line or section of a composition. In popular song, a refrain is sometimes called the chorus.

Renaissance A European historical period that lasted from the early 15th century to 1600 (in music; in other fields, these dates may vary somewhat).

Requiem Mass A funeral Mass. Its liturgy is slightly different from a daily Mass, most notably in the addition of the Dies Irae (Day of Wrath) chant.

Retrograde A melody played backwards.

Rhythm The systematic arrangement of musical beats, accents, and durations.

Riff In popular music, a short, repeated phrase or harmonic progression.

Ritornello A recurring instrumental refrain.

Rondel A French poetic form (ABba abAB abbaA).

Rondo form A musical form with a recurring refrain that alternates with new material (e.g. ABACA or ABACADA).

Rounded binary form A musical form consisting of two main sections (ABa) where the beginning material returns briefly at the end.

Sam In Hindustani music, the first beat of the rhythmic cycle (tala).

Samā' A multi-sectioned and highly formalized Mevlevi worship ceremony that calls the practitioners' attention to God.

Sampling The process of taking a sound from one recorded medium and inserting it into a new one.

Santería A religion that combines tenets of the Catholic and Yoruba religions.

Sarod A North Indian fretless lute. The resonating body of the sarod is covered with goat skin. The sarod has four to six melody strings, one or two drone strings, and as many as thirteen sympathetic strings.

Sataro A speech-like verse that includes praise, proverbs, and other commentary sung by the jalolu bards of West Africa.

Scale The collection of tones (usually arranged in ascending or descending order) that forms the melodic basis of a composition.

Scratching A turntablist technique that produces rhythmic and/or percussive sounds.

Second Wave Feminism A period of feminist activity from the early 1960s to ca. 1980.

Shakuhachi Japanese end-blown bamboo flute.

Shape notes Refers to a system of musical notation that uses note heads in specific shapes. They were designed to facilitate music reading in 18th- and 19th-century America.

Shiva One of the most important gods of Hinduism; the destroyer and transformer in the trimurti (trinity) of Hindu belief.

Shofar A ram's horn trumpet used in the synagogue for Rosh Hashanah and Yom Kippur.

Sitar A North Indian long-necked, plucked lute with resonating gourd on both ends of the instrument. Has melody and drone strings.

Soliloquy When a speaker or singer on stage "speaks" to him/her self.

Sonata A multi-movement work for piano, or single instrument plus piano (i.e. violin and piano), or a single instrument without piano.

Sonata form A compositional form which developed in Europe in the 18th century and consists of three main sections: exposition, development, and recapitulation.

Song A vocal genre performed with or without instrumental accompaniment. "Song" is not a generic word for all pieces of music.

Song cycle A set of songs designed to be performed as a whole.

Sopranist A male singer with a well-developed falsetto who sings in the soprano range.

Soprano Highest female voice. Males who sing in this range are called "sopranists."

Sorog One of three types of tuning in Sundanese music. Similar to "fa mi do si la fa" in the Western scale.

Spotting process The process in which a film's director and composer make initial decisions about where and what type of music should be used. Each such musical insertion is called a "cue."

Sprechstimme ("Speech voice" or Sprechgesang [speech song]) A vocal style between speaking and singing.

Sruti box A small wooden bellows-driven harmonium that provides the drone in Indian classical music.

Staff A set of five parallel lines and the spaces in between on which notes are written in order to transcribe pitch.

Stanza A group of lines in a poem. Groups may be based on rhyme scheme, number of syllables, or topic. Quatrains have four lines, Quintrains have five.

Story ballet Ballet genre with developed plot lines, often based on legends or fairy tales.

String Quartet Music ensemble consisting of two violins, viola, and cello.

Strings A classification of instruments whereby sound is generated by vibrations of a string or strings. Examples are violin, viola, cello, bass, guitar, and lute.

Strophic A song form in which successive stanzas are set to the same music.

Subdominant The fourth tone (or the chord built on the fourth tone) of a major or minor key.

Sufism The mystical branch of Islam.

Suite A collection of dances meant for listening.

Svara One of seven syllables used to designate tones in the South Indian melodic system: sa–ri–ga–ma–pa–dha–ni–(sa).

Syllabic A singing style in which each syllable of text is assigned a separate pitch.

Symbolism A late 19th-century poetic movement characterized by an interest in the subconscious, dreams and emotions.

Symbolist Poets and other writers and artists who, in the late 19th century, expressed ideas through metaphorical and symbolic language. They were interested in the subconscious, dreams, and emotions.

Symphonic poem An orchestral work that depicts a story or theme.

Symphony A large-scale composition for orchestra usually in four movements, the first of which is often in sonata form.

Syncopation The rhythmic displacement of accents or sounds to unexpected positions.

Synthesizer An instrument that generates electronic signals that are converted in sound wave forms. Can imitate standard instruments, natural sounds, or produce new electronic sounds.

Tabla A pair of hand drums used in Hindustani (North Indian) music. The smaller, higher pitched drum (the dahina) is played with the right hand and the larger, lower pitched drum (the bayan), the left.

Taiko A large Japanese double-headed drum; also refers to a Japanese drumming style and ensemble.

Tailpiece The part of the violin that connects the base of the violin to the strings.

Tajwid Refers to highly ornamented Koranic recitation.

Taksim A non-metric instrumental improvisation in classical Turkish music.

Tala The rhythmic system of Indian music.

Tambura A long-necked plucked lute used to provide drone pitches in Indian music.

Tanbur A Turkish long-necked lute.

Tango A sensuous couples dance that originated in Argentina.

Tartil Refers to simple Koranic recitation (as opposed to tajwid, which refers to recitation that is highly ornamented).

Tembang Sunda A classical Sundanese (Indonesia) vocal genre that developed in the mid-19th century.

Tempo The speed at which a piece or passage of music is performed.

Tenor 1) Male vocal line above the bass, 2) a line in music second to the bottom, 3) in Medieval and Renaissance music, the structural line; sometimes using borrowed melodies such as chant tunes.

Ternary form A musical form in three parts, designated as ABA.

Tetrachord A scale of four tones.

Texture The ways in which different musical lines or sonorities fit together.

Theramin Electronic musical instrument. Sound made by two high frequency oscillators with performer moving his/her hands toward and away from the electromagnetic field.

Tihai In Hindustani music, a cadential rhythm repeated three times (similar to Mohra in Karnatic music).

Timbre The character or quality of a sound; sometimes referred to as tone color.

Time signature A notational convention (usually looks like a fraction) that indicates meter; the top number indicates the number of beats per measure and the bottom note indicates what type of note gets the beat (i.e. 2/4 means that there are two quarter notes in each measure).

Tin Pan Alley The area in New York City where the popular song industry was based in the late 19th and early 20th centuries.

Tone A musical sound; especially a particular pitch or note. It can also refer to the quality of sound a musician produces, as in "the flutist has a shimmering tone."

Tonic The first pitch (or the chord built on the first pitch) of a major or minor key, which is considered to be the "home" tone.

Triad A three-note chord built on alternating scale tones.

Trill The rapid alternation of adjacent tones.

Trimurti The Hindu trinity, consisting of Vishnu, Brahma and Shiva.

Troubadours Composers and poets, usually of noble birth, in medieval southern France, who are associated with *fin amours*.

Trouvères Composers and poets, usually of noble birth, in medieval northern France, who are associated with *fin amours*.

Turntablism The use of turntables (usually two) and mixers to create new sounds, sound effects, and/or beats.

Ud (or oud) A Middle Eastern pear-shaped lute.

Usul Cyclic patterns, usually from two to ten beats, that govern the rhythmic system of Turkish classical music.

Vaudeville A theatrical entertainment popular in the United States and Canada from the late 19th century through the early 20th century. Acts included musicians, dancers, comedians, magicians, and trained animals.

Veena (vina) In Karnatic music, a plucked long-necked lute with resonators on both ends.

Venu In Karnatic music, a bamboo transverse flute.

Virtuoso A highly skilled musical performer.

Vishnu One of the most important gods of Hinduism; the preserver of good and guardian of the Earth. Along with Brahma and Shiva, forms the trimurti (trinity) of Hindu belief.

Vocable Syllables with no textual meaning that serve as musical refrains or markers.

Western art music A specific body of stylistically diverse works, composed by individuals and written down. Divided into six historical periods; composed mostly by Europeans and peoples of the European diaspora.

Whole-tone scale A scale that consists entirely of whole steps.

Woodwinds A classification of windblown instruments. Examples include the flute, oboe, clarinet, bassoon, recorder, and shakuhachi.

World/Global music Refers to local or regional music traditions outside the spheres of Western popular and art music genres. Is transmitted orally/aurally, may be commercial or non-commercial and generally categorized by geographic or ethnic origin.

Yang Ban Xi "Eight model plays." These works were promoted by the Chinese government during the Cultural Revolution (1966–1976).

Yoruba Large and influential ethnic group that resides in the eastern and coastal areas of Nigeria.